Zenaide Alexeievna Ragozin

Assyria from the Rise of the Empire to the Fall of Nineveh

Sixth Edition

Zenaide Alexeievna Ragozin

Assyria from the Rise of the Empire to the Fall of Nineveh
Sixth Edition

ISBN/EAN: 9783337169534

Printed in Europe, USA, Canada, Australia, Japan

Cover: Foto ©ninafisch / pixelio.de

More available books at **www.hansebooks.com**

ASSHURBANIPAL HUNTING LIONS

ASSYRIA

FROM THE RISE OF THE EMPIRE TO THE FALL OF NINEVEH

(CONTINUED FROM "CHALDEA")

BY

ZÉNAÏDE A. RAGOZIN

MEMBER OF THE "SOCIÉTÉ ETHNOLOGIQUE" OF PARIS; CORRESPONDING MEMBER OF THE "ATHÉNÉE ORIENTAL" OF PARIS; MEMBER OF THE "AMERICAN ORIENTAL SOCIETY."

"He (Carlyle) says it is part of his creed that history is poetry, could we tell it right."—EMERSON.

"Da mihi, Domine, scire quod sciendum est."—"IMITATION OF CHRIST." ("Grant that the knowledge I get may be the knowledge worth having." *Matthew Arnold's translation.*)

SIXTH EDITION

London
T. FISHER UNWIN
PATERNOSTER SQUARE

CLASSIFIED CONTENTS.

I.

THE RISE OF ASSHUR 1–39

§ 1. Natural boundary of Assyria towards Babylonia.—§ 2. Beginnings of Asshur. First colonies. Assyrian Patesis.—§ 3. Assyria Proper.—§ 4. Asshur—a Semitic nation. Religious affinities with the Hebrews. Asshur, the supreme god.—§§ 5-6. Parallel between passages from Assyrian inscriptions, and from the Bible.—§ 7. Difference between the relation towards the deity of Assyrian and Hebrew kings.—§ 8. The emblems of Asshur on the monuments.—§ 9. Assyrian Pantheon identical with the Babylonian.—§ 10. Early relations between Assyria and Babylon.—§ 11. First appearance of Egyptian conquerors in Western Asia.—§§ 12, 13. Brief survey of earlier Egyptian history. Hyksos invasion.—§ 14. Egyptian conquests in Asia. Acts of retaliation.—§ 15. Battle of Megiddo. First collision between Assyria and Egypt.—§ 16. The Khetas or Hittites. Their power and wealth.—§§ 17-18. Their capitals and empire.—§ 19. The long duration of the Hittite power.—§ 20. Hittite writing and art.—§ 21. Early aggrandizement of Assyria. First conquest of Babylon.

II.

THE FIRST EMPIRE.—TIGLATH PILESER I. . 40–66

§ 1. Lakes Van and Urumieh and the Dead Sea.—§ 2. The "Lands of Nairi."—§ 3. The rock sculpture of Tiglath-Pileser I. by the sources of the Tigris.—§ 4. The cylinder of

PAGE

Tiglath-Pileser I. used for a test of Assyriology.—§§ 5, 6, 7. Tiglath-Pileser's campaigns to Naïri, as narrated on the cylinder.—§ 8. His expeditions to the west. First mention of the Aramæans. Beginning of this race's long political career.—§ 9. Tiglath-Pileser's summing up of his military achievements.—§ 10. His wise home-rule.—§ 11. His hunting exploits and love of sport.—§ 12. His flying visit to the sea-coast.—§ 13. His last years troubled with disasters. Unfortunate expedition to Babylonia.—§ 14. Blank in the history of Assyria after Tiglath-Pileser, and for the space of 200 years.—§ 15. Tiglath-Pileser the real founder of Assyria's greatness.

III.

The Sons of Canaan: Their Migrations.—
  The Phœnicians 67–102

§ 1. Wealth and greatness of the Phœnicians about 1100 B.C.—§. 2. The Canaanitic races. The "Pount" or "Puna."—§ 3. Conjectures about their early migrations.—§ 4. Pre-Canaanitic inhabitants of Syria and Palestine.—§ 5. Conjectures as to "who were these people?"—§ 6. The Phœnicians and their narrow sea-coast home.—§ 7. Rise of their trade and wealth.—§ 8. The purple dye. What a small shell-fish did for a nation.—§ 9. It promotes maritime discoveries and colonization.—§ 10. Voyages for tin.—§ 11. Tarshish.—§ 12. The "Cassiterides." Land route across France and sea route to the English ' Tin Islands."—§ 13. The Pillars of Melkarth. Gades. Tales about Tarshish. § 14. Trade with amber. Land route across Germany.—§ 15. Land routes across Western Asia.—§ 16. Great wealth and splendor of Tyre.—§ 17. Money-making the key to the Phœnician character and historical mission.—§ 18. They are wanting in literary gifts, and lack inventiveness and originality.—§ 19. Their great importance as the agents for spreading material civilization and establishing intercourse between distant countries.—They may be called the Peddlers of the Ancient World. Low moral standard of such a mission.

IV.

THE SONS OF CANAAN. THEIR RELIGION.—SACRIFICE AS AN INSTITUTION.—HUMAN SACRIFICES 103–144

§ 1. Materialism and sensuality distinctive features of the Hamitic races.—§ 2. Materialistic character of their religions, yet with a certain tendency towards monotheism.—§ 3. Dualism of Canaanitic religions. Baal, Moloch and Ashtoreth.—§ 4. Melkarth, the Baal of Tyre.—§ 5. Obscurity of Phœnician myths.—§ 6. Ashtoreth and her different forms.—§ 7. High places, sacred groves and the Ashera.—§§ 8, 9. Baal and his different forms.—§§ 10, 11. Self-torture and human sacrifice features of ancient worship.—§§ 12, 13. The nature of ancient sacrifice.—§ 14. Consecration a form of sacrifice. Sacrifice, to be perfect, demands destruction of the object offered.—§ 15. Victims or offerings, to be acceptable, must be perfect of their kind.—§ 16. Human sacrifices a logical sequence and culmination of the idea of sacrifice; sacrifices of children the most valuable, hence the most perfect of all.—§ 17. The sacrifice of the first born a primeval institution; consecration and ransom substituted at a more advanced and milder stage of culture.—§ 18. Human sacrifices supposed to be of divine institution. Phœnician legend on the subject.—§ 19. The legend illustrated by the sacrifice offered by Mesha, king of Moab.—§ 20. Hindu legends.—§ 21. Greek legend.—§§ 22–24. Intense emotional nature of the Orientals.—Orgiastic religions.—§ 25. Human sacrifices the special due of Baal Moloch, the Destroyer, in times of public calamity.—§§ 26–28. Child-sacrifices at Carthage and among the Jews.—§ 29. Vows. The Jewish "Kherem."—§ 30. Sanchoniatho and the garbled account of Phœnician Cosmogony.—§ 31. The myth and worship of Adonis-Thammuz.—§ 32. The Kabirim.—§ 33. The Phœnicians carry their religion and worship to their colonies.

V.

THE NEIGHBORS OF ASSHUR.—REVIVAL OF THE
EMPIRE 145–174

§ 1. Revival of Assyria.—§ 2. The "Limmu" and the Eponym Canon.—§ 3. State of affairs in Syria.—§ 4. Along the sea-coast.—§ 5. Growth of Israel. The Hebrew monarchy.—§ 6. Idolatry long tolerated. The centre of national worship established at Jerusalem.—§ 7. Solomon's despotism.—§ 8. The division of Israel a consequence of Solomon's harsh rule. § 9. The revival of Assyria favored by the dissensions in Syria.—§ 10. Renewal of Assyrian conquests in the North.—§ 11. King Asshurnazirpal. His campaign in Naïri.—§ 12. His atrocious cruelty. He collects tribute from the Phœnician cities.—§ 13. His constructions. Rebuilds Kalah and makes it his residence.—§ 14. The sculptures of his time.—§ 15. His hunts.—§ 16. The rise of the Kaldu (Chaldeans proper).—§ 17. The princes of Chaldea. Their policy and ambition.

VI.

SHALMANESER II.—ASSHUR AND ISRAEL . 175–212

§ 1. Character of Shalmaneser II.'s reign.—§ 2. Summary of his military career.—§ 3. First campaigns.—§ 4. First Syrian expedition. The Syrian League.—§ 5. Alliance between Ahab of Israel and Benhadad of Damascus.—§ 6. Battle of Karkar.—§ 7. Second Syrian campaign.—§ 8. Third Syrian campaign. Submission of Jehu of Israel.—§ 9. The Black Obelisk.—§ 10. Jehu's submission not mentioned in the Bible.—§ 11. The gates of Balawat.—§ 12. Shalmaneser's retirement. Rebellion of his eldest son. Accession of his other son, Shamshi-Ramân III.—§ 13. Ramân-Nirari III.—§§ 14–16. The Story of Semiramis.—§ 17. Utter historical worthlessness of the story.—§ 18. Urartu and the Alarodians.—§ 19. Rise of the kingdom of Van. Its culture and writing borrowed from Assyria.—§ 20. Second Decline of Assyria. Accession of Tiglath-Pileser II.—§ 21. His double name: Phul or Pul and Tiglath-Pileser.—§ 22. The mission of the prophet Jonah not mentioned on the monuments. Suggested explanation of the whale story.—§ 23. Foundation of Carthage.

APPENDIX TO CHAPTER VI. 212–217
The Stele of Mesha the Moabite.

VII.

THE SECOND EMPIRE.—SIEGE OF SAMARIA . 218–246

§ 1. Assyria's greatness under Tiglath-Pileser II.—§ 2. Political Character of the Second Empire.—§ 3. Annexations. Wholesale deportations.—§ 4. Generals in command. —§ 5. Plan of operations in the West.—§ 6. First Campaigns: in Kaldu, the Zagros and Naïri.—§ 7. Syrian Campaign of 738 B.C. Menahem of Samaria pays tribute.—§ 8. Syria and Israel against Judah.—§ 9. Approaching dissolution of Israel. Ahaz of Judah's embassy to Tiglath-Pileser, entreating aid.—§ 10. Syrian Campaign of 734 B.C. —§ 11. Taking of Damascus.—§ 12. Chaldean Campaign.— § 13. Merodach Baladan of Bit-Yakin pays homage.—§ 14. End of Tiglath-Pileser's reign.—§ 15. Shalmaneser IV.— § 16. Renewed hopes and revolts in the West.—§ 17. Revival of Egypt under Shabaka the Ethiopian.—§ 18. His readiness to support the Asiatic cities and kingdoms. His powerlessness and Isaiah's warning.—§ 19. Revolt of Tyre. Siege of Tyre by the Assyrian's.—§ 20. Revolt of Israel. Siege of Samaria.

VIII.

THE PRIDE OF ASSHUR.—SARGON . . . 247–294

§ 1. Fall of Samaria and transportation of the people of Israel.—§. 2. Sargon's parentage unknown.—§ 3. His vigorous policy at home and abroad.—§ 4. Discontent in the West and intrigues with Egypt.—§ 5. Disastrous rising in Syria.—§ 6. Battle of Raphia.—§ 7. Submission of Tyre.— § 8. Great rising in Naïri. Merodach Baladan, king of Babylon.—§ 9. General conspiracies and repressions.—§ 10. Capture of Karkhemish, the final blow to the Hittite nationality.—§ 11. Campaign against Urartu.—§ 12. Expedition into Media.—§§ 13, 14. Popular rising quelled in Ashdod.—§ 15. Merodach Baladan prepares for war.—§§ 16-17. His "embassy" to Hezekiah, king of Judah.—§ 18. Sargon invades Chaldea.—§ 19. Merodach Baladan flies to Elam.—§ 20. Sargon invited to enter Babylon.—§ 21. His consummate generalship and the capture of Dur-Yakin.—§ 22. He conciliates the cities of Babylonia.—§ 23. He receives the homage of seven kings of Cyprus.—§ 24. His last military and political acts.—§§ 25-27. Construction of Dur-Sharrukin.—§ 28. Marvellous wealth of Sculptures in Sargon's palace.—§ 29. Summary way of peopling the new city.—§ 30. Sargon's wise and beneficent home rule.—31. His invocations for prosperity and long life.—32. His assassination.

IX.

THE SARGONIDES.—SENNACHERIB. (SIN-AKHI-IRIB.) 295-330

§ 1. Sennacherib's name long familiar from the Bible.—§§ 2, 3. General character of his reign.—§ 4. His first successes in Chaldea.—§ 5. Merodach Baladan's flight.—§ 6. Campaign against the Kasshi and Ellip.—§ 7. Preparations for a campaign against the West and Egypt.—§ 8. Hezekiah of Judah revolts.—§§ 9, 10. Siege of Lakhish and submission of Hezekiah.—§§ 11, 12. Messengers sent by Sennacherib to Hezekiah.—§ 13. The King of Judah comforted by the prophet Isaiah.—§ 14. Battle of Altakû.—§ 15. Sennacherib compelled to retreat by the plague breaking out in his army.—§ 16. Second campaign to Chaldea; disappearance of Merodach Baladan.—§ 17. Campaign into Naïri.—§ 18. Maritime expedition across the Gulf into Elam.—§ 19. Unsuccessful expedition into the Zagros.—§ 20. Third campaign against Babylonia. Advance of the forces of Elam and Babylon.—§ 21. Battle of Khaluli.—§ 22. The Bavian rock inscription.—§§ 23, 24. Sack and destruction of Babylon.—§ 25. Last scanty notice of Sennacherib's military career.—§ 26. His assassination by two of his sons.—§ 27. Reconstruction of Nineveh.—§ 28. Sennacherib's palace at Nineveh.

X.

THE SARGONIDES: ESARHADDON (ASSHUR-AKHI-IDDIN.) 331–346

§ 1. Scarcity of monuments of this king's reign.—§ 2. His "addresses" to Ishtar, and Ishtar's "messages."—§ 3. Esarhaddon's brief war against his brothers.—§ 4. Troubles in Bît-Yakin.—§ 5. Reconstruction of Babylon.—§ 6. Expedition against the "distant Medes" in the east and against the Gimirrai (Cimmerians), in the North.—§ 7. Arabian campaign.—§ 8. Rising in Sidon repressed.—§ 9. Esarhaddon receives the homage of twenty-two kings.—§ 10. Construction and inauguration of his palace at Nineveh.—§ 11. Troubles in Syria.—§ 12. Rising in Tyre repressed.—§ 13. Egyptian campaign.—§ 14. Esarhaddon's abdication and death.—§ 15. Appointment of Shamash-Shumukin to the viceroyalty of Babylon.

XI.

THE GATHERING OF THE STORM.—THE LAST COMER AMONG THE GREAT RACES . . 347–370

§§ 1–3. Appearance on the scene of the Aryan race, the last among the four great races.—§ 4. Migrations of the Aryan or Indo-European race.—§ 5. Its great qualities.—§ 6. Ariana.—§ 7. Erân and Turân.—§ 8. The Medes. § 9. Their early social conditions.—§ 10. Their advance towards the West.—§ 11. They supplant nations of other, especially Turanian, stock.—§ 12. Aryan migrations into and across Russia.—§ 13.—The Cimmerians.—§ 14. Their migration into Thrace, driven before the Scythians.—§ 15. Asia Minor early peopled by Hittites.—§ 16. Hittite sculptures in Lydia.—§ 17, in Cilicia.—§ 18, in Cappadocia.—§ 19. Lydia and its early traditions.—§ 20. The Phrygo-Thracian family of nations.—§ 21. The Cimmerians cross the Bosphorus and invade Asia Minor.

XII.

THE DECLINE OF ASSHUR.—ASSHURBANIPAL (ASSHUR-BANI-HABAL) . . . 371–416

§ 1. Brilliant beginnings of Asshurbanipal's reign.—§§ 2–4. Egyptian campaign and sack of Thebes.—§ 5. Rising and submission of Tyre and Arvad.—§§ 6–8. Incident with Gyges, King of Lydia.—§ 9. Uncertain chronology of this reign.—§ 10. Assyria threatened from several points.—§ 11. Danger from the Scythians south of the Caucasus.—§ 12. Defeat of Gôg the Scythian king.—§ 13. First war with Elam: Urtaki, King of Elam, opens hostilities and is defeated.—§ 14. His brother Teumman succeeds. Second war.—§ 15. The Ishtar vision.—§ 16. Battle on the Ulaï and death of Teumman.—§ 17. Tortures and executions.—§ 18. Revolt of Shamash-Shumukin.—§ 19. Encouraging dream of a seer.—§ 20. Revolutions in Elam.—§ 21. Siege of Babylon and end of Shamash-Shumukin.—§ 22. Nabu-bel-zikri of Bit-Yakin goes over to Elam.—§ 23. More revolutions in Elam.—§ 24. Third great war with Elam. Sack of Shushan.—§ 25. Tragic end of Nabu-bel-zikri.—§ 26. Pacification of Bit-Yakin.—§ 27. Last troubles in Elam.—§ 28. Arabian campaign.—§ 29. Asshurbanipal's triumph. His chariot drawn by four captive kings.—§ 30. Uncertainty about the last years of this reign. Asshurbanipal's palace and library.—§ 31. The sculptures.—§ 32. Asshurbanipal—the Sardanapalus of the Greeks.

XIII.

THE FALL OF ASSHUR. . . . 417–432

§ 1. Entire lack of Assyrian monuments for the last years of the Empire.—§ 2. Uncertainty about the last kings of Assyria.—§ 3. Assyria rapidly loses all the conquered provinces.—§ 4. Story of Daökes and the Medes.—§ 5. Probable explanation of the story.—§ 6. Median invasion of Assyria under Phraortes.—§§ 7–8. Kyaxares and the invasion of the Scythians.—§ 9. Descent of the Scythians into Syria. —§ 10. Description of the Scythians by the prophet Jeremiah—§ 11. Another, by the prophet Ezekiel.—§ 12. The Scythians probably overrun Assyria.—§ 13. Kyaxares rids Media of the Scythians.—§ 14. Alliance between Kyaxares and Nabopolassar, the new King of Babylon.—§ 15. Siege and fall of Nineveh.—§ 16. Nahum's prophecy.—§ 17. The prophet Ezekiel's lament over Asshur.—§ 18. Immediate causes that hastened the fall of Asshur.

PRINCIPAL WORKS READ OR CONSULTED IN THE PREPARATION OF THE PRESENT VOLUME.

BABELON, ERNEST. LES ASSYRIENS ET LES CHALDÉENS. Quatrième volume de l' "Histoire Ancienne de l'Orient," de François Lenormant, 9me edit. Paris, A. Lévy. 1885. (Continued from Lenormant by Mr. Babelon.)

BAUDISSIN, W. G. JAHVE ET MOLOCH. Sive de ratione inter Deum Israelitarum et Molochum intercedente. Dissertatio Inauguralis. Lipsiae: 1874.

BUDGE, E. A. WALLIS. History of Esarhaddon. London: 1880. 1 vol.

CORY. ANCIENT FRAGMENTS. London: 1876. 1 vol.

DELATTRE, A. LE PEUPLE ET L' EMPIRE DES MÈDES, jusqu' á la fin du règne de Cyaxare. Bruxelles: 1883. 1 vol.

——— LES CHALDÉENS, jusqu' à la formation de l' Empire de Nabuchodonozor. (Extrait de la "Revue des Questions Historiques.") Paris, 1877.

——— ESQUISSE DE GÉOGRAPHIE ASSYRIENNE (Extrait de la Revue des Questions Scientifiques). Paris: 1883. 55 pages.

——— LES INSCRIPTIONS historiques de Ninive et de Babylone. Paris: 1879. (90 pages.)

DELITZSCH, DR. FRIEDRICH. "WO LAG DAS PARADIES?" Eine Biblisch-Assyriologische Studie. Leipzig: 1881. 1 vol.

DUNCKER, MAX. Geschichte des Alterthums. 5th edition. Leipzig: 1878. Vols. 1 and 2.

HOMMEL, DR. FRITZ. Geschichte Babyloniens und Assyriens. (1st and 2d instalments, 320 pages.) (Allgemeine Geschichte in einzelnen Darstellungen, edited by Wm. Oncken. Lieferungen 95 and 117.) Berlin, 1885 and 1886.

HÖRNING, R. Das sechsseitige Prisma des Sanherib, in

Grundtext und übersetzung, nebst Beiträgen zu einer Erklärung. (Inaugural dissertation.) Leipzig: 1878.
KAULEN, Dr. F. Assyrien und Babylonien nach den neuesten Entdeckungen. Freiburg: 1885. 1 vol.
LAYARD, AUSTEN H. Nineveh and its Remains. London: 1849. 2 vol.
——— Discoveries among the ruins of Nineveh and Babylon. (American Edition.) New York: 1853. 1 vol.
LENORMANT, FRANÇOIS. Les Premières Civilisations, Etudes d'histoire et d'archéologie. Paris: Maisonneuve et Cie. 1874. 2 vol.
——— Les Origines de l'Histoire, d'après la Bible et les traditions des peuples Orientaux. Paris Maisonneuve et Cie., 3 vol. 1st vol. 1880; 2d vol. 1882; 3d vol. 1884.
——— LA LÉGENDE DE SÉMIRAMIS, premier mémoire de mythologie comparée. Paris: 1873.
LHOTZKY, HEINRICH. Die Annalen Asurnazirpals, nach der Ausgabe des Londoner Inschriften-werkes umschrieben, übersetzt und erklärt. (Inaugural-Dissertation.) Munchen: 1885.
LOTZ, DR. WILHELM. Die Inschriften Tiglath-Pileser's I. in transkribirtem Assyrischem Grundtext mit Ubersetzung und Kommentar. Leipzig: 1880. 1 vol.
LYON, DR. D. G. Keilschrifttexte Sargon's, königs von Assyrien. Leipzig.
MASPERO, G. Histoire Ancienne des Peuples de l'Orient. 4e. edit. Paris: 1877. 1 vol.
MEYER, EDWARD. GESCHICHTE DES ALTERTHUMS. Stuttgart. 1884. vol. 1st.
MÜNTER, D. FRIEDRICH. RELIGION DER KARTHAGER, 2te. Auflage. Kopenhagen. 1821. 1 vol.
MÜRDTER F. KURZGEFASSTE GESCHICHTE BABYLONIENS UND ASSYRIENS, mit besonderer Berücksichtigung des alten Testaments. Mit Vorwort und Beigaben von Friedrich Delitzsch. Stuttgart. 1882. 1 vol.
PERROT ET CHIPIEZ. HISTOIRE DE L'ART DANS L'ANTIQUITÉ. Tome II. "Les Assyriens." And Tome III. "Phénicie et Chypre."
POGNON, H. L'inscription de Bavian, texte, traduction et Commentaire. Paris: 1879 et 1880.
RAWLINSON, GEORGE. THE FIVE GREAT MONARCHIES OF THE ANCIENT EASTERN WORLD. London: 1865. 1st and 2d vol.

——— HISTORY OF HERODOTUS, a new English version, with copious notes and appendices, etc. London: 1875. 4 vol.
RECORDS OF THE PAST. Vol. I., III., V., VII., IX., XI.
RENAN, ERNEST. Mission de Phénicie. Paris: 1865. Text, 3 Parts. Plates, 6 Parts.
SAYCE, A. H. FRESH LIGHT FROM ANCIENT MONUMENTS. ("By-Paths of Bible Knowledge" Series II.) 3d ed. 1885. London: 1 vol.
——— THE ANCIENT EMPIRES OF THE EAST. London: 1884. 1 vol.
SCHRADER, EBERHARD. Die Keilinschriften und das Alte Testament. 2d ed. Giessen: 1883. 1 vol.
——— Keilinschriften und Geschichtsforschung. Giessen: 1878. 1 vol.
——— Zur Kritik der Inschriften Tiglath-Pileser's II., des Asarhaddon und des Asurbanipal. Berlin: 1880.
——— "HISTORY OF SENNACHERIB, translated from the Cuneiform Inscriptions. Edited by the Rev. A. H. Sayce, London: 1878. 1 vol.
SMITH, GEORGE. History of Assurbanipal. Translated from Cuneiform inscriptions. London: 1871. 1 vol.
——— ASSYRIA FROM THE EARLIEST TIME TO THE FALL OF NINEVEH. ("Ancient History from the Monuments" Series.) London. 1 vol.
——— Assyrian Discoveries, an account of explorations, 1873-1874. London: 1875. 1 vol.
——— The Assyrian Eponym Canon. London: 1876. 1 vol.
STADE, DR. BERNHARD. Geschichte des Volkes Israel. ("Allgemeine Geschichte in einzelnen Darstellungen.") Berlin: 1881-1886.
TIELE, C. P. Babylonisch-Assyrische Geschichte Erster Theil: von den ältesten Zeiten bis zum Tode Sargons II. Gotha: 1886.
VIGOUROUX, ABBÉ F. LA BIBLE ET LES DÉCOUVERTES MODERNES, en Palestine, en Egypte et en Assyrie. 4e edit. Paris: 1884. 4 vols.
WEBER, A. Indische Streifen.
WRIGHT, WILLIAM. THE EMPIRE OF THE HITTITES. American edition, New York: 1884. 1 vol.
Numerous pamphlets and essays, by Fr. Lenormant, A. Delattre, Sir Henry Rawlinson, A. H. Sayce, Dr. Fritz Hommel and others;

in Mr. Geo. Rawlinson's translation of Herodotus, in the Calwer Bibellexikon, and in various periodicals, such as the "Proceedings" and "Transactions" of the Society of Biblical Archæology, and many more.

LIST OF ILLUSTRATIONS.

	PAGE
ASSHURBANIPAL HUNTING LIONS . .	*Frontispiece*
EMBLEM OF THE GOD ASSHUR	11
WINGED DISK	12
CYLINDER SEAL OF SENNACHERIB . . .	14
ASSYRIAN CYLINDER SEAL	15
HITTITE INSCRIPTION . .	36
DEAD SEA	41
PROCESSION (PROBABLY OF GODS) . .	48
CARRIED INTO CAPTIVITY . .	49
MARCH OF ASSYRIAN ARMY	51
PLUNDERING AND DEMOLISHING A CITY . .	53
SCALING A FORTRESS . .	55
A PASS IN LEBANON	77
SOURCE OF THE RIVER ADONIS . . .	79
SMALL PHŒNICIAN IDOL IN TERRA-COTTA . .	98
ASHTORETH	99
PHŒNICIAN SARCOPHAGUS	101
PHŒNICIAN CYLINDER	107
COIN FROM CYPRUS	111
COIN FROM SIDON	111
ASSYRIAN PORTABLE ALTAR . . .	113
GROUP OF CEDARS IN LEBANON . .	155
ASSHURNAZIRPAL AND OFFICER . . .	160
COUNTING AND PILING UP HEADS OF CAPTIVES	162
PRISONERS IMPALED BEFORE CITY WALLS .	163
LION HUNT (NIMRUD)	167

LIST OF ILLUSTRATIONS.

	PAGE
LION IN ROYAL PALACE	169
ASSHURNAZIRPAL OFFERING SACRIFICE	171
BLACK OBELISK OF SHALMANESER II.	186
FIRST FACE OF BLACK OBELISK	188
SECOND FACE OF BLACK OBELISK	189
THIRD FACE OF BLACK OBELISK	192
FOURTH FACE OF BLACK OBELISK	193
TRIBUTE BEARERS BRINGING MONKEYS	195
GATE OF BALAWAT	197
STELE OF SHAMSHI—RAMÂN III.	199
SEMIRAMIS CHANGED INTO A DOVE	202
SEMIRAMIS CHANGED INTO A DOVE (BACK VIEW)	203
THE "MESHA STELE"	214
FLOCKS AND CAPTIVE WOMEN CARRIED AWAY	220
CAPTIVES AND PLUNDER	221
ASSYRIAN SOLDIERS DESTROYING A PLANTATION	234
STORMING A FORTRESS (FACE)	236
CITY AND PALACES	244
PORTRAIT OF SARGON	248
SARGON'S STANDARD	252
SARGON PUTS OUT PRISONERS' EYES	257
THE MOUND OF KHORSABAD	279
SARGON'S PALACE AT KHORSABAD	281
WALL AND GATE OF DUR-SHARRUKIN	282
GATEWAY OF DUR-SHARRUKIN (RESTORED)	284
SCULPTURES ON WALLS OF DUR-SHARRUKIN	286
FACE VIEW OF WINGED BULL	288
BATTLEMENTS OF TERRACE WALL	289
DECORATION IN ENAMELLED TILES	290
THRESHOLD SLAB IN SARGON'S PALACE	291
LION WEIGHT	292
TRANSPORT OF TIMBER FOR SARGON'S PALACE	293
SENNACHERIB ON HIS THRONE IN GALA APPAREL	296

LIST OF ILLUSTRATIONS. xix

	PAGE
SENNACHERIB RECEIVING SUBMISSION OF CONQUERED PRINCE	301
SENNACHERIB RECEIVES SPOILS OF CITY OF LAKISH (FACE)	312
WILD SOW WITH YOUNG	316
CAPTIVES BUILDING PLATFORM MOUND	323
FINISHED WINGED BULL	325
HALF-SCULPTURED WINGED BULL	327
ATTENDANTS CARRYING DESSERT TO THE BANQUET HALL	329
ROCK STELE OF ESARHADDON	332
HITTITE ROCK SCULPTURE (KAKBEL)	361
HITTITE ROCK SCULPTURE (IBRIZ)	363
ASSHURBANIPAL IN HIS CHARIOT	372
ASSHURBANIPAL CROSSING A RIVER	376
SCENE FROM THE BATTLE ON THE ULAI	389
ASSHURBANIPAL FEASTING	402
ASSHURBANIPAL FEASTING	403
DYING LION	405
DYING LIONESS	407
TABLET FROM ASSHURBANIPAL'S LIBRARY	411
TAME LION AND LIONESS	412
TERRA-COTTA DOG	413
THRESHOLD OF ASSHURBANIPAL'S PALACE	414
LEASHED HOUNDS GOING TO THE CHASE	415

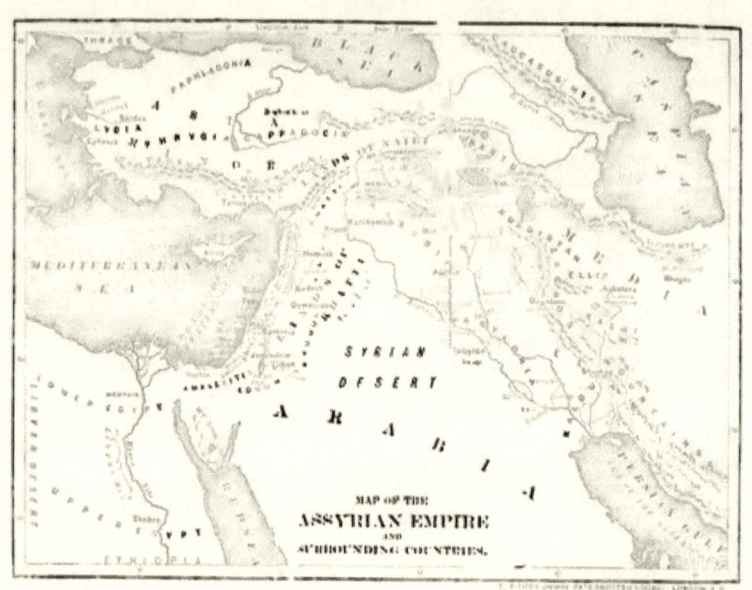

THE STORY OF ASSYRIA.

I.

THE RISE OF ASSHUR.

1. THERE is, on carefully drawn maps of Mesopotamia, a pale undulating line (considerably to the north of the city of Accad or Agadè), which cuts across the valley of the two rivers, from Is or Hit on the Euphrates,—the place famous for its inexhaustible bitumen pits,—to Samarah on the Tigris. This line marks the beginning of the alluvium, *i. e.*, of the rich, moist alluvial land formed by the rivers,* and at the same time the natural boundary of Northern Babylonia. Beyond it the land, though still a plain, is not only higher, rising till it meets the transversal limestone ridge of the Sinjar Hills, but of an entirely different character and formation. It is distressingly dry and bare, scarcely differing in this respect from the contiguous Syrian Desert, and nothing but the most laborious irrigation could ever have made it productive, except in the immediate vicinity of the rivers. What the country has become

---

* See "Story of Chaldea," p. 37.

through centuries of neglect and misrule, we have seen.* It must have been much in the same condition before a highly developed civilization reclaimed it from its natural barrenness and covered it with towns and farms. It is probable that for many centuries a vast tract of land south of the alluvium line, as well as all that lay north of it, was virtually unoccupied; the resort of nameless and unclassed nomadic tribes, for Agadè is the most northern of important Accadian cities we hear of.

2. Yet some pioneers must have pushed northward at a pretty early time, followed at intervals by a steadier stream of emigrants, possibly driven from their populous homes in Accad by the discomfort and oppression consequent on the great Elamite invasion and conquest. At least there are, near the present hamlet of Kileh-Sherghat, on the right bank of the Tigris, the ruins of a city, whose most ancient name is Accadian—AUSHAR—and appears to mean, "well-watered plain," but was afterwards changed into ASSHUR, and which was governed by king-priests—*patesis*—after the manner of the ancient Chaldean cities.† There are temple-ruins there, of which the bricks bear the names of ISHMI-DAGAN and his son, SHAMASH-RAMÂN, who are mentioned by a later king in a way to show that they lived very close on 1800 B.C. The colony which settled here and quickly grew, spreading further north, appropriating and peopling the small but fertile region between the Tigris, its several tributary streams, and

---

* See "Story of Chaldea," pp. 6, 7, and Ch. II. of Introduction.
† See Ibid. pp. 203 and 235.

the first hills of the Zagros highlands, was Semitic;
their first city's name was extended to all the land
they occupied, and they also called themselves by it.
They were the "people of Asshur"; their land was
"the land of Asshur"; and not many centuries
elapsed before all their neighbors, far and wide, had
good reason to know and dread the name. This
sheltered nook, narrowly circumscribed, but exceptionally well situated as regards both defence and
natural advantages, may well be called the cradle of
the great Assyrian Empire, where the young nation
built its first cities, the stronghold in which, during
many years, it gathered strength and independence,
gradually working out its peculiarly vigorous and
aggressive character, and finding its military training
in petty but constant conflicts with the surrounding
roving tribes of the hill and the plain.

3. Accordingly, it is this small district of a few
square miles,—with its three great cities, KALAH,
NINEVEH, and ARBELA, and a fourth, DUR-SHAR-
RUKIN, added much later,—which has been known
to the ancients as ATURIA or Assyria proper, and to
which the passage in the tenth chapter of Genesis
(11-12) alludes. At the period of its greatest ex-
pansion, however, the name of "Assyria"—"land of
Asshur"—covered a far greater territory, more than
filling the space between the two rivers, from the
mountains of Armenia to the alluvial line. This
gives a length of 350 miles by a breadth, between
the Euphrates and the Zagros, varying from above
300 to 170 miles. "The area was probably not less
than 75,000 square miles, which is beyond that of

the German provinces of Prussia or Austria, more than double that of Portugal, and not much below that of Great Britain. Assyria would thus, from her mere size, be calculated to play an important part in history; and the more so, as, during the period of her greatness, scarcely any nation with which she came in contact possessed nearly so extensive a territory."*

4. That the nation of Asshur, which the biblical table of nations (Gen. x. 22) places second among Shem's own children, was of purely Semitic race, has never been doubted. The striking likeness of the Assyrian to the Hebrew type of face would almost alone have sufficed to establish the relationship, even were not the two languages so very nearly akin. But the kinship goes deeper than that, and asserts itself in certain spiritual tendencies, which find their expression in the national religion, or, more correctly, in the one essential modification introduced by the Assyrians into the Babylonian religion, which they otherwise adopted wholesale, just as they brought it from their Southern home. Like their Hebrew brethren, they arrived at the perception of the Divine Unity; but while the wise men of the Hebrews took their stand uncompromisingly on monotheism and imposed it on their reluctant followers with a fervor and energy that no resistance or backsliding could abate, the Assyrian priests thought to reconcile the truth, which they but imperfectly grasped, with the old traditions and the

---

* G. Rawlinson, "Five Ancient Monarchies," Vol. I. p. 227 (edit 1862).

established religious system. They retained the entire Babylonian pantheon, with all its theory of successive emanations, its two great triads, its five planetary deities, and the host of inferior divinities, but, at the head of them all, and above them all, they placed the one God and Master whom they recognized as supreme. They did not leave him wrapped in uncertainty and lost in misty remoteness, but gave him a very distinct individuality and a personal name: they called him ASSHUR; and whether the city were named after the god or the god after the city, and then the land and people after both,—a matter of dispute among scholars,—one fact remains, and that the all-important one: that the Assyrians identified themselves with their own national god, called themselves "his people," believed themselves to be under his especial protection and leadership in peace and war. His name almost always heads the lists of "great gods" who are usually invoked, sometimes alone, sometimes with their "great" or "exalted consorts" at the beginning of long inscriptions. Here is such an invocation, the opening of a very famous inscription, in which Tiglath-Pileser I., a mighty king and Assyria's first great conqueror, narrates some of his campaigns: "*Asshur, the great lord, who rules the host of the gods,* who endows with sceptre and crown, establishes royalty,—Bel, the lord, the king of all the Anunnaki,[*] father of gods, lord of countries,—Sin, the wise, lord of the crown, the exalted in luminous brilliancy,—Shamash, the judge

---

[*] See the "Story of Chaldea," p. 250; "Five Monarchies," Vol. I. p. 300.

of heaven and earth, who sees the evil deeds of the enemies. . . . . Ramán, the mighty, who floods the countries of the enemies, their lands and their houses,—Ninéb, the strong, who destroys evil-doers and enemies and lets men find what their heart desires,—Ishtar, the first-born of the gods, who makes battles fierce;—Ye great gods, the governors of heaven and earth, whose onslaught is battle and destruction, who have exalted the royalty of Tiglath-Pileser, the great one, the belovèd of your hearts," etc., etc. We shall have to return to this inscription, for many reasons one of the most important. But this extract is sufficient to show the precedence and supremacy to which Asshur is considered as unquestionably entitled.

5. Quite as often he is mentioned alone. Indeed, when a king tells of an expedition, undertaking, or public act of his of any importance he generally refers it in some way to Asshur as the distinctive and representative national and supreme God,—to his service, or law, or direct command or inspiration. And herein again, as Mr. G. Rawlinson justly remarks, the Assyrian spirit shows itself nearly akin to that of the Hebrews, who, in the same manner, refer all their public acts, from a raid on a neighboring tribe to a wholesale slaughter of prisoners, to the service and command of Yahveh (Jehovah). The Assyrian kings never fail to attribute their victories and conquests to Asshur, whose emblem precedes them in battle, borne aloft on their standards. (See No. 1.) Indeed, there are two or three standing expressions used to record such events: they are

these: "The majesty of Asshur, my lord, overwhelmed them; they came and kissed my feet;" or, "The fear of Asshur overwhelmed the inhabitants: my feet they took;" or, "Exceeding fear of Asshur my lord overwhelmed them: they came and took my feet." These extracts are taken from inscriptions of different kings and centuries widely removed from each other, and might be multiplied without end. They answer exactly to the biblical phrase, "Yahveh delivered them into their hands;" or this: "The fame of David went out into all the lands, and Yahveh brought the fear of him on all nations." An expedition to conquer a neighboring territory or to punish rebels is undertaken at the express command of Asshur, or of "Asshur and the great gods"; and in order to propagate their laws, or to chastise those who "did not keep their oaths to the great gods," or "hardened their hearts and disregarded the will of Asshur, the god, my creator." Thus Tiglath-Pileser I. says, in the inscription already mentioned: "Asshur, and the great gods who have exalted my royalty, who have endowed me with strength and power, *commanded me to enlarge the boundaries of their land, and gave into my hand their mighty weapons*, the whirlwind of battle: countries, mountains, cities, and kings, *foes to Asshur*, I overthrew, and conquered their territories." Another king, who reigns five hundred years later, represents Asshur and the gods as speaking to him by a direct message: "Then to Asshur, to Sin, Shamash, Bel, Nebo, Nergal, Ishtar of Nineveh, and Ishtar of Arbela I lifted my hands. They accepted my prayer. In their gracious favor an encouraging message they sent to me: 'Go! fear not! We march at thy side! We aid thy expedition.'" All this forcibly recalls to the mind such biblical passages as the following: "And the Lord said unto Joshua, Stretch the spear that is in thine hand toward it, for I will give it into thine hand" (Joshua, viii. 18); or still more this one, to which, moreover, many parallel ones might be found with little searching: "And David inquired of God, Shall I go up against the Philistines? And wilt thou deliver them into mine hand? And the Lord said to him, Go up, for I will deliver them into thine hand. . . . David, therefore, did as God commanded him, and they smote the host of the Philistines" (1 Chronicles, xiv. 10, ff.).

6. Further, the Assyrian kings, when they inflict more than usually cruel treatment on their captives, be they individuals or nations, are wont to justify it by their religious zeal, nay, to glory in the thoroughness with which they fulfil what they represent as the direct commands of Asshur and the gods of Assyria. "They revolted against me," says the often-quoted Asshurbanipal of the people of Accad, Aram, and others, "and by command of Asshur and Belit, and the great gods, my protectors, on the whole of them I trampled." Immediately after this he mentions that he had, in a former expedition, cut off the head of his captive enemy, the king of Elam, "by command of Asshur." As to the rebels in Accad, he boasts that "those men who uttered curses against Asshur, my god, and devised evil against me, the prince, his worshipper, their tongues I pulled out" (a common form of torture

repeatedly represented on the sculptures); of the rest of the rebels, he threw a large number alive into a deep pit or ditch, dug in the midst of the city, among the stone lions and bulls of the palace gates, after cutting off their limbs and causing these "to be eaten by dogs, bears, eagles, vultures, birds of heaven, and fishes of the deep." "By these things which were done," he concludes with religious complacency. "I satisfied the hearts of the great gods, my lords." And when he further relates how he bound another captive chief in chains with dogs and thus kept him "in the great gate in the midst of Nineveh," he calls this treatment a "judgment on him to satisfy the law of Asshur and the great gods, my lords." We see the exact parallel to this in the annals of the Jews' wars and conquests. They are continually enjoined, in the name of the Lord, by their leaders and priests, to put to the sword the vanquished populations, as a preservative against the contagion of their idolatrous religions. "Then you shall rise up from the ambush," says Joshua to the Israelite warriors, "and seize upon the city, for the Lord your God will deliver it into your hand. And it shall be, when ye have taken the city, that ye shall set the city on fire: *according to the commandment of the Lord shall ye do*" (Joshua, viii. 7–8). Perhaps the most memorable occasion is that on which King Saul is declared to have forfeited the crown and the favor of God for having saved one life and reserved some cattle. These are the instructions which the prophet Samuel delivers to Saul as he sends him on an expedition against the Amalekites, prefacing his words with the usual solemn "Thus saith Yahveh Shebaoth (the Lord of hosts)," which stamps them as divine orders: "Now go and smite Amalek, and utterly destroy all that they have, and spare them not ; *but slay both man and woman, infant and suckling*, ox and sheep, camel and ass." Saul did smite the Amalekites, and "utterly destroyed all the people with the edge of the sword," but spared Agag their king, who had been taken alive, and the best of the herds. For this disobedience Samuel declared to Saul : "Thou hast rejected the word of the Lord, and the Lord hath rejected thee from being king over Israel," then calling for Agag to be brought to him, "*Samuel hewed Agag in pieces before Yahveh*" (1 Samuel, xv.).

7. But if both the Hebrews and Assyrians referred their military acts to direct divine command and guidance, the immense power thus created was very differently distributed in both. With the Hebrews it was all in the hands of the priesthood and prophets, and scarcely any of it rested with the kings when royalty was established. The kings were but instruments, one might almost say servants, of the priests and prophets, elected, anointed by them, and by them deposed if not found sufficiently submissive. Even to offer a sacrifice before the people was not lawful for the king ; it was the priest's privilege, and Samuel sternly reproves Saul for his presumption in taking the office on himself on one occasion (1 Samuel, xv.). Things were very different in Assyria. The king was also the priest—still the *patesi* of old times. He sometimes expressly calls

himself "High-priest of Asshur." But only of Asshur, the one supreme god. Royalty on earth is the representative of the ruler in heaven. The national god and the national leader together are the greatness and safeguard of the state; they are in direct communion with each other, and nothing can come between them. The monuments give the amplest and most conclusive proof of this relationship.

8. In the sculptured scenes representing incidents from the career of a monarch—whose person is always known by his rich robes, high head-tire, and his beardless attendants — we often see hovering above his head, or just in front of him, a peculiar object : mostly a human figure, ending in a feathered appendage like a bird's tail—a dove's, it is thought—from the waist downwards, and framed in, or passed through, a circle or wheel furnished with wings. It is the emblem of Asshur, and it is seen, if not above that of the sacred tree or an altar on which sacrifice is being offered, accompanying only the king, never any one else. Its attitude also answers to the character of the scene in the midst of which the god appears to protect and consecrate the royal presence. If a battle, he is represented as drawing a bow before the king; the arrow which he is send-

I.—EMBLEM OF THE GOD ASSHUR.
(Perrot and Chipiez.)

ing into the midst of the enemies plainly symbolizes the destruction and fear which the inscriptions describe him as bringing on all his foes. If a peaceful solemnity—for instance, a triumphal procession, a religious ceremony—the bow is lowered and one hand uplifted unarmed, an attitude in which the king himself is frequently represented on similar occasions (see Nos. 1 and 2); or there is no bow at

2.—WINGED DISK (EMBLEM OF ASSHUR).
(Perrot and Chipiez.)

all, and one hand holds out a wreath, probably an emblem of peace and prosperity. Sometimes the human figure is absent, and the simplified emblem consists only of a winged circle or disk, with the bird's tail, which is never omitted. In this form it strikingly resembles the Egyptian symbol of the supreme deity, which is also a winged disk, but without the tail, while the wings are those of the sparrow-hawk, which was the sacred bird of the Egyptians, just as the dove was that of the Assyrians, and of several other Semitic and Canaanitic nations. The two peoples were known to each other, and came in contact at an earlier date than the earliest to which any sculptures can be referred, and it is not impossible that the Assyrian priests, wishing to embody with the rest of their religious system a conception which they did not inherit from the old Chaldean home, borrowed the emblem from the Egyptians, whose fame for wisdom in such things was of long standing. It may perhaps not be too bold to conjecture that the Asshur-emblem may in reality have been a compound one, intended to convey the idea of the universe embodied in its ruling powers—its gods, to speak the language of antiquity—being contained in the one supreme Godhead. The disk, we must remember, symbolizes the sun in all mythologies; the dove is the bird of Ishtar, the goddess of earthly productive nature—Heaven and Earth, the eternal couple! And when we see the sacred emblem hovering over the mystic tree of life (as in Nos. 3 and 4), the intention seems more obvious still and the presentation of it complete. Within the disk we sometimes see five smaller balls:—the suggestion of the five planets, strikingly emphasizing the conception of heaven, is almost irresistible; and the unique form—a small head on each wing—in which the emblem appears on the cylinder seal of King Sennacherib (No. 3) could scarcely be explained at all on any other grounds; while, if we see in it a personation embracing the Supreme Triad and the feminine form of Nature—*i. e.*, of the entire universe in its twofold essence, masculine and feminine—it explains itself, and almost seems to correspond in deep significance to the Hebrew plural " Elohim," as a name for the one indivisible God.* A no less remarkable instance of the compound nature of the Asshur emblem is a cylinder of, it is thought, the ninth century B.C. The king, (represented, for symmetry's sake, in double), attended by one of those eagle-headed winged-protecting genii so familiar to students of the sculptures, worships before the sacred tree, above which hovers the emblem of Asshur in its completest form; from the circle depends a sort of string in a wavy line, and as it ends in a well-drawn *fork*— the undoubted emblem of Ramân, the god of the atmosphere—it may be reasonably supposed to represent the lightning. That the king holds it in his hand unharmed only expresses the sacredness of his person and his intimate connection with the national god. This supposition would by no means contradict the explanation commonly given of the strings as symbolizing the bond between the god and king created by prayer. Both explanations are perfectly compatible. It is the *fork* which so strongly sug-

3.—CYLINDER SEAL OF KING SEN-NACHERIB.
(Perrot and Chipiez.)

---

* See " Story of Chaldea," p. 354.

gests Ramân. The sacredness of the symbol is impressed on us even by the robes he wears on the sculptures, and which have as much a priestly as a royal character, since not only the embroidery on his breast reproduces the winged disk and sacred tree, but even accessory details of his costume are ornamented with symbolical designs of the same religious nature (see No. 4), which supply much of the decorations also of his dwelling, at least of the public apartments therein. It would almost seem that the king was himself ranked with the gods, as subject to Asshur alone, or at least held worthy to associate with them, if we judge from a cylinder on which a royal wor‑

4.—ASSYRIAN CYLINDER SEAL.
(Perrot and Chipiez.)

shipper is faced on the other side of the sacred tree by no less a personage than Êa-Oannes, that ancient and much revered divine being who, like him, does homage to the holy emblem. Officiating and sacrificing priests are frequently encountered on sculptures and cylinders, but never in the presence of the sovereign, or then only as following and attending on him: nothing and no one could ever come between the king and "Asshur, his lord." Yet the other "great gods" were also called upon to protect and consecrate the royal persons; we see kings wearing, as a necklace, the five secondary divine emblems, probably in gold. These were: a sun, a moon-crescent, a star, Ramân's lightning-fork, and Bel's horned cap—the headdress adorned with bull's horns, which is not only associated with Bel, but generally symbolizes divine lordliness and power, and as such is worn by Asshur himself, by the winged bulls and lions, the mighty guardians of the palace gates, and by the winged good genii (see No. 35). The same emblems we see encircling the head of kings on their sculptured images (see No. 46). One such royal slab or "*stele*," as such representations are technically called, is of additional interest from the altar which was found in front of and just below it, and which seems to suggest that the monarch, either in his lifetime or after his death, received divine honors, or at least was considered as presiding over religious ceremonies in effigy when not present in person. There would be nothing improbable in either supposition after all the indications we have of the royal sacredness; and, truly, Shakespeare might have had the Assyrian monarchs in his mind when he spoke of the divinity that doth hedge a king.

9. After dwelling so long and amply on the most important and distinctive feature of the Assyrian religion,—the conception and worship of Asshur,—the rest of the pantheon can be considered in very few words, since it is mainly unchanged from the Babylonian, and only a few deviations have to be pointed out. In the first place, Gibil, the Fire-god, is heard

of no more. Then Bel-Marduk, transformed from the benevolently busy Meridug, so dear to old Shumir,—Bel-Marduk, the chief and tutelary deity of the later Chaldean empire and of the great Babylon, where his temple was reckoned and long remembered as one of the wonders of the world,—had to be content in the sister kingdom with a very secondary position, that of ruler of the planet Jupiter. Very early Assyrian kings include him in their opening invocations, and sometimes even make separate mention of him in their inscriptions; but it is only from old associations, and the habit dies out as the national Asshur increases in importance. Marduk does not receive the compliment of a single temple in Assyria, and though the latest kings once more make his name prominent in their documents, they pay him this respect on account of their renewed close connection with Babylon and partly to conciliate the Babylonians. His father, Êa, fares even worse. Though he retains his place in the great triad —Anu, Êa, Bel—he practically is consigned to oblivion, and the very rare and cold, if respectful, mention which is made of him only makes the fact more apparent. He also cannot boast a single temple in Assyria, while Anu, who in a great measure shares this neglect, had one at least. True, that one was not in either Nineveh or Kalah, the modern capitals, but in Asshur, the old-empire city, and pointed to a time when the connection with the mother country and its traditions had scarcely as yet been loosened. "There is, however, reason to believe," according to some writers, "that Anu was occasionally honored with a shrine in a temple dedicated to another deity."* Ishtar, on the other hand, was as great a favorite with the Assyrians as with the empire of the South. Her two principal temples were in Nineveh and Arbela (ARBA-ILU, "the city of four gods"). In the latter she was worshipped pre-eminently in her martial character as the goddess of war and battle, the inspirer of heroic deeds, and the giver of victory; while in Nineveh, it was her feminine, voluptuous aspect which predominated, and she was essentially the goddess of love, of nature, and all delights. So marked became this division, that she, so to speak, split herself into two distinct deities, and the mention of her in the invocations is generally twofold,—as "Ishtar of Nineveh" and "Ishtar of Arbela,"—and the two fortnights of the month are alternately consecrated to her. This distinction must have been assisted by the difference of the goddess's garb and attributes in the two characters, and thus have slipped into pure idolatry. As she was, in the astronomical-religious system, the ruler of the planet we call Venus, the star among the five divine emblems (see above) must have been specially intended for her. It is the more probable, that her name originally means "the goddess" *par excellence*, and that in the Assyro-Babylonian writing (the same for both countries, like the language) the sign of a star stands for the idea and the word "deity," whether "god" or "goddess." When the real, visible stars are meant, the sign is

---

* G. Rawlinson, "Five Monarchies," Vol. II. p. 241.

repeated three times in a peculiar group, a very conclusive proof of the originally astral (or astronomical) nature of the religion. Another interesting detail in the same direction is that, the planet Venus appearing in the evening, soon after sunset, and then again in the early morning, just before dawn, it was called Ishtar at night and Bêlit at dawn, as a small tablet expressly informs us; a distinction which, apparently confusing, rather tends to confirm the fundamental identity between the two.—Ishtar, "the goddess," and Bêlit, "the lady." * The other gods changed little in their migration from the Persian Gulf to the foot of the Zagros and the Armenian Mountains; and besides, we shall occasionally meet them as our narrative advances, when it will be time enough to note any peculiarity they may display, or influence they may exert.

10. Whether Assyria in its infancy was a mere dependency of the mother country, ruled, may be, by governors sent from Babylon, or whether it was from the first an independent colony (as the young bee-swarm when it has flown from the old hive), has never yet been ascertained. There have been no means of doing so, as there is no narrative monumental inscription earlier than 1100 B.C. Still, all things considered, the latter supposition appears the more probable one. The Semitic emigrants who retired to the distant northern settlement of Aushar, possibly before the Elamitic conquerors, took their departure at a time when the mother country

---

* See the "Story of Chaldea," p. 245.

was too distracted by wars and the patriotic struggle against the hated foreigners to exercise much control or supervision over its borders; and they will have experienced as little of both as did their brethren of Ur, when they wandered forth into the steppes of Canaan. The bond must have been merely a moral one, that of community in culture, language, and religion—a bond that could not prevent rivalry as soon as the young country's increasing strength allowed it, and, as a consequence, a frequently hostile attitude. At all events, border feuds must have begun early and proved troublesome, from the indefiniteness of the natural boundary, if the slight elevation of the alluvial line may be so termed, and the first positive record we have of Assyria as a political power is one which shows us a king of Assyria and a king of Kar-Dunyash (Babylon)* making a treaty in order to determine the boundaries of the two countries, and giving each other pledges for the observance thereof; this happened about 1450 B.C., and the successors of the two kings renewed the treaty about 1400 B.C. The friendship was so close at the time, that BURNA-BURYASH, the Babylonian king † (of the Cossaean dynasty), ‡ married the Assyrian's daughter; an event which was the indirect cause of Assyria's first armed interference in the affairs of the South. For after Burnaburiash's death there was a revolt among the Kasshi. They rose against his son

---

* See the "Story of Chaldea," p. 286.
† See Ibid. p. 228.

(perhaps on account of his half-foreign parentage?) and slew him, after which they raised to the kingdom a usurper,—"a man of low parentage," the tablet calls him. ASSHUR-UBALLIT, the then reigning king of Assyria, made a descent on Babylon to avenge his kinsman's fate, defeated the rebels, and placed another son of Burnaburiash on the throne. Having inflicted this neighborly correction he returned to his own realm, and things remained as they had been. He may possibly not have been displeased at this opportunity of asserting the northern kingdom's power and importance and of establishing a precedent flattering to its new-born dignity.

11. Not quite two hundred years before these events, we are confronted by the name of Asshur in a rather unexpected quarter. It occurs on an Egyptian list of Asiatic nations who sent tribute or presents to the great Egyptian conqueror DHUTMES III., who repeatedly overran the immense region between the Nile and the Euphrates—not twice or three times, but fourteen times in seventeen years. Egypt was just appearing on the world's stage in the character of an invader and conqueror, and, though a very old nation, the part she played so brilliantly was new to her. The Egyptians, from their remotest antiquity (and that, as we saw,[*] takes us back quite or nearly as far as the antiquity of Chaldea), had always dwelt secluded in their wonderful Nile-valley. This valley, making up in length

---

[*] See "Story of Chaldea," p. 304.

what it wanted in width, gave them sufficient room in which to live and increase, to be industrious and prosperous, and to develop, in the course of some three thousand years, that magnificent civilization, that profound national wisdom, which have been the marvel of the world, and are becoming more and more so with every conquest of the pickaxe and shovel—those humble instruments which are as magicians' wands in the hands of the modern explorer, to call the dead to life and reconstruct cities and kingdoms. Not only were the Egyptians proud of their race, they considered it as something sacred, and themselves as a nation set apart from the rest of the world for purity and holiness. With such an opinion of themselves they naturally had a horror of foreigners, mere contact or intercourse with whom was to them pollution, and that alone would have sufficed to deter them from travelling or annexing other lands.

12. But absolute seclusion is unnatural and an impossibility, as well for nations as for individuals, and the Egyptians had to open—grudgingly, ungraciously, but still to open—at least one corner of their sacred land to their Canaanitic and Semitic neighbors —the north-east corner by the sea, which, moreover, it would have been difficult to close against stray wanderers from the desert coming across the sandy wilderness of the Sinai peninsula, since, on that side, Egypt has absolutely no natural barrier or protection. That district, then, rendered very fertile by the many arms of the Nile, had been for centuries inhabited in great part by foreigners. No-

madic tribes who came, in times of drought, with their thirsty, dwindled flocks, were admitted and allotted pastures, on which they settled permanently, unless they preferred, after awhile, to return to their steppes in Syria or their oases in Arabia. It was thus that Abraham visited Egypt: "And Abram journeyed, going still toward the South. And there was a famine in the land, and Abram went down into Egypt, to sojourn there; for the famine was grievous in the land" (Genesis, xii. 9-10). Thus also his descendants went the same way, Jacob and his sons, when they entered the land,—a small tribe, little more than a family,—whence they were to go forth, four hundred years later, a nation. They say to the Pharaoh: " Thy servants are shepherds, both we and also our fathers. . . . To sojourn in the land are we come ; for there is no pasture for thy servant's flocks ; for the famine is sore in the land of Canaan : now therefore, we pray thee, let thy servants dwell in the land of Goshen " (Genesis, xlvii. 3-4). Traders, in all probability mostly Phœnicians, dwelt in the cities, their ships coming and going between the mouths of the Nile and the cities along the Mediterranean coast, their caravans carrying the treasures of Africa and Asia back and forwards along the great high-road which, skirting the sea, ran off northward into the country of the Lebanon and across Aram to the Euphrates.

13. Thus a large and powerful population was formed, looked on by the native Egyptians with suspicion and dislike, but tolerated as a necessary evil.

until a day came when their prophetic instinct was justified and a great disaster befell them from that obnoxious quarter. The country was invaded and conquered by a swarm of those Semitic tribes, rovers of the desert, like the Bedouins of the present day, whom the Egyptians contemptuously designated by the sweeping name of SHASUS, *i. e.*, "thieves, plunderers." They entered through the foreign district in the north-east, from the peninsula of Sinai, and surely must have been assisted by their wealthy and cultured kinsfolk, for without such assistance semi-barbarous nomadic tribes could scarcely have managed more than a clever plundering raid, certainly not organized a systematic invasion. Much less could they have established a permanent rule and supplanted the native kings by a dynasty of their own, which maintained itself several hundred years. This dynasty is familiarly known in history as the "SHEPHERD KINGS," a translation of the Egyptian HYKSOS ("*hyk*"—king, "*shôs*"—shepherd), a name probably given them in scornful allusion to their former pastoral habits. It is impossible to fix the date of this important revolution, for lack of inscriptions. The Egyptians, after the expulsion of the Shepherds, were not fond of recalling this long period of national humiliation, and vindictively erased all traces of it from their monuments, so that hardly more than a few names of these foreign kings have been preserved, as though by mistake, and a reconstruction of their times is not to be thought of, at least until new discoveries be made. Historians have to be content with vaguely placing the Hyksos conquest anywhere between 2200 and 2000 B.C. This date, even thus dimly defined, coincides remarkably with a momentous epoch of Chaldæan history,—that of the Elamitic conquest and rule,—and involuntarily leads to the question whether there may not have been a more than casual connection between the two events. The ravaging expeditions of Khudur-Nankhundi and his successors down to Khudur-Lagamar,* must have created a great commotion among the half-settled or wholly nomadic tribes of Aram and Canaan, and brought about more migrations than the two which we found to be probably attributable, more or less directly, to that cause. Once set in motion, such tribes would naturally be drawn rather to the South, vast and flat, than to the hilly North, because of their flocks, and thus, descending from year to year, meeting, and gathering numbers, would come on the more warlike and aggressive Shasus of Arabia and Sinai. These, knowing the way into Egypt, were very likely to propose a grand raid in common, and the two united masses must have borne down everything before them at first by sheer force of numbers. It was under one of the last Hyksos kings that Joseph was sold into Egypt, and his extraordinary career is in great part explained by this fact. Under a native Egyptian monarch it would have been impossible for a foreigner to become prime minister—" governor over the land " (Genesis, xlii. 6). The Semitic affinities between the Pharaoh and the young stranger must

---

* See " Story of Chaldea," pp. 219–225.

have been as much in the latter's favor as his skill in interpreting dreams—(this accomplishment, by the way, an inheritance from Chaldæa). The coming into Egypt of the small Hebrew tribe (now already called ISRAEL)—Jacob, his sons and grandsons, seventy souls in all, besides his sons' wives (Genesis, xlvii. 26–27)—is placed about 1730 B.C. The war of independence, carried on by native princes in the South, was already in progress: nor was the day of the national triumph very far: the Shepherds were expelled and the native monarchy restored soon after 1700 B.C.—1662 is given as a probable date.

14. But mere deliverance from the foreign yoke did not satisfy the Egyptians' long pent-up feelings of mortification. They thirsted for revenge, for retaliation, and it was this passionate desire which transformed them from a peaceful, home-abiding people into a race of eager, insatiable invaders. Kings and people became alike possessed with this aggressive spirit, and for several centuries lines of warrior-monarchs succeeded each other on the throne, among whom were some of the mightiest conquerors the world has seen. Year after year they marched into Asia and overran as well populous countries as the desert with its scattered nomadic tribes, which fled before them, more fortunate in being able to do so than the dwellers in cities and owners of farms. Of these, some thought themselves strong and fought, but were generally vanquished and heavily ransomed. Those who felt weak or timid from the possession of great wealth, brought gifts and purchased safety. These triumphant ex-

peditions were really nothing but plundering raids on a gigantic scale, for the Egyptian monarchs annexed politically none of the countries they subjected,—never attempted to turn them into Egyptian provinces, only occasionally building a fort or leaving a garrison,—but returned again and again, partly to revel in this avenging of the old national grudge —to "wash their hearts," as the Egyptian inscriptions expressively put it—partly to gather the immense periodical spoils which they had come to regard as their due. The people at home got into the habit of looking for the return of their victorious armies, and would have thought themselves defrauded, had many years elapsed without bringing round the dearly loved delights of a triumph with all its warlike pageantry, its processions of captive princes, of prisoners bound in gangs, its exhibitions of booty. And right willingly did the Pharaohs indulge them. Fourteen victorious and well-paying campaigns in seventeen years—which, as we saw above, was the figure attained by Dhutmes III., a conqueror mighty among the mightiest—surely must have satisfied both the direst thirst of vengeance and the most inordinate covetousness.

15. In one of these campaigns he encountered a more than usually well organized and obstinate resistance from a coalition of Canaanite princes, who waylaid him in the passes of the Southern Lebanon. There was a great battle near the city of MEGIDDO, situated between the Jordan and the sea, and the victory which the Pharaoh won on this occasion laid the land open before him to the Euphrates, perhaps even

—but that is by no means certain—to the Tigris. Tribute came pouring in at every place where he halted, and among those who sent gifts the "chieftain of Assuru" (Asshur) is set down on the list for fifty pounds and nine ounces of real lapis-lazuli, for imitation lapis-luzuli of Babylon (quantity not mentioned, as being less valuable), and "much gear of . . . . stone of Asshur." In the catalogue of tribute collected two years later, the "chieftain of Assuru" again figures as having sent 50 hewn cedar trees, 190 other trees, several hundred chariots, many armlets, and various other articles that have not been clearly made out. That these things are classed under the head of "tribute," not "booty," proves that Assyria did not show fight, probably not feeling equal as yet to face so formidable a foe. The battle of Megiddo took place about the year 1584 B.C.,—let us say not much later than 1600,—and Assyria had not yet reached a very noticeable place among its Western neighbors. It has been remarked that, if the Egyptian inscription be read right, the fact of the king of Assyria being denied this title, and mentioned only as "chieftain," goes as far as his submissive attitude to show that his country did not as yet rank high as an independent state. Things were to change considerably within the next three hundred years.

<small>Battle of Megiddo ab. 1600 B.C.</small>

16. On the same Egyptian lists of booty and tribute gathered in the great Pharaoh's Asiatic campaigns we find the name of another nation, occupying a prominent position, which strikingly contrasts with the bare mention of Assyria: it is that of the

KHETAS, whom we know from the Bible as HITTITES —a great and powerful people, spreading over an immense territory, far beyond the bounds of the lands we have thus far surveyed, and who were reaching the height of their glory just as Assyria began to emerge from insignificance. It is always the Khetas against whom the Pharaohs' expeditions are principally directed, and from whom they encounter the most heroic and well-regulated resistance; and though they generally defeat them, the Khetas are the only enemies with whom they occasionally treat on equal terms, and whom they mention with respect, as foes worthy of themselves. The coalition which nearly had stopped Dhutmes III.'s progress at Megiddo was composed of Hittite princes with their allies, and the spoils of the field sufficiently testify to their wealth and magnificence. Among them figure a royal war-chariot entirely of gold and thirty-one chariots plated with gold, statues with the heads of gold, thousands of pounds of golden and silver rings, jewels of all descriptions, large tables of cedar-wood, inlaid with gold and precious stones, thrones with their footstools of cedar-wood and ivory, etc., etc. Their tribute, too, when they paid it, the Khetas mostly sent in precious metals and stones. Silver was the metal they most affected, and when, after an intermittent warfare of four hundred years, a lasting peace was at last concluded between them and the Egyptian Pharaoh RAMSES II. of the nineteenth dynasty, the treaty was engraved on a large plate or disk of silver. This happened in the first part of the fourteenth century B.C. (soon after the interference of Assyria in Babylonian affairs; see p. 20), in consequence of a very famous battle fought near the Hittite capital KADESH on the river ORONTES, and in which Ramses II. indeed gained the victory, but at a cost and after a long doubtful struggle, which made it amount almost to a defeat. At least he accepted a reconciliation as eagerly as his adversary sought it.

<small>Battle of Kadesh ab. 1380 B.C.</small>

17. Like the Egyptians, the Hittites belonged to the great Hamitic division of mankind—"Heth, son of Canaan," Chapter X. of Genesis (v. 15) calls them, and Heth comes immediately after Sidon, the "firstborn." This at once locates them,—since both Canaan and Sidon were, as we have seen, geographical terms,*—and places them just where history finds them: in very early possession of the greater part of Canaan (Syria), in compact masses or scattered tribes. But they were only the southern branch of a vigorous Hamitic stock which had its headquarters in the TAURUS range, its continuation, Mount MASIOS, and the Armenian Mountains. At what time or by what route a migrating body of Hamites reached this wide streak of mountain land is, indeed, beyond the power of even conjecture to surmise; but it is quite plain that, once they got there, they stayed for long years. For locomotion is not as easy in roadless mountain passes and narrow, shut-in mountain valleys as on the open plain, and once fractions of races get wedged into such nooks,

---

* See "Story of Chaldea," p. 134.

they stay until forced, by increasing numbers or by want, to send forth new swarms in search of other quarters. That is why mountain races develop very marked individual qualities, which, having had time to become rooted habits of body and mind—a second nature, as it were—never are entirely lost, even under the influence of totally different conditions. Thus it is that the Hittites, long after their descent into the hot plains of Canaan, still preserved in their attire—the use of boots, of the close-belted tunic—certain signs betraying a Northern origin. This is very plainly shown on the Egyptian wall-paintings which represent the battle of Kadesh and reproduce with great accuracy the distinctive traits of the nations that took part in it.

18. The Hittites had another and still more important capital than Kadesh—KARKHEMISH on the Euphrates, a city as strong, from a military point of view, as it was powerful and wealthy, being situated at the junction of the two commercial high roads—that from Egypt to the mountains of Armenia (south to north) and that between Babylon and Nineveh, on one side, and the rich trading cities along the sea on the other (east to west). This city in time became their principal capital, the great national centre. So that the King of Karkhemish is frequently styled by the Assyrians "King of the Hittites" in a general way, although the Hittites, like all ancient nations, were split into a great many larger or smaller principalities, the petty rulers of which all rejoiced in the title of "king." It would seem, however, that in the course of time, he of

Karkhemish came to exercise a certain supremacy over them all, could summon them to follow him to wars, and could rely on their services as one entitled to command them. Next to him in power and importance was undoubtedly the King of Kadesh. These two appear to have controlled, between them, the Hittite cities and tribes scattered all over the northern part of Syria, but were separated by various alien peoples, with names familiar from the Bible—Amorites, Hivites, Jebusites, etc.—from a southern branch of their nation, the Hittites of Hebron, between the Dead Sea and the Mediterranean—the same whom we found selling to Abraham, for a sum of money (in silver again!), the piece of land of which he made his family burying-place.* These southern Hittites reached in an intermittent chain to the boundaries of Egypt, and as they cannot but have had connections with the Shasus of Sinai, it is very probable that they took part in the great invasion. Indeed, some eminent scholars more than suppose that one of the unknown Hyksos dynasties was Hittite. This, if proved, would account still more fully for the bitter enmity which could not vent itself sufficiently through four centuries of war.

19. On the whole, the Hittites of the South had a more difficult position than those of the North. Not only did they have to bear the first brunt of an Egyptian invasion, but they were scattered and wedged in amidst various hostile tribes, and in the territory of the most powerful and compact nation

---

* See "Story of Chaldea," pp. 347-348.

of this region, the confederation of the PELISHTIM, so well known to us as PHILISTINES, and from whose name the modern one of the whole country—PALESTINE—is derived. It is no wonder that the weight of the national greatness and power should gradually have retired from them and centred in the more solid Northern empire with its more numerous Hittite population. As Assyria increased in might and became more aggressive towards its Western neighbors, the glory of the Hittites, weakened as they were by the long wars with Egypt and harassed by the Amorites and other peoples of Syria, began to wane. At the time of the battle of Kadesh they were perhaps at their culminating point. The decline after that was neither sudden nor even marked, yet the records of Assyria's warlike career show it to have been steady and sure; and seven hundred years after the battle, the empire succumbed under the persistent attacks of a long line of Assyrian conquerors, the confederation dissolved, and the King of Karkhemish made place for an Assyrian governor. The race was, however, not destroyed, nor even its rule extinct: the greatness that departed from one branch of it shifted to another. Already at the time of their greatest prosperity—from the fifteenth century B.C.—the Hittites had begun to reach out towards the west, or, rather, north-west. From the cold, rugged mountain region, their oldest known home, they passed into the vast peninsular region of Western Asia, known as ASIA MINOR, pushing onward to the beautiful littoral of that loveliest portion of the Mediterranean. There they founded or conquered cities and states. There we shall find their traces again when those countries, in their turn, take their places in the panorama which the history of the East slowly unrolls before us; but there, for the present, we must leave them.

20. At all events, when the Hittite empire finally perished, about 700 B.C., it cannot be said to have met with an untimely end. It had endured, from first to last, about three thousand years, a term of existence nearly double that fated to its con-conquerors. For already in the great astrological work associated with the name of Sargon of Agadè[*] we find the following item entered in a list of astronomical observations in connection with events on earth: "On the 16th day (of the month Ab) there was an eclipse; the King of Accad died; the God Nergal (*i.e.*, war) devoured in the land.—On the 20th day there was an eclipse; *the king of the land Khatti attacked the country and took possession of the throne.*" As "KHATTI" is the name invariably given to the Hittites in the Chaldean and Assyrian inscriptions, there can be no doubt but that this is a record of an early Hittite invasion in Mesopotamia. From which it follows that they were then already settled in the region between the Orontes and Euphrates (in other words, between Mesopotamia and Phœnicia), *i.e.*, virtually in the same regions which they occupied later on, towards the end of the fourth and the beginning of the third thousand B.C., with the difference that at this early period the

---

[*] See "Story of Chaldea," p. 209.

central point of their power lay probably rather in the southern part of their territory than in Karkhemish, their later capital.

21. Still, their relations to the ancient Chaldæan states cannot always have been hostile. They must, at some time, have been closely connected with those venerable seats of civilization, if they have not, in their migrations, actually passed through the great valley between the rivers and sojourned awhile in it. For their own culture, as regards both religion and art, bears the unmistakable stamp of a Chaldæan origin. Of the former, indeed, little is yet known, save that they gave to their highest god the name of SUTEKH, "king of heaven and earth," and that the goddess Ishtar, as worshipped in Karkhemish, bore the name of ATARGATIS (Hittite corruption of her Chaldæan name), and was ministered to in her temple by a large band of girls and women, her consecrated, or "sacred," priestesses. As to their art, sculptured monuments of theirs have been discovered which clearly prove its affinity with that of early Babylon (see No. 5), although for their writing they made use of signs or hieroglyphics entirely of their own invention, and unlike either the cuneiform or Egyptian writing. Little has been done as yet for the decipherment of such Hittite inscriptions as have been recovered. But when we consider that as late as ten years ago no one yet dreamed of the existence of a great Hittite nation, and a Hittite empire reaching from the frontiers of Egypt to the shores of the Bosphorus, we shall wonder not that so little should be accomplished, but rather that so

much new knowledge should have been partly secured and partly indicated. It is to Professor A. H. Sayce of Oxford, to his wonderful ingenuity, his

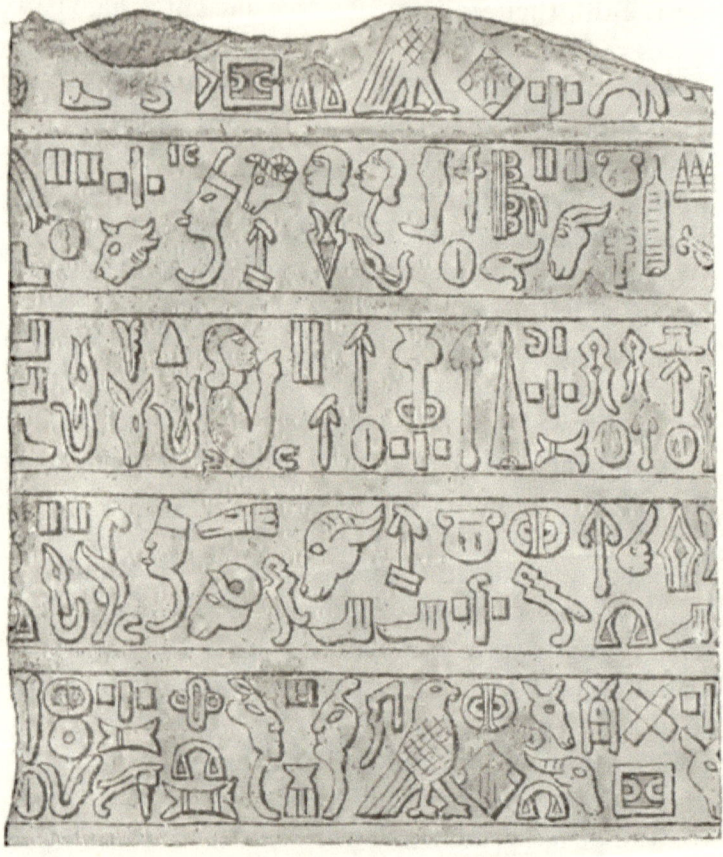

5.—HITTITE INSCRIPTION.
(Hommel.)

untiring industry, and passionate pioneering zeal in opening new fields of investigation, that we owe a revelation which even now may already be termed a revolution, so startling is the light it has unexpectedly thrown on a vast tract of ancient history hitherto obscure and utterly neglected.

22. From their position, the Khatti, or Hittites, were the natural foes of Assyria—formidable neighbors to a rising power, obnoxious to an ambitious one. Accordingly, they were the first against whom the young but already aggressive nation tested its weapons. Asshur-Uballit (the king who marched down to Babylon to avenge the murder of his grandson about 1380 B.C., see p. 21) directed short expeditions to the west and north-west of Nineveh, against mountain tribes, who were either Hittite outposts or closely adjoined the territory of the Hittites proper. His successors followed the same impulse, only they pushed further into the mountains and descended lower southward, not only firmly establishing their dominion over all the land from the Tigris to the Euphrates,—which latter might be considered Assyria's natural western boundary,— but gradually extending their invasions far beyond it, into the plain-land of Syria. As booty abounded and population increased, new cities sprang up around the two older capitals, Asshur and Nineveh. Each raid, too, brought thousands of captives, who had to be disposed of in some way—and what better employment for them than to build those gigantic mounds and ponderous palaces, the cost of which, as valued in human labor, gives such bewildering figures?* Thus we find King SHALMA- NESER I., shortly before 1300 B.C., founding the great city of Kalah, which became a third capital, and the favorite residence of sev-

<small>About 1300 B.C.; foundation of Kalah;</small>

---

* See "Story of Chaldea," p. 48.

eral of the most powerful later monarchs. This is the city which Layard brought to light at Nimrud, the deserted and dismantled "Larissa" of Xenophon. Separated from each other only by a few miles, and moreover united by the course of the Tigris, these three cities almost appear like separate quarters of one vast capital, and it is hardly to be wondered at that the first explorers much inclined to this view. This date of 1300 B.C. is a notable one in Assyrian history. It is about that year—probably a few years later—that the first conquest of Babylon by an Assyrian king is recorded, a feat of arms associated with the name of TUKULTI-NINÊB, son of Shalmaneser I., who had a signet ring made bearing his name and title, with the in-scription "*Conqueror of Kar-Dunyash.*"

First conquest of Babylon;

His success, however, cannot have been a permanent one, as it appears that he lost this very signet ring, which the Babylonians, with pardonable vanity, preciously preserved in their royal treasure, possibly in memory of the conqueror's precipitate and disastrous retreat, flattering to their national pride. Six hundred years later it was found and carried home by one who achieved the same conquest far more thoroughly—King SENNACHERIB, who thought the recovery of this ancient trophy of sufficient importance to record the occurrence and the ring's history in his annals, thus enabling us to secure one more among the few authentic dates of early history; a date the more interesting to us, that it coincides almost exactly with that of the exodus of the Jews out of Egypt under the leadership of Moses. Thus

Exodus of the Jews from Egypt.

the beginning of the thirteenth century B.C. shows us Assyria not only fast approaching the period of her glory, but already confronted, in various stages of their development, by the three powers which of all others were to be connected, for good and for evil, with her future destinies: the power of Babylon, that of the Hittites (then already on the wane), and that of the Jews—the latter as yet only a speck on the horizon, undiscernible to the eyes of the high and mighty rulers of Asshur.

II.

THE FIRST OR OLD EMPIRE.—TIGLATH-PILESER I.

1. IN the south and south-east portion of the vast mountain region which spreads between the great chain of the Caucasus and that of the Taurus with its prolongations, in more or less parallel ridges varying in height and ruggedness, there are two of the most remarkable lakes in the world: LAKE VAN and LAKE URUMIEH. In the first place, they are situated at an elevation at which one hardly expects to find such large sheets of water, the former over 5000 and the latter over 4000 feet above the level of the Mediterranean; and Lake Urumieh, the larger of the two, is, at a rough estimate, not very much inferior in size to Lake Ontario. Secondly, they have a peculiarity unusual in lakes: their water is salt. That of Lake Urumieh especially is far more so than that of any sea, enough to materially increase its weight and buoyancy, or, to use the scientific expression, "specific gravity." Sir Henry Rawlinson gives the following account of it: "The specific gravity of the water, from the quantity of salt which it retains in solution, is great; so much so indeed, that a vessel of 100 tons burthen, when loaded, is not expected to have more draught than three or four feet at the utmost. The heaviness

6.—DEAD SEA (WHERE IT RECEIVES THE RIVER ARNON).
(Stade.)

of the water also prevents the lake from being much affected with storms. . . . A gale of wind can raise the waters but a few feet; and as soon as the storm has passed they subside again into their deep, heavy, death-like sleep." Of course no fish or living thing of any sort can exist in such brine. What makes these peculiarities doubly striking is that they are the very same for which the great lake of Palestine, the so-called Dead Sea, has always been famous: a salt-water bottom, perhaps the lowest in the world, since it lies 1300 feet *below* the level of the Mediterranean. These two lakes, with a difference of 5500 feet between their levels, yet identical in nature, are equally remnants of former seas, pools of that immense ocean of which the Caspian Sea is but a more gigantic memorial, and which once upon a time, ages before man had appeared on the earth, covered the greater part of Asia, Europe and Africa, with only the very highest mountain ridges—such as the Himalaya, the Caucasus, the Atlas, and, partly, the Alps—rising above the waters and forming solitary and widely scattered islands. The time will come when all these salt pools will dry up and leave nothing but banks of salt, like those deposits which are frequently met with in the sandy steppes of Central Asia and South-eastern Russia, and from a distance startle the traveller, parched with heat and half spent with thirst, with the appearance of snow-drifts.

2. Both Lake Urumieh and Lake Van were well known to the Assyrians, and the peoples who lived around them again and again were subjected to

their inroads and depredations. Of the two, Lake Van was perhaps the most familiar to the indefatigable conquerors. The exceedingly rough and severely cold country in which it is situated—part of the region now known under the name of KURDISTAN—belonged to the vast mountain-land somewhat vaguely designated by the Assyrians as NAÏRI, or LANDS OF NAÏRI. The valleys between the different mountain spurs were inhabited by independent tribes, each calling itself a nation, while their chieftains are all awarded the title of "king." Loosely, if at all, connected with each other, they were an easy prey to the compact and well-trained armies which, year after year, pushed further into their fastnesses, and before which they generally fled deeper and higher into the mountains—"like birds," in the expressive phrase of the historical inscriptions. There they would hide until the invaders, who had too much to do in many places to linger long in one, had departed, or else, pressed by hunger and cold, compelled by the destruction of their homesteads and the massacre of their warriors and such of their people as had stayed behind, they would come down, and, to put an end to the present misery, submit and pay tribute.

3. At one of the sources of the Tigris, somewhat to the west of Lake Van, there is a sculpture on a natural rock, smoothed for the purpose, representing a king in the attitude of pointing the way, with the following inscription: "By the help of Asshur, Shamash, Ramân, the great gods, my lords, I, TUKULTI-PALESHARRA, King of Assyria, son of . . ."

(here follow the names of his father and grandfather, with their titles)—" the conqueror from the great Sea of the West to the sea of the land of Naïri, for the third time have invaded the land of Naïri." This monument, the oldest memorial of Assyria's conquests in the North, is also the earliest specimen of Assyrian bas-relief sculpture yet found, and represents the first really great king of that country, at least the first whose doings are, owing to a series of lucky chances, well known to us. The manner of its discovery, too, is of unusual interest, as it did much in its time to finally silence the doubts which were for a long while entertained by over-cautious and sceptical scholars concerning the reliability of cuneiform decipherment. At the reading of a long inscription of Ashurnazirpal, a much later king, whose palace Layard laid open at Nimrud, some lines were made out to mention this very sculpture, with an exact description of its location. With no other guide than this, the place was explored and the sculpture found, a result which established beyond a doubt the claim of Assyriology to be real science, dealing with positive facts and systematic researches, and not merely with ingenious and more or less plausible guesses, as had by many been thought probable. However, this confirmation ought already to have been superfluous, for the discovery happened in 1862, and in 1857 an experiment had been made which ought itself to have been sufficient.

4. At the exploration of a vast mound at Kileh-Sherghat (ancient Asshur) the excavators had ex-

tracted from the four corner-chambers in the foundations * four cylinders, in the form of octagonal prisms,† about eighteen inches in height, which bore the name of Tukulti-palesharra, while the inscription stamped on the bricks revealed the fact that the mound had once been a temple of Raman, restored by the same king. Two of the cylinders were in excellent preservation; of the two others only a few fragments were available; but the loss was not great, as they all were but the repetition of the same inscription. As this was the first unbroken text of considerable length—over a thousand lines—which had as yet been recovered, the arrival of the cylinders at the British Museum created much excitement, and it was determined to make them the subject of an experiment which should be a decisive test of the value of the new science. When the inscription had been lithographed, copies were sent to the four scholars who were then foremost in the work of decipherment: Sir Henry Rawlinson, Mr. Fox Talbot, Dr. Hincks, and Mr. J. Oppert. Each was to contribute a translation of the text independently of the others, and at the end of a month the work was completed and the manuscripts were sent in to the Royal Asiatic Society, which was to officiate as umpire. When the four translations were printed in four parallel columns, no layman but must have seen at a glance that they were the rendering of the same text, the

---

* See " Story of Chaldea," p. 114.
† See Ibid., illustration No. 51.

discrepancies between them being only in details, and such as were to be expected from the still imperfect knowledge of the language. The translation has since been rehandled and improved several times, and the latest and most perfect version is in many particulars very different from those first attempts; yet these were too convincing, on the whole, not to have been considered by most as final proof in favor of cuneiform research, and inveterate doubters, if such remained, had to yield to the evidence of the sculpture and inscription so strangely discovered five years later.

5. The inscription, as it happened, proved of the greatest interest in itself, apart from the philological use to which it was put. It gives a minute account of the first five years of TIGLATH-PILESER I. (for this is the common, though corrupt, reading of the name), and brings before us this warrior king with the vividness of a full-length portrait, at the same time that it gives us a complete picture of the greatness Assyria had reached in his reign, which covers the end of the twelfth century B.C.—1120–1100. Its beginnings were most brilliant, and it is no idle boast when he declares, with more truth than modesty, in the long and elaborate preamble of which the opening paragraph has already been quoted (see pp. 5 and 6): "No rival had I in battle. To the land of Assyria I added land, to its people I added people. I enlarged my territory, all their countries I subdued" (his enemies). That he was not the first to do these things, and that Assyria's con-

Tiglath Pileser I.— about 1100.

quests had already extended far beyond the original district on the Tigris, both to the north and west, is proved by the fact that most of the expeditions which occupied the first five years of his reign were directed against rebellious provinces and unsubmissive neighbors. Of these latter the first to feel his might were certain Hittite tribes of the mountains between the sea and the Upper Euphrates, whom he attacked in their own country,—" a land difficult of access,"—and defeated with their five kings and twenty thousand warriors. "With their corpses," says the king, "I strewed the mountain passes and the heights. I took away their property, a countless booty. Six thousand warriors, the remnant of their army, who had fled before my arms, embraced my feet. I carried them away and counted them among the inhabitants of my own land." This was only a beginning. From one mountain district to another the king marched laboriously but victoriously, through rugged, pathless countries, which are vividly portrayed in a few scattered notices. In one place the inscription mentions that a way had to be cleared with the axe through dense undergrowth and full-grown trees; in another again we read: "I entered high and steep mountains, that had crests like the edge of a dagger, impracticable for my chariots. I left my chariots, and climbed the steep mountains;" or else: "Through mighty mountains I made my way in my chariot as far as the ground was even enough, and where it was too rugged, on my feet."

6. The king prides himself on having "passed

through precipitous defiles, the inside of which no king before him had beheld," and on having travelled high and far, where no road was ever made. Indeed, he seems to have pushed very nearly as far north into the Armenian ranges as any Assyrian ever did; many of his successors followed his footsteps, but

7.—PROCESSION (PROBABLY OF GODS).
(Perrot and Chipiez.)

none much advanced on them in this direction. And as he attacked successively and separately the various independent kingdoms located among the highlands around the Upper Euphrates and Upper Tigris, the result was everywhere the same: monotonously terrible and disastrous to the mountaineers ; monotonous too in the reading, as the same horrible details are repeated in the same almost stereotype phrases of cold, matter-of-fact narrative, which make the picture of devastation all the more impressively ghastly. Forests, passes, heights filled and covered

8.—CARRIED INTO CAPTIVITY.
(Perrot and Chipiez.)

with the bodies of their defenders, corpses thrown into the Tigris or carried into it by its affluents; cities burned and destroyed, palaces robbed and "made heaps of"; the families of kings led away captive with thousands of their subjects, or, if the kings submitted and their homage were graciously accepted, carried to Assyria as hostages ; then minute enumerations of spoils in horses, chariots, cattle, plate, and bars of bronze, etc., not forgetting "the gods" of the vanquished—these few lines sum up pages of Tiglath-Pileser's triumphant inscription. Of the first half of it almost every paragraph recounts the conquest of some one country or kingdom, and generally concludes with one of the following statements : " I carried away their possessions, I burned all their cities with fire, I demanded from them hostages, tribute and contributions;" or, " I laid on them the heavy yoke of my rule, and commanded them to bring me yearly tribute to my city of Asshur;" or, "I conquered the land in all its extent and added it to the territory of my country ;" or, lastly, "I pardoned them, imposed tribute on them, and made them subject to Asshur, my lord." From one country he took " their twenty-five gods," and, having brought them to " his city of Asshur," placed them in its principal temples,— very much in the same spirit with which he would have incorporated royal prisoners in his own household as slaves.

7. One expedition must have been fraught with more than ordinary difficulty and danger, to judge from the particulars into which the inscription enters and the peculiar solemnity of the preamble, which is, on a smaller scale, almost a repetition of the great opening paragraphs. Tiglath-Pileser had to deal on this occasion not with separate tribes or nations, but with a coalition of nearly all the kings of the land of Naïri. At least he gives a list of twenty-three, to whom he adds sixty more in a

9.—MARCH OF ASSYRIAN ARMY THROUGH A WOODED MOUNTAINOUS REGION. (SHOWS PART OF A FORTRESS AND CAPTIVES CARRIED AWAY.)
(Lenormant)

lump—eighty-three in all. Even though the magnitude of this figure is a positive proof that the so-called "kings" were in reality no more than chieftains of mountain tribes (perhaps something like the great Highland "clans" of old Scotland), still their union must have made them formidable, especially in a wild region of wooded mountain fastnesses and narrow passes, as familiar and friendly to them as they were unknown and dangerous to the invaders. For this is the paragraph in which particular mention is made of the fact that no king before Tiglath-Pileser had ever before entered that region. The entire relation of this remarkable campaign is so lively and entertaining, so full of characteristic details, that it may stand here, almost unabridged, as a specimen of the early monumental literature of Assyria at its best.

"In those days, . . . Asshur, the Lord, sent me, who knows no victor in war, no rival in battle, whose rule is righteous, over the four quarters of the world, towards distant kingdoms on the shores of the Upper Sea, which knew not submission, and I went forth. Across impracticable heights and through precipitous defiles the inside of which no king had beheld before, I passed. Through sixteen mighty mountain ridges "—(the names are given)—" I marched in my chariot where the ground was good; where it was inaccessible, I cleared a way with axes, and bridges for the passage of my troops I constructed excellently well. I crossed the Euphrates. The kings of . . . . "—(here follows the list)—" together twenty-three kings of the lands of Naïri, assembled their chariots and troops in the midst of their countries and came forth to do battle against me. By the impetuous onslaught of my mighty arms I conquered them. I destroyed their numerous armies like Ramân's thundershower; with the corpses of their warriors I strewed the mountain heights and the enclosures of their cities as with straw. Their 120 chariots I destroyed in the battle; sixty kings of the lands of Naïri, with those who had come to

16.—PLUNDERING AND DEMOLISHING OF A CITY IN A MOUNTAINOUS COUNTRY.
(Lenormant.)

their assistance, I pursued to the Upper Sea. Their great cities I took, their spoils, their possessions I carried off, their towns I burned with fire, I destroyed, laid them waste, made heaps of them and land for the plough. Numerous herds of steeds, colts, calves, and implements without number I carried home. The kings of the lands of Naïri my hand captured alive, all of them. To these same kings I granted favor. Captive and bound, I released them before Shamash, my lord, and made them swear the oath of my great gods for all coming days, made them swear allegiance forever. Their children, the offspring of their royalty, I took as hostages. I imposed on them a tribute of 1200 steeds and 2000 bulls and dismissed them to their respective countries. Sini, king of Dayaïni"—(one of the twenty-three)— "who did not submit to Asshur, my lord, I brought captive and bound to my city of Asshur. Favor I granted him, and from my city of Asshur dismissed him, a devoted servant of the great gods, to live and be submissive. The vast lands of Naïri I took in all their extent, and all their kings I brought low to my feet."

It is impossible not to notice the remarkably mild treatment which Tiglath-Pileser awarded to the King of Naïri, a treatment so strongly contrasting with his usual summary proceedings as plainly to indicate a conciliatory intention. He could not but admit that Assyria could not afford continual repetitions of such adventurous campaigns into remote and inaccessible mountain wilds as he had just successfully carried out, and was wisely content with turning unruly and perhaps aggressive neighbors into vassals and tributary allies, without attempting actually to annex their countries or letting the hand of "Asshur, his lord," weigh too heavily on them.

8. These conquests in the North seem to have been his principal occupation and most important achievement. An expedition to the South-east, into the outposts of the Zagros Mountains, is mentioned indeed as successful and profitable, but with-

11.—SCALING A FORTRESS, AND CARRYING AWAY CAPTIVES.
(Lenormant.)

out much emphasis. Neither does the inscription dwell with any excessive complacency on a campaign in the West, directed against the "Aramæan Riverland," and which extended the rule of Assyria to the Euphrates, where the river bulges out in an immense bow, furthest towards the Mediterranean. Yet this very paragraph is of great interest, as being the first official mention of a people who were destined to great power. For only a few hundred years after the time of Tiglath-Pileser I., the Aramæans, a purely Semitic race who had probably also halted in the land of Shinar and migrated thence, occupied the whole of modern Syria, forming a single kingdom, of which Damascus, originally a Hittite city, became the capital. This is one of the very few cities in the world which never entirely perished. Essentially a Semitic centre, it retained its splendor and leading position all through antiquity; in the Middle Ages, when the Arabs — Semites also — went abroad conquering land after land as they preached the religion of their prophet, Mahomet, Damascus became one of their chief seats of power and learning, little inferior to Baghdad itself; and even when the barbarous Turks had swept over all the fair countries of Western Asia and engulfed them in their upstart empire, Damascus still held its own, and to this day is a far from unimportant place. This sums up for it a continuous existence of 3500 years at least, more, perhaps, than any other living city can boast. Though not founded by the Aramæans, to this nation it was indebted for its greatness. But here, about 1120 B.C.—from the passing mention of the "Aramæan riverland" which the Assyrian conqueror crosses, to make a sudden and rapid razzia into the land of the Khatti, where he surprises and " plunders Karkhemish in one day "—we find that it was as yet only an unimportant tribe, which had not ventured beyond the sheltering river. Evidently they were the successors of the Hittites in the land we call Syria, gathering strength as these lost it, treading close on their heels, and occupying territory and cities as fast as the Hittites evacuated them in their retreating movement towards their mountain strongholds.

9. After going over each of his campaigns more or less minutely, Tiglath-Pileser thus sums up the result of them in a concise yet comprehensive statement, the utterly unadorned simplicity of which lends it a certain impressive grandeur:

"Forty-two countries altogether and their princes, from beyond the lower Zab, the remote forest districts at the boundaries, to the land Khatti beyond the Euphrates and unto the Upper Sea of the setting sun"—(the Mediterranean above the mouth of the Orontes) —" my hand has conquered from the beginning of my reign until the fifth year of my rule. I made them speak one language, received their hostages, and imposed tribute on them."

10. So far the warrior and conqueror. But there is another side to his character, which is pictured with equal life-likeness in this invaluable record. He shows himself to us as a prudent sovereign, who devotes the leisure he has so hardly earned to works of peace and to the increase of his country's power: " I made chariots and yokes, for the greater

might of my country, more than there were before, and provided them with teams of horses. To the land of Asshur I added land, to its people I added people; I improved the condition of my subjects, I made them dwell in peaceful homesteads." He tells us that he "fortified ruinous castles," filled the royal granaries throughout Assyria, and collected into herds, "like flocks of sheep," the wild goats, deer, antelopes, which he had caused to be caught in the forests of the mountainous countries through which he passed; they multiplied and furnished choice victims for the altars of the great gods. Nor did he omit to care for the adornment of his capital and of his country generally. Even while on the march, he found time to admire the beautiful forest trees, and order numbers of them to be carefully taken out of their native ground, transported to Assyria, and there planted in the royal gardens and parks. He mentions cedars and two other kinds of trees, of which the names have been deciphered but not identified, and says of them: ". . . . these trees which in the times of the kings, my fathers of old, no one had planted, I took and planted them in the gardens of my country; also precious garden grapes which I had not yet brought into my country, I got and enriched with them the gardens of Assyria."

11. The king also makes us witness his favorite pastime, the chase, in which he seems to have indulged on an imposing scale during his various expeditions. All the countries he visited, as well as Assyria itself, swarmed with lions and other wild

beasts, differing according to the different regions; so that the abundance of game was as unlimited as was the royal huntsman's ardor to pursue it. That the distinction gained in this way was considered most kingly and glorious, is evident from the pride with which he recounts his exploits in the chase, tendering due thanks always to "his patrons," Nineb and Nergal, the two tutelary deities of war and hunting, especially Nergal, whose sacred emblem seems to have been the human-headed winged lion. Of four wild bulls which he killed in the desert, on the border of the land of the Khatti, with his own bow and sharp-pointed spear, he carried the hides and horns as trophies to "his city of Asshur," as also the hides and tusks of ten male elephants killed by him in the desert, while four elephants he took alive and brought to his capital. "Under the auspices of Nineb, my patron," he goes on to say, "I killed 120 lions in my youthful ardor, in the fulness of my manly might on my own feet, and 800 lions I killed from my chariot. All kinds of beasts and fowls I added to my hunting spoils."

12. So great was this king's fondness for curiosities in natural history that when the King of Egypt wished to cement a courteous interchange of friendliness by some acceptable gift, he could think of nothing more acceptable to send than a large river animal—surely a crocodile of the Nile—and some "beasts of the great sea." This curious incident, however, we know, not from Tiglath-Pileser's own cylinder, but from a fragment of a much later inscription, in which another famous conqueror-king

goes over the deeds of his great predecessor. Though extremely concise, this account reproduces the essential statements of the lengthy original, and even adds a few particulars, among which the most interesting is a mention of the fact that Tiglath-Pileser "mounted ships of Arvad and killed a .... (perhaps a dolphin?) in the great sea." Now ARVAD (or ARADUS) is the most northern of the Phœnician cities, on the shore of that part of the Mediterranean which the Assyrians called "the Upper Sea of the setting sun," and it would seem from this passage that our king was the first of his nation to go out to sea. From what we already know of him we can well fancy that he took no little pride in this pleasure-sail, both as a political demonstration, a sort of taking possession of the new element,—considered until then as the exclusive domain of the sons of Canaan along the shore,—and also as an opportunity to indulge his passionate love of sport by a novel experience. It must have been a memorable and festive occasion, and one wishes one might have a glimpse of the pageant, graced as it doubtless was by all the gorgeousness of Oriental costume in its richest display and by the blue splendor of those wonderful waters and skies.

13. We thus take leave of Tiglath-Pileser at the height of his power and glory, with a feeling of admiration for his heroic and brilliant personal qualities; and it is not without regret we learn that towards the end of his reign that power was somewhat shaken and that glory dimmed. Like all the other Assyrian kings of whom we possess records, he

had wars with Babylonia, and this was always their unlucky direction. Even during the period of Assyria's highest fortunes, when she was invariably successful against the nations that surrounded her to the west, north, and east, she often was roughly checked in the South—very naturally, since Babylonia, once her metropolis and teacher, was now her equal in the arts of peace and war, her equal—if not her superior still—in culture. Yet, ever since Tukulti-Nineb I. had entered Babylon in triumph and written himself "conqueror of Kar-Dunyash," the younger monarchy seems to have claimed supremacy over the mother country, and the claim to have been, at most times and in a general way, acknowledged. The kings of Babylon, too, from that very epoch, suddenly appear with Semitic names instead of the Accadian or Cossæan ones that had succeeded each other in a long line; and this alone more than suggests a change of dynasty effected by the Assyrian conquerors with a view to their own interests. Some kind of allegiance, some form of homage must have been agreed upon, though we have no documents to throw light on the subject, for we often hear of "tribute" from Babylon; and when the kings of Assyria march down into the country it is generally to repress what they are pleased to term a "revolt." At all events, the kings of Babylon never ceased to assert their independence, alternately, as circumstances prompted, changing their attitude from one of self-defence to one of aggression, with intervals of submission and outward inactivity when fortune had been too much against them. The relations of the two Mesopotamian monarchies during the six hundred years which elapsed between the first conquest and the final struggle for life may be described as an unending game, with alternating vicissitudes, in which each player, when winning most sweepingly, was liable to sudden defeat, and when losing most deeply, was ready for his revenge. Tiglath-Pileser I., like his ancestor, Tukulti-Ninêb I., had to take his turn at the losing game, and, like him, left a trophy of his defeat in his adversary's hands—a pledge which the renowned Sennacherib, when he finally captured Babylon, 400 years later, redeemed at the same time as the former conqueror's signet ring. In this case, as in the other, it is only from Sennacherib's statement that we learn anything of the disaster of which he was the final avenger. It appears that Tiglath-Pileser, who in almost every sentence of his great record betrays an uncommonly religious turn of mind, and seems to take more pride in the building and restoration of temples than even in his warlike deeds, carried with him in his campaign to Babylonia the statues of his favorite god Ramân with the consort-goddess, Shala; that the "king of Accad" "took them away and dragged them to Babel," whence Sennacherib "brought them forth" and restored them to their own temple.

14. This completes the information, so unexpectedly abundant, which we have concerning Tiglath-Pileser I., and to which by far the greatest part he has himself contributed in his great cylinder, as

he distinctly intended to do when he had four copies of it deposited under the four corner-stones of his most important building—" for later days, for the day of the future, for all time!" he exclaims in the closing paragraph. The mighty figure of the warrior king stands forth the more colossal and imposing that it stands alone, like a solitary, finely finished statue in a vivid ray of strong light, against a dark background. For all is darkness around him, scarce relieved by a few vaguely flitting shadows. As nothing is known of Assyria under his predecessors, except the few morsels of facts about Ashur-Uballit and Tukulti-Nineb, so for two hundred years nothing again comes to light of his successors. His name embodies for us an entire revelation. His is the first important historical and literary record that the Assyrian ruins have yielded us; his the first monument of Assyrian art we know; after him—a blank. We have no artistic relics whatever, and, as to history, nothing more than, after an interval of nearly two centuries, a list of a few royal names, with not a scrap of reality about them. "Nothing is known at present of the history of these monarchs," says Mr. G. Rawlinson in his "Five Monarchies." "No historical inscriptions belonging to their reign have been recovered; no exploits are recorded of them in the inscriptions of later sovereigns. They stand before us, mere shadows of mighty names,—proofs of the uncertainty of posthumous fame, which is almost as much the award of chance as the deserved recompense of superior merit."* These lines are certainly forcible and impressive; but, are they equally true? *Are* those really "mighty names" that are transmitted to us without a faintest record of any achievement attached to them? Deeds of moment, greatness of any kind, generally survive in *some* way, leave *some* trace or memory, occur indirectly in later records if contemporary monuments are wanting. Assyrian kings, absorbed as they were in their own exploits and given to self-glorification as they show themselves throughout their monumental literature, were not forgetful of their more eminent predecessors, and often refer to them with reverence and admiration, or at least, as we have already repeatedly seen, mention this or that fact connected with their reigns. That no such posthumous mention occurs of any of those who succeeded, during the next two centuries, to the power so firmly established by Tiglath-Pileser, is perhaps in itself rather conclusive proof that there *was* little to record, nothing especially noteworthy, either as event or personal character, to stand out prominently in the memory of posterity and break the monotonous if exciting routine of petty warfare, hunting, building, and despotic home-rule which made up the average career of an Assyrian monarch.

15. At all events, Tiglath-Pileser I. embodies for us the first period of Assyria's rise and greatness, known as "the First or Old Empire," because the

---

* "Five Monarchies," Vol. II. p. 336.

line of sovereigns who founded it had apparently been as yet unbroken, through probably as much as 800 years. This remarkable fact is indirectly pointed out by Tiglath-Pileser himself, who, after naming, in a paragraph of his great inscription devoted to his royal genealogy, his own father and his ancestors up to the fourth generation back, mentions his remotest ancestors, Ishmidagan and Shamash-Ramân (the first known *Patesis*, not yet "kings," of Asshur), the latter as the original builder of the Temple of Anu and Ramân which he takes so much pride in having reconstructed with greater splendor than before. It is evidently under his rule, and mainly by his efforts, that Assyria may be said to have reached her normal extent and boundaries. In the North, the conqueror's own sculptured effigy, stern and commanding, seems to be forever silently pointing from its rock by the source of the Tigris to the mountain ridge known to later antiquity as MONS NI-PHATES (" Snowy Mountains ") as the frontier he gained for her. To the west the Euphrates seems her most natural boundary, while to the east the Zagros chain of many ridges is an unmistakable barrier; to the south alone the boundary, though well marked by the line of the alluvium, is made fluctuating by the uncertain relations between Assyria and Babylonia. This region Mr. G. Rawlinson defines "the country actually taken into Assyria," covered by undoubted remains of Assyrian cities and towns, as distinguished from " that which was merely conquered and held in subjection." The same author then continues:

"If Assyria be allowed the extent which is here assigned to her, she will be a country not only very much larger than Chaldea or Babylonia, but positively of considerable dimensions. Reaching on the north to the 38th and on the south to the 34th parallel, she had a length diagonally to the alluvium of 350 miles, and a breadth between the Euphrates and Mount Zagros varying from above 300 to 170 miles. Her area was probably not less than 75,000 square miles, which is beyond that of the German provinces of Prussia or Austria, more than double that of Portugal, and not much below that of Great Britain. She would thus, from her mere size, be calculated to play an important part in history; and the more so, as during the period of her greatness scarcely any nation with which she came in contact possessed nearly so extensive a territory."*

---

* G. Rawlinson, "Five Monarchies," Vol. I. p. 227.

III.

THE SONS OF CANAAN: THEIR MIGRATIONS.—THE PHŒNICIANS.

1. WHEN we read of Tiglath-Pileser I.'s holiday sail in ships of Arvad, and of his killing that big sea-fish, there is something in the whole occurrence, a certain inappropriateness, which involuntarily compels a smile, as at some boyish freak. Maritime honors sit awkwardly on the hero of a hundred land battles, the adventurous invader of unknown, impassable mountain regions, and Assyria was so eminently a continental power that her king and armies appear out of place on the sea-shore amidst a people of traders and sailors. At all events, this was but a passing excursion, a military visit, and the Phœnician merchant-princes who on this occasion no doubt entertained the royal intruder and did him courteous lip-homage,—not unaccompanied, we may be sure, by costly gifts,—probably considered it in no other light, nor dreamed that the hour was not so far distant when the iron rule of Asshur should stretch to their luxurious homes by the sea, their docks and ship-yards, their warehouses and factories, and lie long and heavy on the necks of their descendants. The Assyrians, one of whose chief characteristics was insatiable greed, were not

likely to forget such a glimpse of boundless wealth and overflowing prosperity as now dazzled their astonished, coveting eyes. For the Phœnicians, at this very time, had already reached the towering point of their career, and while their unbidden guests were wonderingly enjoying the novelty of a sail and a bit of sea-sport, they ranged and reigned as masters over the blue element as far as human knowledge went and ships would bear—both knowledge and ships being exclusively their own. Indeed, the date which has been ascertained as that of Tiglath-Pileser—1100 B. C. and thereabouts—is also given approximatively as that of the foundation of the remotest Phœnician colony and one of their most important stations—GADES (now Cadiz) in Spain, on the other side of the Strait of Gibraltar. To arrive there they must have touched and gained firm footing at a great many intermediate points; and it must have taken them many centuries, for the way is long from the Persian Gulf to the Atlantic Ocean, and all ancient authors agree that their original starting-point was a group of small islands in that gulf,—"the Great Sea of the Rising Sun," as Assyrian geography names it. Such was also their own account of themselves.

Foundation of Gades—about 1100 B.C.

2. This group of small islands, now known by the name of BAHREIN ISLANDS, is situated about the middle of the western shore of the gulf, close to the coast of Arabia, a tract, as nearly everywhere along the sea, fertile and habitable, being separated by mountains from the sands and parching winds

of the inland deserts. Here seems to have been the first known home of the Hamites of Canaan before they separated and multiplied into the numerous tribes which overspread all the pleasant and fruitful portions of Syria and were to play so important a part in the fortunes of the Hebrews, for which reason the biblical historian gives so full and particular a list of them. (See Genesis, x. 15-19.) Here, not on the islands alone, but also on the littoral, they must have dwelt for centuries. One of these Hamitic tribes was even then of sufficient pre-eminence to have received a separate name, that of PUNT or PUNA, (the PHUT or PÛT of Genesis, x. 6), later corrupted under Greek influences into PHŒNICIANS, and to have been personified as one of Ham's own sons. They retained their separate identity through the great westward migration, while their kindred took their generic name from the land of Canaan, over which they spread, receiving their special denominations from the districts or cities they inhabited. The Puna were essentially a commercial race, and preferably chose for their settlements such regions as offered fair play to this peculiar instinct of theirs. An important branch of them gained possession of the finest portion of Arabia—the present YEMEN, the south-eastern corner of the peninsula by the Strait of BAB-EL-MANDEB and the opposite protruding corner of Eastern Africa, now known as the SOMALI coast—a position which evidently commands the commerce of the Red Sea, the Arabian Sea, and even the more distant Indian Ocean, and was, moreover, as it still is, a point of attraction and departure for caravans. Besides which, both Yemen and Somali are themselves exceedingly rich in numbers of costly Oriental products, such as rare woods, frankincense, spices, etc. Here the Puna lived and traded, principally with Egypt, long before we hear of the Phœnicians. Some think that the latter were a later branch of these Puna, which separated from them at some time and wandered northwards. Others, again, are of opinion that the people who settled on the Syrian sea-shore were Puna, who migrated, by a more northern road, directly across the desert into the Syrian land from their old home by the Persian Gulf, whence their Canaanite brethren had departed before them, so that they found them already as builders of cities and founders of communities. Among these and the Semitic tribes who continued nomadic longer,—some forever,—they must have tarried by the way, until, by long intercourse and unhindered intermarriages, the differences wore away and they were numbered among the "sons of Canaan," and their first capital, SIDON, came to pride herself on being "the first-born of Canaan."

3. There are no events of greater moment in the history of remote antiquity than the early migrations of races, and none to which, from their very nature, it is more difficult to assign even an approximative date. Races generally migrate when they are at a stage of culture that does not as yet create many monuments, and the creation of monuments takes time. At a given moment a people is mentioned in the inscriptions of some more

advanced nation as living in certain places, and that is the first we hear of it. All we can say is, "At such a time they were there, for here is the proof;" How long? is often a question impossible to answer. Yet in some favorable cases indirect indications may be gathered which will help to place the event correctly—within a couple of hundred years or so, a trifle which at our distance from it scarcely comes into account at all. Now in Genesis (chap. xii. 5-6), where we are told how Abram, with Saraï, his wife, and Lot, his brother's son, and all their substance and families, departed from Harran towards the south and came into the land of Canaan, we read this little annotation: "And the Canaanite was then in the land." The qualifying word "*then*" seems to imply that they had not been there long. Whether they had sojourned, as had the Hebrews, in the land of Shumir itself, or confined themselves to the adjoining fertile tracts by the Gulf, they seem to have preceded the Hebrews in their westward migration. According to one tradition they had been driven from their seats in consequence of a quarrel with the King of Babylon. The time thus indicated corresponds more than approximatively with the famous Elamite conquest of Khudur-Nankhundi, to which we are continually led back, and there is nothing improbable in the supposition that the dispersion of the Canaanites, like the migration of the Hebrew and Assyrian Semites, was caused by the shock of that invasion, the reaction of which was felt in wider and wider circles, even before it reached the

Dead Sea itself under the enterprising Khudur Lagamar,* until, as we saw in a former chapter (see p. 24), it threw the Hyksos hordes into Egypt. In the Hyksos invasion the Canaanite, especially the Hittite, element was strongly represented, as strongly as the Semitic, and both acted so much in concert as to be almost undistinguishable from each other, owing to the many and close affinities which have always subsisted between the two races of Shem and Ham, and the ease with which they always amalgamated, as though by mutual attraction. Thus everything concurs to show the Elamite invasion to have been one of the most momentous as well as authentic events of remote antiquity, and a point of departure for revolutions which affected the Oriental world far beyond the countries immediately concerned, and helped shaping it into those conditions which have until lately been considered as the very earliest that history could deal with. Nothing could be established with much certainty previous to 1000 B.C., and, fantastical as the saying may seem, all the ground we have gained in our backward progress has been conquered by the labors of the pickaxe and shovel, within the last thirty or forty years.

4. We have seen † that it is a law of history that no country is found desert by an invading or migrating race when it takes possession of it; also that no race, however long established and however

---

* See "Story of Chaldea." p. 221.
† See Ibid. p. 126.

indigenous it may deem itself, but will be shown to have come from somewhere else, if we can get back far enough to find out. Of course, behind everything we have found out stands the next thing which we have not, and which we may, or may not, find out in the future, since no one can tell beforehand *where* the limit of knowledge and discovery lies, though it is certain that there *is* such a limit somewhere, in every branch and direction of knowledge. As we pursue the destinies of migrating races, we often come upon populations which we have no means to track further up into the past, and the very names of which, given them by the new comers, show them to have been as great a puzzle to these new comers as they are to us. Thus we are told that " Palestine, when entered by the Canaanites, was not a wilderness. The greater part of its towns were already built and the country round about them inhabited by a numerous population, who were either exterminated or forced to emigrate by the Canaanites. Some remnants, however, of the primitive races still existed when the Israelites conquered the land. Some of the names given by the Bible to these primitive races of Palestine indicate men of large stature and great strength, and thus popular tradition in after ages has termed them giants." * Such were the ANAKIM, the EMIM (the latter name meaning " the terrible," " the formidable "); such also the people whom the

---

* Fr. Lenormant. "Ancient History of the East," translation of E. Chevallier, Vol. II., p. 146.

Canaanites called Zuzim and Zamzummim, names simply indicative of a language which sounded to the foreigners like a monotonous gibberish, an unintelligible buzzing. The last remnants of these primitive races were destroyed by the Hebrews; but even then they were numerous enough, and report represented them as sufficiently terrible to inspire the new conquerors with even greater misgivings than the Canaanitic nations they came to dislodge. When Moses sent twelve men of trust and high standing, one from each tribe of Israel and " every one a ruler among them," to " spy out the land of Canaan " and " see the land, what it is, and the people that dwelleth therein," " whether they be strong or weak, whether they be few or many," they came back disheartened, and declared to Moses and the assembled tribes : " We be not able to go up against the people, for they are stronger than we. . . . There we saw the giants, the sons of Anak, which come of the giants: and we were in our own sight as grasshoppers, and so we were in their sight " (Numbers, xiii.). And of the land of the Moabites by the Dead Sea (at its southern end) it is further said : " The Emim dwelt therein aforetime, a people great, and many, and tall, as the Anakim, which also were accounted giants, as the Anakim : but the Moabites call them Emim." And again of the people that preceded the Ammonites, a little to the north of the Moabites: ". . . . the Ammonites called them Zamzummim ; a people great, and many, and tall, as the Anakim ; but the Lord destroyed them before them, and they (the

Ammonites) succeeded them and dwelt in their stead" (Deuteronomy, ii. 10-11, 20-21). In fact, the physical power of these last descendants from the old owners of the soil had become proverbial: "Who can stand before the children of Anak!" was a common saying, and it took two conquests, that of the Canaanites and that of the Hebrews, finally to exterminate them. The account of the latter concludes with the express statement, "There was none of the Anakim left in the land of the children of Israel," certain districts of the Philistines alone excepted.

5. Now, when we ask the question that naturally suggests itself: "Who were these very remarkable primitive races? Under what division of the human family should they be classed?" we have no means of answering it by anything but conjectures. If they have attained any notable degree of culture, they have left no monuments of it, and the great table of the tenth chapter of Genesis itself furnishes no clew, leaving us completely at fault; for while it minutely enumerates the members of the Canaanitic family, it passes over in silence their predecessors, who have been aptly called "the pre-Canaanite races of Syria." This silence itself is, perhaps, a sort of indirect clew, for it is manifestly intentional. It cannot proceed from ignorance or inadvertence, since they are so frequently and pointedly mentioned afterwards. They are voluntarily and consistently ignored, as are the entire yellow and black divisions of mankind. It does not, therefore, appear improbable that they should have belonged to the former, especially when

we remember the traditions as to the long occupation of all Western Asia by Turanians, and the fact that wherever any one of the great white races, which alone the biblical historian ranks among Noah's posterity, arrives in the course of its migrations, it seems to find a Turanian population in long established possession.*

6. Of all the "sons of Canaan" the Phœnicians achieved the widest renown and performed the most universally important historical mission. They conquered the world—as much of it as was known—not by force of arms, but by enterprise and cleverness. And they knew more of the world than any other people, for they alone possessed a navy and ventured out to sea,—into the open sea, out of sight of the land. They were the connecting link between the most distant shores, the most uncongenial peoples, the founders of that amicable intercourse which commerce creates and fosters, because it satisfies mutual needs. They were the first wholesale manufacturers, and—greatest boon of all!—they gave the alphabet to the world. And all this greatness, power, wealth, these achievements they owed, next to their distinctive national bent of mind, to the peculiar disadvantages under which they labored with regard to their location. Not that their country was unproductive or in any way undesirable. There is, perhaps, no fairer strip of land than that between the Mediterranean and the Lebanon chain. But it is just only " a strip," so narrow that the gigantic

---

* See "Story of Chaldea," Chapter II., "The Great Races."

12.—A PASS IN LEBANON.

mountains that overtop it with the eternal crown of snows which gave them their name ("Lebanon" means "White Mountains"), have no room to descend to the shore in easy steps and gracious slopes, as they do on their eastern side into the Syrian plain, but tower rugged and precipitous, with rocky ledges sometimes jutting and beetling on the very edge of the water. At its widest, the coast-land has only a few miles to expand in, so that even the streams are not really rivers, but rather rushing, leaping torrents. Never had nation so scant space to grow and multiply in, with such utter impossibility of spreading on any side. It was a cup which, when too full, could overflow, literally, only into the sea. The harbors along the shore were many and good, and around them the Phœnician fishing settlements grew into populous, active cities, forming a sort of ladder, with the promontory of MOUNT CARMEL at the bottom, and the island city of Arvad at the top. To this day the lines of steamers, as they ply their service along the Syrian coast, stop for passengers and freight at all the great maritime stations of the Phœnicians: ACRE, SÛR, SAIDA, BEYROUT, DJEBEL are the ancient AKKO, TYRE, SIDON, BERYTUS, GEBAL, each of them once an independent township or principality, with its own territory and subject villages, its own king and council of noble and wealthy elders; all rivals, jealous and envious of each other, sometimes hostile, yet bound fast together by the ties of race, language, religion, common customs, institutions, and pursuits, till to outsiders and later generations all distinctions were blurred,

13.—SOURCE OF THE RIVER ADONIS IN THE LEBANON.

all differences merged in the one collective name of "Phœnicians." Stinted for space on dry land, these communities early betook themselves to the water, became the best mariners and shipwrights in the world, built almost as many ships as houses, and must have come to look on the sea as their real home, since even their very dwellings were in great part constructed more on water than on land. Arvad rose on a rocky islet quite some distance from the coast; Tyre was built on a group of small islands artificially connected by filling the shallow straits between them, and though the oldest quarter of the city continued to exist on dry land, it was degraded into a suburb of warehouses and landing-places for freight, while the palaces and temples, the arsenals and docks graced the later island quarter. The real uncorrupted name of Tyre is TsÔR, *i. e.*, "the Rock." Sidon occupied a small peninsula, connected with the coast by a narrow neck or causeway, and endowed with the unusual luxury of three harbors, facing the north and south.

7. It was during the four or five centuries of the Hyksos rule in Egypt that the Phœnician cities rose to their full development; indeed, most probably in consequence of that rule, which, being in the hands of kindred races, must have created very favorable conditions for their commerce. It was then, too, that Sidon achieved a pre-eminence among them, which, while not amounting to actual sovereignty, yet must have become a real leadership or supremacy, and gained for her the proud surname of "first-born of Canaan," even though, in point of

date, some other cities may have been of older foundation still,—so that during a long period foreign nations often used the name "Sidonians" indiscriminately, applying it to the whole Phœnician people. For this distinction Sidon may very likely have been indebted originally, as her name suggests, to her purple fisheries, the most profitable along the shore. For of all the staple articles of the Phœnicians' export trade, the one which created the widest demand and fetched the highest prices was their purple dye,—an article, too, which could be had only from them. They supplied the markets also with many other most valuable products of their industry, but there was none so distinctively their own. They were skilful workers in metals, and produced exquisite cups, dishes, ewers, and ornaments of all sorts in gold, silver, and bronze; their glasswares were as famous as Bohemian and Venetian glass is nowadays; their looms were not idle. But in all these branches they could be imitated and rivalled, in some outdone. Thus the works of the Egyptian jewellers are marvels of art, and the Egyptians also manufactured glass, while many countries and cities might have disputed the prize in weaving fine stuffs and beautiful carpets. But the purple dye the Phœnicians had discovered, invented, they possessed, and jealously guarded the secret of it, and no one else could make it. Through all the gradations of color, from delicate crimson to the richest blood-red, the softest amethyst-purple, the deepest black, they could manage the wonderful substance, till the costliest, most perfect piece of woollen goods increased in value tenfold on emerging from their vats. And robes of Sidonian or Tyrian purple became an almost necessary attribute of royalty and of worship, the adornment of temples, the distinctive badge of the high-born of all nations, so that the less wealthy or more thrifty, as in later times the Romans, if they could not afford or condemned the expense of the lordly luxury, still adorned at least the hem of their garments with a more or less wide band of purple, according to the wearer's rank.

8. Never before or after did tiny shell-fish—for that was the humble scale in creation occupied by the giver of the precious dyeing substance—come to such high honor or play so princely a part in the affairs of the mighty of this world, unless we except the pearl oyster; yet even pearl fisheries, though they have enriched companies and fed whole populations, have not been the making of great states, while it may be said, with very little exaggeration, that the purple mussel *was* the making of Phœnicia, first by the discovery of it, then—and still more—by its disappearance. The dyeing substance is a fluid, secreted by the mussel in almost microscopic quantity, each animal yielding just one small drop. Of this fluid, the raw material, it is recorded that three hundred pounds were needed to dye fifty pounds of wool. Clearly, at this rate the home fisheries, however abundant, *had* to be exhausted some day, and when the mussel began to grow scarce, the fishers followed it up the coast in their boats. It was soon discovered

that the entire coast of Asia Minor swarmed with the precious shell-fish; then ships were equipped and sent on fishing tours, much as whalers are now. Thus, from station to station, fishing, trading, exploring, they were drawn far to the north, as far as the Hellespont. But this was not all. It appears that in those days that particular kind of mussel absolutely filled the waters not only of the Asiatic coast, but of all the islands between that and Greece, the straits, and bays, and gulfs of Greece itself, nay, of Sicily, and, further still, the coast of Northern Africa and Southern Spain in the entire Mediterranean. From island, then, to island the Phœnicians advanced, always in pursuit of their invaluable " raw material " ; on, onwards to the west, till the shores of Africa and Spain became to them as familiar as their own. Thus this same insignificant little animal, after founding the wealth and prosperity of the nation, lured it into enterprise and became the direct cause of the first voyages of discovery that were ever made and which enlarged the world, as then known, by all the expanse of the Mediterranean, with all the countries that enclose it, and all the islands scattered over it ; for of these, surely, there is not one that was not first stepped upon by the Phœnicians.

9. But even this is not all that marvellous mussel did for them. It founded their first colonies. For it would have been highly unpractical and wasteful to bring home shiploads of the mussels for the sake of the one drop of fluid to be obtained from each. It was much simpler to extract it on the

spot and leave the shells to rot or dry upon the shore, as the pearl-fishers do with the oysters. That such really became the general practice we have evidence in the mounds of shells still occasionally found on the beach of this or that island. This obvious calculation gave rise to the establishment of counting-houses and factories at the principal landing points; these in their turn, and at the more important stations, gradually expanded into permanent settlements. Contact with the native populations, as yet very rude and uncultured, was inevitable; native labor had to be employed, as being both cheap and handy. The islanders were quickly trained to fish for the purple-mussel themselves and to trade it to the strangers for manufactured wares—pottery, glass, woollens—and there is no doubt that the foreign merchants drove many hard bargains and cheated their semi-barbarous customers quite as systematically and successfully as the modern traders who grow rich on the gold and ivory of African tribes, obtained for handfuls of beads, bottles of whiskey, and poor cutlery. Single Phœnician ships would enter some harbor or anchor in some well-sheltered cove, and, displaying an attractive array of goods on the shore, draw out the natives and organize an extempore fair, which seldom lasted more than five or six days, the seventh day being generally devoted to rest by the Phœnicians as well as by the Babylonians and Assyrians.* Not unfrequently the ship-owner and

---

* See "Story of Chaldea," p. 256.

crew would invite the islanders to a grand festive winding up of business, perhaps promising the women presents or bargains, and, when the sails were set and all was ready for their departure, seize upon as many girls, boys, and children as they could without too great risk, and carry them away, to be sold for slaves in their own country, or in Egypt, or Asia Minor, or even on other distant islands—again very much after the manner of European dealers on the coast of Africa before the abomination of slave-trade was abolished.* However, the islanders of the Greek seas were not stolid African tribes, but the ancestors of the Greeks, the most gifted race in all the ancient world. So they learned from their foreign visitors; learned not only what these taught them, but far more, so that in time they could treat with them on equal terms, barter their fishing, their timber, their ore to them in fair exchange, and in the course of a few hundred years supplant the Phœnicians' navy by their own and become their rivals in many arts, yet never in the production of the purple dye, although the Greeks did attempt to imitate even that, and not unsuccessfully. But all this belongs to a far later period of history than that we have as yet arrived at, and which is that of active Phœnician colonization.

10. The prosperity of most of the Greek islands

---

* That the Phœnicians never quite abandoned the practice we can gather from the reproof addressed to them by the prophet Joel: "The children of Judah and Jerusalem have ye sold unto the sons of the Grecians" (Joel, iii. 6).

dates from the establishment on them of Phœnician colonies. Of these the oldest, falling into the age of Sidon's supremacy and sent out principally by that city, are naturally the nearest to the mother-country. By far the most important ones were those on the neighboring island of CYPRUS, then on that of CRETE, the two largest and most southern of the Greek islands. Cyprus's chief attraction lay in her copper mines, which were so abundant that the island itself was named after the metal,*—a most valuable discovery to skilful workers in bronze, since about nine parts in ten of bronze are copper. Now bronze, in those early times, was the staple metal out of which every kind of implements, tools, and household articles was manufactured, and even weapons—swords, daggers, the heads of arrows and lances—the use of iron having been introduced only later, at least on a large and general scale. But if copper is the main ingredient of bronze, the other ingredient, tin, is no less necessary, though only in the proportion of one tenth or little more. Yet it is much less plentifully supplied by nature; there are, in the world, several copper mines to one of tin; these are few and far between, and where they do occur they are comparatively scant and quickly exhausted. It is this difficulty which probably first led to adopt iron, though it is more difficult to work, for its great superiority could be revealed only by the use and labor of centuries. But in the time

---

* Hebrew *Kopher;* Greek, *Kupros;* German, *Kupfer;* our *Copper*.

of the earlier Phœnicians bronze still reigned supreme, and they had to provide the tin both for their own foundries and those of other nations, for instance, the Egyptians. For awhile they used to get it in the mountain regions of the Taurus, north of their own country, but the supply was insufficient, and soon ceased entirely. They then went for it to the Caucasus, sending their ships all the way round Asia Minor, through the Hellespont and the Bosphorus into the Black Sea, along the southern coast of which they scattered several settlements. And in their westward navigations, extended as much in pursuit of the precious ore as of the no less precious shell-fish, they carefully explored every point at which they touched land.

11. It was thus they came on a land which was to be for many centuries one of their richest possessions—the south of Spain, which they called TARSHISH, and which is often given in the later and corrupted form of TARTESSUS. Here the rivers carried gold sand; the mountains generously opened their silver-laden sides and yielded such treasures of pure ore as many centuries of assiduous working scarcely succeeded in exhausting; and not silver alone, but also copper, lead, and, in small quantities, tin, while the fertile plains known to this day, under the name of Andalusia, as one of the gardens of the earth, literally flowed with honey, oil, and wine, and were a very granary of wheat and other grains, besides sheep of finest fleece and several lesser products. The most extravagant tales, as of fairyland, were circulated of this blessed

region, and many have been wonderingly and half believingly transmitted to us by various writers of note. Thus one tells how the first Phœnicians who came to Tarshish received so much silver in exchange for worthless articles that the ships could not carry the weight; so all the implements and utensils, even to the anchors, were left on the shore and new ones made of silver. Another gravely reports that once on a time the forests got on fire, when the gold and silver bubbled up from below the earth, melted by the tremendous conflagration, for that every hill and mountain was a solid mass of gold and silver. The same story is told of the Pyrenees, where numerous rivulets of pure molten silver were said to have formed and run down the mountain sides on a similar occasion. In the north-western corner of the Spanish peninsula the Phœnicians found tin in rather larger quantities than in the South.

12. But the great and only reliable tin mart of the world in the bronze ages was England, especially its south-western extremity, now known as Devon and Cornwall, and the islands of the Channel, the first recorded name of which is a Greek one, signifying "TIN-ISLANDS" (CASSITERIDES). When or in what way the Phœnicians ever heard of so remote a nook, so totally out of the beat and beyond the horizon of all the nations then of any note, must ever remain a mystery. But certain it is that already long before the foundation of Gades (about 1100) they in some manner regularly drew thence their supply of tin by a continental route

which traversed the whole of France. Probably they did not at first go over to the islands, but the natives brought the tin to them where their caravans waited to receive it, somewhere about the mouth of the Seine, and even further inland, if not as far as the Pyrenees themselves. A glance at the map will show how easy it was, by sailing up the Seine as far as it is navigable, then transferring the freight by a short land journey to the Saône, then drifting down to that river's junction with the Rhône, and again down the latter's deep and swift current, to take any amount of wares to any of the numerous harbors on the Mediterranean by the mouths of the Rhône, where would be stationed some of the so-called " Tarshish ships,"—vessels of unusual size and peculiar build, adapted for long navigations and heavy freights.

13. Still, this route must have been hampered by many expenses and delays. For the country it traversed was occupied by a great many tribes, each of whom, of course, learned to make an easy profit out of the foreign traders by levying a toll on their ships or wagons as the condition of allowing them free and safe passage through their own respective territories. The Phœnicians were not a fighting people and always submitted to exactions, even extortions, having early learned the power of wealth and its extraordinary capacities for smoothing every path ; besides, their profits were so enormous that they could well afford to sacrifice some portion of it for the sake of being allowed to pursue their business unmolested. At the same time,

they were never slow to find and take ways and means to elude irksome obligations. So it was in this case; they discovered that there was a way to the "Tin Islands" round by sea, the route we now know as that from Gibraltar by the Bay of Biscay and the Atlantic. But to take this route required more than ordinary pluck, not to say recklessness; not so much on account of any deficiency in the ships or in the skill of the mariners, as because the Phœnicians had an idea that the straits which separated Spain from Africa marked the end of the world. The great waste of waters beyond was to them the mysterious Western Ocean, into which their national deity, the great BAAL-MELKARTH, the glorious Sun-God, plunged every night at the end of his career, and whither no mortal was to follow him. He had protected his people in their distant wanderings; he had led them, in the wake of his own westward course, to these gates of the outer world, but here was the end, the limit, where he said "No further!" The two gigantic, towering rocks which mark the entrance into the straits from the Mediterranean, he had himself set up as signs and boundaries; they were, and for all ages were to be, "THE PILLARS OF MELKARTH," beyond which to pass to further explorations would be little less than sacrilegious. Gades, indeed, the headquarters of their western commerce, wealthy and splendid, a miniature Tyre, built, like the metropolis, on a rocky islet at some distance from the land,—Gades rose on the outer side of the sacred landmarks, but then that was only a continuation of a coast belonging to them along its whole extent; and besides, the city was said to have been founded by the god's own order, imparted in a dream. Had they not been held back by this feeling of superstitious awe, who knows what further discoveries they might have made. One they did make, but it was only accidental, and nothing came of it except a few fables, which the Greeks later took hold of, and, touching them up with their marvellous fancy, worked out into beautiful stories. It appears that some Phœnician ships were carried out into the Atlantic by violent winds, and, losing control of their movements, "were driven by the tempest, after many days, to a large island opposite the shores of Lybia (Africa), blest with such fertility and such delicious air as to appear destined for the abode of gods rather than the dwelling of men." Evidently the island of Madeira! But the Phœnicians did not return thither, and left the group to be re-discovered a couple of thousand years later. The love of gain, however, seems to have overruled even religious scruples, for the next thing we hear of are the regular trips of Phœnician ships to the "Tin Islands," and if they did not found any permanent settlements in that remote and uncongenial clime, there is no want of traces to attest their presence. Thus, they had a station on the Isle of Wight, in the centre of the island, where it rises to a considerable eminence, commanding the rest. The site was so cleverly chosen, that when the Romans came, a thousand years later, they built a fort on the same spot, and that again was succeeded in due time by a strong castle of Norman construction, the noble ruins of which are much visited and admired under the name of Carisbrooke Castle. The knowledge of the sea-route to the "Tin Islands" the Phœnicians kept strictly to themselves, and were jealously watchful that no one should follow and supplant them there, as the Greeks had supplanted them nearer home. A characteristic story has been preserved of a Phœnician captain, who, finding himself pursued by some Roman ships which had accidentally strayed into those unfamiliar waters, and being unable to escape by stress of oars and sails, deliberately ran himself aground and drowned his whole crew and cargo, so as not to be questioned and found out—a deed which was considered at Tyre an act of patriotic heroism. All this, however, relates to a much later period than that we have to deal with now.

14. Tin was not the only commodity the adventurous traders brought from their northern voyages. They were the only importers of another northern produce, the yellow amber of the Baltic—merely a fancy article, it is true, an ornamental luxury, but not the less in great and general demand, and fetching extravagant prices, for it had become universally fashionable in the then civilized world on account of its scarcity and the mysterious charm which distance lent it. It is well known that the resinous substance we call amber, the produce of inaccessible forests of submarine plants, washed ashore by high tides and tempest-beaten waves, is gathered all along the coast of Prussia. It has therefore been con-

jectured and given out almost as a certainty, that the Phœnician ships must have visited those secluded and most inhospitable seas. Later and more accurate study, however, has shown the improbability of their having confronted the dangers of a navigation round Denmark, and ventured into strange and nearly always stormy waters, so bristling, moreover, with obstacles in the shape of reefs and cliffs, shoals and shallows and straits, as to make them nearly impracticable to any but native sailors. It has further been shown that, in very ancient times, amber was found off the coasts of Holland, very easily accessible from England, and, lastly, that the Phœnicians had established a caravan route across the whole of Germany, from the Adriatic to the Baltic. It is along this route, which offered them many convenient points for bartering their Asiatic wares against local products, that the greater part of the amber was brought to the mouth of the river Po in Northern Italy and then shipped down the Adriatic.

15. For the Phœnicians, although their chief renown is based on their maritime expeditions, were quite as intrepid travellers by land as by sea. On the Asiatic continent they practised caravan trading on an immense scale; the great caravan routes of the East were almost entirely in their hands: from the Black Sea to the Nile, over Karkhemish and Damascus; from their own cities, through the land of Judah to the southern marts of Arabia; across Syria, through Damascus, to the Euphrates, and down the river to Babylon, or by a

short cut through the desert to Assyria proper —Nineveh, Kalah, and the rest; lastly, from Babylon, across the continent, even to India itself, at least to the mouth of the Indus. The latter point, however, they probably reached more frequently in large armed vessels of the same build as the Tarshish ships. They were the privileged traders of the world; the wealth of nations passed and repassed through their hands in its transfer from country to country, and in its passage enough stuck to these hands to have made the cities by the sea rich and prosperous beyond all others, even without the ever flowing source of income which their own factories supplied, and which, again, would have sufficed for a nation's prosperity without the addition of foreign commerce on such a scale.

16. As it was, the wealth and boundless luxury which the Phœnicians enjoyed at home passes all description and almost imagination. "Tyrus did build herself a stronghold," says one of the Hebrew prophets,* "and heaped up silver as the dust and fine gold as the mire of the streets." But the most complete and striking picture of Tyre in her greatest glory we find in some of the prophet Ezekiel's wonderful pages. This picture breathes and lives before our enraptured eyes, and we scarcely know what most to marvel at,—the poetic beauty of the description, or its almost dazzling vividness and gorgeousness. The prophet apostrophizes the queen of the Phœnician cities;

---

* Zechariah, ix. 3.

"O thou that dwellest at the entry of the sea, which art the merchant of the people unto many isles . . . . thou, O Tyre, hast said, 'I am perfect in beauty.' . . . By thy wisdom and by thine understanding thou hast gotten thee riches and hast gotten gold and silver into thy treasures. By thy great wisdom and by thy traffic hast thou increased thy riches, and thine heart is lifted up because of thy riches, ... and thou hast said, 'I am a god, I sit in the seat of God, in the midst of the seas.' . . . Thy borders are in the heart of the seas, thy builders have perfected thy beauty. They have made all thy ship boards of fir trees from Senir; they have taken cedars from Lebanon to make a mast for thee. Of the oaks of Bashan they have made thine oars; they have made thy benches of ivory inlaid in boxwood from the isles of Kittim (Cyprus). Fine linen with broidered work from Egypt was thy sail, that it might be to thee for an ensign; blue and purple from the isles of Elishah (the Greek islands) was thine awning. The inhabitants of Sidon and Arvad were thy rowers; thy wise men, O Tyre, were in thee, they were thy pilots . . . all the ships of the sea with their mariners were in thee to occupy thy merchandise. . . . Tarshish was thy merchant by reason of the multitude of all kind of riches; with silver, iron, tin, and lead they traded for thy wares. Javan, Tubal, and Meshech (the Ionian Greeks and the mountain peoples of the Taurus), they were thy traffickers; they traded the persons of men and vessels of brass for thy merchandise. They of the house of Togarmah (Armenia) traded for thy wares with horses and war-horses and mules. . . . Many isles were the mart of thine hand: they brought thee in exchange horns of ivory and ebony. Syria was thy merchant, by reason of the multitude of thy handiworks: they traded for thy wares with emeralds, purple and broidered work, and fine linen, and coral and rubies. Judah and the land of Israel, they were thy traffickers: they traded for thy merchandise wheat . . . . and honey and oil and balm. Damascus was thy merchant for the multitude of thy handiworks, by reason of the multitude of all kinds of riches; with the wine of Helbon and white wool. . . . Arabia " (the prophet enumerates a number of Arabian tribes from the Persian Gulf to the Red Sea) " . . . they traded for thy wares in lambs, and rams, and goats . . . . with chief of all spices and with all precious stones, and gold . . . . in choice wares in wrappings of blue and broidered work, and in chests of rich apparel, bound with cords, and made of cedar. . . . When thy wares went forth out of the seas, thou filledst many people; thou didst enrich the kings of the earth with the multitude of thy riches and of thy merchandise. . . . The ships of Tarshish were thy caravans for thy merchandise; and thou wast replenished and made very glorious in the midst of the seas."*

17. "Thy wisdom and thine understanding."—"Thy great wisdom and thy traffic."—The wisdom of the money-maker, the understanding of the cunning trader—such indeed is the summing up and the culmination of the Phœnicians' moral worth. Money-making, the love of gain and accumulation, is not only the key to their national character, it is their character itself, and their whole character. Motive, incentive, sustaining power—all is there; they develop great qualities: enterprise, endurance, industry, ingenuity—but these are all begotten of and animated by the love of lucre, and success to them is wealth, and therein is their pride, their joy: "Thine heart is lifted up because of thy riches." Truly, if ever nation has been a worshipper of Mammon, has made its choice and clung to it, the Phœnicians have been that nation. They were lacking in all the qualities which have won for other races the name of heroic and intellectual; their ambition ran in but one channel. They were not a warlike or conquering people, not even a patriotic or freedom-loving people. Ever ready to meet an invader with tribute and submission, they invariably preferred to pay rather than fight. They were not alive to the shame of foreign rule, and bore it with equanimity so long as its demands on their treasu-

---

* Ezekiel, chs. xxvii. and xxviii.

ries were moderate and it did not interfere with their commercial operations. They had no army, but foreign hired soldiers for emergencies; in the words of Ezekiel (xxvii. 10), "They of Persia and Lud (Lydia) and of Put (Libya) were in thine army, thy men of war: they hanged the shield and helmet in thee." When actually attacked within their cities, their homes, or subjected to excessive extortion, they *could* fight, like wild beasts at bay in their dens, and this they did more than once. But they were seldom put to such a test, being far too valuable subjects, too convenient agents and middlemen not to be treated, as a rule, with consideration. Thus they came through the five hundred years of Egyptian dominion and invasions unscathed and unimpoverished, rarely refractory, never openly rebellious. Even when they founded colonies, they were quite willing to pay ground rent for their settlements, if the native population met them in a determined spirit and asserted their rights, and they frequently continued to pay such rent long after the colonies had grown into powerful communities, simply to avoid unpleasantness.

18. They were not a literary or intellectual people. Although they invented the alphabet, they used it chiefly for purposes of book-keeping and short inscriptions. They have left no poetry, no historical annals, no works of science or speculation. They do not seem to have cared even to publish their own very remarkable experiences and exploits: these brought them wealth, what cared they for the fame? Had Assyrian conquerors visited such

remote and unfamiliar regions as the coast of Spain, that of the Baltic, the "Tin Islands," what interesting records would have been left for our perusal! How the monotony of the military narrative would have been relieved with touches of description, giving briefly but graphically the most marked peculiarities of the land and the people, accounts even of their plants and animals! Nothing of the kind seems to have occurred to the Phœnicians, whose silence is especially tantalizing in the case of the "Tin Islands": We *should* like to know what England was like two thousand years B. C. They were not an imaginative or creative people, but merely clever learners and imitators. Of the many arts they cultivated, not one was their own. Their only original invention was the purple dye—and that is a craft, not an art. Their sculpture, of which many specimens have been preserved, was only a transformation of Babylonian and Assyrian art. Nothing can be more hideous and shapeless than the images of their principal deities, mostly in clay, which they

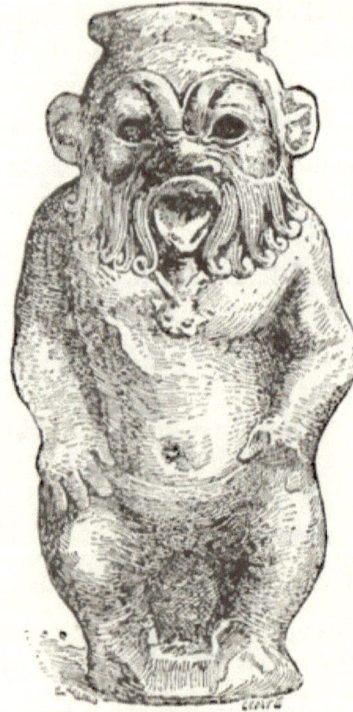

14.—SMALL PHŒNICIAN IDOL IN TERRA-COTTA (CLAY).

carried with them on all their expeditions. Of their architecture we cannot judge, for when the day of destruction came, it was utter and complete, and not stone on stone was left of their buildings.

It came to pass, as we read in the prophet Ezekiel: "They shall destroy the walls of Tyre and break down her towers . . . and they shall break down thy walls and destroy thy pleasant houses; and they shall lay thy stones and thy timber and thy dust in the midst of the waters. . . . *I will make her a bare rock: she shall be a place for the spreading of nets in the midst of the sea.*" *

19. Thus through the cycle of what the Phœnicians were *not*, we are forcibly brought back to what they eminently *were*, to the vocation wherein they displayed unrivalled genius and boundless capabilities —that of business men and money-makers. And as it seems to be a wise and invariable dispensation that people, in laboring, however selfishly, to benefit themselves, should in some way, and independently

15.—ASHTORETH, SMALL PHŒNICIAN IDOL IN TERRA-COTTA (CLAY).

---
* Ezekiel, xxvi.

of their own will, necessarily benefit others also, so the Phœnicians have been the bearers, if not of spiritual culture, at least of material progress to countless tribes and places, which, but for them, but for their awakening and stirring contact, might have slumbered for ages longer in unconsciousness of their own powers and resources.

"In this respect," says François Lenormant, the scholar so often quoted already, "it is impossible ever to overrate the part which the Phœnicians played in the ancient world and the greatness of their influence.... There was a time, of which the culminating point may be placed about twelve centuries before the beginning of our era, when the counting-houses of the sons of Canaan formed an uninterrupted chain along all the shores of the Mediterranean to the Strait of Gibraltar, while another series of similar establishments were stationed along the sea route that stretched from the southern extremity of the Red Sea to the shores of India. These counting-houses exercised an immense influence on the countries wherein they were established. Every one of them became the nucleus of great cities, for the natives quickly rallied around the Phœnician commercial settlement, drawn to it by the advantages it offered them and the attractions of civilized life. Every one, too, became a centre for the propagation of material civilization. A barbarous people does not enter into active and prolonged commercial relations with a civilized one without gradually appropriating the latter's culture, especially in the case of races so intelligent and capable of progress as were those of Europe.... New needs make themselves felt: the native covets the manufactured products which are brought to him, and which reveal to him all sorts of refinements of which he had no idea. Soon the wish arises in him to find out the secret of their fabrication, to master the arts which create them, to profit himself by the resources his own country yields, instead of giving them up in the shape of raw material to the strangers who know so well how to make use of them...."*

20. If we will try to imagine how reviving, bene-

---

* Fr. Lenormant, "Premières Civilisations," Vol. I., p. 158.

ficial, truly civilizing, even in our own days, would be the regularly recurring trips of a pedler with a judicious selection of wares to a remote and secluded neighborhood somewhere on the outskirts of civilization, especially if that pedler be willing to barter his goods not always for money, but more often for such simple local products and materials as his customers can supply, we shall, by magnify-

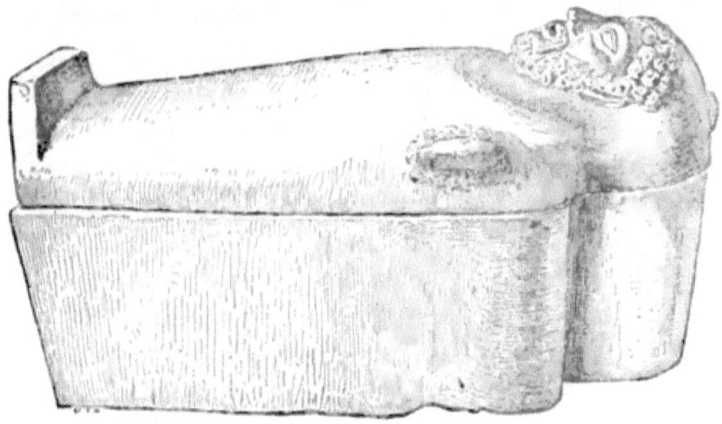

16.—PHŒNICIAN SARCOPHAGUS (COFFIN). (OF LATE PERIOD.)

ing the whole thing a hundredfold, form a tolerably fair idea of the blessings that everywhere followed in the wake of the Phœnicians. The resemblance would be the closer from the fact that our pedler would certainly cheat his customers as hard and as long as they would let him, that is, as long as they had not gained some knowledge of the market value of their own wares, and, probably some skill in manufacturing them, so as to become comparatively independent of their itinerant trader. If they were wise and just, however, they would not grudge him his past exorbitant profits, even while reducing them for the future within reasonable bounds, but would consider that all schooling must be paid for. Thus as each one of the great nations that have in succession played prominent parts on the historical stage of the world seems to have had allotted to it a special mission, in accordance with its own particular powers and gifts, we really might define that of the Phœnicians by entitling them, in a certain sense, without disrespect and without undervaluing their immense importance, the Pedlers of the Ancient World. It was in its time undoubtedly a most necessary, most beneficent mission; yet one would hesitate to call it either noble or glorious, as those epithets can never apply to a pursuit so entirely selfish and grossly material as that of wealth for its own sake. Such a pursuit, even while calling into play many splendid qualities, debases them by the use it puts them to, and the only sides of human nature which it develops fully and permanently are its lowest ones—unscrupulous craftiness, deceitfulness, brutality, and, on occasion, cold-blooded cruelty.

IV.

THE SONS OF CANAAN: THEIR RELIGION,—SACRIFICE AS AN INSTITUTION,—HUMAN SACRIFICES.

1. IT is but fair to admit that the Phœnicians had by no means a monopoly of those qualities the combination of which goes far towards making up a rather repulsive national character. An exceeding sensuality,—*i. e.*, attachment to all the material pleasures and advantages of life,—a proneness to exclusively material views of both visible and invisible world, with a strange absence of loftier instincts and spiritual aspirations, resulting in gross immorality and dulness of conscience,—such were the common features generally characteristic not only of the various branches of Canaan, but of the entire Hamitic race, with the solitary and striking exception of the Egyptians, than whom there never has been a more spiritually inclined, contemplative nation. All the numerous people gathered into one group under the generic name "Sons of Canaan" shared this remarkably well-defined common character with the Phœnicians, but without their genius —for to genius the latter certainly can lay claim in their own particular line. This is why, with a hankering after material prosperity as absorbing, a spiritual callousness as impenetrable, the other Ca-

naanitic nations never, even distantly, rivalled their brethren of the sea-shore,—favored, too, as these were in the peculiar conditions under which they developed,—in either power or wealth, the Hittite confederacy alone excepted, and that only during a few centuries. This same character of materialism and sensuality pervades the Canaanitic religion as well, and stamps it with the unmistakable mark of the race, as is but natural. For if there is a thing in which a race expresses itself most fully, and in its innermost qualities, that thing is its religion. What a people is, that, in a heightened and intensified degree, a magnified form, its gods will be, its worship will embody. This is an inevitable consequence of the anthropomorphic tendency which is a necessity of the limited human nature,[*] and which an ancient Greek writer expressed most strikingly, if somewhat coarsely, by saying that if horses and oxen had gods, they would certainly imagine them in the shape of more perfect and powerful horses and oxen. A general sketch of the religious conceptions of the Sons of Canaan will include the Phœnicians, although, as is the wont of all polytheistic races, different communities did particular homage to this or that particular deity, and some local names, some local forms of worship produce at times the illusion of separate religions. It *is* an illusion. The religion of Canaan—Phœnicia and Syria—is in substance one and the same.

2. The religion of Canaan, like that of Babylonia, like that of every race and nation in the world, is

---

[*] See "Story of Chaldea," pp. 355–357.

originally based on the primitive conception of the powers of nature as living and divinely endowed immortal beings—or gods. But beyond this similarity, which extends to all mankind universally, it has a far closer connection, manifested in many exact coincidences, both of general features and of details, with the Babylonian religion,—a connection which will easily be explained on the ground of kindred, when we remember that the Hamitic race must have been strongly represented in the mixed population of the old land of Shumir and Accad. In one way the religious ideas of the Canaanites may be said to have been an advance on the Babylonian ones, since, not having the background of Turanian goblin-worship to work into their own system, and being moreover of a far less contemplative turn of mind, that system was much simpler, and, if still polytheistic, reduced the number of deities to a degree at least approaching monotheism. We find here no elaborate superstructure of sacred triads, of puzzling but profound import ; no beautifully ordered system of planetary divinities, with their many-colored spheres and subtle influences on the fate of men and states. To the Canaanites the world was a far less complicated affair. These dwellers in a land where barren sandy wastes and bald, rocky highlands alternate with the most luxuriant, fertile plains and cool, wooded slopes, the unreclaimable aridity of the desert with the eternal freshness of the sea,—where dewy, balmy nights follow on burning, breathless days,—where the surpassing loveliness of a showery, flowery spring is quickly succeeded by the merciless, destructive blaze of a torrid mid-summer,—the children of such a land seem to have been especially impressed with the contrasts in nature, or what has been called the DUALISM of things, *i. e.*, their twofold aspect, the opposite extremes which face and balance each other. They saw that there was good and evil in the world, (both to them of a purely physical nature.) There was heat and coolness; drought and moisture; the rude glare of day and the mild glory of night, the former set apart for labor and hardship, the manly toil of mind and body, the latter inviting to soft indulgence, effeminate repose in the midst of all the luxuries and pleasures that wealth can buy and leisure enjoy. And, in another order of ideas, there was the eternally creating and the eternally producing and nourishing power,—the masculine and feminine principle into which all living creation, pervaded by the law of sex, naturally separates itself, the division which rules and harmonizes the universe.* Of this abstract division, the material one of heat and moisture, fire and water, seemed an apt embodiment and rendering; and in carrying out the idea, the fiery element, as the fiercer, more actively energetic, was naturally identified with the masculine principle, while that of moisture, as the milder and quieter, answered well to the feminine principle; the necessary union of the two to form a complete world, being perfectly symbolized by the fact that moisture is productive of life only when subjected

---

* See "Story of Chaldea," pp. 242-245.

THE RELIGION OF CANAAN. 107

to the influence of heat, while heat is barren, unless tempered by moisture.

3. In the material world, this dualism had its visible representatives in the two great rulers of the heavens, the Sun and Moon : the Lord of Day and the Queen of Night ; the source of all heat and the dispenser of coolness and dew, (as the moon was long supposed to be); luminaries both, hence of a kindred nature, yet how different in their ways and attributions ! It was the sun, then, whom the Canaanites worshipped, calling him now BAAL ("Lord," the same word as the Babylonian BEL), now MOLOCH (king), with occasional variations, such as "Lord of Heaven," or "King of the City,"—and when BAALIM are spoken of ("gods," in the plural), it is only the sun-gods of the different cities or communities that are really meant,—the same one sun-god, localized and appropriated by the addition of city names. As to the female deity of the Canaanites, ASHTORETH (whom the Greeks have called ASTARTE), she is the ISHTAR and MYLITTA or BELIT ("BAALATH," "Lady,") of the Assyro-Babylonian cycle of gods, scarcely changed either in name or nature ; the goddess both of love and of war, of incessant production and laborious motherhood, and of voluptuous, idle enjoyment, the greatest difference being that Ashtoreth is identified with the moon and

17.—PHŒNICIAN CYLINDER.

wears the sign of the crescent, while the Babylonian goddess rules the planet Venus, the Morning and Evening Star of the poets. We have a Phœnician cylinder of carnelian, representing the Baal in the shape of a tree or post, the rays which surround it characterizing it as the symbol of the Sungod, and accompanied by the Crescent. The cylinder which so clearly brings before us the joint worship of Sun and Moon, the male and female principle, is supposed, from the place where it was found by a peasant, to represent the Baal of Aphaka, a city on the western slope of Lebanon, east of Byblos (Gebal), which had an ancient and very famous temple.

4. As was but meet, the two principal cities of the Phœnicians had respectively placed themselves under the patronage of their two great national deities: Sidon did special homage to Ashtoreth, while Tyre invoked Moloch under the local name, already mentioned above more than once, of MEL-KARTH ("King of the City"). The temple of the god was the pride of the New, or island-Tyre, and stories were told of its magnificence which almost surpass in extravagance those current about the great temple of BEL-MARDUK in Babylon. HERODOTUS, the celebrated Greek traveller and historian of the fifth century B. C., tells us that he made a voyage to Tyre expressly to see this temple, of which he had heard as "very highly venerated." "I visited the temple," he continues with perfect good faith, "and found it richly adorned with a number of offerings, among which

were two pillars, one of pure gold, the other of emerald, shining with great brilliancy at night." Pillars of gold there have been; but *pillars* of *emerald*, and that too of such perfection as to emit light in the dark, manifestly belong to fable. The pillar was probably made of the famous Egyptian green glass which mimicked the emerald,—a stone, ancient writers inform us, the easiest of all to imitate. Even in this shape, the ornament must have been one of immense value.

5. Neither the Phœnicians nor any of the Canaanitic nations were literary people; they were not even poetical people; at least not in the sense of writing down and collecting in a poetical form the legends popularly current about their own gods. Thus they have left us, properly speaking, no mythology, and, naturally, no Epos.* Yet the poetical or imaginative faculty is never totally absent in any, either race or individual. So the Canaanites, like all other races, of course, did have myths,—*i. e.*, presentations of natural phenomena in the form of poetical images,†—only these myths did not crystallize into stories; indeed, they were not generally expressed in words, but rather in ceremonies, customs, forms of worship, attempts at artistic representations. There is, therefore, no nation at whose myths it has been more difficult to get. They have had to be collected from the stamps of coins, fragments of monuments, few and insignificant, but

---

* See "Story of Chaldea," pp. 298-299.
† See *Ibid.*, p. 294.

principally from the notices scattered through the works of a great many writers, some of whom spoke as eye-witnesses, and others only as reporters and compilers of traditions and of other people's evidence. Among these the compilers of the Bible-books hold an eminent position. Also some of these myths the Phœnicians, in their wanderings, transmitted to the Greeks, and these,—the great story-tellers of the world,—quickly condensed them into shapes of almost tangible reality; into tales of wonder and beauty, transforming, yet scarcely obscuring their foreign features. Thus, from all these manifold and incoherent materials, the mythical conceptions of the Canaanites could be gradually reconstructed,—piecemeal, so to speak, but with a completeness of outline which makes their peculiar characteristics stand forth very vividly and unmistakably.

6. Like her Babylonian double, the Canaanite goddess was especially served and honored by women. Her temples were crowded with beautiful girls,—dancers and musicians,—and her altars were ministered to by priestesses, frequently recruited from the noblest families. But the temple-building was of secondary importance; it was the temple-grounds, the sacred groves which surrounded it that were the principal sanctuary: the goddess of nature was best worshipped in the open air, under bowers of vegetation, which symbolized her eternal youth and productiveness better than any effort of art. Hence the finest trees were sacred to her, especially the evergreens, and of these particularly the cy-

press, which we have already learned from Babylonian religion to know as essentially an emblem of everlasting life.* The pomegranate was her own especial fruit, because of the thousands of seeds its pulp encloses, making it a striking emblem of fertility. For the same reason fishes were sacred to her; in many places it was considered sacrilege to eat or kill fish; a well-filled, religiously-tended fishpond usually occupied some part of the temple-

18.—COIN FROM CYPRUS, REPRESENTING THE TEMPLE AT PAPHOS.

19.—COIN FROM SIDON, REPRESENTING A PORTABLE TEMPLE OR SHRINE, PROBABLY USED IN PROCESSIONS.

grounds, and in ASCALON, where the goddess was worshipped under the name of DERKETO (see p. 114), she was represented under the form of a woman ending, from the hips, in the body of a fish. There was, besides, near that city a lake, very abundant in fish. A still more invariable and favorite attribution, however, was the white dove; it was looked upon as an essentially holy bird, which it was sinful to kill for food or sport. On the few representations of her temples which we have (mostly on coins of

---

* See "Story of Chaldea," p. 268.

Greek islands, whither the worship of the goddess had been carried by the Phœnicians), we see doves fluttering above the roof and around the stone of tall conical shape, which strangely and rudely personifies the divinity herself.*

7. But the principal feature of the worship of Ashtoreth has always been the sacred grove, whether of artificial planting or of nature's own providing, in wooded dells or on the slopes of Lebanon,—as altars to Baal were erected by preference not so much within the walls of temples as under the open sky, on the top of hills, or any convenient eminence. Near the altar was usually planted a "sacred tree," the ASHERAH,† either a real tree or an imitation of conventional shape. In this manner the Baal was not served unaccompanied by the Baalath, and the worshipper was forcibly reminded of the dual nature of the One First Principle, or—to reverse the definition—of the real unity of the divine couple. We see this symbol—the altar of the god and the tree of the goddess—on many Assyrian sculptures representing scenes of worship. These are the "high places" and the "asherahs," so frequently and wrathfully denounced in the Bible, the heathen abominations into which Judah and Israel continually

---

* This is the very oldest Canaanitic and Semitic idol-form, sometimes, as on the illustration No. 18, furnished with rude appendages, simulating a head and arms; but this is a later innovation. See also No. 17.

† Another form of the Sacred Tree, the holy Life-Symbol, familiar to us from Babylonian and Assyrian sculpture, and the signification of which has been fully explained in "Story of Chaldea," p. 268, ff.

lapsed, and for which the prophets as incessantly reproved them, till there would, from time to time, arise a pious or repentant king who would sweep

20.—ASSYRIAN PORTABLE ALTAR WITH ASHERAH. (INTERIOR OF A CAMP OR FORTRESS.)

them from the land—to be restored by his successors, generally by his own son. Thus it is said of Josiah, king of Judah, a great religious reformer (2 Kings, xxiii.), that he burned all the vessels that had been made for the service of Baal, "and for the *asherah*, and for all the host of heaven,"—"and he put down the idolatrous priests whom the kings of Judah had ordained to burn incense *in the high places* in the cities of Judah and in the places round about Jerusalem; them also that burned incense unto Baal, to the sun, and to the moon, and to the planets, and to all the host of heaven . . . and he brake down the houses where the women wove hangings for the *asherah*. . . ." These hangings were of the richest tissues, mostly of fine purple, lavishly embroidered; some served to make tents and pavilions in the sacred groves, luxurious resting-places for the worshippers who flocked thither as on some delightful pilgrimage or excursion, and who could think of no better way to honor the goddess of joy and sensual pleasure than spending whole nights in feasting and inordinate revelry within the sacred precincts, waited on by the women and girls devoted to her service, and for whom this was an essential part of their religious duties.

8. To the Canaanites, the Sun and Moon—the masculine and feminine principles, as represented by the elements of fire and moisture, the great Father and Mother of beings—were husband and wife. So with the Baal of Tyre, Melkarth, Ashtoreth was associated with the title of "Queen" (MILKATH), while in Ascalon and the other cities of the Philistine confederation they both assumed the peculiarity noted above, together with other names, and became, she, the fish-goddess, Derketo, and he, the fish-god, DAGON (from *dag*, fish, in the Semitic languages). In a temple of Dagon there was a statue of the god

which is described as having the face and hands of a man, the body of a fish, and below that again human feet. It is not difficult to recognize in this description an exact double of the Babylonian Oannes,* a resemblance enhanced by a tradition current at a very late period, and which attributed to Dagon the invention of the plough, making him the protector of agriculture generally and the dispenser of food. The name of one of the earliest Assyrian *patesis*, Ishmi-Dagan (see p. 2), further points to a closer connection between the two myths than can as yet be actually proved by documents.

9. This, however, was only a fanciful local transformation. The genuine Baal-Moloch of Syria and Phœnicia was a far mightier and more active being. The most remarkable feature about him is his double nature, combined of good and evil qualities, of which now the former, now the latter become predominant, until the one being splits itself into two, decidedly hostile to one another. The excessive heat of summer, which dries up the land and kills, that is Moloch, the terrible, the devourer, the fierce Sun-god. The moderate warmth of spring, with its frequent mild and vivifying showers, the warmth that coaxes the seed into life and fosters the growth of the crop; or the gentle glow of autumn, which brings back the clouds, absent for months from the inflamed atmosphere, which feeds the thirst-parched, panting earth, clothes her with a second robe of green, and mellows her fruits—

---

* See illustration No. 56 in the "Story of Chaldea."

that is Baal, the benignant, the beneficent, the good Sun-god. When his strength decreases and his glory pales; when his beams visit the earth for a shorter space each day, distant and slanting, and powerless to stir the sap in the trees, the seed in the earth—then Baal sleeps, or travels far away, somewhere in the West, and there is mourning for him among men, until the course of the months brings him back, and his return, or awakening, is hailed with tumultuous rejoicings, a festival which fell in our month of March.

10. There is a famous passage of the Bible bearing on this myth. It is that which tells how, in the reign of King Ahab, there was a sore famine, and four hundred and fifty priests of Baal, accompanied by four hundred priests "of the Asherah," assembled on Mount Carmel in the sight of the people of Israel, and were challenged by the prophet Elijah to make the fire of heaven descend on their sacrifice by their prayers. "And they took the bullock which was given them, and they dressed it, and called on the name of Baal from morning even until noon, saying, O Baal, hear us. But there was no voice, nor any that answered. . . . And they leaped about the altar that was made. And it came to pass at noon, that Elijah mocked them and said, Cry aloud: for he is a god; either he is musing, or he is gone aside, *or he is in a journey, or peradventure he sleepeth, and must be awaked*" (1 Kings, xviii. 26-27). The prophet's taunt is not merely a masterly piece of sarcasm, as which it is often quoted, but a direct allusion to the myth. It is

followed by a very remarkable verse, which brings before us the most extraordinary peculiarity of Canaanitic worship: "*And they cried aloud, and cut themselves after their manner with knives and with lances, till the blood gushed out upon them.*"

11. The meaning of this, to all appearance, insane performance is this: the priests, seeing their prayers and offering unheeded, proceeded to *emphasize* both, by adding to them their own blood and voluntary suffering, in the not unnatural supposition that the blood of men, and of his own servants at that, must be more precious in the Baal's sight than that of a mere senseless animal, and the pain which they inflicted on themselves of their own free will in his honor must have more persuasive virtue than the dying pang of a stupidly passive victim. Supposing the disappointment and fervid excitement to go on for some time increasing at the same rate and to reach absolute desperation, the next step would be to offer their own life, or that of one or several human victims, as a last means of moving the Baal's pity. This is a logical necessity contained in the very idea of "sacrifice," in the sense which the entire ancient world gave to the word. And accordingly, the horrible practice of human sacrifices has, in very remote ages, been universal. Not one of the ancient religions has been exempt from it. But most of them, as far as our knowledge reaches, show only rare survivals, half-obliterated traces of it, while it was reserved for the sons of Canaan to retain it not only down to historical times, not only to a comparatively

late period, but to a period so absolutely recent as the first century of our era (A.D.).

12. The word "sacrifice" is Latin, and means merely "a sacred act," any rite connected with worship. But it came to be applied exclusively to the rite which was felt to be the most holy, awe-inspiring, mysterious, to bring man most directly into the presence of the deity, into personal communication with it—that of offering gifts to it. Now gifts among men are offered on one of two impulses: that of love,—tokens of gratitude and general friendliness,—and that of fear,—gifts of propitiation; the latter naturally being by far the more copious and costly. There is a third class of offerings which cannot properly be called gifts; they are meant as a bribe to induce the receiver to do a certain thing which lies outside of his ordinary functions, to confer an extra favor. The costliness of such gifts would be proportionate to the favor demanded, and might be gradually increased if the receiver were found indifferent or obdurately unwilling to exert his power on behalf of the petitioner. Such a transaction is manifestly more a bargain than a sacrifice. Then there are the offerings regulated by law as to time, quality, and quantity, which come more properly under the head of dues, taxes, tribute, and which are cheerfully awarded to the ruler of the land on the understanding that he shall have of the very best that the land produces, and in sufficient quantity, but shall abstain from taking more or all, as he has the power and is admitted to have the right to do. It is evident that for all these gifts, of

whatever class, a return is expected in the form of material goods and advantages. Even love-gifts are no exception, for the giver certainly feels himself entitled to kindliness and friendly benevolence on the part of the receiver, and the powerful generally express these feelings by acts of graciousness and favor. It is only charity which bestows its gifts without looking for a return, even in thanks. But that is a virtue which was unknown to the ancient world, and which therefore could not be reflected in its religions.

13. Sacrifices to the gods exactly answer to these several classes of gifts to men; the feelings that prompt both, their motives, their objects, are the same. In order thoroughly to realize the very practical, entirely unromantic nature of the institution, we must put ourselves in the ancient worshipper's place, identify ourselves with his mode of thinking, and adopt the absolute, intense anthropomorphism which pervades his conception of the deity.* The god to him is a king, "only more so,"— more benevolent, more beneficent when in a kindly mood, infinitely more powerful, and proportionately more terrible in his wrath when offended. He claims certain dues and watches jealously that they shall be rendered him. He owns the land wherein he allows his worshippers to dwell. He has given it to them with all it contains and bears, to use and to enjoy. But of these good things a fair share is due to him, the Supreme Landlord, in common gratitude.

See "Story of Chaldea," pp. 355-357.

His should be at least the male first-born of every domestic animal, the first-fruits of every crop, and a portion—generally the tenth—of all the products both of the soil and of men's industry, to be paid in at stated periods, solemnly consecrated as festive at the nearest temple. Festive such occasions must be, and times of rejoicing, lest the deity receive the impression that the debt was grudgingly and unwillingly paid, and in its anger at the slight and ingratitude, may withdraw its bounties, or even inflict chastisement. It is easy to see that the quantity of live-stock and produce thus accumulated periodically at the various places of worship must have been something enormous. It is also understood that a portion of the booty made in war—not less than the tenth—of right belongs to the gods, whose favor has prospered the nation's arms.

14. There were two ways of performing the sacrifice: the thing offered could be either destroyed, consumed on the altar by fire, or only consecrated to the use of the sanctuary. The first way, the so-called burnt-offering, was of course the most complete and direct. It was supposed to convey the gift and the prayer or the thanksgiving straight to the deity. Hence the expression constantly used, "The gods *smell* a sacrifice"; if they "smell a *sweet* savor" the sacrifice is acceptable. "YAHVEH (JEHOVAH, "the Lord,") smelled a sweet savor," says Genesis.* "Let Yahveh smell an offering," says

---

* We find the identical expression in the Izdubar Epic: "The gods smelled a savor; the gods smelled a sweet savor." See "Story of Chaldea," pp. 316, 359.

David. On ordinary occasions it was only the live stock—the bullocks and the calves, the kids and the lambs—that were thus offered whole, with some of the produce of the earth, especially grain, flour, oil. But even that was rare. The more customary way was to slay the victim, to burn some choicest portions of the flesh and fat on the altar, then to lay aside an abundant supply for the priests and temple ministers, and let the people feast on the rest. Of the liquid offerings—milk, wine, oil—some would be poured into the altar flame or on the ground,—(that was the drink-offering or libation),—and the rest would be "consecrated" like the fruits, and the greater part of produce of all sorts, for the use of the sanctuary and its servants. Thus an income was formed, sufficient to defray the repairs and adornment of the buildings and shrine, to provide for the priests and attendants on a scale of great magnificence, and to keep the temple treasury always well filled. On extraordinary occasions, when the sacrifice offered by an individual or a community was an "expiatory" one—*i. e.*, offered in atonement for some crime, in deprecation of the deity's wrath for some offence or omission in the observances of worship,—or when the object was to obtain some great and uncommon mercy, personal or national, "consecration" was deemed insufficient: the sacrifice must be complete; nothing short of absolute renunciation could satisfy the offended majesty or merit a special divine interference. On such occasions whole herds and flocks and ship-loads of precious wares have frequently been consumed by the sacrificial flames, fed with the costliest perfumes, oils, and spices.

15. It stands to reason that the thing offered in sacrifice, whatever it is, whether living or inanimate, must be the best of its kind, unsullied by use, unimpaired in beauty, and unbroken in spirit and strength by work. Would a man present to his superior or to his friend a cast-off garment, a shorn sheep, a galled ox, a horse sore from the harness or saddle? And if he did, would not the receiver turn on him in well deserved anger, and instead of favor deal vengeance to him? Therefore the victim reserved for sacrifice must be perfect and without a blemish, the fairest in form and color; the heifer and the steer must not have known the ignominy of the goad and plough, nor the steed the humiliation of obedience, or the female animals have been wearied with the cares and labors of motherhood. Besides, it would be irreverent to offer an animal after having drawn profit from it, in the shape of either work or increase. Naturally, too, if the animal is a favorite, or an especially valuable one from rareness and excellence of breed, the sacrifice will be all the more acceptable, and probably the more efficacious, as manifesting the greater and more ungrudging zeal.

16. It is but according to human nature that the zeal and lavishness displayed should be in proportion to the emergency or to the cause of especial gratitude. In ordinarily prosperous times, a god-fearing man would make it a point to do all that was right in the way of regulation sacrifices and family thank-offerings—for births, marriages, safe

return from journeys, successful enterprise, and the like—but would not feel called upon to exceed the measure demanded of him by custom and law. It is when the heart overflows with joy or is wrung with anguish and terror that men cease to calculate, that they in a measure lose count of their wealth and the relative value of things. There are mercies so great and evils so overpoweringly terrible, that to requite the one and avert or obtain relief from the others, men under the influence of excessive excitement would hold all they own a cheap price, all their possessions, their own lives, their own flesh and blood. From these premises: first, the conception of a deity that can be won by gifts to perform or abstain from certain acts, and who is influenced in proportion to the value of the offering; and, second, a state of feeling so overwrought as to have temporarily slipped from the control of reason, the necessary logical consequence will be—human sacrifices, human life being man's most precious possession. The line of logical sequence being strained to the uttermost, the sacrifice of babes, of children, nay, of favorite children, not only as the purest of all possible victims, but also the most effective, since their immolation carries to the throne of the deity, in addition to their own worth, the superadded sum of sacrifice wrung from their parents' tortured feelings.

17. Strictly speaking, the sacrifice of children was the deity's due in all cases and at all times, as a portion of the nation's wealth and increase. If the first-born of every domestic animal are demanded,

why should those of the master be excepted? This obligation we find formally and unconditionally recognized by the Hebrews, the only Semitic people whose laws are before us in their entirety. This is the notable passage (Exodus, xxii. 29) wherein this important point is laid down: "Thou shalt not delay to offer the abundance of thy fruits and of thy liquors. *The first-born of thy sons shalt thou give unto me. Likewise* shalt thou do with thine oxen and with thy sheep: seven days it shall be with its dam, on the eighth day thou shalt give it to me." Considering that human sacrifices, and especially of children, were a standing institution among other Semitic and the Canaanitic races, there can be little doubt that originally, in prehistorically remote times, this decree was understood literally and acted upon. When the Jews make their appearance on the historical stage of the world, however, their conception of divine goodness as overbalancing divine sternness is already too advanced to allow of such barbarous literalness, and we see sacrifice, as regards the human first-born only, modified into consecration. Still, enough of the original meaning of the law lingers in the people's consciousness to make a ransom necessary, which we see fixed at the uncostly rate of a pair of turtle-doves or two young pigeons—an offering within the means of the poorest. (See Luke's Gospel, ii. 22-24.)

18. Human sacrifices are so inevitably an outcome of the coarsely material and anthropomorphic conception of the deity common to the entire an-

cient world, that we cannot be surprised if we find them accredited as of directly divine institution. It was but natural that the gods who gave men laws and taught them the practices of religion and all that pertains to a state of civilization should have instituted this most sacred and awful of rites. There are among the various nations several stories and legends which embody this idea. One of the most remarkable is a Phœnician one which we find in some fragments quoted by late writers out of a large work on Phœnician cosmogony and theogony attributed to an ancient priest, SANCHONIATHO, said to have lived over a thousand years before Christ. In one of these fragments we are told that the supreme god himself, once, "when a plague and mortality happened, offered up his only son as a sacrifice to his father, Heaven"; and in another the same account is given in a less meagre form, wherein the origin of it can be plainly discerned: "It was the custom among the ancients in times of great calamity, in order to prevent the ruin of all, for the rulers of the city or nation to sacrifice to the avenging deity the most beloved of their children, as the price of redemption. They who were devoted for this purpose were offered mystically" (*i. e.*, with ceremonies of mysteriously sacred—or mystical—significance, in memory of, and allusion to, the divine origin of the practice). For—the text goes on to say—the god (Il) had an only son, and "when great danger from war beset the land, he adorned the altar, and invested this son with the emblems of royalty, and sacrificed him." It is evident that the legend has been invented in order to explain the custom and lend it the consecration of divine authority, without which so monstrous a violation of the laws of nature could never have obtained. Such legends, purporting to give the origin or cause of some particular custom, name, belief, etc., have been so numerous throughout antiquity as to have been classed under a special name, that of AITIOLOGICAL MYTHS (from the Greek word *aitia*, " cause ").

19. It is extremely startling to find in the Bible a description, terribly impressive because so simply given, of an undoubtedly historical occurrence, which is the exact reproduction on earth of the act which, according to the ancient tradition, takes place somewhere among the gods. It is an incident of a war —(about 850 B.C.)—between the Israelites and MOABITES, a Semitic people very nearly akin to them, whose king, MESHA, has left a famous inscription showing him to be a very zealous worshipper of his national god, KHEMOSH.* "The Israelites rose up and smote the Moabites, so that they fled before them ; and they went forward into the land smiting the Moabites. And they beat down the cities ; and on every good piece of land they cast every man his stone, and filled it ; and they stopped all the fountains of water, and felled all the good trees, until in Kir-Haresheth only they left the stones thereof (a city a little to the east of the southern end of the Dead Sea); howbeit the slingers went about

---

* See Appendix to Chapter VI.

and smote it. And when the king of Moab saw that the battle was too sore for him, he took with him seven hundred men that drew sword, to break through unto the king of Edom: but they could not. *Then he took his eldest son that should have reigned in his place, and offered him for a burnt-offering upon the wall.* And there came great wrath upon Israel, and they departed from him and returned to their own land." (2 Kings, iii. 24-27.)

20. The ancient Hindus had a legend of somewhat similar import. It was very old, and we nowhere find it formally related. But it is alluded to in one of their sacred hymns as something well known. It appears that they had imagined the universal masculine principle in the form of a gigantic male being who is called Man (*par excellence*), yet is represented as divine, the master of the universe, who is all things that are, have been, and will be, and from whom all things proceed. When the gods offered up the Divine Man as a sacrifice, says the hymn, spring was its clarified butter (poured over the victim), summer its fuel, and autumn its accompanying oblation (offering of fruit and cakes). "This victim, born in the beginning of time, they immolated and sprinkled with water on the sacrificial grass. . . . When the gods, in performing the sacrifice, bound him as a victim, seven bars of wood were placed around him, thrice seven layers of wood were piled for him. . . . *These were the first institutions.*" By the immolation of the Divine Man all the worlds and all contained therein is said to have been created. Accordingly the sacred books of the

Hindus contain the most formal and detailed instructions about human sacrifices, on what occasions and with what ceremonies they are to be offered,—sometimes on an enormous scale, as many as 150 human victims at one sacrifice. Of course, with greater enlightenment and milder manners, these barbarities came into disuse. The divine will was supposed to have declared against them and opened an escape for the victims, and the popular feeling was, as usual, embodied in parables and stories. One of these tells of a youth who, when already bound to the stake and awaiting the mortal blow, prayed to all the gods in succession, and his bonds were miraculously loosened. Another story tells of a woman in a similar predicament, in answer to whose prayer a shower of rain was sent down on the already blazing pyre and fell only on that one spot. And when bloody sacrifices, even of animals, were in great part abolished, and offerings of cakes of rice and wheat were substituted, the humane change was authorized by a parable which told how the sacrificial virtue had left the highest and most valuable victim, man, and descended into the horse, from the horse into the steer, from the steer into the goat, from the goat into the sheep, and from that at last passed into the earth, where it was found abiding in the grains of rice and wheat laid in it for seed. This was an ingenious way of intimating that henceforth harmless offerings of rice and wheat cakes would be as acceptable to the deity as the living victims, human and animal, formerly were. That the change could not be made without alleging authority higher than men's own feelings is obvious, for necessarily divine sanction was needed to abrogate a custom divinely instituted.

21. This, of course, is the true meaning also of the biblical legend of Abraham sacrificing his son Isaac. God demands the sacrifice, but at the decisive moment stays the uplifted knife and substitutes a ram, thereby signifying his willingness to be content with the less precious victim, and spare the children of men. The same legend appears scarcely altered among those of the ancient Greeks: there it is a fair and favorite daughter whom a great king, her father, is commanded to immolate for the good of the people, and for whom a white doe is substituted. Other instances might be quoted from the legendary lore of various peoples, all tending to show how increasing culture taught men a nobler and purer faith, the certainty that the deity, bounteous giver of life and human affections, could not delight in wanton slaughter and the trampling out of the very feelings it inspired as the holiest and sweetest in nature.

22. Not so, however, with the heathen Semites and the Canaanites. Their fierce religion knew no relenting, their culture no softening influence. Owing to a peculiarly ruthless and sanguinary bent of their nature, a strange fervidness and readiness to intense excitement, they seem to have luxuriated as much in excess of pain as in excess of joy. It is ever thus with natures both sensual and emotional to excess. They are strongly inclined to effeminacy, and, by a strange but natural rebound,

to revolting cruelty, and, on occasions, self-torture. The emotional nature has an insatiable craving for strong, even violent sensations. The effeminate indulgence in luxury and material enjoyments of every sort, by producing satiety, blunts the capability for receiving sensations. Yet they must be procured at all costs, so the cloyed and wearied nerves seek them in more and more powerful irritants. Every natural feeling of the human breast, to be felt at all, must be heightened and intensified a hundredfold. Ecstasies of joy, ecstasies of terror, ecstasies of mourning; otherwise—a blank, apparent apathy, an almost lifeless calm, superficial and deceptive, however.

23. Such Orientals have always been, such they are now. This is the secret of the majestic impassibility, the scant and compassed words, the few and measured gestures which strike with a sort of wondering awe all who have any intercourse with them. They are not less capable of being roused to frantic excitement than were their ancestors of three thousand years ago, but the modern conditions of life offer fewer occasions, therefore the quiescent intervals are longer, and when outbreaks do occur they take the unreflecting world by surprise, as something incongruous and unexpected. Now as then, too, these outbreaks are mainly due to overwrought religious feeling. Massacres and wars are all prompted and inspirited by fanaticism, aided by the maddening effects of the powerful opiate stimulants in which they immoderately indulge.

24. The ancient Asiatics found their supply of excitement mainly in the rites of their religion. They entered into it with the intenseness of nervous exaltation which was their breath of life. Whether they were celebrating the joyful spring festival, the reunion of the young Sungod risen from the dead and the long widowed goddess of Nature, or mourning his untimely end at the hands of Winter or torrid Midsummer and her bereavement, they excited themselves and each other, in the processions which were a principal feature of every festival, with shouts and wails, and noisiest demonstrations of sorrow or exultation, as the occasion required, to the verge of insanity. The priests, leading the way, gave the example, and quickly reached the stage at which neither shouts, nor wails, nor tearing of clothes could satisfy the emotional nature let loose, when blood and pain alone could allay the nervous irritation arrived at its height. Then they would tear their flesh with their nails, wound and gash it with knives and lancets. The contagion spread, and in the crowds that followed great numbers vied with them in self-laceration, in inflicting tortures and mutilations on themselves. Nay, it was no unfrequent occurrence to see some unfortunate fanatic fall into a sort of trance, and seek death under the wheels of the ponderous chariot that carried the idol. Thus a day begun with the dignified solemn ceremonial and gorgeous display so dear to the Oriental fancy, was sure to end in a tumult of unbridled, licentious merry-making if the occasion were

a joyful one, of hideous bloodiness and inordinate lamentation if sorrowful. This kind of religious frenzy was stamped by the Greeks with the very apt name of ORGIES—the Greek word "*orgé*" meaning "violent passionate emotion"—and the religions which bore this violent character—*i. e.*, all the Canaanitic and Semitic religions of Syria and Western Asia generally—are often called ORGIASTIC. It scarcely needs demonstration that human sacrifices were but a necessary culmination of such a state of mind.

25. Nor will it be wondered at that the culture of these nations should have failed to humanize and purify their religious conceptions and practices. For, as was said above, what a people is, that, emphatically, its religion is, its gods will be; and, besides, culture brings out a race's inborn gifts, develops its natural qualities to their greatest perfection. Thus, then, we see that, far from falling into disuse, the practice of human and child-sacrifice increased in frequency and virulence. From being confined to times of war, drought and pestilence, as we are expressly told it originally was, we see it become a permanent and regularly recurring feature of Canaanitic worship. Human sacrifices took place yearly in Phœnicia and in its colonies. In times of public calamities, extra sacrifices were ordered. It would not, however, be reasonably expected that such cruel offerings should have been laid on the altar of any divinity indifferently. Gentle deities—the beneficent Sun-god, or Ashtoreth, the mild fosterer of life—could not rejoice in the de-

struction of the existence which they gave; such an offering would have been rather an offence and an insult than a propitiation. But it was a meet one for the Baal Moloch, the destroyer, the fierce Sun-god (see p. 115). Drought and pestilence were of his sending, and war, with its bloodshed and suffering, was his delight. When one of these plagues visited the land, or—as is so frequent in the East—all three together, with their accompaniment of impending or actual famine, then Moloch reigned supreme. The kindly deities were forgotten, their rites left in abeyance, their priests and priestesses, for the time, unhonored. Then was the grim harvest gathered for him, and the more desperate the danger, the heavier the visitation, the more lavishly was the god entreated.

26. Owing to the scantiness of literary monuments left by the Phœnicians, we should know nothing of the manner in which these dreadful rites were accomplished, had not the Greek writers described with ample details what took place on such occasions in Carthage, the Phœnicians' greatest and most powerful colony, as wealthy as the mother-city, Tyre, herself, with which she never entirely severed her connection. Even when full-grown and wholly independent, Carthage sent a yearly voluntary tribute to the temple of the Syrian Melkarth, as well as a large percentage of the booty made in war. We may therefore safely presume that the religious bond was kept intact, and that the colony had, for what it did, the authority of the example and traditions of the metropolis.

27. It appears that there was in Carthage a statue of Moloch specially destined to receive human burnt-offerings. It was colossal in size, made entirely of brass, and hollow inside. It had a bull's head, the bull being a favorite emblem of physical might, and therefore of the male principle in nature, of the Sun-god at his fiercest. The statue's arms were of monstrous length, and in its huge outstretched hands the victims were laid, which the arms, worked by chains and pulleys placed behind its back, lifted up to an opening in the breast, till they rolled into the furnace blazing inside of the statue, on an invisible grate, through which the cinders and ashes fell, forming a gradually increasing heap between the colossus' legs. It is supposed that grown-up victims were first killed, but it is certain that children were consigned living to the horrible red-hot hands. No sorrow was to be shown. While being prepared for immolation, the children's cries were to be soothed with caresses. Most hideous and incredible as it seems, the mothers had to be present, and to repress their tears, their sobs, every sign of grief, as otherwise they would not only have lost all the credit reflected on them by the great honor thus publicly paid them, but might have drawn down the anger of the vengeful god on the community, and one unwilling offering, one begrudged victim might have defeated the entire sacrifice, nay, made matters worse than they were before. So weak-minded a mother would have been branded for life as unpatriotic and un-

worthy. An incessant noise of drums and flutes was kept up, not only to drown the little victims' cries, but also to heighten the public exaltation. The rite was doubtless accompanied with solemn dances, at least in Syria this was certainly the case; and hymns of praise and invocations were sung, as customary in Phœnicia and Canaan,—a sort of litany wherein the name of the god constantly recurred. And if the priests had any doubts of the sacrifice being acceptable to him, they were bound to support and emphasize it by shedding their own blood. The Bible-writers, in speaking of such sacrifices, mostly use the expression: "To cause their children *to pass through the fire* unto" or in honor of Moloch or Baal. Hence it has been supposed that in most cases a ceremony of consecration through fire took the place of actual immolation. But there seems to be nothing to support this hypothesis; indeed, many passages are explicitly against it. In speaking to Jerusalem in the name of the Lord, to reprove the royal city for her backslidings and iniquities, Ezekiel says: ". . . . *thou hast slain my children* and delivered them up, in *causing them to pass through the fire* unto them;" and, a few verses further on: ". . . . because of all the idols of thy abominations, and for the blood of thy children which thou hast given unto them. . . ." For the Jews had so thoroughly adopted the custom of their neighbors and kindred nations, that they had a place outside the walls of Jerusalem, the valley of Tophet, specially devoted to the worship of Baal, where the sacrificial pyres were constantly kept blazing and were often fed with child-victims.*

28. On the principle that the gift is acceptable in proportion as it is precious to the giver, the national sacrifices were to consist of none but children of the noblest houses, and when parents were convicted of eluding the demand the punishment was terrible. Once when the Carthaginians had been beaten in a very important battle, the loss of which endangered the commonwealth, we are told that a severe investigation showed that the city nobles had for some time been in the habit of purchasing and fattening low-born children and substituting these for their own offspring. To this impiety the anger of the god was attributed, and a national expiatory sacrifice was ordered on an unusually large scale: two hundred boys of the noblest ruling families perished, and of the parents, some authors say that three hundred who had been guilty of the accursed malpractice voluntarily gave their own lives. One shudders to think what opportunities were thus presented to priests and to others for the indulgence of family feuds and personal grudges. Not until the reign of the Roman emperor, Tiberius, a contemporary of Christ, was the execrable custom officially put a stop to in Carthage. The Romans, then the rulers of the world, were not noted for gentleness or tender-heartedness. Yet when a Roman legion under the reign of that emperor

---

* See 2 Kings, xxiii. 10; Jeremiah, vii. 31; xix. 5-7.

came upon the priests of Moloch in the midst of a child-sacrifice, so great was their horror and pity that they not only dispersed the crowd, and released the victims, as many as were still living, but hung every one of the priests; after which a law was issued, forbidding the repetition of the unnatural rite in future. But there can be no doubt that it was indulged in occasionally and surreptitiously for another hundred years or two—in fact, until Christianity gained a firm hold on the African provinces of the Roman Empire.*

29. Sometimes human sacrifices were offered in gratitude, or in accomplishment of a vow. The Carthaginians sacrificing their fairest women-captives to Moloch after a victory give us an instance of the former custom, while the latter is strikingly exemplified in the famous story of Jephthah and his daughter. "And Jephthah vowed a vow unto Yahveh and said: If thou wilt indeed deliver the children of Ammon into mine hand, then it shall be that whosoever cometh forth of the doors of my house to meet me, when I return in peace from the children of Ammon, it shall be Yahveh's, and I will offer it up for a burnt-offering" (Judges, xi. 30–31). But a wholesale form of this kind of sacrifice, "vowing" or "devoting" things, animals and persons to the deity as a thank-offering for the reception of a certain boon petitioned for, was long

---

* See Münter, "Religion der Karthager." For a thrilling and most learned description of a child-sacrifice on a large scale see the chapter "Moloch" in Gustave Flaubert's Carthaginian novel "Salammbo."

preserved among the Jews, who called it the *Kherem*. It consisted in promising to "devote" to Yahveh this or that city, if he would deliver it into their hands,—a promise which meant that the city with all its wealth should be destroyed and all that had life in it should be killed—all in honor and for the glory of Yahveh. The most complete instance of such a *Kherem*, or "devotion," we have in the command laid on Saul by Samuel, as he sent him against the Amalekites. (See p. 10.) And how strictly the fulfilment of it was demanded we see from the denunciation hurled against him for sparing the life of the king and the finest cattle. Knowing this, we can well understand why Saul's plea that "the people spared the best of the sheep and of the oxen to sacrifice unto the Lord," availed him naught before the prophet: what sense or merit was there in sacrificing a part, since the whole was "devoted"? In Deuteronomy (xx. 13-14) we find the "devotion" of conquered cities erected into a law and sacred precept. Only, as this book was written at a much later time (about 800 B.C.), the rigor of the "kherem" is somewhat moderated and the law of death applies only to the males of the population; slavery and confiscation are the lot of the rest. Here is the entire passage: "And when Yahveh thy god delivereth it (the city) into thine hands, thou shalt smite every male thereof with the edge of the sword, but the women, and the little ones, and the cattle, and all that is in the city shalt thou take as a prey unto thyself, and thou shalt eat the spoil of thine enemies which the Lord God hath given thee." Accordingly we continually come across passages like the following: "If thou wilt indeed deliver this people into my hand, then I will devote their cities" (Numbers, xxi. 2-3). "And Yahveh hearkened to the voice of Israel and delivered up the Canaanites, and they devoted their cities" (2 Kings, iii. 27). So little doubt is there about the sense in which the word "devote" is used in all these passages, that the translators of the Bible have rendered it in the popular version by "utterly destroy."

And now we can at last close this digression, long, but most necessary for the right comprehension not only of the very important group of kindred religions that has been called "Syrian," or of Western Asia, but of that most puzzling and intricate side of all ancient religions which bears on what has always been considered the great Mystery of Sacrifice.

30. It is a pity that Sanchoniatho should be neither so late nor so authentic a writer as Berosus. He is said to have been, like the latter, a priest of one of the principal sanctuaries in his own country. Many doubt whether Sanchoniatho, as an individual, really did exist, there being no evidence thereto but a name bare of all personal traits or details. But what is certain is that the fragments preserved under that name contain teachings handed down by the priestly colleges of GEBAL (Greek BYBLOS), a city only second to Tyre and Sidon in commercial and political greatness, and superior to them in sanctity. It appears to have

been a sort of headquarters of priestly lore, of religious legends and observances and sacerdotal authority. Even in their sadly imperfect condition they give a very elaborate system of the Cosmogony,* said to be that of the Phœnician nations. Unfortunately the account, transmitted in an abbreviated yet intricate form by a Greek writer of the early Christian period, himself a Christian,† is so corrupted and inextricably confused by the admixture of late Greek ideas and by most of the names being rendered into Greek, unaccompanied by the Phœnician originals, that it is scarcely possible to disentangle the two elements. The result is very puzzling. A great deal has been written on the subject without as yet producing much clearness. This is therefore not the place where we can discuss those nevertheless most valuable and interesting relics, for at the present stage of our studies we strive mainly to unravel and record the genuine, original religious conceptions and traditions of the several peoples. This, as already remarked (see p. 70), is especially difficult in dealing with the Phœnicians and Canaanitic nations generally, and there is no likelihood of any monuments forthcoming to throw such light on the so-called "Sanchoniatho fragments" as those of the Mesopotamian states shed on the more authentic Berosus.

31. That both the Cosmogony of the Phœnicians and their principal myths were nearly akin to those

---

* For the meaning of the word see "Story of Chaldea," p. 259 ff.
† Eusebius.

of ancient Chaldea is as certain as that their art was in great part derived from that of Babylonia. It is therefore without very much surprise that we meet with the Chaldean Dumuzi making his home, under the name of ADONIS-THAMMUZ, in the holiest seat of Phœnician worship, Gebal. ("Adonis" simply means "lord, master," and is identical with the Hebrew word "Adon," much used by the Hebrews as a title of God.) However unsympathetic and coarse the Canaanites' moral tendency, they could not rob of its poetry and pathos the beautiful story of the lovely Sun-Youth tragically done to death. He was beloved by the goddess BAALATH (Greek BELTIS), the local equivalent of Ishtar and Ashtoreth, and taken from her by a cruel accident : * killed while hunting in the forests of Lebanon by the tusk of a fierce boar, sent, according to some, by his deadly foe, Baal-Moloch, the Fiery. It was in midsummer, July, a month sacred among the Semites to the young slaughtered god. The river that flows by Gebal was named after him, Adonis, and it was said that in his month it flowed red with his blood. This pretty conceit was suggested by an actual fact: the springs of the river flow through certain red clay passes, which, becoming dry and crumbling in the hot season, are partly washed down by its waters. The mythical sense of the story is evident. It is the victory of the fierce and wicked Sun-god, the Destroyer, over the beneficent Sun, the fair Spring-

---

* See "Story of Chaldea," pp. 323-326.

god, the bridegroom of Nature in her prime. Of course he comes to life again. His festival was celebrated in early spring. It began in mourning, with processions of wailing women, tearing their hair and clothes, crying out that the god was dead, calling on his name and repeating, "*Ailanu! ailanu!*" ("Woe is us!") They laid a wooden effigy of him, clothed in regal robes, on a bier, anointed it with oil and performed over it the other rites for the dead, fasting severely all the while. The bier was carried in procession, followed by an ever increasing crowd, with the usual extravagant demonstrations of grief. Then the god's resurrection was celebrated with equally extravagant rejoicings, after the fashion of the race, and the air resounded with the triumphant cry of "Adonis is living," instead of the universal wail, "Thammuz is dead!" It need scarcely be remarked that this festival in its double aspect was of an essentially orgiastic character. One very pretty custom was connected with it: that of the so-called "Adonis-gardens." It consisted in sowing seeds of several garden herbs and early plants in wooden boxes, so as to have them green and in bloom for the festival, to greet the awakening of the god, to whose renovated power they moreover bore witness. These must have been something like our window gardens.

32. The nearest approach to a moral conception of the divine nature that we can credit the Phœnicians with is the creation of the divine group of the Seven KABIRIM ("Mighty ones"). They are no

new creations. Melkarth and Ashtoreth were of the number, and it is very probable that the five others were originally planetary powers. If so, they underwent some transformations, and even received names significant of the moral qualities ascribed to them. One is "the Orderer," and invents the art of working iron; another is "Law." And all seven are said by Sanchoniatho to be the sons of "SYDYK, the Just," or, as we might perhaps render the idea, if not literally the name, of Justice. The most original feature about this group is the addition to it of an eighth Kabir, higher still and greater than the rest, although called their brother. His name was ESHMUN, (the word means simply "the Eighth"), and he was understood as concentrating in himself the essence and power of all the others —a desperate but lame effort towards monotheism. The Kabirim represented the divine Intelligence and All-wisdom in every aspect, and while they were the guardians of the nation's political and social organization, the inventors of the arts which ensured its prosperity, above all of ship-building, navigation and the working of iron, they were also its religious teachers. The fragment of Sanchoniatho closes with the declaration: "These things the Kabirim, the seven sons of Sydyk, and their eighth brother, Eshmun, first of all set down in their records . . . . and they delivered them to their successors and to foreigners. . . ." Consequently the Phœnicians considered their sacred writings as revealed by the Kabirim, just as the Babylonians ascribed the revelation of their own to their most ancient god, Ea, the Oannes of Berosus. These "records" must have been preciously treasured, since they had priestly colleges, and even a city called "the City of Books" (Kiriath-Sepher), and it is very strange that not the least trace of them should have turned up.

33. It is scarcely needful to state that wherever the Phœnicians had commercial settlements or colonies they carried their gods and their worship. This was the case with all the Greek and Italian islands, and many portions of the Greek continent also, especially along the eastern shore of it. The pliant and receptive mind of the Greeks adopted them in a great measure, and amalgamated them with their own beliefs and ideas, bringing to bear on them their own poetical genius, and thus subjecting them to a transformation which made the old, rude, barbaric forms unrecognizable, except to the eye of practised scholarship.

V.

THE NEIGHBORS OF ASSHUR.—REVIVAL OF THE EMPIRE.

1. THE blank of nearly two hundred years which occurs in the monumental history of Assyria after the brilliant incident of Tiglath-Pileser's reign (see p. 63), gave us an opportunity of taking a long excursion to the cities of the sea-shore without doing an injustice to our master-subject. When next we turn our eyes to the valley of the Upper Tigris, the 10th century B.C. is drawing to its close, the cloud has lifted from Nineveh, and the Assyrian lion is stronger and hungrier than ever. An uninterrupted line of mighty warrior-kings now holds the throne, perhaps a new dynasty, with fresh energies and a vigorous military organization. These we can follow in their succession and their exploits with an ease and certainty very refreshing after the almost hopeless gropings of early chronological research, thanks to a peculiar and very practical institution of the Assyrians, contrived by them for the express purpose of keeping up a system of reliable dates.

2. It appears that, from very remote times, it was usual to name each year after one of the great magistrates of the state. The year was then designated

as the "LIMMU" of So-and-So. It is thought by many that the magistrates themselves, in their capacity of time-keepers, had the special title of LIMMU in addition to the title they held from their office. Modern scholars have rendered the word by EPONYMS.[*] This office seems to have been considered a great distinction, for we find none but the highest dignitaries invested with it. Every king was *limmu* at least once, generally the second full year of his reign. (The king counted his regnal years not from the day of his accession, but from the beginning of the next year; whatever remained of the old year was simply called "the beginning of the reign.") In his second year, then, the king was *limmu;* after him came, in more or less regular rotation, the *turtan* or general of his forces, then his chief minister of state, then a functionary whom George Smith supposes to have been the head of the priesthood, then an officer whom the same scholar defines as a sort of *aide-de-camp* to the king; after these followed the governors of provinces and important cities, Assyrian or conquered. Of course lists of the eponyms with their respective years were carefully kept, and the manner of dating was something like this: "Fourth year of Shalmaneser, *limmu* So-and So;" or "Second year of Shalmaneser, *limmu*—the King." How far back this custom began we do not know, for the lists which have been found take us only to about 900 B.C. No less than four copies of *limmu* lists have been exhumed, greatly injured and even erased in places, but the fragments fitting into

---

[*] See explanation of the word in "Story of Chaldea," p. 134.

each other and completing one another so beautifully that, by the simple expedient of writing them out in four parallel columns, an uninterrupted and fully reliable scheme of reigns has been obtained, covering over two hundred years (about 900 to 666 B.C.). This is the famous so-called Assyrian EPONYM CANON, *i. e.*, "authentic table of Eponyms." A further and still greater help has been derived from the discovery of tables of eponyms with a short notice attached of the principal feature of each year; for instance, "(Expedition) to Babylon," or "to the land of Naïri," or "to the land of Cedars," or "In the land," the latter meaning that the king had not gone out of Assyria that year—a very unfrequent notice. An eclipse opportunely mentioned in one of these tables furnished the means of firmly locating the entire row of dates. This result was especially desirable for this particular period, because it is the period when the history of Assyria and that of the Jews are in constant collision. Almost every event connected with Assyria mentioned in the Bible is faithfully recorded in the historical inscriptions of the Assyrian kings, and the Eponym Canon enables us to correct the somewhat loose chronology of the Jewish historians, who kept no such yearly record and were too much given to deal in averages and round figures for perfect accuracy.

3. When Assyria emerged from that long spell of inactivity and obscurity, and once more stepped forth aggressively upon the stage of the world—*her* world—that stage was greatly altered. The Hittite

power, which even in the time of Tiglath-Pileser I. had virtually ceased to exist as an independent empire,—or, more correctly, as a compact confederacy,—is now altogether broken up, and though Karkhemish still retains considerable importance, it is more as a wealthy station on one of the great commercial high-roads (see p. 31), and as a seat of national worship, than as a political centre. The Aramæans have come to the front, everywhere supplanting the Hittites and driving many of them north, towards the passes of the Amanus and Taurus ridges. Aram has become a powerful and united nation, under the rule of kings who have established their seat of empire in Damascus. (See p. 56.) But it is not only the Aramæans' steady pushing from the Euphrates westward that has displaced or overruled the ancient Hittite power. They have been pressed upon from the south by the Jews, who have gradually, in the course of several hundred years, occupied the lands around the Dead Sea and along both sides of the Jordan, that "land of Canaan" which they firmly believed to be their own promised patrimony by right divine, and of which they took possession by dint of stubborn determination and ruthless cruelty. Thus, although the historical inscriptions of this period make frequent mention of the "cities of the Khatti" (Hittites), the "land of the Khatti," the word has become a vague geographical designation, meaning in a general way the land and cities of what has later been called Syria, the people thus designated being as often of Aramæan as of Hittite race.

4. A change has also come over the great trading communities of the sea-shore. The supremacy of Tyre, which had begun to supplant that of Sidon among them, has become more and more confirmed, and the people are no longer known, as in the oldest times, under the general name of "Sidonians." The colonizing process is going on more actively than ever; only whereas the first colonies which followed on the exploration of the Greek seas and islands were for the most part Sidonian, the later and more distant ones (see p. 90 on Gades and Tarshish) were sent out from Tyre. More and more distant they were, because the Greeks had ousted the Phœnician traders from their own waters, and had, very naturally, established there their own commerce and merchant navy. More and more frequently, too, the old hive sent out new swarms, because more and more closed in and cramped for room by the advance and spreading of Aram and Israel in the East, and in the South of another nation, the Pelishtim (Philistines), new comers of a different and probably European race. In the Bible they are said to have come from KAPHTOR, an island far away in the West. This is thought to be none other than CRETE, the largest and most southern of the Greek islands, but not with any degree of certainty. It is the more hopeless to obtain anything like reliable authority on the origin of this warlike people, so interesting from its long conflict with the Jews, because they appear to have been promptly Semitized, as shown by their proper names and by their religion. We have already seen

that they worshipped principally Dagon and Atargatis (Derketo), the Fish-god and Fish-goddess. (See p. 111.) In one of their cities, Akkaron, the Sun-god was honored under a peculiar name and aspect, that of BAAL-ZEBUB, "the Lord of Flies," *i.e.*, the "breeder of corruption," the corruption of death and decay, from which new life springs in another form. Still the Philistines are said to have retained many peculiarities, and never to have adopted certain customs and ceremonies very current in the Semitic world. All this would point to a probability of their having originally been a band of foreign adventurers, who took possession of an already settled and organized Semitic country, and established there a military royalty and aristocracy, or ruling class. However that may be, history finds them as a strong and united confederacy of five principalities, with five capital cities: GAZA, ASHKALON, ASHDOD, GATH and AKKARON (EKRON). These are "the five kings" of the Philistines who kept Saul and David so busy, and so harassed the Jewish farmers with their depredations that they lost all courage to till and to sow, knowing they would not reap, and began to hide in caverns and in woods.

5. But the greatest change in the general scene-shifting that had taken place in the Semitic and Canaanitic world was that which had converted a few wandering tribes of the desert first into a settled rural population and holders of cities, with valiant chieftains and princely ruling families, then into a powerful kingdom, organized after the model of the most pompous and absolute Oriental monarch-

ies. Yet it was a popular monarchy too; for it arose out of the struggles of the nation for liberty, and the crown was the reward of its deliverers, enthusiastically bestowed, not begrudged, nor bowed to in servile abasement. The century that elapsed after Tiglath-Pileser I. (1100–1000 B.C.) saw the conflict between the Philistines and the Jews reach a climax most disastrous to the latter, since they actually had to suffer the presence of Philistine governors within their strongest cities, and, according to one, perhaps exaggerated, tradition, were forbidden by their haughty oppressors to bear arms or exercise the smith's and armorer's craft. It was by killing one of these governors that Saul and his son Jonathan, princes in the tribe of Benjamin, began their heroic and adventurous career. But not for them to taste were the sweets of royalty. Theirs the toil of constant warfare, not against the Philistines alone, but other neighboring peoples as well; theirs the arduous cares, the heavy responsibilities of national leadership in critical, dangerous times, theirs the bitter death of the vanquished on the battle-field. For David, the chosen of Judah, the royal outlaw and freebooter, it was reserved to wear in peace and prosperity the crown which had had naught but thorns for Saul, which he had voluntarily laid down with his life in weariness and hopelessness of spirit. To David it was given to accomplish the task of deliverance, and to unite the scattered forces of a people, conscious indeed of its unity of race, but politically inefficient from being broken up into many independent communities—the tribes. This he achieved by girding the land around with fortresses, by substituting a standing organized army for the temporary, irregular armaments, always eager to disperse again, of the time of the Judges, and a central government for the old patriarchal rule of the councils of elders. These changes he most effectually achieved by building himself a royal city on a well situated hill, JERUSALEM, and especially by setting up his own royal sanctuary as the only holy place of the nation.

6. For hitherto there had been many holy places of worship and pilgrimage, and to each had offerings flowed unceasingly, and some were held peculiarly sacred by one tribe, some by another. Also, monotheism, though professed in theory, was as yet far from being consistently conformed to in practice. Even idolatry was not yet strictly abolished ; it was, by the Bible's own showing, at least tolerated. Private men, if wealthy and influential, could have chapels or sanctuaries of their own, dedicated of course to Yahveh, not to any of the foreign Baals —" abominations," as they were popularly spoken of—and maintain priests of their own to minister at their altars; and it must have been by no means unusual to enshrine in them idols, meant as images of Yahveh.* The establishment of the

---

* See Judges, viii. 24-28 (story of Gideon); xvii. and xviii. (story of Micah, his teraphim and his priest); 1 Samuel, xix. 10-17 (story of David's escape).

royal sanctuary for the enthronement of the great national shrine, the Ark, in Jerusalem, was not only a necessary religious move in the right direction, but also a wise and deep-laid political measure. Nothing keeps communities so enduringly apart, even when professing a common faith, as separate sanctuaries; nothing more quickly and solidly cements them into one nation than a common sanctuary. People whose best feelings, highest thoughts, and most sacred hopes tend towards one centre, meeting and blending there on common ground, weaned for the time from worldly rivalries and animosities, cannot but become enclosed in a strong bond of brotherhood and good-will. When David's son and successor, Solomon, built the temple on Mount Moriah, and it was proclaimed the only high place at which it was lawful for Yahveh's people to pray and sacrifice, the seal was set on the work begun by his father, a work which endured through all ages down to our own day. But for that command, and but for that memory, the Jews might in after times, like all conquered people, have amalgamated with the conquerors and lost their political consciousness. As it is, that memory and that command, which they consider as binding even yet, have kept them apart from all the nations among which they have been scattered, so that dwellers in many lands as they have been and are now, they still keep together morally, all distances notwithstanding, and consider themselves emphatically a separate nation.

7. The reign of Solomon (middle of tenth century B.C.) represents the climax of splendor and power reached by Hebrew royalty. He is the ideal of the peculiar kind of ruler that may be called the Oriental despot of the grand type, with its strange mixture of large qualities and vainglorious love of display, of wisdom and cruelty. His passion for building, the scale on which he indulged it, and the manner, remind one of the Babylonian and Assyrian monarchs. Pressed gangs of laborers —"strangers that were in the land of Israel"— worked under thousands of overseers; 70,000 as "bearers of burdens," 80,000 as "hewers in the mountains," besides which a levy of 30,000 men was sent into Lebanon to cut cedars and break stone; and the burdens which he laid on his people were very heavy, as they needs must have been to meet the outlay. For he had more to defray than the actual expense of building: he had to get foreign artists to decorate his constructions, the Jews having been refused by nature the inventive faculty in the arts, with the exception of music and poetry. He applied to his ally, Hiram, king of Tyre—"for Hiram was ever a lover of David"—to send him artists and skilled workmen to teach his own people, and do the finest work themselves, engaging to maintain them at his own cost. Hiram did all that he was asked, furnished the cedar and fir-trees, and even supplied his friend with loans in gold, "according to all his desire." For which, after twenty years, when all the building was done, both "the house of Yah-

Solomon and Hiram of Tyre middle of tenth century B.C.

veh" and "the king's own house" (the former taking seven years and the latter thirteen), Solomon, unable after so great a strain on his finances to pay in money, was fain to give up to his royal creditor twenty cities near their mutual boundaries. It is a great misfortune for the history of art that Solomon's constructions should have been so utterly

21.—GROUP OF CEDARS IN LEBANON.

destroyed, for the detailed description preserved in the Bible (1 Kings, vi., vii.; 1 Chronicles, iii., iv.) is somewhat confusing and very difficult to imagine without something to illustrate it, and these two buildings must have been masterpieces of that Phœnician art which we know to have been borrowed in about equal parts from Babylon and from Egypt, and to have been very perfect in its workmanship, but of which so little is left for us to judge by.

8. In thorough, far-seeing statesmanship Solomon was probably inferior to his father, David. His policy was to make friends far and near, and to secure himself a peaceful reign, and, though he succeeded very fairly, yet the result was neither so complete nor so lasting as he surely wished it to be. He strove to accomplish his plans after a characteristically Oriental fashion: by numerous marriages with daughters of all the surrounding princes. His chief queen was an Egyptian princess, for whom he built a separate palace near his own. His harem became unusually extensive even for an Oriental sovereign, for whom, according to Oriental notions, a numerous harem is a necessary and seemly mark of royal state, and contained princesses of the Sidonians and the Hittites, of the Moabites, Ammonites, Edomites—of all the nations with whom Israel had waged war. From this he was led to build "high places" to foreign gods: "And so did he for all his strange wives, which burned incense and sacrificed unto their gods." But it certainly was done quite as much for the sake of conciliating his wives' families and countrymen, and foster international intercourse and commerce, for Jerusalem quickly became a notable mart of trade. Of this condescension, though apparently dictated by sound policy, the effects were disastrous, for the friendship was not maintained a moment longer than convenient to all parties, while the Jews' indomitable hankering after the worships of their Semitic and Canaanitic neighbors was fatally encouraged, and Jerusalem became the headquarters

of the very abominations which her founders so strongly deprecated and denounced. And the yoke which Solomon had laid on a people hitherto independent and masterful had been so exceeding heavy that the sinews that had borne it relaxed the moment his hand was taken from their necks by death; and when his son refused in insulting language to lighten their burdens, the war-cry was raised: "To your tents, O Israel!" and ten tribes seceded from the house of David, choosing a king for themselves, and only Judah followed David's grandson and his sons after him. Henceforth, then, there were two kingdoms, that of Israel and that of Judah. Revolts, palace revolutions and violent changes of dynasties were of frequent occurrence in the former, while the house of David reigned in the latter to the end, son after father, uninterruptedly. The mutual attitude of the two kingdoms was generally hostile, often bursting into open war. This afforded a welcome chance of aggrandizement to the new monarchy of Damascus, which followed the simple and practical policy of playing one off against the other, and to all the older enemies of Israel, especially Moab, who at this period became extremely ambitious and aggressive, displaying qualities which are concisely hit off in a couple of lines of the prophet Isaiah: "We have heard of the pride of Moab, that he is very proud; even of his arrogancy, and his pride and his wrath."

9. If, as has been thought likely, the temporary abasement of Assyria, of which the causes are un-

known, was indirectly brought about, or at least assisted, by the aggrandizement of so many neighbors on whom Tiglath-Pileser would have looked down with contemptuous wonder had he been made aware of their humble beginnings, it is also not improbable that the splitting of the Jewish monarchy and the dissensions that were rife between all these restless and jealous nations may have in some degree favored the resumption by his remote successors of his conquering career. "The people shall be oppressed," says the prophet, "every one by another, and every one by his neighbor"; and, lo! Asshur stands before them, and "it is in his heart to destroy, and to cut off nations not a few." (Isaiah, vii. 2; x. 7.)

10. Yet it is not west of the Euphrates but in the North that we once more catch a distinct view of the Assyrian warrior-kings, in that mysterious mountain region of Naïri, of which the exact extent and boundaries have never been determined, but which clearly formed the bulwark beyond which no branch of the Semitic race ever established a home or political dominion. TUKULTI-NINÊB II., the third of the new series of kings, about the middle of the tenth century B.C., is recorded by his son as having placed a stele with his own effigy by one of the sources of the Tigris, alongside of that of Tiglath-Pileser I. But it was that son, ASSHURNAZIRPAL, who fully revived the ancient splendor of Assyria and greatly added thereto, both by his deeds of war and by his works of peace.

11. "I am the king, the lord, the exalted, the strong, the revered, the gigantic, the first, the mighty, the doughty, a lion and a hero— Asshurnazirpal, the powerful king, the king of Asshur." Thus he announces himself in the long inscription which has been called his "Annals," and goes on for many lines glorifying himself as a "resistless weapon," a "destroyer of cities," a "treader down of foes," etc., etc., before he enters on the narrative of his campaigns. The first one was directed into that same indomitable land of Naïri, which appears to have taken up a good third of the Assyrian king's energies and time, almost leading one to suspect that their frequent expeditions into it were a matter of self-defence even more than of conquest. It is very possible that those mountaineers would, after the fashion of highland tribes in all countries and ages, have harassed their great neighbor by perpetual inroads and depredations had they not been kept in constant fear of an invasion. As it is, they are continually said to have "rebelled," and thus called down on themselves dire coercion. Asshurnazirpal repeatedly boasts that in this his first campaign he "advanced whither none of his royal ancestors had arrived," to a mountain which pierced the sky "like the point of a dagger," to which "not even the birds of heaven find access," and that the people who had built a stronghold there "like an eagle's eyrie" he threw down from the mountain, having "climbed it on his own feet" and "dyed the mountains with their blood like

*Asshurna-
zirpal,
884–860
B.C.*

22.—ASSHURNAZIRPAL IN CONFERENCE WITH AN OFFICER.

wool." This particular fastness, however, cannot have been very populous, since the massacre " laid low" only two hundred warriors. The king had his own likeness hewn in the rock, in the same cave by the source of the Tigris as that of Tiglath-Pileser and Tukulti-Nineb, and it was found there by Mr. Taylor with the former; the second was destroyed in some way, perhaps, it has been suggested, by the falling in of the cave. So Asshurnazirpal, notwithstanding his boast, can scarcely have gone much further than his predecessors, or he would not have failed to place his likeness at the uttermost point he reached.

12. One wishes there might have been as much exaggeration in the recitals of the unheard-of cruelties which he details with a vaunting complacency that makes one shudder even more than the acts themselves, unfortunately common enough in Eastern warfare, not in antiquity alone. A few specimens from this first campaign will more than suffice to illustrate the revolting character of the narrative. After taking another stronghold which " hung like a cloud on the sky," he built a pyramid of the heads of its slain defenders. The " prince of the city" he took home with him to his city of Arbela, and there flayed him alive and spread out his skin on the city wall. Another chieftain, "the son of a nobody," *i. e.*, not of princely lineage, met the same fate at Nineveh after having witnessed the slaughter of his companions: "I erected a pillar opposite the gate of his city," says the king; " the nobles, as many as had

rebelled, I flayed and dressed the pillar in their skins; some I walled up inside the pillar; others I impaled on stakes planted on top of the pillar; others again I had impaled on stakes all around the pillar. . . ." He seems to have been in the habit of cutting off prisoners' hands and feet, noses and ears, and making piles of them, putting out captives'

23.—COUNTING AND PILING UP HEADS OF CAPTIVES.

eyes, burning boys and girls in the fire. The only respite from these horrors is the long dry catalogues of booty, tribute and presents. On the whole, this document is more tedious and repulsive than most others of the same kind. The narrative gains but slightly in interest when it takes us (ninth campaign) into the "land of the Khatti" (Syria), to the skirts of Lebanon and the sea-shore: "In those days I occupied the environs of Lebanon; to the great

24.—PRISONERS IMPALED BEFORE CITY WALLS.—ASSYRIAN BATTERING-RAM.

sea of Phœnicia I went up; up to the great sea my arms I carried; to the gods I sacrificed, I took tribute of the princes of the sea-coast." Tyre, Sidon, Gebal, Arvad, are among the names, and thus the great merchant-people once again purchased safety with wealth—silver, gold, tin, copper, woollen and linen garments, etc., also "strong timber," of which the king stood much in need for his numerous constructions, and of which he next informs us that he cut much for himself in the Amanos Mountains.

13. Ten campaigns in six years carried on in this vigorous spirit secured submission for a time, and gave the king leisure to attend to matters at home. The North was quelled, Assyria's dominion in the West materially enlarged, and successful expeditions in the South-east and South kept Kar-Dunyash and the hill tribes of the southern Zagros in a respectful attitude, so that during the remaining fifteen years of this reign we hear of but one more campaign, to the North again, where, notwithstanding the 250 towns taken and destroyed, resistance never died out. This long interval of quiet Asshurnazirpal mainly devoted to rebuilding and adorning his city of Kalah, formerly founded by Shalmaneser I. and since somehow destroyed or fallen into decay, which he now chose for his favorite residence and the second capital of the Empire. He employed on the gigantic works all the captives he had brought from "the other side of the Euphrates," and what those works were Layard's labors on the Nimrud

Mound have shown to our astonished age.* It is the so-called "North-west Palace" which was Asshurnazirpal's own, flanked by the temple of Nineb, his favorite deity, and the Ziggurat belonging thereto, now marked by that pyramidal mound which forms the most conspicuous feature of the Nimrud landscape. He constructed an important canal, meant not only to supply the city with pure mountain water more directly than it could be supplied by the Zab and its affluents, but also to be distributed over the surrounding fields by means of dams and sluices. It is the only Assyrian work of the kind sufficient traces of which have been preserved to make us understand the principle on which it was carried out. The new capital must have grown with magic rapidity. In Mr. George Rawlinson's lively and picturesque words: "Palace after palace rose on its lofty platform rich with carved woodwork, gilding, painting, sculpture and enamel, each aiming to outshine its predecessors, while stone lions, obelisks, shrines and temple-towers embellished the scene, breaking its monotonous sameness by variety. The lofty Ziggurat dominating over the whole gave unity to the vast mass of palatial and sacred edifices. The Tigris, skirting the entire western base of the mound, glassed it in its waves, and doubling the apparent height, rendered less observable the chief weakness of the architecture. When the setting sun lighted up the whole with the gorgeous hues seen only under an Eastern sky,

---

* See "Story of Chaldea," Introduction, Ch. I.-III.

Kalah must have seemed to the traveller who beheld it for the first time like a vision from fairyland."*

14. Of the historical slab-sculptures with which Asshurnazirpal's palace is decorated throughout, specimens are given in the illustrations presented in this chapter. When first discovered, they were a revelation concerning the luxury and refinement which the Assyrians had attained in their costumes, military equipments, and other belongings. Here again Mr. George Rawlinson will permit us to borrow a page from him; it is forcible, and exactly to the point:

"What chiefly surprises us in regard to them (the sculptures) is the suddenness with which the art they manifest appears to have sprung up, without going through the usual stages of rudeness and imperfection. Setting aside one mutilated statue of very poor execution and a single rock-tablet" (the often mentioned one of Tiglath-Pileser), "we have no specimens remaining of Assyrian mimetic art more ancient than this monarch. (Some signet cylinders of Assyrian workmanship may be older, but their date is uncertain). . . . Asshurnazirpal had undoubtedly some constructions of former monarchs to copy from, both in his palatial and his sacred edifices; the old palaces and temples at Kileh-Sherghat (Asshur) must have had a certain grandeur, and in his architecture this monarch may have merely amplified and improved upon the models left him by his predecessors; but his ornamentation, so far as appears, was his own. The mounds of Kileh-Sherghat have yielded bricks in abundance, but not a single fragment of sculptured slab. We cannot prove that ornamental bas-reliefs did not exist before the time of Asshurnazirpal; indeed, the rock-tablets which earlier monarchs set up were sculptures of this character; but to Asshurnazirpal seems at any rate to belong the merit of having first adopted bas-reliefs on an extensive scale as an architectural ornament, and of having employed them so as to represent by their means all the public life of the monarch. . . .

---

* "Five Monarchies," Vol. II., pp. 356-357.

25.—LION-HUNT. (NIMRUD.)

"... The evidence of the sculptures alone is quite sufficient to show that the Assyrians were already a great and luxurious people; that most of the useful arts not only existed among them, but were cultivated to a high pitch; and that in dress, furniture, jewellery, etc., they were not very much behind the moderns." *

15. Of these sculptures perhaps the most remarkable in point of artistic beauty are the representations of the royal hunts. They are most spirited in composition, perfect in detail, and the animals are treated with a boldness and truth to nature which makes them, in variety of attitude and finish of form, much superior to the conventional rendering of human figures, with their exaggerated play of muscle, eternal profile-turn, and sameness of motion. Nothing but long and loving observation of nature could have produced such results, and there can be little doubt that the artists accompanied the king for the express purpose of witnessing his prowess and taking studies on the spot. The passion of the chase was a distinctive taste of the Assyrian kings, and they attached as much importance to their hunting exploits as to their warlike deeds, and were quite as anxious to have them portrayed for the benefit of posterity. Lions and wild bulls seem to have been Asshurnazirpal's favorite game,—probably the most plentiful, so that the royal amusement must have been a public benefit as well. The king is always represented as engaging his lion single-handed, either on foot or from his chariot; one or more attendants, it is true, are close behind,

---

* "Five Monarchies," Vol. II., pp. 351-353.

but inactive, and, so to speak, respectfully observant, ready with a reserve of spears or arrows. One can easily imagine that it must have been as much as their life was worth to interfere with the master's sport unbidden, or before imminent danger threatened his sacred person. Asshurnazirpal is as particular as Tiglath-Pileser in recording his most nota-

26.—LION IN ROYAL PALACE, LET OUT OF CAGE TO BE HUNTED.
(PALACE OF ASSHURBANIPAL.)

ble hunts, the number of animals killed or captured by him, for he too used to keep menageries at home, or, more probably, parks sufficiently vast to hunt in, for which purpose lions, kept in cages, would be let out. But perhaps this was done only by later kings, when the lordly game had become scarce. (See illustration No. 26.) A successful hunt was an occasion for thanksgiving as well as a victory, and we have several scenes representing the monarch in the act of pouring a drink-offering over dead lions or wild bulls, dutifully laid, with limbs composed in seemly posture, as of rest, at the foot of the altar. (See ill. 27.)

16. In this king's "Annals" there occurs this phrase: "The fear of my dominion reached unto Karduniash; the progress of my arms filled the LAND KALDU with terror." "Kaldu" is our "Chaldea," and it is a somewhat startling fact that this is the very first time the name appears on any monument, either Babylonian or Assyrian, and in a way which expressly separates it from Kardunyash or Babylonia proper. We are forced to admit that the name as *we* use it, embracing the whole of Lower Mesopotamia as distinguished from Assyria, is, strictly speaking, a misnomer. It is neither so ancient nor so comprehensive. It applies legitimately only to the lowlands around the Gulf and their population; in this sense it is continually used from this time forth and contrasted, not confounded, with Babylon with its particular district, the land of Accad, and the north of Shumir with its great cities. It is necessary to know this in order to secure a more accurate understanding of the later revolutions in which the Chaldeans, in this restricted sense, play a principal part. Yet the word will probably continue to be used in its wider and improper acceptation. There is nothing more difficult to correct than a form of speech originating in insufficient knowledge, but sanctioned by long use. Thus

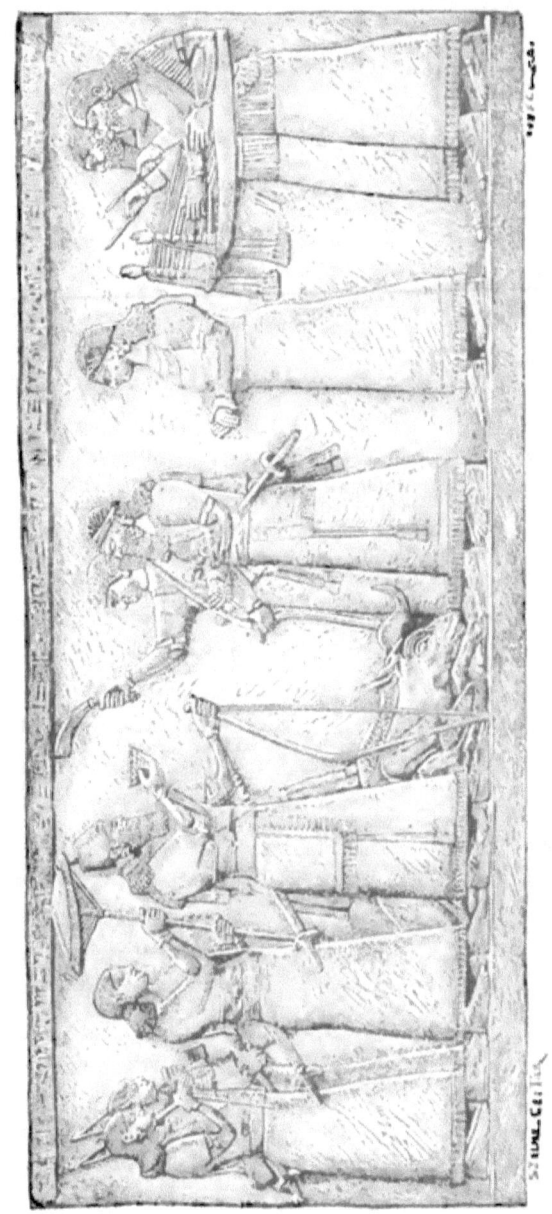

27.—ASSHURNAZIRPAL OFFERING SACRIFICE AFTER BULL-HUNT.

every child nowadays knows that the sun neither "rises" nor "sets," yet no one expects "sunset" and "sunrise" to be discarded from our vocabularies.

17. The Chaldeans proper, then, were the people of the lowlands by the Gulf, divided into a number of small principalities, *i. e.*, of tribes very patriarchally governed by their own chieftains, who ambitiously called themselves "kings," and probably were originally the heads of families which had grown into powerful clans or tribes. This seems indicated by the fact that each such principality was called "the house of So-and-so,"—"Bît . . . ." By all accounts the most important was that founded by YAKIN—BÎT-YAKIN. The princes of this "house" exceeded the others in wealth and influence, and when the time came for the great national rising, which was slowly preparing, they naturally assumed the part of leaders. It is not clear when these tribes began to gather strength and to form a political body, but it does not seem improbable that the movement may have begun somewhere in the tenth century, during the period of Assyria's abasement and obscurity. From the moment they do appear, they are Assyria's uncompromising foes,—hardened rebels, from her point of view, always spoken of with a bitter rancor, betokening some degree of respect and fear. Not so with Babylon, the relations to which, if not always smooth and peaceable, were, on the whole, patronizingly neighborly. The kings of Babylon are unmistakably vassals of Nineveh; as such they are

chastised when refractory, but received into favor again the moment they send in their tribute and submission. The Assyrian kings sacrifice in state at the great sanctuaries—to them also national ones, —at Babylon, Borsip, Sippar, Kutha, and they esteem it a favor of the "great gods" to be permitted to do so. It is like going on pilgrimages. It has been suggested that Babylon and the other great cities had become, in a great measure, resigned to a rule, which, after all, could not exactly be called a foreign one, since there was the bond of race and religion to take the greatest odium from it, while the people of the lowlands and the sea-coast had maintained a feeling of independence which kept them stubbornly on the defensive, until the moment when they should be able to assert themselves aggressively. When we remember that the ancient culture of Shumir and Accad had its oldest seats in this very region, and thence spread gradually northward, it does not seem improbable that this sea-coast population should have more particularly belonged to the older Turanian stock of the mixed and much stratified nation, and treasured the consciousness of an older and purer race, as well as the traditions of immemorial national greatness, together with an ardent and inspiriting longing to restore that race to independence and, indeed, to sovereignty. They developed great qualities in the conflict on which they entered perhaps imprudently, but which they carried on against all odds through two centuries and more. When the prophet Habakkuk (i., 6) calls them "that bitter and hasty nation, terrible and dreadful," it is the strongest possible testimony; he had but too much opportunity to study them, for they were triumphant in his time; theirs was the Empire, and Babylon, "the glory of kingdoms," was "the beauty of the Chaldeans' pride" (Isaiah xiii., 19), so dazzling to the world that the Greeks, with their usual carelessness of historical accuracy, applied the name "Chaldea" sweepingly to the whole of Lower Mesopotamia. This is one of the many current misnomers for which they are responsible.

VI.

SHALMANESER II.—ASSHUR AND ISRAEL.

"And the people shall be oppressed, every one by another, and every one by his neighbor."—ISAIAH, iii. 5.

1. WE now come to one of the longest and most monotonous reigns of which we have any record,—that of Asshurnazirpal's son, SHALMANESER II. (Shalmanu-usshir). Were it not for some highly interesting monuments belonging to him and for the fact that under him took place the first direct collision between Assyria and Israel, his thirty-five years (860-824) might be dismissed in a very few lines. Not that this monotony was one of inaction or ingloriousness. Quite the contrary. Assyria under this king attained her full growth and highest power, and his father's boast that he had ruled from the sources of the Tigris to the Lebanon and to the great sea became a reality. It is the sameness of those eternal expeditions, with the same details of horrors and cruelties (although these are not dwelt on at such length, or with such sickening complacency as in the preceding "Annals"), which makes the reading of this king's historical inscriptions so trying a performance. The conqueror appears to us as a sort of martyr or drudge of military greatness. The campaigns

Shalmaneser II., 860-824 B.C.

in their order—" in my tenth year, ..." "in my twenty-third year, ..." " in my thirty-first year " —succeed each other with oppressive regularity, like the operation of some baleful law of nature from which there is no escape, and make one take in the full significance of this matter-of-fact remark of a Bible-historian: "And it came to pass, at the time of the return of the year, *at the time when kings go out to battle*. . . ." (First Chronicles, xx. 1). It was the proper thing to go to war in spring, as it is now to shoot grouse or ducks in autumn, and one almost expects to see an "opening day" fixed for the one, as there is in most countries for the other. Shalmaneser does not seem to have had leisure even for hunting; at least no mention is made of any hunting feats. But we gather from his records that he cut timber in the Amanos Mountains eight several times, and crossed the Euphrates no less than twenty-four times in person, more than once " in its flood," which must have much increased the difficulty. What greatly enhances the tediousness of the narrative is the abominably dry, utterly unadorned style, peculiar to the annalists of this period, unrelieved by any little picturesque expression or touch of reality, such as we shall find in abundance two hundred years later. The only poetical expression in two long inscriptions is one likening a mountain peak to a dagger that cuts the sky; and *that* is copied from the annalist of Asshurnazirpal.

2. Yet it is not difficult to a trained reader to peel out of this mass of prickly burrs a kernel, if not sweet and palatable, at least substantial enough to yield a

great deal of valuable and very interesting information. The main fact, too, of this reign at once discloses itself; it is that its heaviest and most continued stress was directed against the West, while the North and South are attacked only occasionally and incidentally, just enough to keep them in subjection. Shalmaneser mentions that he went up into the land of Naïri, reached the head springs of the Tigris, where he, in imitation of his predecessors, placed "the image of his royalty," and invaded Armenia proper (by the lakes Van and Urumieh), but evidently without succeeding in definitely enslaving those stubborn highlanders. On another occasion he took the opportunity of a quarrel in the royal house in Babylon to display his power there, to sacrifice at the great sanctuaries, and to frighten the princes of Chaldea into sending him tribute, "striking terror unto the sea (the Persian Gulf) by the might of his arms." Then again he describes a descent he made from the countries by the great Armenian lakes, along the eastern boundary of Assyria, down the Zagros; whether in a purely aggressive spirit, intent on tribute and booty, or to prevent those highland "kingdoms" from becoming troublesome neighbors, does not very clearly appear. At all events, all these are secondary features of his career; his great object was to secure the permanent subjection of the roving tribes of the Syrian Desert, and especially to put a stop to the independence of the various Syrian kingdoms, whose growing prosperity and wealth made them very desirable vassals, but most objectionable rivals. Their inferiority in size, as well as their mutual jeal ousies and bitter feuds, made the enterprise practicable. Nevertheless, it is probable that the Assyrian conqueror found the work somewhat less easy and rapid than he had counted on.

3. Shalmaneser commenced operations, not at random, nor with a view merely to immediate plunder, but after a well-laid and practical plan. He began by scouring both banks of the Euphrates, and, after taking the strongest cities, he deprived them of their defence by carrying the inhabitants away to Assyria, while he settled Assyrians in them and changed their very names. Karkhemish, so important both strategically and commercially as to be the key of the great highroad from Egypt to the North, admitted his sovereignty without protest, and its Hittite king sent him not only large gifts in cattle, gold, silver, iron, bronze, purple cloth, etc., but his own daughter for his royal harem, with more presents, together with the daughters of a hundred of his nobles. Then, after crossing the Orontes, he marched northward through the whole of northern Syria, traversed the Amanos, collecting on his passage a goodly tribute in "cedar beams," the local ware of greatest value, and actually descended on the other side into Cilicia, where he effected a short, but profitable raid. On his return he tarried awhile on the Euphrates, to receive the tribute sent by "the kings of the sea-coast" and the "kings of the banks of the Euphrates."

4. These ostentatious military promenades must have been watched with anything but comfortable feelings by the kings and petty princes of Lower

Syria, who could not be blind to the fact that they boded them no good. The king of HAMATH especially, being the nearest, (on the eastern side of Lebanon, a little north of Arvad), felt himself the first on the list for the expected invasion. But their time had not yet come. The preparatory campaign was ended, and it was only in the following year—Shalmaneser's sixth, 854 B.C.—that the storm burst over their devoted heads. They made good use of the respite, to organize a coalition for common defence and resistance. It was a formidable array. At its head were the three most powerful rulers of Lower Syria: the king of Damascus, HADIDRI (or DADIDRI), called in the Bible BENHADAD II. (First Kings xvi., xvii., and other places), with 1200 chariots, 1200 horsemen and 10,000 infantry; the king of Hamath ("Hamath the Great," as one of the prophets calls him), with 700 chariots, 700 horse and 10,000 infantry; and AKHABBU SIRLAÏ (Ahab of Israel), with 2000 chariots and 10,000 men. Shalmaneser names nine more princes who brought or sent smaller contingents; among them we find a king of Arvad, a king of Ammon, an Arabian (probably Bedouin) prince with 1000 camels, and—rather startling—1000 men sent by the king of Egypt. This last circumstance tends to show that the terror of the Assyrian name already began to spread considerably further than its immediate surroundings, and that Egypt, although she could not possibly dream as yet of being actually overrun and conquered by the Assyrian arms, began to fear their approach towards her boundaries, and was willing to assist in the general effort to keep them off

5. It is not a little surprising to see the king of Israel in league with some of Israel's bitterest and most ancient foes: Ammon and Hamath and Damascus. Nothing can be more incongruous than the elements thus assembled, and nothing but the most imminent common peril could have brought about such a suspension of feuds and such a fusion of conflicting elements. This common danger, and this alone, fully explains the reconciliation between Ahab of Israel and Benhadad of Damascus, related at length in the Bible, First Kings, xx. There had been a fierce war between them, and several battles, in the last of which Israel gained a decisive victory, and Benhadad was taken prisoner. It is quite unexpected, at this point, to see Ahab, instead of proceeding with so important a prize according to the good old custom—"hewing him down before the Lord"—call him "his brother"; and make a covenant with him. What the articles of the covenant were we are not told, only that "they continued three years without war between Syria and Israel" (First Kings, xxii. 1). But the blank in the biblical narrative is admirably filled by the Assyrian contemporary monuments, the two great inscriptions of Shalmaneser II. One of them gives the entire list of the allies, the other merely speaks of them collectively as "Dadidri of Damascus, Irkhulina of Hamath, with the kings of the land Khatti, and of the sea-coast"—a passage which well shows in what a sweeping sense the name "Khatti" was used at that time.

6. Not since the times of the great Hittite con-

federacy against Ramses II., and the battles of Megiddo and Kadesh, had there been so strong and united an armament of Asiatic nations. The allies felt so confident and buoyant that they marched to meet the Assyrian, and offered him battle by the city of Karkar, near the Orontes. Whatever the issue, he should at least be kept away from their own countries. That issue appears to have been somewhat doubtful. He declares in one inscription that he killed of them 14,000 men; in the other and later one the figure grows to 20,500; he asserts that, by the help of Asshur the great Lord, he defeated them. "Like the god Ramân I thundered down on them." . . . "In that battle I took their chariots, their horses, their teams." Plunder and slaughter there may have been enough. But we do not see that the Assyrian army advanced further than the Orontes, and there is not the slightest mention of vassalage and tribute. An Assyrian king never acknowledged a defeat; but his silence is sometimes very significant —as in this case. It is evident that the victory at least cannot have been as complete as Shalmaneser claims, and the fact that it was five years before he returned to the charge, makes the repulse he encountered look suspiciously like a defeat. This interval is partly filled by his expedition "to the head of the river, the springs of the Tigris, the place where the waters rise," and where he set up "an image of his royalty of large size," and by that to Babylon and the land Kaldu." After that, he hovered for two years about the Euphrates, before

Battle of Karkar, 854 B.C.

he made another decisive move and marched down into Hamath. There he met his old opponent, Benhadad, with "twelve of the kings of Khatti," as before,—and was again repulsed.

7. One is tempted to suspect that the number "twelve," which is again repeated on a later occasion, is given somewhat at random, as a round and effective figure. They were, at all events, not always the *same* twelve. At the time of the second Syrian campaign, Ahab of Israel was no more, and the unnatural alliance with Damascus had been broken the moment that the pressure of an immediate common danger had ceased. In the recoil, Ahab had thrown himself into the arms of the king of Judah, and both had united their forces against Benhadad ; there was a great battle, and in that battle Ahab fell. With him ended the rule of a house which had bid fair to be a prosperous and powerful dynasty in the land of Israel. His father Omri, a valiant soldier and a bold usurper, had taken the crown to himself in the midst of conspiracy, murder, civil war, favored and upheld by the army which he commanded. He was an energetic and statesmanlike sovereign, and his great care had been the consolidation of the northern Jewish royalty and nation (Israel). Like David, he bought a hill and built on it a royal city, SAMARIA, which at once became the capital of Israel. His son was fully as capable and energetic as he had been, and sought to strengthen his house and throne by marriage with a Tyrian princess. It was probably in the time of these

monarchs that the fame of Israel reached the
Assyrian kings, who must have been strongly impressed by the reports of their power and splendor,
since the whole kingdom became to them "the
house of Omri,"—BIT-KHUMRI, according to the
Assyrian fashion of naming countries after the
founders of their reigning houses.

8. A third Syrian campaign did not bring about
any more decisive results. The coalition still existed and held its own, although Shalmaneser this
time brought down an apparently overwhelming
force.

"In my fourteenth year" (846 B.C.), he reports on one of his colossal winged bulls, "I called together an innumerable force from the whole wide land. With 120,000 men I crossed the Euphrates in its flood. In those days, Dadidri of Damascus, Irkhulini of Hamath, with twelve kings of the coast of the Upper and Lower Seas (portions of the Mediterranean) assembled their great, their numberless troops, and advanced against me. I gave them battle and put them to flight, destroyed their chariots, their cavalry, took their baggage from them. To make their lives safe they departed."

His principal opponent was still old Benhadad, undaunted as ever, supported this time principally
by the "kings of the sea-coast," *i. e.*, the Phœnicians, and, possibly, the Philistines of the five
cities. (See p. 150.) We note also the old tactics:
to meet the foe, to bear the brunt, and break his
onslaught, keeping him at a distance,—successful,
but for the last time. A revolution, of which the details are unknown, but which placed an usurper on
the throne of Damascus—the Syrian palace officer,
HAZAEL, who murdered his aged master Benhadad
II. (see Second Kings, viii. 7-15),—appears to have

dissolved the coalition. For when, after another respite of four years, the Assyrian perseveringly returns to the charge, he mentions only one opponent, KHAZAILU of Damascus, who, perhaps made timid by his isolation, awaits him in his own country, amidst the strongholds of the mountains opposite the Lebanon range (Anti-Lebanon), and there suffers so signal a defeat, with such grievous loss of men, chariots, cavalry and baggage, that he is fain to retreat to his capital, whither the conqueror follows him. Shalmaneser, however, does not say that he took it, only: " In Damascus, his royal city, I besieged him ; I destroyed his plantations." Immediately afterwards he marches to the sea-coast, there to receive the repentant submission and the tributes of Tyre and Sidon, and—of " YAHUA, THE SON OF KHUMRI." This latter is no other than JEHU, the new king of Israel. He was in no sense a "son of Omri," *i. e.*, a member of Omri's house, but, on the contrary, the destroyer of that house,—an adventurous captain who, having had himself proclaimed king by his soldiers, drove furiously to the capital, put to death the young king and his mother, and ordered the massacre of King Ahab's entire family,—seventy young sons, the biblical historian tells us, who were under the care of various noble elders of the nation. (Second Kings, ix.-x.) There is a strange incongruity in seeing this man called " son of Omri" on two Assyrian monuments. It may have happened either from ignorance of the events, or because the name of Omri, having once strongly impressed itself on the Assyrian politicians' minds, became a fixed tradition, so that the land of Israel remained to the end "The House of Omri," and the kings of Israel, quite irrespective of any changes of dynasty, the successors, and therefore the sons, of Omri.

9. In the ruins of Shalmaneser's palace, which occupy the centre of the great Nimrud mound, Layard found a very remarkable monument, a pillar in hard black stone, about seven feet high, of the shape known as "obelisk." Owing to the hardness of the stone it was in excellent preservation, far better than that of another and larger monument of the same shape, in white soft stone, belonging to Asshurnazirpal. The four faces are covered with sculptures and writing, five rows of the former and a great many lines of the latter. (See Ill. No. 28.) This is the so-called "Obelisk-Inscription," which presents a record of Shalmaneser's wars to nearly the last year of his reign. The sculptures represent processions of tribute-bearers from five nations. On one of the faces (see No. 29), we see certain personages presented to the king by his palace officers, one of whom holds a scroll—probably a list of the articles composing the tribute. The attitude of these personages shows that there is no exaggeration in the phrase so frequently recurring on the monuments: "My feet they took," or "They kissed my feet." The prostrate personage on the second row has been thought to be the ambassador of Jehu, but it seems more probable, from the tenor of the inscription overhead, that it is Jehu him- *Jehu, King of Israel, pays tribute to Shalmaneser II. King of Assyria, 842 B.C.*

28.—BLACK OBELISK OF SHALMANESER II.

self. This is a literal rendering of the inscription: "Tribute of Yahua, son of Khumri: silver, gold, basins of gold, bottles of gold, vessels of gold, buckets of gold, lead, ... (?) wood, royal treasure, ... (?) wood, I received."* Most of these different articles can be identified on the sculpture, which also admirably renders the cringing, fearful attitude of the bearers, as well as the unmistakably Jewish cast of their features. Although this row of sculpture is of course the most important from its biblical associations, yet some others are, in themselves, more amusing, from the number of various and uncommon animals represented; the elephant, the antelopes, the two camels, the monkeys, are evidently destined to enrich the royal parks and menageries, and one cannot help admiring the lively touches with which the artist has reproduced their most taking and characteristic features. (See Nos. 29-33.)

10. It is to be noted that in neither of the biblical historical books referring to this period, *i.e.*, neither in Second Kings, nor in Second Chronicles, is there the slightest mention of two such important events as the participation of Ahab in the Syrian league and the war against Shalmaneser II., and the submission of Jehu. It is difficult to imagine a reason for so strange an omission, unless it be that these events were duly narrated in a book which has apparently been lost, and to which we are continually referred.

---

* Prof. D. G. Lyon, to whose kindness we are indebted for the translation, is of opinion that the prostrate personage is Jehu himself.

29.—FIRST FACE OF BLACK OBELISK. (JEHU OF ISRAEL ON THE SECOND ROW.)

30.—SECOND FACE OF BLACK OBELISK. (JEWISH TRIBUTE-BEARERS ON SECOND ROW.)

under the title of "The Book of the Chronicles of the Kings of Israel." "Now the rest of the acts of Jehu, and all that he did, and all his might, are they not written in the Book of the Chronicles of the Kings of Israel?" This formula is used, almost unvaried, at the death of every king. But the book itself is missing.

11. Another monument belonging to this king, of great interest and artistic value, and moreover quite unique of its kind, was discovered about ten years ago by Mr. Hormuzd Rassam (formerly Layard's assistant, now his successor in the field of Assyrian excavations). We will leave the explorer to speak for himself:

"In 1877, in a mound called BALAWAT, about 15 miles east of Mossul, and 9 from Nimrud, I found scrolls of the copper plating of an Assyrian monument. The copper " (more properly bronze) " was very much injured from the immense time it had been buried. The top part was 3–4 feet from the surface of the ground, the bottom 15 feet. It is now in the British Museum. It is thought to be the coating of a huge gate with double leaves, the thickness of which must have been about four inches, as shown by the bend of the nails that fastened the plates to the wooden frame."

These scrolls or strips are covered with bas-reliefs of the usual type, not cast in moulds, but hammered out from the inside, the kind of work now known as *repoussé*. The sockets were found on the spot, and it was easy for a skilful draughtsman to imagine the gates in their original aspect. An inscription, concisely rehearsing the events of the first nine years, ran around it. It belonged to a city built by Asshurnazirpal, and must have been very imposing and massive, but not clumsy, owing to its fine proportions. (See No. 34.)

12. The last seven or eight years of his life Shalmaneser spent in well-earned repose, mostly in Kalah, building, repairing, ministering to the "great gods." It was he who completed the great Ziggurat of the temple of Nineb, begun by his father,—that very "pyramid" the ruins of which puzzled Xenophon when he halted by Larissa.* His wars meantime were conducted by his general-in-chief, victoriously it would appear. But they were comparatively unimportant, now the great work of this indefatigable monarch's reign—the subjection of Syria—was accomplished. He was not permitted, however, to enjoy the power he had so much enlarged, undisturbed to the end. His eldest son rebelled against him, and succeeded in enlisting on his side a large portion of Assyria proper. As many as sixteen cities are said to have declared for the rebel prince. It was therefore another son, SHAMSHI-RAMÂN III., who succeeded to the throne after quelling the rebellion. (See No. 35.)

13. Nothing much of note is recorded of this king, while his son and successor, RAMÂN-NIRARI III., reproduces in great part his grandfather's glorious career, not only by the length of his reign, which nearly equals Shalmaneser's, but by the number and importance of his campaigns, especially those against Syria. To enumerate or describe them would be most tedious and unprofitable iter-

---
* See "Story of Chaldea," p. 3.

31.—THIRD FACE OF BLACK OBELISK. (JEWISH TRIBUTE-BEARERS ON SECOND ROW.)

32.—FOURTH FACE OF OBELISK. (JEWISH TRIBUTE-BEARERS ON SECOND ROW.)

ation, the general character being always the same. Suffice it to say, that he completed the subjection of Aram, by actually taking the capital, Damascus, a triumph which Shalmaneser never quite succeeded in achieving, and imposing on it a tribute which almost passes conception, besides the booty taken in battle and on the march. For the rest he fairly sums up his own career when he says: "West of the Euphrates I subdued the land Khatti, the whole of the land Akharri (Phœnicia), Tyre, Sidon, Bit-Khumri, Edom and Philistia, unto the shore of the Sea of the Setting Sun, and imposed on them tributes and contributions." Neither Israel nor the cities of the sea-coast were conquered as yet by force of arms, but they had sent presents. That was a dangerous precedent, for, according to Assyrian ideas, sending presents was tantamount to declaring one's self a vassal, and whoever, having done so once, did not repeat the act of homage,—in fact pay regular yearly tribute,—was held a rebel, and treated as such. "All the kings of Kaldu" are mentioned as obediently paying tribute, but Naïri does not seem to have been much visited. In compensation, we find the names of a great many hitherto scarcely or not at all noted "kingdoms" and "nations,"—"tribes" would be less misleading,—on the north-east and the east, *i. e.*, among the spurs and outer ridges of the Zagros, from the great lakes down to Elam. Among these names we particularly mark that of the MEDES, (MADAÏ), of whom a great deal more hereafter.

14. Râman-nirari III. was married to a princess of

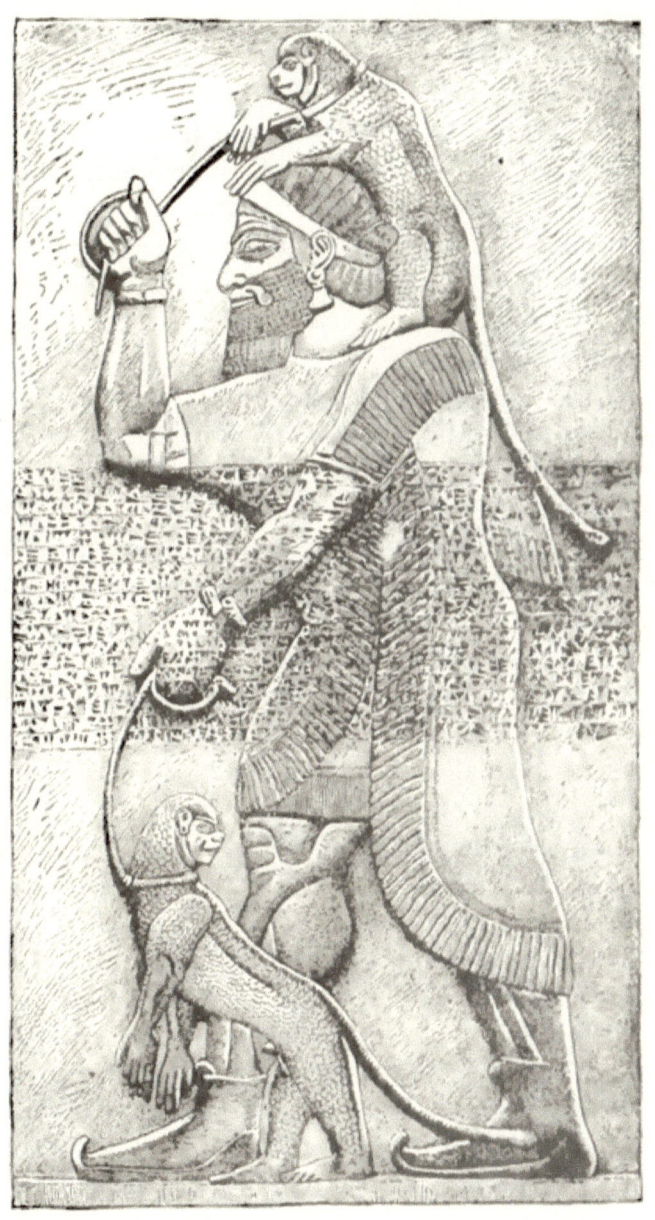

33.—TRIBUTE-BEARERS BRINGING MONKEYS (SEE NO. 32, THIRD ROW.

the name of SHAMMURAMAT. This the Greeks corrupted into SEMIRAMIS. It is the name of a fabulous queen, about whom the most extravagant stories were current, and being transmitted by several Greek writers were taught as actual history down to the time of cuneiform discoveries, *i. e.*, as late even as some thirty years ago. This is the story in briefest outline.

In very ancient times there were kings in Asia; but they did nothing worthy of note, and no records of them existed, until in the number there arose a mighty man of war, the Assyrian NINUS. He began to make conquests right and left, and founded a vast empire. The whole of Asia Minor to the sea, Armenia and Media were subject to him. He conquered all the lands around the Black and Caspian seas, even to portions of Southern Russia, and all the countries which compose modern Persia, not to speak of Arabia. Then he built a magnificent capital for himself, to which he gave his own name, Ninus—even the city of Nineveh. He had a trusty general, ONNES, or OANNES, and this general's wife, Semiramis, was the most beautiful of all women. Indeed she was something more than mortal woman. She was the daughter of the Syrian fish-goddess, Derketo, and had been nurtured as a babe in a rocky wilderness, not far from her mother's sanctuary at Ascalon (see p. 111 and p. 114) by doves, until she was found by shepherds. They took her to their chief, SIMMAS, the overseer of the royal flocks, who brought her up as his own child. One day the royal governor, Onnes, accidentally met her, and as it was

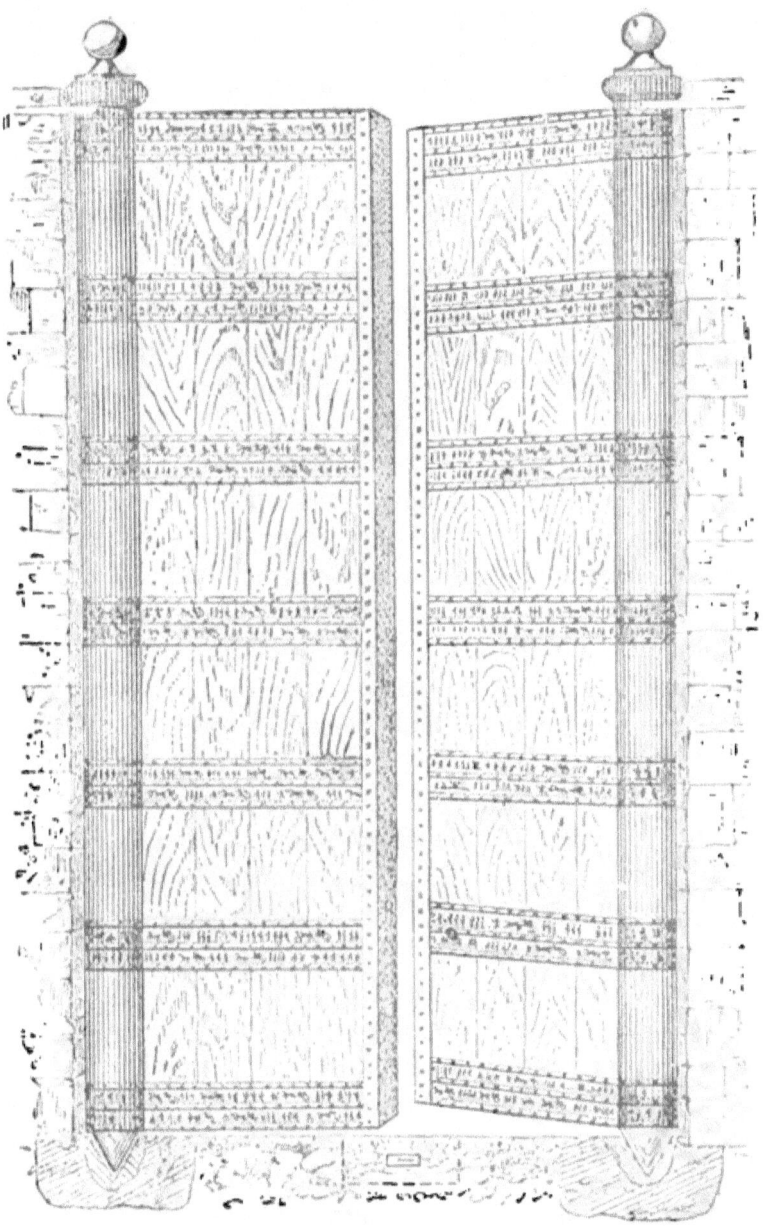

34.—GATE OF BALAWAT. (RESTORED.)

impossible to see without loving her, he immediately lost his heart to her and made her his wife. She proved as wise and brave as she was beautiful, and on one occasion, by her personal prowess, helped her husband and King Ninus to take a strong fortress, which had long resisted them. The king at once succumbed to her fatal gift of beauty, and took her from Onnes, who killed himself from grief. Semiramis became Ninus' queen, and so fondly did he dote on her to his end, that when he died, after a reign of 52 years, he left his whole empire to her, although they had a son, NINYAS.

15. Semiramis now showed herself a greater sovereign than even King Ninus had been, for to a most royal ambition and great deeds of war she joined a noble genius for the useful works of peace. She built the city of Babylon, with its hanging gardens, mighty walls and towers, the great temple of Bel, and the wonderful bridge over the Euphrates. She ordered the seven-ridged chain of the Zagros to be broken through to construct a direct and commodious road into Media, where she built the capital, Egbatana, with a fine royal castle, and supplied it with water brought down from some mountain lakes through a tunnel. There is in the Zagros highlands a tall, almost perpendicular, three-peaked rock-mountain, near a place anciently called Bagistana. She ordered the face of that rock to be carefully smoothed and covered with sculptures, representing her with one hundred of her body-guard. Her warlike expeditions surpassed in boldness those of the king, her lord; she not only conquered

35.—STELE OF SHAMSHI-RAMÂN III. (IV. ACCORDING TO SOME)

Egypt, Ethiopia and part of Libya, but organized and led a campaign against India. She had reached and actually bridged the river Indus, and was preparing to advance into the country, when she was met by an Indian force, defeated, and compelled to retire with heavy loss. This disaster did not much affect the queen's haughty spirit. She returned to her dominions, where she gave herself up to a life of pleasure and luxury, in which she indulged as passionately as in war and work in her intervals of leisure. Her unearthly gift of beauty was not impaired by age ; a look from her made men her slaves, and her court was brilliant beyond words. But her son, Ninyas, tired of his obscure and inglorious lot, conspired against her. The queen discovered the conspiracy and remembered an old prophesy, according to which she was to be gathered to the immortals and receive divine honors when her son should rebel against her. So she made over the empire to Ninyas, and ordered all her nobles and generals to swear allegiance to him. As for herself, she turned herself into a dove and flew out of the palace with a flock of doves. From that time the Assyrians honored Semiramis as a goddess, and held the dove sacred. Assyrian art repeatedly represented this transformation. There are, however, also other versions of her death.

16. Ninyas proved as feeble and contemptible a monarch as his parents had been ambitious and active. He shut himself up in his palace, spent most of his time in the harem in effeminate idleness, never showed himself in public, and governed en-

tirely through his generals and dignitaries. And long as the Assyrian Empire endured, until it fell into the hands of the Medes, *i. e.*, over 1300 years, all his successors lived and governed in the same inglorious way, and not one of them left a name or a deed worthy to be recorded.

17. The facts of history, as they have been revealed by the cuneiform monuments, make it almost superfluous even to point out the utter incongruity of the whole narrative. The Greeks learned it not from the Assyrians themselves, but from their successors, the Medes and Persians, under circumstances which are better reserved for another volume. It is a story of the kind that belongs, not to history, but to folk-lore, and perhaps in part to national epos, in so far as Ninus, the eponym of Nineveh, and Semiramis, the dove-woman, are persons from the Assyrian pantheon transferred to earth in human form. Ninus is most probably a heroic form of Nineb, one of the most popular protecting deities of the Assyrian kings, while Semiramis (whose Assyrian name, "Shammuramat," means simply "dove")* is, beyond doubt, none other than the goddess Ishtar in her double character as Lady of War and Queen of Love and beauty—Ishtar of Arbela and Ishtar of Nineveh in their original unity. It may be just pointed out that the names of Onnes and Simmas strongly suggest two more

---

* Fr. Lenormant, in a private letter, formally retracting the elaborate interpretation of the name which he attempted in his "Légende de Sémiramis," in favor of this simpler and so much more obvious one.

divine beings, Oannes-Ea and Shamash. This part of the story, therefore, is unmistakably and transparently mythical. As for the gross historical incongruities of the whole, this is not the place to explain them. We shall have to return to the subject. One thing is sure: that the only historical Shammuramat or Semiramis is Ramân-nirari III.'s

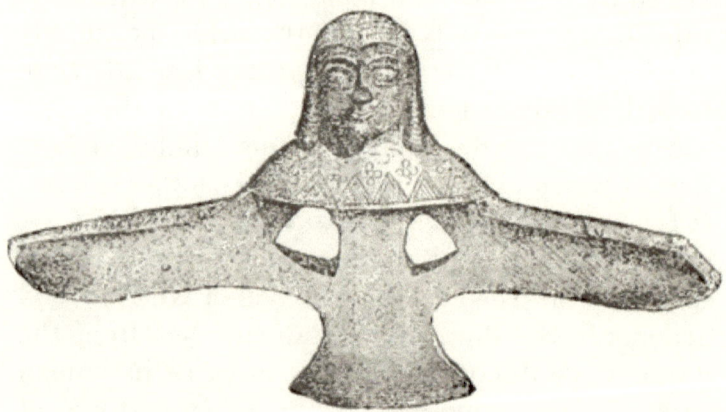

36.—SEMIRAMIS CHANGED INTO A DOVE. (BRONZE ORNAMENT BENT TO FIT THE SHAPE OF A DRINKING-CUP, AND SERVE AS HANDLE.)

queen,—the only Assyrian queen, by the way, whose name is recorded in monumental inscriptions. It occurs on the pedestals of two statues of the god Nebo, which are said to be consecrated by the governor of Kalah to Nebo, "the protector of Ramân-nirari, king of Asshur, his lord, and of Shammuramat, the consort of the palace, his lady." Nothing has been discovered as yet to account for this departure from universal Oriental custom. It has been suggested that the queen may have been a princess of

Babylon, and as such have exercised some power in her own right.

18. Ramân-nirari III.'s reign of twenty-nine years (811–782) takes us over into another century, and at his death the eighth century B.C. is well under way. The next forty years or so are filled by three monarchs who do not seem to have added anything to

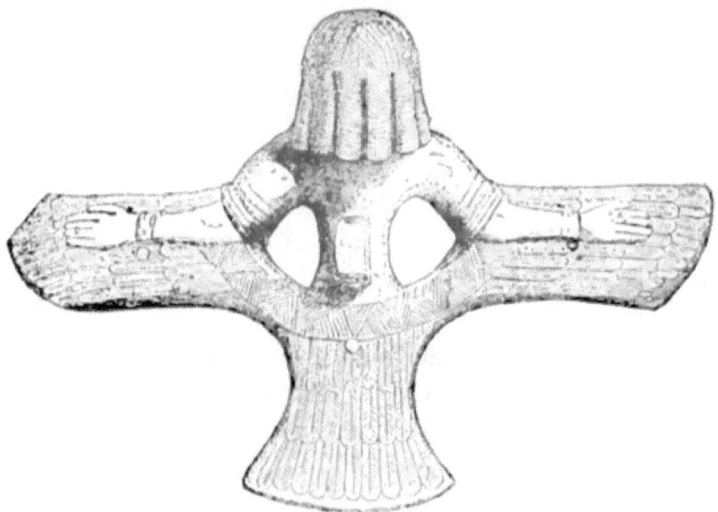

37.—SEMIRAMIS CHANGED INTO A DOVE. (BACK VIEW.)

the lustre of their country's name, or rather appear to have suffered it to become obscured once more. True, we do not read of risings in the West, the Syrian countries being probably too much weakened to muster so soon a sufficiency of men and means, nor are the lands of Naïri conspicuous; but the far North-east, URARTU, *i.e.*, Armenia proper, the mountainous countries around the great lakes,— becomes troublesome and threatening. Ramân-nirari's son, Shalmaneser III., in a reign of only ten years, records six expeditions against Urartu, without any very apparent results. The reason was that a kingdom of some extent and importance was forming in that region, probably out of many loose tribes of kindred race, who felt the need of greater compactness, for purposes of independence, defence, and perhaps aggression. This was the kingdom which has been called VAN, the name of Armenia being of much later date. That of Urartu, given to it by the Assyrians, must really have been the original one, or very near it, as we are led to conclude by that of MOUNT ARARAT, which still belongs to the highest mountain of Armenia. The people who inhabited this intricate land of mountains, the exact extent of which towards any side it is impossible to determine, are called by the later Greek geographers ALARODIANS, an obvious corruption of Urartu, no whit more unlike the original than any transcriptions left us by the Greeks, who were detestable linguists and were never known to catch the sound of a foreign name, to which peculiarity of theirs we owe a number of historical and geographical puzzles, not half of which have been fully solved as yet. The capital of the new kingdom was the city of VAN. Some traces of it have been found, consisting of native monuments, with inscriptions in cuneiform characters, also some sculptures, on slabs or steles, or on convenient surfaces of live rock smoothed for the purpose, showing that the new nation borrowed the forms of Assyrian culture, even while carrying on an unceasing warfare with the Assyrian nation.

19. Urartu at first appears only as one of the

kingdoms of Naïri. It is highly probable that it was the most considerable one among them, as well as the most inaccessible, and thus gained a sort of supremacy, which may have developed into actual sovereignty, for the kings at Van, in this their period of growth, call themselves "Kings of Naïri" generally, while they tell of conflicts with the Khatti, (the Hittites south of the Amanos), and sundry victories over the Assyrians—a detail we should vainly look for on the records of Ramânnirari's successors. These inscriptions, in which the familiar wedge is forced into new and strange combinations, to express a new and uncongenial language, have only very lately begun to yield to the efforts and ingenuity of Professor A. H. Sayce, that great pioneer and decipherer, but for whom this earliest Armenian kingdom, with its very powerful native dynasty, might never have been revealed. This people, the Alarodians, he frequently, on that account, calls PROTO-ARMENIAN, (*protos* is a Greek word, meaning "first," earliest), to distinguish them from the later Armenians, who were invaders of entirely different race and culture. Mr. Sayce has conclusively shown from the language of the monuments at Van that the Proto-Armenians were not Semites; neither were they Turanians. He thinks —and the conclusion is gaining wider and firmer ground—that they were a branch of the great Hittite family, which occupied the whole of Naïri, broken up into innumerable independent tribes, and at various times, not to be determined historically, hived off in different directions into the vast and in viting valleys of Asia Minor. It is certainly remarkable that the mountaineers of that entire region to this day wear the high fur cap, boots with upturned points, and belted *kaftan*, which we see on the Hittite sculptures. (See Nos. 67, 68.) Mr. Sayce is of opinion that the westward extension of the Hittites may be located between the fifteenth and thirteenth centuries B.C., *i.e.*, in the first period of Assyrian greatness.

20. Of Ramân-nirari's three successors, the first, Shalmaneser III., might have done more had he lived longer; but the two last seem to have gradually sunk into inaction. At least, it has been noticed that the annotated eponym canon more and more frequently has the note: "In the land," meaning that the king had stayed at home that year. It has even been surmised that this may have been the cause of discontent in the army, used to yearly campaigns, which never failed, at all events, to enrich the soldiers and the country generally with booty; a plausible explanation, it must be admitted, of the revolts that broke out in several cities, even in Asshur and Kalah itself, and ended in a revolution which placed a usurper on the throne, putting an end to a line of kings, which, if a very explicit statement in an inscription of Ramân-nirari III. has been correctly interpreted, traced its descent uninterruptedly to the founder of the Assyrian monarchy, through, it would appear, something like a thousand years. Of the manner in which this revolution took place, we have unfortunately not the slightest indication. Political events at home find no place in

the royal annals, for the historical inscriptions are avowedly composed for the glorification of the respective monarchs whose reigns they relate, and would, in all cases, be extremely reticent on any matter of a disastrous or disagreeable nature. So we have no means of knowing even who the usurper was, whether only an adventurer, an ambitious and unscrupulous general, like Omri and Jehu and Hazael, and almost all the Oriental founders of new dynasties, or a pretender at least collaterally connected with the ancient royal house. True, he speaks of "the kings, his fathers," but as he never mentions his own father and grandfather, the word may stand, in a not unusual Oriental acception, for "elders" or predecessors, and he may be the son of the old Assyrian kings after the same fashion that all the kings of Israel were "sons of Omri." However that may be, one thing is sure, and that by far the most essential, that in this usurper we have to do with one of the mightiest conquerors in history.

21. He reigned under the name, familiar from the biblical history of the Jewish kings, of Tiglath-Pileser II., a name to which he did ample justice, whether it were his own, or assumed at his accession, as a glorious omen, or as a declaration of the illustrious model he had proposed to himself. For it is very curious that this king's name itself has for years been a subject of dispute, and an apparently hopeless problem. The confusion was caused by the mention (Second Kings, xv. 19) of a king of Assyria, PHÛL or PUL, while the same chapter, ten verses lower, speaks of Tiglath-Pileser. Now, thanks to

the Eponym Canon, we have a complete and unassailable authentic list of the Assyrian kings for this whole period, and in the number there is no Phûl. On the other hand, Berosus gives for this same time a Phûl as king of Babylon, and the name is repeated by a Greek writer, corrupted into POROS. It was at length proved, by chronological calculations and various circumstantial evidence, that the two were one. Tiglath-Pileser did conquer Babylonia, and assume the full title of the Babylonian kings. For what reason he should have been inscribed on the royal list there under a different name from that he bore as Assyrian monarch, is what has never been found out. One explanation suggested is that Phûl was his own original name, and the other an assumed one.

22. If one set of important events affecting the people of Israel—the first Syrian league, the battle of Karkar and Jehu's tribute—is missing in the Jewish historical books that have come down to us, there is another, affecting Assyria, given at length in the Bible and unrecorded on the monuments; it is the journey of the prophet Jonah to Nineveh and his preaching there. It is difficult to know just what to make of the narrative. It seems such a strange thing for a Jew to do, especially as it never was the Jews' wont to go out of their way for the spiritual welfare of any other people. In other respects, the incongruity is perhaps not as great as at first sight appears. Jonah's date—this side of 800 B.C.—coincides with the disastrous period of weakness and intestine troubles which immediately precedes the

second Tiglath-Pileser, when the monarchy itself seemed threatened with dissolution. Then, the proclamation of a public fast and penance in times of national danger and calamity is not incompatible with the Assyro-Babylonian, nor indeed with the spirit of any Semitic religion, and we know of other cases. Also, the Assyrians had prophets or "seers," in whom they placed much faith. Lastly, the very fable which is such a stumbling-block to the intelligent reading of the whole book becomes most unexpectedly cleared of its hitherto impenetrable obscurity, when Assyriology informs us that the Assyrian name of the "great city" is NINUA, a word very like NUNU, which means "FISH"; the connection being moreover indicated by the oldest sign for the rendering of the name in writing, which is a combination of lines or wedges plainly representing a *fish in a basin or tank*, thus: 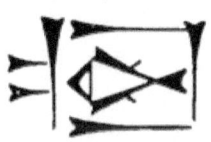 The origin of both name and figure are as yet unexplained, so much only being suggested, that they must be in some way connected with the Semitic and still more Canaanitic fish-myth (see p. 111 and p. 114), and the consequent sacredness of fishes. However that be, enough is apparent to suggest a solution of the whale story. The big fish that swallowed Jonah was no other than Nineveh, the Fish-City itself, where he must surely have been sufficiently encompassed by danger to warrant his desperate cry for deliverance, in a strain that forcibly recalls the old "penitential psalms" of Shumir and Accad.* The whole extraordinary story thus assumes its proper character, that of an Oriental parable, somewhat exceptionally high in color, it is true, and adorned with foreign additions, but *that* came from repeated tellings, and possibly in the final writing down, the scribe who did so being probably ignorant of the myth underlying the original parable. Hence the attempted flight in a ship—to account for the prophet's getting into the fish's belly at all. Furthermore, we have seen that local tradition has attached the memory and name of the prophet to one of the mounds which contain the ruined palaces and temples of Nineveh (Nebbi Yunus †). But then that tradition is probably to be ascribed to the Arabs and Turks, since the Mussulmans know the biblical prophets and hold them in honor. Altogether it must be admitted that the book of Jonah is in many ways puzzling.‡

23. Before passing over to the second and more tragic phase of the conflict between Asshur and Israel, a conflict which this time directly involved the Phœnician cities, let us pause to record an

---

* See "Story of Chaldea," pp. 177-179.

† See lower, p. 341 ; also "Story of Chaldea," p. 49.

‡ This solution of the famous Jonah story was suggested to the author by a passage in Fr. Lenormant's "Légende de Sémiramis," and is offered only *as* a suggestion, which it were desirable, however, to pursue and develop until a thorough research either confirmed it or proved it to be erroneous. If confirmed, it would certainly do away with a huge and puzzling incongruity.

event which, though of little immediate importance, is forever memorable from the consequences that were to arise from it in a not very remote future: this is the founding of a city on the northern shore of Africa by a Tyrian colony, in 814 B.C., the tenth year of Shamshi-Ramân, the successor of Shalmaneser II. There had been a revolution in Tyre. Two children, the boy, Pygmalion, and his somewhat older sister, Elissa, were left joint possessors of the throne, the power virtually belonging to their uncle, the high-priest of Baal-Melkarth, to whom Elissa had been married by her father. When Pygmalion grew up, he rebelled against this tutelage, and having the people on his side, put his uncle to death and proclaimed himself sole king. Elissa then, accompanied by a number of her husband's followers, presumably older men of noble families, seized on ships which were lying in the harbor ready to sail, put to sea, and landing on the northern coast of Africa, at a point where there were already Phœnician settlements, some prosperous, some decayed and deserted, founded on the site of one of the latter, a city which, famous under its corrupted name of Carthage, would scarcely be recognized under its original one of Kart-Hadascht ("New City"). This whole story, being transmitted through Greek channels, is anything but authentic in the details. The names are both Greek, not Semitic, in form, and the narrative has been worked over again and again by Western poets, till the Tyrian princess somehow exchanged

Foundation of Carthage, 814 B.C.

her first name for another, that of DIDO, under which she became a standing character of ancient fiction. In point of historical fact, however, the two solid landmarks remain: there was a revolution in Tyre, and, in consequence thereof, a colony departed and founded this African city, Tyre's last-born but most illustrious daughter. As for the name of the foundress, Elissa, it may very possibly have been an eponym for all those regions, colonized from Phœnicia, which the Bible calls Elishah, and which may have included, besides Greek islands and coast tracts, also the not very distant settlements on the northern point of Africa.

APPENDIX TO CHAPTER VI.

THE STELE OF MESHA THE MOABITE.

THE destinies of Moab, like those of all the small states and principalities that form the group of Palestine, lie too much outside the orbit of Assyria to be introduced separately or at any length in the great historical drama of which that country has the title part. In that drama they have a place in so far only as they come in contact or collision with the chief actor. The Jewish kingdoms themselves would make no exception, were it not for the peculiar interest which attaches to them for us, and which makes us refer to them principally the events in which, to an indifferent eye, they played in reality but a subordinate part. As it is, Israel and Judah must always take in a history of Assyria a prominent place, which would be disproportionate, but for their importance on other than strictly political grounds.

Not so with Moab. Yet one monument, discovered about twenty years ago, has given it a claim to attention. It is a stone in the shape of a stele, covered with a long inscription, which seems to have been set up by King Mesha, in memory of his country's deliverance from the rule of Israel, to whom it had been subject and had paid tribute for about forty years. Moab, like Edom and some other nations of Palestine, was so nearly akin to the Hebrews in race as to speak the same language, so the inscription " is written in the Moabite dialect, *i. e.*, in a language which is, with slight difference, that of the Bible. . . . The characters are the ancient Hebrew characters, the so-called Samaritan or Phœnician ones."* It is not only the oldest Hebrew literary monument in existence, but the most ancient specimen of alphabet writing. The stele was standing, half buried in the ground, at the foot of a hill by the side of Dibon, the ancient capital of Moab, and was unfortunately broken in the digging, so that it had to be patched out of twenty pieces, and the surface was so badly injured that half the writing would have been irrecoverably lost had not the discoverer had the forethought of ordering a stamping to be taken before the stele was removed. This enabled the scholars at the Louvre,

---

* Vigouroux, " La Bible et les Découvertes Modernes," Vol. IV, p. 59.

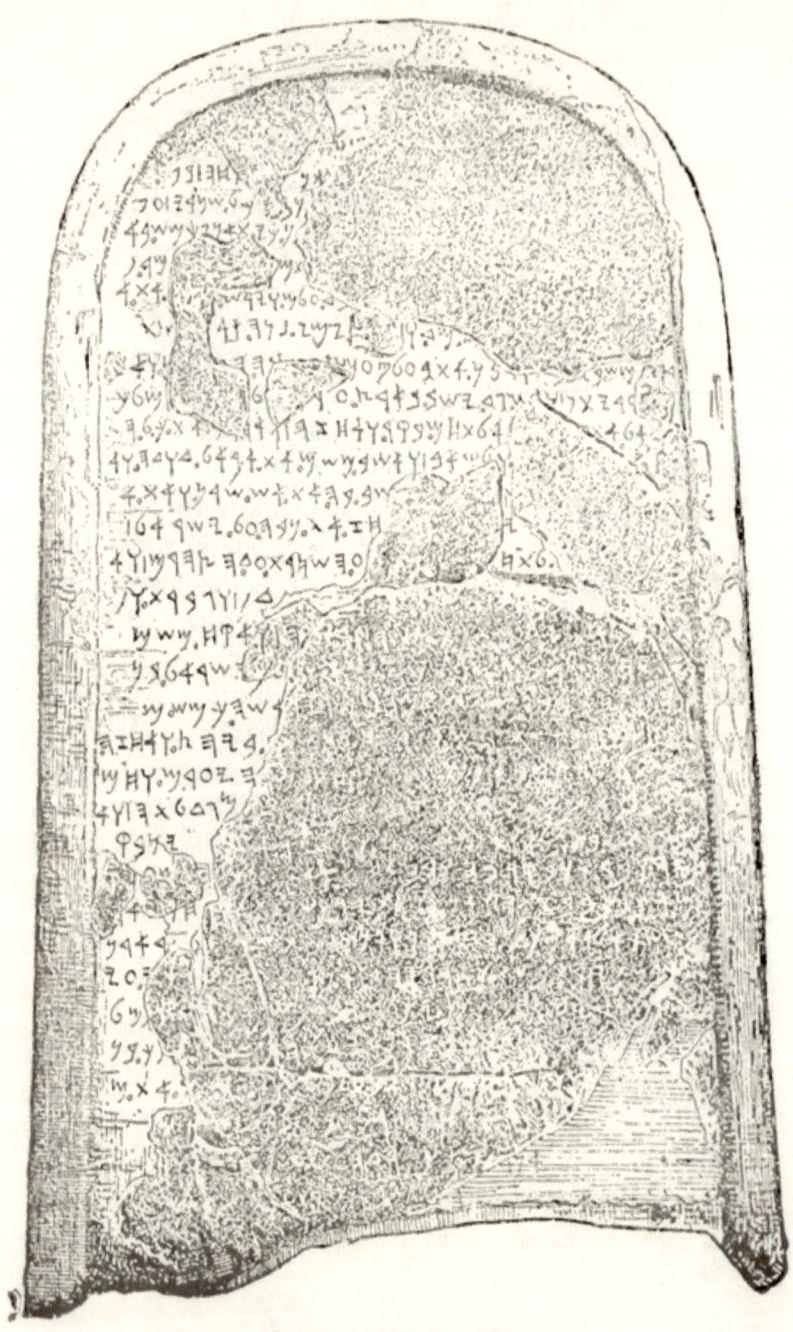

38.—THE "MESHA STELE."

where it now stands, to complete the text by reproducing the lost parts on a layer of plaster applied on the damaged portions of the surface. The difference shows very clearly.

But great as is the philological importance of this "find," its historical contents are at least as interesting. The inscription relates to a time and to events so familiar from Bible history, that a Sunday-school child who knew its lesson well would have no trouble in placing it, and connecting it with the story told in Second Kings, iii., the tragical end of which was given in a preceding chapter. (See p. 127.) There we are informed that "Mesha, king of Moab, was a sheepmaster, and he rendered unto the king of Israel the wool of an hundred thousand lambs and of an hundred thousand rams. But it came to pass when Ahab was dead that the king of Moab rebelled against the king of Israel." Then we read, in a vivid narrative, how the kings of Israel and Judah joined their forces against Moab, and pressed it sorely, and how King Mesha, in the hour of despair, resorted to the last horrible appeal of the Canaanitic religions and sacrificed his eldest son,—to Khemosh, the god of Moab, although the name is not given,—and how the Israelites were seized with a great horror and departed to their own land. It is this great deliverance which he celebrates in his inscription, but without mentioning at what price he bought it.

"I am Mesha, the son of Khemoshgad the Dibonite. My father reigned over Moab thirty years, and I reigned after my father, and erected this sanctuary to Khemosh in Karkha * . . . . because he assisted me against all my foes, and let me feast my eyes on all my haters.—*Omri, the king of Israel, oppressed Moab many days, for Khemosh was wroth with his land.* And his son followed him, and he also spake: I will oppress Moab. In my days he spoke thus, and I feasted my heart on him and his house. And Omri had taken possession of the land Medeba and dwelt in it . . . . the days of his son, forty years. *And Khemosh restored it in my days.* And the men of Gad had dwelt in the land Atarot from of old. And the king of Israel had built Oltarot for himself. And I fought against the city, and took it and slew all . . . . to rejoice the eyes of Khemosh and Moab. . . . *And Khemosh spoke to me: Go, take Nebo from Israel. And I went* at night, and fought against it from the rising of the morning dawn until midday, and I took it and slew all, 7000 . . . . women . . . . and maidens I consecrated to Khemosh's Ashtoreth" (or "to Kemosh, Ashtoreth"?), "and I took thence the vessels of Yahveh and dragged before Khemosh. . . .

"And I built Karkha. . . . I built its gates and its towers. And I built the royal palace. . . . And there was not a cistern inside the city in Karkha. Then I spoke to all the people: "Make each a cistern in your houses. . . ."

Then follow more constructions. The last intelligible fragment is: "*Khemosh spoke to me: Go down, fight against Khoronan*, and I . . . . Khemosh in my days. . . ." The inscription breaks off at the thirty-fourth line.

The similarity of this inscription to the Assyrian ones in manner and spirit is almost too striking to be pointed out. But it reminds one at least as strongly of countless passages in the Bible. Substi-

---

* The discoverer of the stele, Mr. Clermont Ganneau, thinks that "Karkha, mountain and city in one, is the Sion of Dibon, the Moabite Jerusalem; it is the city of Mesha, which contains the temple of Khemosh and the citadel. I cannot make my meaning clearer than by likening Dibon to Rome, Karkha to the Capitol, and the sanctuary of Khemosh to the temple of Jupiter Capitolinus."

tute "Yahveh" for "Khemosh" in any of the passages given in italics, and the name of Edom or Ammon or any of Israel's enemies for that of Israel, —and they might be written by the most ardent Hebrew monotheist. In the same manner likewise the Assyrian speaks of Asshur,—a distinctively Semitic relation to the Supreme Deity. (Compare pp. 11, 12.)

VII.

THE SECOND EMPIRE.—SIEGE OF SAMARIA.

"Ah, the uproar of many peoples, which roar like the roaring of the seas! And the rushing of nations, that rush like the rushing of many waters! . . . Behold the Lord bringeth up upon them the waters of the River, strong and many, even the king of Assyria and all his glory; and he shall come up over all his channels, and go over all his banks: and he shall sweep onward into Judah; he shall overflow and pass through; he shall reach even to the neck; and the stretching out of his wings shall fill the breadth of thy land."—ISAIAH.

1. THE prophet Isaiah, when he described the career of an Assyrian conqueror in such magnificent poetry, likening it to that of Asshur's own Euphrates in high flood time, spoke of what his eyes were sorrowfully beholding almost every year. And not of one king only might he have thus spoken, but of four, whose contemporary he was, mighty conquerors all of them, for Assyria was now reaching the noonday zenith of her greatness, that giddy point of excessive elevation on which no mortal thing can do more than remain poised a little while, to descend almost immediately, oftener headlong than by slow degrees. That point she undoubtedly attained under the second Tiglath-Pileser, who, while quite as much the robber, had more of the statesman than his predecessors, and greatly changed the character of the Assyrian power.

Tiglath Pileser II., 745-727 B.C.

2. "The accession of Tiglath-Pileser II.," says an eminent historian,* "marks a turning-point in the history of Western Asia. His first task was to regain the position held by his predecessors, but much impaired since in many ways, and especially by the Alarodians; but he went far beyond that. While the Assyrian kings had hitherto virtually contented themselves with the subjection of Mesopotamia and the lands of Naïri, and only plundered or raised tribute on remoter territories, like Babylonia and Syria, the new ruler began systematically to build up a great political empire."

"This second empire," to borrow the words of another eminent Assyrian scholar, Professor Sayce,† differed essentially from the first. The usurper was an organizer as well as a conqueror, and sought, for the first time in the history of Western Asia, to give his conquests a consolidated and permanent character. The conquered provinces were no longer loosely connected with the central power by the payment of tribute, which was refused as soon as the Assyrian armies were out of sight; nor were the campaigns undertaken by the kings of Nineveh mere raids, whose chief objects were prestige and plunder. They were made with a purpose, and in pursuance of a definite line of policy, and, once made, they were tenaciously preserved. The conquered nations became subject provinces, governed, wherever possible, by Assyrian satraps (governors), while turbulent populations were deported to some distant parts of the empire. Each province and capital city had its annual contribution to the imperial treasury fixed and regulated, and centralization superseded the loose union of mutually hostile states and towns. . . . The second Assyrian empire was essentially a commercial one. It was founded and maintained for the purpose of attracting the trade and wealth of Western Asia into Assyrian hands. . . ."

3. Accordingly, two novel features strike us in the

---

* Ed. Meyer, "Geschichte des Alterthums," p. 416, § 305.
† A. H. Sayce, "Herodotus," p. 376.

second Tiglath-Pileser's inscriptions. The formula for announcing a conquest is no longer, "The land So-and-so I plundered, I devastated the whole of it," but "To the boundaries of Asshur I added," *i. e.*, I annexed. Asshurnazirpal had made a beginning in this direction, and occasionally mentions appointing

39.—FLOCKS AND CAPTIVE WOMEN CARRIED AWAY.

a governor over a conquered city or district. The difference is that what was formerly done occasionally was now done systematically. The same king had in some instances transported part of a conquered but unsafe population into Assyria (see p. 159), but Tiglath-Pileser introduced such deportations on principle, and carried them out on an astounding scale. On an average, a fourth of every subjugated popula-

40.—CAPTIVES AND PLUNDER.

tion may be assumed to have been transferred either into Assyria proper or into remote provinces and dependencies of the empire, while their place was filled with Assyrian families or, at least, with people from kindred and loyal districts. That the object was to effect a general fusion of races, and obtain, in time, uniformly submissive and contented subjects, is shown by the fact that deportations of thousands of women are specially mentioned, who could not possibly be sent into the middle of Assyria except for the purpose of being there married and settled, and bringing up a generation which, from their mixed origin, should be free from very decided patriotic leanings—unless, indeed, to the country of their birth. Such deportations *en masse*, being a measure of policy, not of punishment, and one which generally took place after the full measure of chastisement had been meted out to a rebellious province or resisting city, do not appear to have been carried out in a spirit of wanton cruelty and humiliation. The sculptures of the second empire show us many scenes bearing on this strange accompaniment of war: we see women, with their children and household goods, riding on asses, or on chariots drawn by, probably, their own teams of ploughing oxen, the men walking indeed, but seldom fettered, the flocks and baggage carts following, the whole escorted and superintended, of course, by Assyrian warriors. Such processions are very different from those of prisoners led before the king after a battle or capture of a city, their feet in chains, their arms bound behind their backs at the elbows, their captors driving them on with uplifted stick or spear-shaft.

4. Another feature of the new policy inaugurated by Tiglath-Pileser II. is that the kings entrust many of their expeditions to experienced generals, whom we may well suppose to have been their own tried companions in arms, trained in all the branches of higher military tactics. Shalmaneser II., it is true, did not often take the field himself in the seven last years of his life, but sent out his general, whose name he frequently mentions with respect and praise. But it was not until nearly thirty years of unintermitting marching and fighting must have broken the old warrior's strength that he resigned his staff of command, while he himself sat down at Kalah to attend to his buildings and inscriptions. Now, however, the Turtan (general-in-chief) appears in the very beginning of the new reign, and henceforth comes to the front more and more frequently. The boundaries of the Empire, as they widened on all sides, were becoming more insecure, and if aggressive warfare was carried into the neighboring countries, it was often only as a more dignified, and, on the whole, safer and more profitable form of self-defence, the choice mostly being between invading and being invaded. Thus military expeditions had to be incessantly and vigorously pushed to so many points at once that the presence of the sovereign at all became out of the question, and they were compelled to concentrate their own personal efforts against those which were of most importance in the general scheme of their policy.

5. Now, in this scheme, by far the most essential item was the entire subjugation of the West—the vast region between the Euphrates and the Mediterranean, bounded on the north by the Taurus and Amanos ranges, and towards the south losing itself indefinitely in the sandy wastes which finally touch upon Arabia and Egypt. The immediate and material incentive of securing, in the shape of tribute and plunder, the immense wealth of that peerless cluster of ancient and highly cultured states, sweepingly designated as Syria, Phœnicia and Palestine, was equalled by the more statesmanlike desire of controlling the great commercial highroad so often referred to, while beyond Egypt opened a flattering vista of still further conquests and booty—which, however, may not yet have been distinctly contemplated at this period. Egypt herself, at all events, felt the danger, and, by an aggressive bearing, wholly out of keeping with her now rapidly waning power, angered the full-grown northern lion and probably hastened the very fate which she feebly labored to avert.

6. Like Shalmaneser II., Tiglath-Pileser first cleared the way for his Syrian campaigns by securing himself from attacks in the rear and on the flanks, and dealing out to his neighbors of Urartu, the Zagros and Chaldea enough punishment to keep them quiet at least for a few years. Babylonia was reduced to the condition of an avowedly vassal state, and the Assyrian king, for the first time since Tukulti-Nineb's temporary conquest, could again call himself by the ancient titles of " King of Shu-

mir and Accad" and "King of Kar-Dunyash"—titles which his successors retained to the end of the northern monarchy. The princes of Kaldu were subdued for awhile by a rapid and successful inroad, and by the execution of one of their number before his own city gates. Some Aramæan tribes, too, which had for some time back been settling along the Euphrates in the southern part of Babylonia and were inclined to be troublesome, were energetically put down, a certain number of families being transferred to other parts of the empire. In the East, the mountain tribes of the Zagros were made innocuous for some time to come by an invasion which penetrated further into the highlands than any preceding one, and even seems to have pierced through the sevenfold range into the country beyond, held by tribes of Medes. This campaign brought the Assyrian army as far as the foot of a high mountain which the monuments call BIKNI, which it has as yet proved impossible to identify with any degree of certainty. The conduct of this expedition, begun by the king himself, was made over to his Turtan, his personal presence being more needed in the North, where he now marched against the kingdom of Van, so dangerously increased in power and influence that it actually had organized a league of the—probably kindred—highland chieftains so often collectively spoken of as "Kings of Naïri," and even, it would appear, had secured the co-operation of some princes of Northern Syria, especially the important and wealthy city and principality of ARPAD. This Armenian campaign was so far successful that Tiglath-Pileser drove back the troops of the Urartian, pursued them into their fastnesses farther than any of his predecessors, and so effectually frightened minor kings that they obediently returned under the yoke, and the Alarodian coalition dispersed. But the royal capital by Lake Van was not taken yet, as Tiglath-Pileser could not spare the time just then for a long and difficult siege. So he contented himself with erecting "an image of his royalty" in view of the city gates— as a reminder and a warning.

7. These preliminary operations took up three years, and the results, though on the whole satisfactory, were not particularly brilliant, as nothing very decisive was accomplished in any direction. The next years the king devoted exclusively to his enterprise against the western countries, which required considerable perseverance, since the city of Arpad alone delayed him three years. When that siege was ended, things progressed more rapidly, but it was not till the fifth year of the expedition that the northern portion of Syria, *i. e.*, the entire valley of the Orontes, and the corresponding sea-coast, was virtually annexed to the Assyrian Empire, in token whereof great numbers of the inhabitants were transferred into some of the loyal Naïri districts, while Aramæans from Babylonia were brought to take their place. In the same year the other Syrian princes, whose hour had not struck yet, sent tribute and paid their court. We find on the list the kings of Damascus, of Karkhemish, of Hamath, Tyre, Gebal (Byblos), a queen of Arabia—probably

of some northern districts adjoining the Syrian desert—and, lastly, a familiar-sounding name: MINIHIMMI IR SAMIRINA, *i. e.*, MENAHEM OF THE CITY OF SAMARIA, the then reigning king of Israel. This Menahem, having obtained the throne by the not unusual means of murdering its occupant, had just come out of a civil war, and therefore did not feel very secure. So he bethought him of buying the protection of the conqueror, and gave him a thousand talents of silver, "that his hand might be with him to confirm the kingdom in his hand. And Menahem exacted the tribute of Israel, even of all the mighty men of wealth" (Second Kings, xv. 19 20. This is the place where Tiglath-Pileser is called Phul).

Tribute of Menahem of Israel, 738 B.C.

8. The hundred years which had elapsed between the submission of the usurper Jehu, the murderer of Omri's grandsons, and that of the other usurper, Menahem, had been a century of decline for both the Jewish kingdoms. That of Israel was the first to suffer. "In those days" (of Jehu), pithily sums up the biblical historian (Second Kings, x. 32), "Yahveh began to cut from Israel." Moab, after King Mesha's dearly-bought success in the war of deliverance (see p. 126), had again become a formidable neighbor and harassed them in the south-east; but their most ruthless foes were the kings of Damascus. Hazael and his son, BEN-HADAD III., gradually conquered and annexed almost the whole country east of the Jordan—the rich, hilly woodland and pasture lands of Gilead and Bashan. Of all the might which had enabled

Ahab to send so great a force into the field (see pp. 126-127), nothing was left but 50 horsemen, 10 chariots, and 10,000 footmen : " for the king of Syria destroyed them and made them like dust in the threshing" (Second Kings, xiii. 7). The same fate would have befallen Judah, but that the king bought off Hazael, when he already had "set his face to go up to Jerusalem : " he " took all the hallowed things that his fathers, kings of Judah, had dedicated, and his own hallowed things, and all the gold that was found in the treasures of the house of the Lord, and of the king's house, and sent it to Hazael, king of Syria; and he went away from Jerusalem" (Second Kings, xii. 18). But the fate from which the king of Judah had saved the sacred city at such heavy cost, he drew on it himself at the hands of the king of Israel, whom he unwisely and gratuitously provoked into a war which ended most disastrously for himself. " Judah was put to the worse before Israel, and they fled every man to his tent." The king of Judah himself was made captive ; the king of Israel entered Jerusalem by a breach made in the city wall, " and he took all the gold and silver, and all the vessels that were found in the house of the Lord and in the treasures of the king's house, the hostages also, and returned to Samaria" (Second Kings, xiv. 14). It strikes one as a little singular that there should have been so much to take, after we have just been told that *all* had been taken out of both temple and royal treasure-house to be given to the king of Syria. This only shows that one must be cautious in dealing with Oriental phraseology and not accept sweeping statements without mental reservations.

9. Those were dreary times for both Jewish states which, not content with the wars they had to support unceasingly against all their surrounding neighbors, could not keep the peace with each other, so great was their ever-increasing mutual hatred and jealousy. But Judah, at least, with the exception of an occasional family tragedy and family conspiracy, enjoyed some measure of internal security under the unchanging rule of the House of David, while Israel, founded by an adventurer, was fated from the first to be the prize of any hand bold enough to seize the crown, and at this period had finally plunged into a tangle of lawlessness and civil strife, to which there was only one possible end —rapid and inglorious dissolution. And indeed, scarcely had Menahem, soon after his abject submission, rather suddenly died and his son PEKAHIAH ascended the throne, when the latter was in his turn murdered by "PEKAH, his captain," son of Remaliah, who straightway made alliance with the new king of Syria, REZÎN, that they might jointly fall on Judah. The king who then reigned at Jerusalem was AHAZ, very young and newly come to power. His inexperience may have been an incentive to his enemies, who, moreover, had reason to consider him as being in the bad graces of the Assyrian conqueror, since the name of the king of Judah was not among those of the princes who did homage to him in 738. Yet the grandfather of Ahaz, AZARIAH (also called UZZIAH), is mentioned

in an inscription as having paid tribute some time during the long siege of Arpad, probably during the last year of his own reign. The absence of Judah from among the tribute-paying countries must, therefore, have been looked upon in the light of a revolt, and is the more significant, that its immediate neighbors, Edom, Moab, and Ammon, are also absent. This seems to point to some feeble attempt of Judah at a temporary defensive alliance with her hereditary and unrelenting foes. Such an attempt at independence at that time, under the very outstretched wings of the Assyrian lion, even as they "filled the breadth of the land," was sheer folly. The young king of Judah understood this, "and his heart was moved, and the heart of his people, as the trees of the forest are moved with the wind" (Isaiah, vii. 2). But the prophet spoke comfort to him in the name of Yahveh: "Be quiet; fear not, neither let thine heart be faint, because of these two tails of firebrands, for the fierce anger of Rezin of Syria and of the son of Remaliah, saying let us go up against Judah and vex it, and let us make a breach therein for us.... It shall not stand, neither shall it come to pass" (Isaiah, viii. 4). "Before the child" (who has just been born) "shall have knowledge to cry, My father and my mother, the riches of Damascus shall be carried away before the king of Assyria" (ix. 11-12). "The Lord will cut off from Israel, head and tail, palm-branch and rush in one day." So Ahaz took heart, and of many pressing evils chose the least, and averted the imminent harm, at least for the time being, by imploring the conqueror's assistance, for Judah was sore beset, not only by Israel and Syria in the north, but by Edom and the Philistines in the south. (See Second Chronicles, xxviii. 17 18.) "So Ahaz sent messengers to Tiglath-Pileser, king of Assyria, saying, I am thy servant and thy son: come up and save me out of the hand of the king of Syria, and out of the hand of the king of Israel, which rise up against me." Such a message would have been wasted breath, unless weighted with great gifts; so "Ahaz took the silver and gold* that was found in the house of the Lord, and in the treasures of the king's house, and sent it for a present to the king of Assyria. And the king of Assyria hearkened to him" (Second Kings, xv. 7 9).

10. We are not told where the messengers of Ahaz found Tiglath-Pileser. The last two years he had been away in the North and East, where disturbances in Urartu and the Zagros claimed his personal attention. Victorious as usual, he was, however, at liberty to turn his mind once more to the affairs of the West, which were shaping themselves very much to his liking. This expedition, which all but dealt Israel the long impending death-blow, is called in the annotated Eponym Canon "To Philistia," probably because the king did pass through the Jewish lands into those of the Philistines. Moreover, the description very well covers what we would mean by saying "To Palestine." Israel's resistance was

---

* Another version (Second Chronicles, xxviii. 21) says, "*a portion.*" This more moderate estimate must be the true one.

quickly broken. Pekah was assassinated, perhaps for having involved the country in this unequal struggle; perhaps for refusing to end it by submission. At any rate, the usurper who succeeded him, HOSHEA, formally acknowledged himself as the vassal of the king of Assyria, holding the throne at his pleasure and under him. Of this revolution, which surely took place spontaneously and only sought the conqueror's sanction when accomplished, the Assyrian claims all the credit: "PAKAHA (Pekah), their king, *I killed*," he says; "AUSI (Hoshea) *I placed* over them." In the same vaunting spirit he exaggerates the completeness of his conquest. "The distant land of Bit-Khumri . . . . *the whole of its inhabitants*, with their goods, I carried away to Asshur." The biblical historians (Second Kings, xv. 29) specify several cities and districts, making in all about half of Israel, adding, however, in perfect accordance with the inscriptions, "and he carried them captive to Assyria." There is another tribute-list for this year (734 B.C.), which includes all the kings so conspicuously absent from that of four years before—TAHUHAZI MÂT JAUDAÏ (Ahaz of Judah), those of Ammon, Moab and Edom, a document sufficiently eloquent in its bareness. The same list contains the names of the kings of Arvad, Ascalon and Gaza; Tyre is omitted this time, and not without reason, as we shall see.*

<small>Hoshea established king over Israel and tribute of Ahaz, king of Judah, 734 B.C.</small>

---

* This is one of the places where biblical chronology is hopelessly at variance with the dates given by the monuments and the Eponym Canon. The compiler of the Book of Kings says that Pekah reigned

11. Having delivered Ahaz from one of his foes, and left him to reign in Jerusalem as his son and servant, *i. e.*, his humble vassal, Tiglath-Pileser turned all his force against the other and more formidable one, Rezin of Syria. The inscription wherein the siege of Damascus (which lasted two years) and the taking of it are described is unfortunately so fearfully mutilated that very few whole sentences can be made out. There is enough, at all events, to show that the Syrian army was completely routed, chariots, infantry, cavalry and all; that Rezin, "to save his life, took to flight all alone, and entered his capital through the great gate;" that Tiglath-Pileser captured some of his captains alive and had them impaled, then "shut him in like a bird in a cage," destroyed the magnificent plantations of trees "not to be numbered," which surrounded the capital, "not leaving as much as a single tree." All this confirms and completes the simple statement in Second Kings (xv. 9): "And the king of Assyria went up against Damascus and took it, and carried the people of it captive to Kir (not identified) and slew Rezin."

---

twenty years. Now it has been seen that Menahem was still reigning in 738, and Pekah was put to death, and succeeded by Hoshea in 734. These dates, unequivocally established by the Canon (see Schrader's "Die Keilinschriften und das Alte Testament," 1883, pp. 251-258, and page 475), leave no room for dispute. But there is nothing astonishing in this, since the parallel dates given by the Bible historians themselves for the two kingdoms of Judah and Israel often disagree. Besides, as monuments, Canon, and Bible history entirely agree in the date of a most important event,—the fall of Samaria,—we have hol l of a principal landmark, and the mutual confirmation of the different sources can be pronounced amply satisfactory *on the whole*.

41.—ASSYRIAN SOLDIERS DESTROYING A PLANTATION.

"And King Ahaz went to Damascus to meet Tiglath-Pileser," further relates the Jewish annalist. Had we a completer and more uninjured set of this king's inscriptions, we should probably find that the Jewish monarch came not alone to "meet" face to face his terrible ally and master. It was becoming an accepted custom for vassal and friendly sovereigns, not only to send their tributes and gifts to any part of the empire where the king might be at the moment, or even into enemies' countries, but to gather at some important point where he might be stopping for a longer time, to do him personal homage. It is probable that such gatherings took place by royal appointment and invitation, not to say command, and that non-attendance would have been looked upon as a mortal offence and breach of allegiance and punished accordingly. What a pity we have no description of any of these princely convocations! They must have been festive occasions, celebrated with a splendor and display of which we would fain evoke a vivid picture before our minds' eye, and we may fancy that the grim and dreaded host would, if only out of vanity and policy, unbend to outward graciousness and entertain his not always willing guests right royally, even while making them feel the rod and yoke. That the guests, on their side, would not be behindhand with courtly demonstrations and dissembling lip-homage stands to reason, and we have an example in the flattery practised by King Ahaz of Judah, when he professed such admiration for the royal portable altar at which he saw Tiglath-Pileser sacrifice at Damascus, that he sent to the high-priest at Jerusalem "the fashion of the altar and the pattern of it, according to all the workmanship thereof," desiring him to order an exact copy of it and set it up in the house of Yahveh against his return, and to use it entirely, instead of the old brazen altar of Solomon, which was placed on one side for less important ministrations. And when he returned to Jerusalem and saw that all had been done according to his orders, he carried his imitation of Assyrian customs so far, that he "drew near unto the altar, and offered thereon. And he burnt his burnt-offering and his meal-offering, and poured his drink-offering, and sprinkled the blood of his peace-offerings upon the altar," although it was contrary to Jewish custom for the king to officiate himself.*

12. The contumacy of Tyre was neither forgotten nor condoned; but the king's presence was becoming necessary in other parts, and the West was in no condition to inspire much fear, so he left his Turtan to deal with the merchant city, and inflict on her an enormous fine, while he himself turned his steps once more to the South, for the Chaldean princes were vigorously pushing their aggressive policy against Babylonia, where they were bent on establishing a Chaldean monarchy; and not unsuccessfully, for already one of their number,

---

* As Max Duncker judiciously remarks: "No one can seriously mean to assert that Ahaz remodelled his own national worship and changed his god's altar in imitation of Rezin the arch foe's of both Judah and Assyria, who had but just been overthrown." ("Geschichte des Alterthums," 5th edit. vol. ii., p. 318, note.)

46.—STORMING A FORTRESS. (ASSYRIAN SOLDIERS WITH FIRE-BRANDS SETTING FIRE TO IT FROM THE BASE. FLAMES ISSUING FROM THE BATTLEMENTS.)

UKÎNZIR, (corrupted by the Greeks into CHINZIROS), was actually king of Babylon. It appears, therefore, that Tiglath-Pileser was received by the capital and the great Babylonian cities like a deliverer; his progress through the country was triumphal, and at each ancient shrine he paid the customary sacrifices to the ancestral gods. His expedition against the sea-side princes was, on the whole, successful. Energetic it certainly was. One of the rebellious princes was impaled before the gate of his own city, which was then razed to the ground. Ukinzir's principality, too, was laid waste, but his capital, SAPIYA, could not be taken, and was entered at last, not by force, but treaty, while Ukinzir continued to reign at Babylon, jointly with Tiglath-Pileser for the last four years of the latter's reign,—at least nominally; in reality he probably was his obedient vassal. At Sapiya the Assyrian held one of those royal levees which were becoming an institution, and which enabled the kings to number their servants and adherents, and test their loyalty by that primitive and fallacious test—the splendor of the presents they brought.

13. On this occasion the Assyrian received the voluntary submission of a very exalted and powerful personage, MARDUK-HABAL-IDDIN (usually called MERODACH-BALADAN, as his name is rendered in the Bible), the ruler of BÎT-YAKIN, the largest and wealthiest of the Chaldean principalities, commanding so large an extent of coast on the Gulf, and thereby affording such commercial advantages that the sons of the House of Yakin went by the flattering

designation, " Kings of the Sea," or " the Sea-coast." How important the Assyrian conqueror deemed this particular addition to the number of his vassals we can measure by the complacency and stress with which he records the occurrence. " Marduk-habal-iddin, son of Yakin, king of the sea-coast, from which to the kings, my fathers, formerly none came and kissed their feet,—terrible fear of Asshur, my lord, overwhelmed him and to Sapiya he came and kissed my feet; gold, the dust of his country, in abundance, cups of gold, instruments of gold, the product of the sea, . . . costly garments, gums, oxen, and sheep, his tribute, I received." Tiglath-Pileser had, indeed, reason to exult, judging by his lights. But to us, judging by the light of subsequent events, it is clear that the ambitious, crafty schemer curbed his proud neck to the humiliating act of homage only to gain time and mature his far-reaching plans. For of all the unfortunate princes who tendered their allegiance from helplessness or compulsion, surely none meant less to keep it; all bitter foes of Assyria as they were at heart, he was the only one in whom was danger, and the arrogant conqueror, whose foot perhaps scarcely refrained from spurning the princely form that prostrated itself in well-feigned self-abasement, might have shuddered in his seat of power could a prophetic flash have revealed to him that he had before him the man who, for fifty years to come, was to be the evil genius of Asshur, nay, one of the indirect causes of Asshur's fall, since he was to loosen and set in motion some of the stones that were to crush the northern kingdom's too-uplifted head. But it is probable that no foreboding or warning could at that moment have shaken "the stout heart of the king of Asshur," or dimmed "the glory of his high looks. For he hath said: By the strength of my hand I have done it, and by my wisdom; for I am prudent: and I have removed the bounds of the peoples, and have robbed their treasures, and I have brought down as a valiant man them that sit on thrones; and my hand hath found as a nest the riches of the peoples; and as one gathereth eggs that are forsaken, have I gathered all the earth: and there was none that moved the wing, or that opened the mouth or chirped" (Isaiah, x. 12-14).

14. Here ends the political and military career of the second Tiglath-Pileser. The year 730 is marked "In the land," *i.e.*, the king remained in Assyria. The two following years he seems to have gone again to Babylon, but on peaceful and even religious errands. The annotated Canon has this rather obscure note for both those years: "The king takes the hands of Bel." It is supposed to allude to some peculiarly solemn and festive sacrifices and ceremonies, in the course of which the king received the highest religious consecration. It would be most interesting to find out the exact meaning of the phrase, but it is very doubtful whether anything will turn up to enable us to do so. In 727 Tiglath-Pileser II. died. There seems to have been peace during the last three years of his reign, but a revolt just at the end.

15. He was succeeded by SHALMANESER IV. In

what manner, on what grounds, by what claims is utterly unknown. Whether he was his predecessor's son, as advanced by some scholars,* or an heir by a side branch, or merely an usurper, we have no means whatever of ascertaining. If the suggestion just made by an eminent scholar,† that this king and one who stands on the list of Babylon under the name of ILULAI are one and the same, just as Tiglath-Pileser and Phul are one, there would be great probability in favor of the first of these conjectures. Then it might be supposed that Phul had a son, Ilulai, who, on coming to the throne, changed his own private name to a royal one, in imitation of his father. But these are as yet nothing but conjectures. Strangely enough, we are not much better informed on any other point concerning this king, further than to have his existence duly attested by the Eponym Canon, and his short reign—five years—determined by the same document. He has left no monuments, or, more probably, none have as yet been found, and what we do know of his deeds we learn from foreign sources,—the Bible and a late Tyrian historian. For so much seems sure, that he occupied himself with only two important wars, one against Tyre and the other against Samaria.

16. It seems very startling to find another king engaged in conquering those same countries to which a warrior of Tiglath-Pileser's stamp had

---

* Ed. Meyer, C. P. Tiele, Geo. Rawlinson.
† C. P. Tiele, " Assyrisch Babylonische Geschichte."

dealt so many, and, it would seem, finally crushing blows. But the fact is, their resources were still great, and if the coalition of Ahab's and Shalmaneser II.'s time could have been enlarged and maintained they might have stood their ground to the end. But the hatred and jealousies between them were too inveterate for that, and the temptation to use the conqueror's might to compass each other's ruin too great to be resisted by races for whom politics were a question of purely local and selfish interests, with a short-sighted range narrowly limited to the present, and to whom patriotism was an unknown quantity. Still, when actually perishing, partial and short-lived alliances would still be brought about between the implacable rivals and foes. But, on the whole, theirs was the case of the bundle of sticks, which, being untied, fall apart and are easily broken individually, while the whole bundle would have been strong enough to withstand any effort. At this moment, however, a new actor had appeared on the stage and brought a revival of energy, brief and deceptive, it is true, but sufficient to stave off the final catastrophe yet a little while.

17. That actor was Egypt, so long inactive, so long out of sight; Egypt, whose long race was well-nigh done, whose sands were running very low, and who was never more to stand foremost in the place of honor among free and progressing nations. The long course of conquests in Asia, by which she avenged the thraldom she had endured under the rule of Asiatic invaders (see p. 26, ff.), had been

stopped by dissensions and intestine troubles at home. Originally welded together out of many small principalities, the monarchy of the Nile had gradually dissolved back into its component parts, and become divided among as many petty rulers as there were great cities, with their temples, colleges of priests and surrounding districts. These princes, more often than not, were all at war with each other and therefore exposed, exactly like the kings and cities of Syria, Palestine and Phœnicia, and for the same reasons, to the attacks of any neighbor or invader. But the danger this time did not come from Asia, where kings and peoples had enough to engage their whole powers and attention. There was, nearer home, a country and race which had to avenge many centuries of oppression and contempt. Ethiopia, the "Vile Kush" of the inscriptions in the times of Egypt's glory, saw her opportunity and took it. As the Alarodians of Urartu and Naïri had borrowed the culture of their most inveterate foes, the Assyrians, so the Kushites of Ethiopia had assimilated that of their hated masters and had become a match for them, not only in material strength, but also in intellectual and political attainments. Under able and ambitious leaders their progress was slow, but it ended in the subjugation of all the Egyptian principalities until the Ethiopian king, SHABAKA, could call himself, without boasting, king of Egypt also. He was a wise and moderate ruler, and governed the country with a strong and firm, yet also a mild hand. He left most of the petty princes in their places, but kept them in due subjection, and Egypt could rejoice, not only in a new era of material prosperity, but, to a certain extent, in a renewal of her political importance.

18. This king (the So or Sou of the Bible), no sooner had established himself on his double throne than he realized the impending danger threatened by the ever approaching Assyrian thunder-cloud. When all the intervening nations had been gathered, "like eggs that are forsaken," it was not likely that so rich a nest as Egypt should be overlooked. And now that even the Arabs, that movable but effective bulwark, had been subdued the intervening nations, were few indeed: the two Hebrew kingdoms and the cities of the sea-coast; and those few more than half undone, especially Israel. Therefore Shabaka at once manifested his readiness to support such of the still surviving states as had not yet lost all vital energy and force of resistance. But there he overrated his own powers. No single adversary could be a match for Asshur at this heyday of her greatness, and the time had not yet come when the iron-mailed giant with the feet of clay would collapse with its own weight. Naturally, all that still hoped against hope and still feebly writhed in the lion's paws clutched at this unexpected and, as they fondly fancied, still timely aid; but it proved to them a delusion and a snare, and the more clear-sighted among statesmen were not deceived. "Woe to them that go down to Egypt for help, and stay on horses," warns Isaiah the prophet and prime minister of Judah; "and trust in chariots because

they are many, and in horsemen because they are very strong. . . . Now the Egyptians are men, and not God; and their horses are flesh, and not spirit" (xxxi. 1-3).

19. Thus matters stood at the death of Tiglath-Pileser. Shabaka had seated himself in the throne of Egypt the year before. This coincidence favored, indeed suggested revolt. On which side the

43.—CITY AND PALACES. (SOLDIERS WITH BOOTY.)

overtures were made, we do not know. But very soon we find Tyre refusing tribute and preparing for the consequences. But what the proud queen of the seas was perhaps *not* prepared for, was to see her own sister-cities all along the coast join not in her support, but for her destruction. Whether from abject fear for themselves, or from a low and spiteful jealousy, they all arrayed themselves under Assyrian command and went to sea against Tyre with 60 ships and 8000 oarsmen. Tyre at that moment had only 12 ships to dispose of, and with this insufficient force held out for five years on her rocky islets, vigorously blockaded by sea by her own country-people, while the Assyrians placed military out-posts on the coast at the mouth of the river and at all the waterworks, to prevent any desperate sally for water. Fortunately, the besieged were able to procure water on the islands by digging cisterns and boring wells.

20. How great and general were the hopes raised by the death of Tiglath-Pileser we see from the warnings addressed by Isaiah to all the nations of Syria in turn. To Philistia he says: "Rejoice not, O Philistia, all of thee, because the rod that smote thee is broken; for out of the serpent's root shall come forth a basilisk and his fruit shall be a fiery flying serpent. . . . Howl, O gate! Cry, O city! Thou art melted away, O Philistia, all of thee! for there cometh a smoke out of the North. . . ." (xiv. 29-31). Israel also foolishly rejoiced, and fell to conspiring. When Shalmaneser, the Book of Kings tells us, first "came up" against Hoshea, the latter "became his servant and brought him presents." But soon after, the king of Assyria "found conspiracy in Hoshea; for he had sent messengers to So, king of Egypt, and offered no present to the king of Assyria, as he had done year by year; therefore the king of Assyria shut him up and bound him up in prison." This is the last we hear of the last independent king of Israel; whether he died in prison, or was slain, or lived in bondage, we do not

know. "Then the king of Assyria came up throughout the land, and went up to Samaria, and besieged it three years. . . ." (Second Kings, xvii. 4–5).

VIII.

THE PRIDE OF ASSHUR.—SARGON.

1. "IN the ninth year of Hoshea the king of Assyria took Samaria." These words immediately follow those with which the preceding chapter closes. Yet they had to be reserved for the beginning of a new chapter, for between the two lay—the beginning of a new reign, as the king of Assyria who "went up against Samaria" was not the same who took it. It was Shalmaneser IV. who began the siege and carried it on for three years,—whether personally or through his generals, we are nowhere told,—but it was Sargon who completed it. One of the first entries in Sargon's annals is this: "In the beginning of my reign I besieged, I took by the help of the god Shamash, who gives me victory over my enemies, the city of Samaria (*ir-Samirina*). 27,280 of its inhabitants I carried away. I took fifty chariots for my own royal share. I took them (the captives) to Assyria and put into their places people whom my hand had conquered. I set my officers and governors over them, and laid on them a tribute as on the Assyrians." * To what portions of the Assyrian

<small>Fall of Samaria and Accession of Sargon, 722 B.C.</small>

---

* Another inscription says, "As the former king."

44.—PORTRAIT OF SARGON. (KHORSABAD.)
(For another portrait of Sargon see "Story of Chaldea," ill. No. 64.)

empire the captives were transferred we are not informed, but the Book of Kings specifies some of them. There we find that the conqueror "carried Israel away into Assyria, and placed them in Halah, and in Habor the river of Gozan, and in the cities of the Medes." Habor is the river Khabour, and Gozan the portion of Mesopotamia watered by it. Halah is thought by some to stand for the city Kalah, and by others for an Eastern province not very clearly identified, while the general location of the "cities of the Medes" cannot be mistaken. What people were brought to Samaria the same book tells us, at least in part. They were, in the first place, people from Babel, Kutha, Sippar, then from Hamath, and from Avva (unidentified). The same passage (xvii. 24-33) further informs us that the newcomers were frightened at the lions which, it appears, abounded in their new quarters, having probably multiplied, unchecked, during the late disastrous times, and that, some of their own number having been devoured, they attributed the visitation to the anger of the god of the country, whom they therefore determined to serve along with their own gods, to pacify him, and they sent a message of that purport to the king. "Then the king of Assyria commanded, saying, 'Carry thither one of the priests whom ye brought from thence, and let him go and dwell there, and let him teach them the manner of the god of the land.'" This was done, and the result was a very mixed religion, judging from the simple statement: "They feared Yahveh, and served their own gods, after the manner of the nations from among whom they had been carried away . . . their children likewise, and their children's children, as did their fathers, so do they unto this day." The foreign nations represented in this manner in the land of Israel were many more than the Bible history mentions by name, and we are enabled to complete the list from the Assyrian monuments of the time. Sargon in his annals informs us that, in the seventh year of his reign he "made subject several remote Arabian tribes that dwelt in a land which no wise men and no sender of messengers knew, a land which had never paid tribute to the kings his fathers, and *the remnant of them he transported and settled in the city of Samaria.*" No wonder, then, that the later Jews of Jerusalem, who prided themselves on the purity of their race and worship, should have looked down on this strange medley of nations and gods, the "Samaritans," with the utter contempt and disgust which we repeatedly find reproved by Jesus in word and deed in the name of humanity and charity.

2. Who and what was Sargon? It is not improbable that he was the general who conducted the siege of Samaria, either under Shalmaneser IV. or in his absence, and that he had won the army's regard to an extent that enabled him to proclaim himself king on that monarch's death, in firm reliance on their countenance and support. There is nothing to prove that such was not the case. As to his rank and birth, he speaks of "the kings his fathers." But so did Tiglath-Pileser II., and the evidence is not considered conclusive in his case,

because he does not mention either his father or grandfather, as is the invariable custom of other kings. We notice the same omission in Sargon's documents. His name yields no indication one way or the other. It is the same as that of the ancient Sargon of Agadé, and he may have assumed it with the royal power. This name, in its original Semitic form, SHARRU-KÊNU, is translated "the established" king, or "the true, faithful" king. It is probable that he himself attached a moral significance to the name, besides the prestige of a glorious memory, for he repeatedly plays on the word *kênu* in his inscriptions, calling himself "the true," or "faithful (*kênu*) shepherd," and generally showing more sense of moral obligation towards his people than any of his predecessors.

3. Under the reign of this king Assyria maintains herself, outwardly, on the pinnacle to which the last two monarchs had raised her, and still further extends her dominion. We note this difference, however, that the wars are more than ever conducted on all the boundaries at once, and, except in the East, where the Assyrian arms are pushed far beyond the Zagros, they are not wars of conquest, but of defence and of repression. The Assyrian policy is that vigorously centralized despotism so characteristic of the Second Empire: rebellious cities and provinces, when conquered, are no longer left to native princes under the mere obligation of paying tribute, but placed under Assyrian governors, who are strictly controlled and directed from home, and only the remoter principalities are suffered to retain

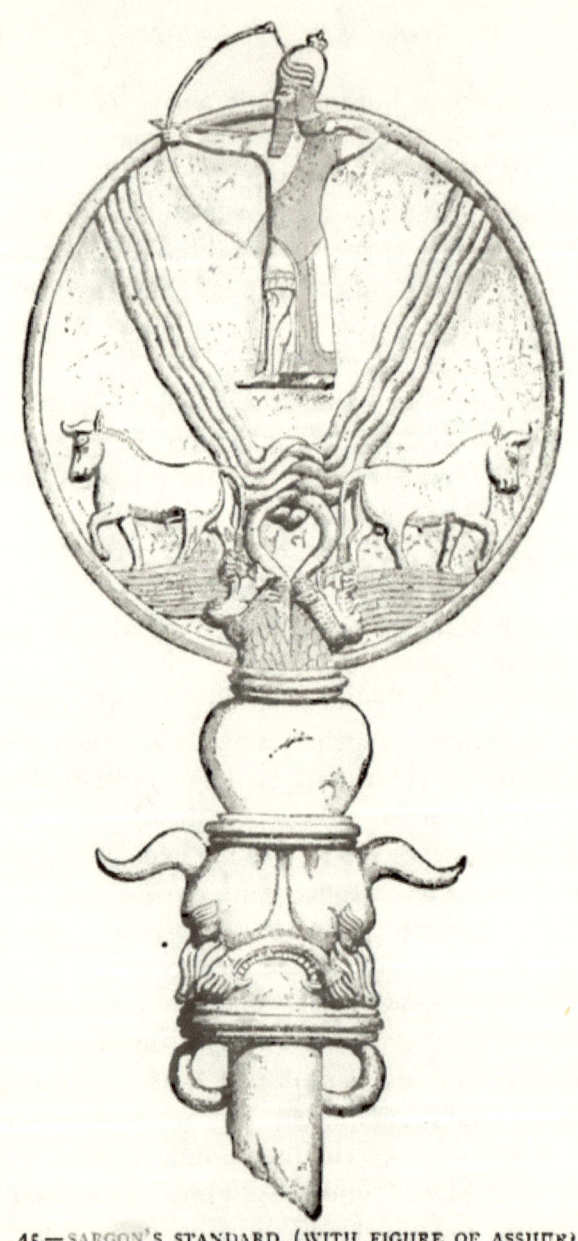

45.—SARGON'S STANDARD (WITH FIGURE OF ASSHUR)

some show of independence, under vassal rulers, either confirmed or imposed by the distant, yet ever present and watchful "Great King," "king of nations." The correspondence between the governors and the central power is brisk and minute in detail, as we see from numerous reports and despatches which have been found in the royal archives of Nineveh, all addressed directly to "my lord, the king." But not the completeness of this grinding machinery, not the fear of inevitable and ruthless slaughter, torture and captivity, nor the wholesale deportations which continued on an increasing scale, could keep the subject provinces quiet. Coalitions were constantly forming, more and more extensive, more and more desperately bent on breaking the yoke, and there must have been a lively undercurrent of adventure, of danger, of narrow escapes and mortal failures, consequent on the conspiring, exchanging of secret messages, sending of open embassies under plausible pretences, which were going on throughout the lands that ostensibly owned the Assyrian dominion, only biding their time to throw it off. That time had not come yet, not by a hundred years, and the issue of all these attempts was mostly calamitous, but their persistence under such discouragement and against such fearful odds was a sign of the times,—especially the fact that many of them took the hitherto unknown form of popular risings; the inscriptions of this reign repeatedly mention that the *people* of this or that city dethroned and slew—or "bound"—the tyrant "placed over" them by the Assyrian king, and set up a prince of their own choice who refused tribute and straightway prepared for war. To be sure, these upstart princes generally met a quick and deplorable end, and the rising was quelled in fire and blood; but to little ultimate purpose, for the nations had grown reckless with suffering, and, from standing sullenly at bay, were passing into that desperately aggressive stage in which neither worldly wisdom nor statesmanship find a hearing, and which ends either in total annihilation, or vengeance, full and triumphant—more often the latter.

4. Nowhere was the movement more general, hope more indestructible, than in the West. Egypt was the soul and secret mainspring of the resistance which no amount of punishment could crush, of the outbreaks which no common-sense dictates could stay. Shabaka, remarks one historian, was to the nations of Syria a messiah, always promising, always expected, never coming, because his strength was not equal to his will. Hezekiah, king of Judah, was the only monarch who abstained from conspiring and joining coalitions against the Assyrians, preserving a strictly neutral attitude, and most probably keeping him in good humor by presents, if not by actual tribute, in obedience to the urgent remonstrances of his spiritual and political adviser, the prophet Isaiah, who never ceased to inveigh against the powerlessness of Egypt and the foolishness of putting any reliance in her assistance. The prophet's views, thus far, accord perfectly with those of the Assyrian monarch himself, who speaks with a certain compassionate contempt

of the "embassies," which the princes of Syria were forever sending to the king of Egypt and Ethiopia, "a ruler who could not save them." It should be noted that, in the language of the monuments for these and the following troubled times, "sending embassies" is another word for "conspiring."

5. Under the influence of these deceptive hopes, Syria rose up in arms the very next year after Sargon's accession. All the old ground had to be gone over, all the old battles to be fought over again, and all the old familiar names confront us once more: Damascus, and Arpad, and Hamath, and even Samaria. For the people of Israel had not all been slain or transferred to distant lands; there was a remnant left, sufficient to keep up a strong leaven of national spirit. In the picturesque and bitter language of a prophet (Amos, iii. 12), "As the shepherd rescueth out of the mouth of the lion two legs or a piece of an ear, so shall the children of Israel be rescued that sit in Samaria;" and further (v. 3): "The city that went forth a thousand shall have an hundred left, and that which went forth an hundred shall have ten left;" or, according to Isaiah, the most poetic of prophets: "The remnant of the trees of his forest shall be few, that a child may write them. . . . Yet there shall be gleanings left therein as the shaking of an olive-tree, two or three berries in the top of the uppermost bough, four or five in the outmost branches of a fruitful tree." Hamath seems to have been the headquarters this time. IAUBID (or ILUBID), apparently an upstart usurper, had pos-

sessed himself of the crown, we are told, and incited the others, having occupied the strong city of Karkar. In that city,—the same before which was fought the great battle of the first Syrian league against Shalmaneser II. (see p. 181),—Iaubid was besieged, taken prisoner, and flayed alive by order of Sargon, who had the execution represented in full on one of the sculptures in his own palace. To keep so irrepressible a province under better control, 63,000 Assyrians were brought over to dwell in it, probably in the place of the slain and the prisoners carried into captivity. After that, short work was made of the rebellion, and the condition in which the country was left by the Assyrian army as it marched down to the frontier of Egypt, to meet Shabaka, the "sultan of Egypt"* (*Siltannu Muzri*), on his own ground, before he could come up to the rescue of his unfortunate clients and allies, could not be more aptly and vividly described than in the words of a Hebrew prophet: "That which the palmer-worm hath left hath the locust eaten; and that which the locust hath left hath the canker-worm eaten; and that which the canker-worm left hath the caterpillar eaten. . . . For a nation is come up upon my land, strong and without number; his teeth are the teeth of a lion, he hath the jaw teeth of a great lion. . . . The land is as the garden of Eden before them and behind them a desolate wilderness. . . ." (Joel, i. 4–6; ii. 3).

---

* Probably the earliest known use of the title.

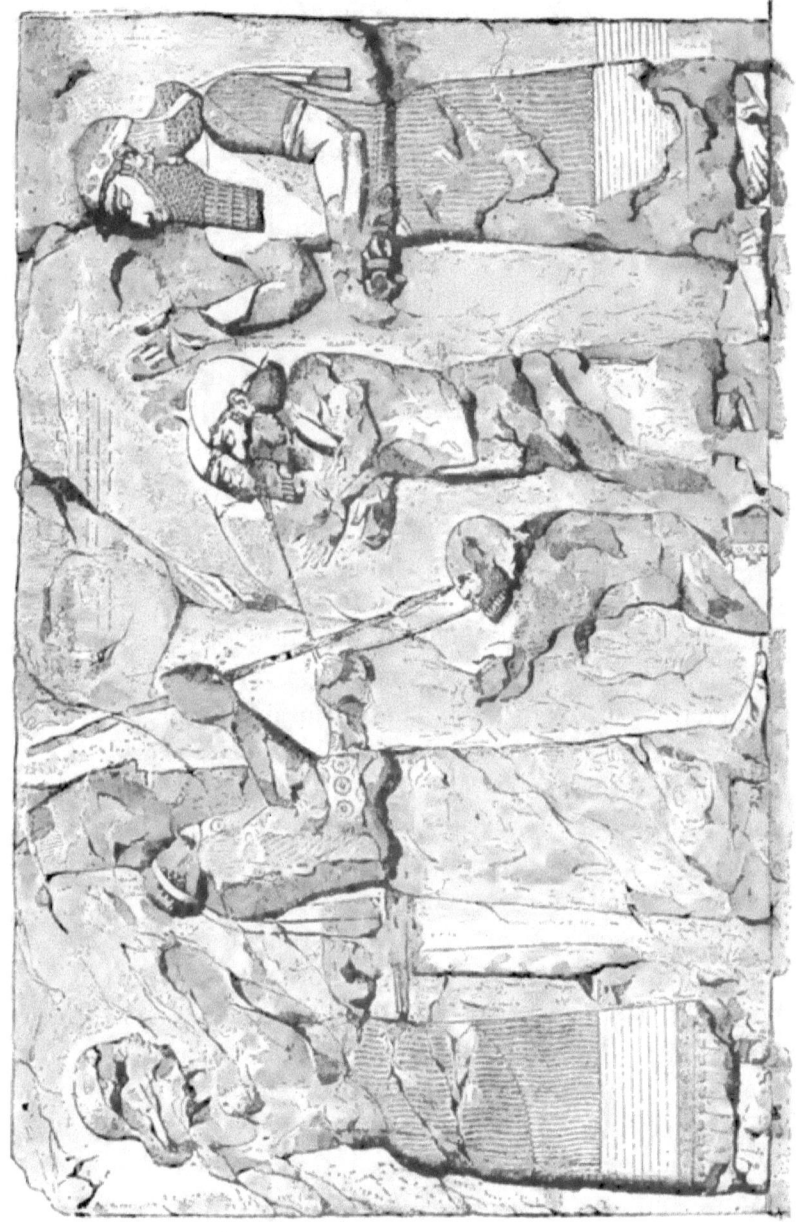

46.—SARGON PUTS OUT PRISONERS' EYES. (THE KING PASSED THROUGH THE LIPS WITH BRIDLE ATTACHED IS TO JERK THE HEAD INTO THE RIGHT POSITION AND KEEP IT FROM MOVING.)

6. The two greatest powers of the ancient world stood face to face for the first time in 720 B.C., before the city of RAPHIA, situated on the seacoast, south of Gaza, the king of which had joined Shabaka. The occasion was a memorable one and full of significance, but not auspicious for the older power, which had long been on the wane, while her younger antagonist was still in the prime of her might, and the flaws which were already at work preparing her rapid ruin, though plainly visible from our remote and elevated point of view, had not begun to impair her vigor perceptibly to contemporaries or to herself. So the struggle was an unequal one, and quickly ended in the complete defeat of Egypt, and the undignified flight of Shabaka, who left the field accompanied by one of his shepherds. Sargon did not, however, follow up his victory by an invasion, as Isaiah had expected, having too much on his hands at the time, and only partially fulfilled the prediction of the Hebrew seer and statesman, whose foresight was not to be fully justified till many years later.

7. It must have been about the same time that the long siege of Tyre, begun with that of Samaria, came to an end. The city does not seem to have been actually taken; it is only said to have been "pacified," and it is very probable that the besiegers, having grown as weary of the protracted and unexciting operation as the besieged, besides being needed elsewhere, offered terms,—heavy, no doubt, but preferable to utter destruction,—and that Tyre took the alternative and paid the random, buying what, after all, proved only a respite.

8. The next ten years were laborious ones for Sargon. A vast and powerfully organized conspiracy which embraced the entire North and Northwest—all the Naïri-lands, with several neighboring countries,—and of which URZA, king of Urartu, was the soul, broke out with the suddenness and violence of a long-latent conflagration, and kept the king and his generals so continually on the alert that he found no time for an expedition which he must have had much at heart, that against the Chaldean, Merodach-Baladan, of Bit-Yakin. This ambitious and crafty politician, after blinding Tiglath-Pileser's eyes by his voluntary homage at Sapiya (see p. 238), and thus securing a long interval of peace and safety, made good use of the ten years that followed. How he paved the way for his far-reaching designs we have no means of finding out ; but we may be sure that he spared neither promises nor intrigues, neither gifts nor diplomatic efforts, for in the very year of Sargon's accession he obtained his heart's desire, the crown of Babylon, and could rely on the support of, at least, one powerful ally, KHUM-BANIGASH, the king of Elam. It would seem, from the sequel of events, that he was not accepted enthusiastically, certainly not unanimously, by the Babylonians. Sargon calls him " Merodach-Baladan, the foe, the perverse, who, contrary to the will of the great gods, exercised sovereign power at Babylon," and it is easy to imagine the ancient capital and the other great cities divided into two parties, the Assyrian and the Chaldean. In his very first year, Sargon had managed to make a rapid

descent on the frontier of Elam and inflict a smart blow on the usurper's ally; but he was so pressed for time, his presence was so imperatively demanded in the West, to stop the progress of Shabaka by marching down on him, that he was not able to follow up this first advantage, and the chance he lost then he could not retrieve till fully eleven years later, Merodach-Baladan peacefully reigning at Babylon during that time, unchallenged and unopposed.

9. It was immediately after the battle of Raphia that the outbreak in the North took place. No ordinary local revolt, aiming merely at deliverance from the Assyrian supremacy and from tribute, but a mighty coalition, which several princes, hitherto friendly, were forced to join out of fear,—one of them having been massacred by his own subjects,—and which would most certainly have ended in a collective descent into Assyria, had not Sargon been so promptly on the scene himself, repressing, punishing and negotiating. Yet, though he was as usual victorious at the moment, filled the highlands with terror, and weeded them of a great number of their inhabitants, whom he sent to dwell in Hamath and other Syrian lands, his success was so far from complete that the conspiracy continued to spread, and the coalition to strengthen itself as soon as he was called away. Indeed, so many were the threads and so skilfully woven, that for several years he never could do his work of repression thoroughly, or advance very far into the Armenian mountains, because some distant member of the coalition would be sure to begin a stir at the critical moment and

operate a diversion, by drawing him away from the headquarters of the conspiracy—the kingdom of Urartu and its immediate neighbors. One year it is the king of Karkhemish who rebels—an unexpected occurrence, for he was an old man, and for thirty years at least had managed to keep on good terms with his terrible neighbor, and his name, all through the reigns of Tiglath-Pileser and Shalmaneser, continually stands conspicuous on the lists of princes who do homage and bring presents. It by no means follows, of course, that he could not, at the same time, have been secretly concerned in the underhand intrigues that were going on at all the Syrian courts, and, like so many others, biding his time. If so, he did not choose it well after all, for the angry lion made, so to speak, just a mouthful of him; he was dragged into captivity, with the greatest part of the people of his capital, while his palace and the city, that centre of traffic, that mart of the world's trade and emporium of wealth, yielded to the royal treasury of Nineveh an amount of booty fabulous even for those times of wholesale plunder. Assyrian colonists were then settled in Karkhemish, and an Assyrian governor sent to rule it. This was the final blow dealt to the Hittite nationality, which, after the fall of Damascus, had still throbbed in the city that held the great national sanctuary and the last national kings, as the blood retreats to the heart and courses through that stronghold to the very last.

10. Another year, the Median districts in the Zagros and on the eastern slope of that mountain range, never quite daunted or submissive, notwith-

standing the Assyrian forts that had been constructed at different times on commanding points and strongly garrisoned, revolted with an unanimity which could come only from previous agreement, and which made an expedition imperatively urgent. The measures which Sargon took, though marked with the usual ferocity, were certainly wise, and calculated to produce a lasting effect. The cities which he destroyed and from which the native population had been transferred to Assyria, he re-built, settling Assyrians in them, and for their protection he provided them with forts, thus creating a complete chain of Assyrian outposts, with characteristic Assyrian names, such as KAR-SHARRUKIN, KAR-NINÊB, etc. (*Kar*, "fortress.") Some of the rebel princes he had executed after the usual cruel manner (flaying alive was the fashion then, rather than impaling), others he pardoned and reinstated, even adding to their territory towns that had voluntarily submitted. Of such submissions there were many. On one occasion he mentions that of twenty-two "chiefs of towns," on another of twenty-eight, then of thirty-four. That these revolts stood in direct connection with the great conspiracy of which Urza held the threads was amply proved; and Sargon, in his dealings with the rebel princes, naturally proportioned his severity or mercifulness to the degree in which he found them implicated or stubborn.

11. It was not until the fifth year since the first outbreak in Naïri, and after several hurried and therefore only partially successful expeditions into the mountains of the North, that Sargon felt him-

self sufficiently strengthened and secure in the rear to plan a great and decisive invasion, not only of the already familiar highlands of Naïri, but the remote and far more inaccessible fastnesses of Urartu itself. By this time Urza found himself well-nigh alone, his allies having been successively detached or cut off, like the limbs of a tree that is to be felled. One of these, however, was still left him, a friend, staunch to share an inevitable fate. This was his nearest neighbor, URZANA, king of MUZAZIR, a country which has not yet been fully identified, and is therefore not to be found on maps, but is thought to have been the next to Urartu in a westerly direction, and to the north of Lake Van. Muzazir seems to have been, as much as Urartu itself, the centre and core of the Alarodian nationality; perhaps more, since it was the capital of Muzazir, which held the chief national sanctuary, that of HALDI, the Alarodians' "great god," the father and chief of the numerous lesser deities, who, like those of their kindred Hittite and Canaanitic races, were probably nothing more than local names and forms of the one deity, as worshipped in the different districts and cities of the race. (See p. 107.) Even after Sargon had "killed quantities without number, people of Urza, and 250 persons of his royal race," and captured all his cavalry,—after Urza himself had fled into the mountains, trusting to the fleetness of his mare to save his life, Urzana still "refused the protection of Asshur." Perhaps he counted on the ruggedness of his country as a last and efficient safeguard against an enemy already tired and partly satiated with slaughter and plunder. Sargon himself calls the country a land of "inaccessible mountains impassable for the horses," and mentions that he "recommended himself to the gods, his helpers," as he started on the venture with a picked corps. When Urzana found that Sargon was actually upon him, he suddenly lost heart, "escaped like a bird and went to the high mountains," *i. e.*, into the passes and caves where no pursuit could follow, where no track or path could betray his hiding-places. Sargon now, probably unresisted, "took the town of Muzazir," seized on all that belonged to Urzana— his wives, his sons, his servants, cattle and treasure of all kinds, and at last "took with him the god Haldi" and other divinities, "and their holy vessels in great numbers." Urza had "for five months wandered about alone in the mountains," going from heights to valleys, waiting and watching for news, of a certainty, more hungrily than even for food. And when the news came they broke his heart. The situation is so highly tragical that even the dry statement in the Assyrian official annals invests it with a great dignity and pathos. "Urza heard the fall of Muzazir, the capture of his god, Haldi. He despaired on account of the victories of Asshur, and with his own hand cut off his life. . . ." It would seem that here was an end of Urartu and Naïri. But nothing can equal the power of rebound which all those old nations seem to have possessed. A very few years later we already find a new king of Urartu brewing mischief in the old way, among his neighbors, and when Sargon's successor dies, assassinated by two of his own sons, it is to Urartu the murderers fly, certain to find there shelter and a friendly reception.

12. The next three years passed in petty warfare, with the object now of punishing several old allies of Urza, some of them on very remote boundaries, as far as Cilicia, now of settling a family quarrel in some loyal vassal country, where two claimants for the throne would appeal to the arbitration of the great king, or one would apply to him for armed assistance,—an occurrence which became quite frequent in this and the following reigns,—or, lastly, for the more important purpose of supporting or avenging a friendly sovereign, whom his own people had risen to deprive of crown or life in hatred of his servility. These popular risings, as before noted, were an ominous sign of the times. It was an errand of this kind which took Sargon once more into Media, this time not into the usual mountain districts, but into a flourishing and fertile country of hills and pastures and plains, a part of what was, later, Media proper—the ELLIP of the monuments. The king of this country, an aged man of the name of DALTA, had at one time been persuaded to join the rebel Median provinces, but had very soon prudently withdrawn from the dangerous game and won Sargon's regard by the steadfastness with which he kept his allegiance. "Dalta of Ellip," he tells us expressly, "was subject to me, and devoted to the worship of Asshur. Five of his towns revolted and no longer recognized his dominion.

I came to his aid, I besieged and occupied these towns, I carried the men and their goods away into Assyria, with numberless horses." "I gladdened the heart of Dalta," we are told by another text, "and re-established tranquillity in his country." On this occasion Sargon pacified several more districts which either had rebelled or been infected by wandering Median tribes from the eastern steppes, and received the submission of as many as forty-five "chiefs" of Median towns, who sent several thousands of horses, and "asses and sheep an innumerable quantity."

13. Not very different was the occasion which drew Sargon's army once more and for the last time to the shores of the Western Sea. The people of Ashdod, the Philistine city, had risen, put to death the king who had been enthroned by the Assyrian and submissively clung to his protection, and placed in his stead a man of their own choice, a certain YAMAN (or YAVAN), "not heir to the throne." They had prepared for defence, fortified the city, enclosed with a deep moat or ditch; supplied it with water by "bringing the springs of the mountains." The people of Philistia, Judah, Edom and Moab "were speaking treason. The people and their evil chiefs, to fight against me, unto Pharaoh, the king of Egypt, a monarch who could not save them, their presents carried and besought his alliance."* Yet with all these preparations, military

---

* Cylinder discovered and translated by Geo. Smith, in "Assyrian Discoveries," pp. 290 ff.

and diplomatic, such was the terror which then attended the Assyrian name, that on the mere report of the army's approach, the upstart king fled to the borders of Ethiopia,—" and no trace of him was seen,"—leaving " his gods, his wife and sons, the treasures, possessions and precious things of his palace, together with the inhabitants of the country to be carried into captivity." The cities, however, according to Sargon's invariable practice, were rebuilt and filled with captives from the East, who were made " the same as Assyrians." As to the help from Egypt, it never came, any more than it had come to Samaria. Indeed, the king of Ethiopia (and Egypt, since the Ethiopian dynasty was still reigning [*]) threw himself on the Assyrian's mercy, bound Yaman in iron chains and delivered him. By this act of arrant treachery, this breach of trust and hospitality, a further respite was gained for Egypt.

14. It appears that the king did not lead this expedition in person, although he speaks of it in the first person in his inscriptions. The prophet Isaiah expressly says that the " Tartan came unto Ashdod when Sargon, the king of Assyria, sent him, and he fought against it and took it " (xx. 1). It is difficult to find out from the monuments every time the Assyrian kings sent generals to conduct a campaign, because they mostly relate the course of it in their own name and take the credit to them-

---

[*] Such is the opinion of E. Schrader; but some other scholars differ from him and think the country named here is not Ethiopia. This is, however, one of those open points, a discussion of which would ill suit a popular narrative.

selves; yet it is certain that Sargon must have spent some of his time in his own kingdom, for he was a sovereign who attended much and wisely to affairs at home; and besides, he found a special attraction in a project and occupation which he had greatly at heart, and of which more anon.

15. There was nothing now any longer to delay the grand closing scene of this stupendous reign: the struggle for Babylon. Twelve years the Chaldean had sat on the throne of the great Southern capital in defiance of Sargon, who, after inflicting a passing chastisement on his ally and supporter, the king of Elam, had been forced to leave him unmolested, and even in a way to acknowledge him, since he repeatedly calls him "king of Babylon." Of course, however, the usurper's insolent success was a thorn in his flesh, and a sore in his eye, and the longer he was compelled to treasure up his revenge, the more terrible it would descend when once he could give his undivided attention to a war which he meant to be crushing and deadly. One thing he found time to attend to even in the midst of the manifold occupations with which those twelve years were crowded. He took care to keep on excellent terms with the priesthood of Babylon and the other great temple-cities,—that wealthy and influential class being at the head of the discontented party, and stimulated their loyalty to Assyria and their hatred to the Chaldean ruler, on whom they looked in the light of a foreigner and intruder, by frequent and great gifts to the different temples, duly recorded in his inscriptions. Merodach-Bala-

dan, on his side, well knew that the day of reckoning must come, and prepared against it, by using all the resources at his command, with great foresight and activity. In the first place, was he not the "king of the sea?" "He had established his dwelling amidst the Sea of the Rising Sun; he trusted in the sea and the retreat of the marshes." This alludes to his hereditary principality of Bit-Yakin, and the marshy tract by the mouths of the great rivers (which were still separate at that time), extending all the way to Elam, and affording him very secret means of communication and flight in case of need. But more than all he trusted to foreign alliances and diplomatic negotiations. The close connection which he had kept up with the king of Elam, SUTRUK-NAN-KHUNDI,—the successor of his former friend, Khumbanigash,—was felt to be insufficient, and Sargon complains that "against the will of the gods of Babylon, the city of Bel who judges the gods," Merodach-Baladan, "the deceiver, the wicked," "had excited all the nomadic tribes of the desert against him," as well as all the countries of Shumir and Accad, and for twelve years had been "sending out embassies." Now we know with what object "embassies were sent" in those days. (See p. 74.)

16. Of one such embassy we find a detailed and life-like account in an unexpected quarter—in the Hebrew Book of Kings. For it seems that Merodach-Baladan, knowing that the king of Judah, Hezekiah, had so far kept a strict neutrality, which he did not break even when the sister-kingdom perished miserably under his eyes, concluded that

the Hebrew monarch would be a useful ally to secure, since his resources, husbanded during a long peace, must amount to something considerable, and if he and the few other unannexed Syrian States could only be brought to act once more in concert, they might, between them, even yet make trouble for Sargon, when he should be engaged in the marshes by the Gulf. Now it so happened that Hezekiah had been ill almost unto death. He had set his house in order, not expecting to live, and his recovery appeared so wonderful as to be considered miraculous. The fame of it spread through all the lands; as well as that of his great wealth and prosperity. The Hebrew Book of Chronicles informs us that he "had exceeding much riches and honor; and he provided him treasures for silver, and for gold, and for precious stones, and for spices, and for shields, and for all manner of goodly vessels; storehouses also for the increase of corn and oil, and stalls for all manner of beasts, and flocks in folds. Moreover, he provided him cities and possessions of flocks and herds in abundance, for God had given him very much substance." Such rumors must have been very tantalizing to one in so great need of treasure and support as Merodach-Baladan, and he determined to find out just how much truth there was in them. The illness and marvellous recovery of Hezekiah supplied him with an opportunity and a plausible pretext for the open sending of "an embassy." So he sent letters and a present to Hezekiah.

17. We can well imagine the stately reception of

the ambassadors, and the great flourishes of Oriental courtesy with which they discharged their ostensible mission. That the conference soon touched on other things, and that the wily Chaldeans began to draw out the Jewish monarch by flattering his vanity, we are left to infer from the statement immediately following: "And Hezekiah hearkened unto them, and showed them all the house of his precious things, the silver, and the gold, and the spices, and the precious oil, and the house of his armor, and all that was found in his treasures; there was nothing in his house, nor in all his dominion, that Hezekiah showed them not." The good king evidently had somewhat lost his head in his pride and self-complacency, and acted on impulse without the advice or even knowledge of his wisest councillor, for we are next told that, "Then came Isaiah the prophet unto King Hezekiah, and said unto him, What said these men? and from whence came they unto thee? And Hezekiah said, They are come from a far country, even from Babylon." This curt and anything but candid answer still further aroused, or rather confirmed the suspicions of the prophet-minister, who then asked the king point-blank: "What have they seen in thine house?" Thus taken directly to task, Hezekiah defiantly told the whole truth: "All that is in mine house have they seen; there is nothing among my treasures that I have not showed them." Then Isaiah was very wroth, for he knew that a great harm had been done, since accounts of the embassy, and the treasures and the secret conferences, were sure to reach the ear of the king of

Assyria, whose spies and agents were at all the allied or vassal courts. And the prophet, in no gentle or measured terms, told the king what the consequences of his folly would be at a not very distant future time: "Hear the word of Yahveh: Behold, the days come that all that is in thine house, and that which thy fathers have laid up in store unto this day, shall be carried to Babylon." And he added that "even the king's sons should be taken away and become servants in the palace of the king of Babylon." By this time Hezekiah had become conscious of his blunder, and his reply to this terrible threat shows some shamefacedness, not untinged with sullenness: "Good is the word of Yahveh which thou hast spoken. Is it not so, if peace and truth shall be in *my* days?" If Judah really was implicated, together with Edom and Moab, in the rising of Ashdod, as we are given to understand on Geo. Smith's cylinder (see p. 36), it was perhaps in consequence of this "embassy." No serious consequences, however, seem to have come of it, at all events until the next reign.

18. The moment Sargon was secure and disengaged on all sides, Merodach-Baladan knew his time had come, and bravely opened hostilities by refusing to send tribute. Sargon, who throughout this campaign elaborately acts the part of champion to the gods of Babylonia and deliverer of the great Southern capital and temple-cities, solemnly prefaces his narrative with the announcement that Marduk himself, the great god of Babylon—(it is noteworthy that Asshur is not mentioned on this occasion, nor

any of the special gods of Assyria)—chose him among all the kings as his avenger, "elevated his head in the land of Shumir and Accad, and augmented his forces, in order to make him prevail against the Chaldeans, a people rebellious and perverse." He knew that he had to do with no despicable foe. Yet in the conflict which now began, the Chaldeans were, from the first, not triumphant. Sargon displayed consummate generalship, marching down with an army divided into two corps, of which he commanded one himself. The fortresses which protected Babylonia from the north yielded to the king's advance, and the nomadic Aramæan tribes, as well as some Babylonian ones, who had been detailed to the north as a sort of light vanguard to receive and detain the enemy, having been beaten, at once dispersed. The other army corps, meanwhile, operating east of the Tigris, was harassing Elam, taking from it fortresses and whole districts, not to speak of captives, cattle and other plunder, and preventing the junction between the Elamite and Chaldean forces. Thus Sargon, cautiously but steadily advancing, crossed the Euphrates and took up his headquarters in one of the Chaldean cities.

19. Merodach-Baladan did not wait for him in Babylon. In the hope that he might even yet obtain the necessary support from Elam, if he went over personally, he left the capital "in the nighttime, like an owl," and reached Elam, by a route which he succeeded in keeping secret. He found Sutruk-Nankhundi, who had fled "into the far mountains to save his life," unwilling to engage any

deeper in so risky a struggle. In vain Merodach-Baladan offered such valuable presents as he could at the moment dispose of: his throne, his sceptre, his royal parasol, all of pure silver, " a considerable weight,"—the Elamite was deaf to arguments and bribes. Then the Chaldean, in his anger, took by violence and drove away as much cattle as he could lay hands on, and returned by the same secret ways by which he had come—not to Babylon, but to his own capital by the sea, DUR YAKIN, which he proceeded to prepare for a last and desperate stand.

20. For Babylon was no longer open to him. No sooner had he left in that abrupt and undignified manner, than a solemn and worshipful delegation from that city and its great suburb, Borsip, composed of high dignitaries and officers, and also " learned men of books,"—doubtless priests,—went forth to seek Sargon at his headquarters, bearing with them images of the two cities' tutelary deities, Bel and Nebo, with their consorts, and to entreat him to take possession of the deserted capital, which he immediately did, and not only offered expiatory sacrifices, but during the interval of calm which followed, was allowed to perform that mysterious and hallowing ceremony which is described as " taking the hands of Bel." This was the work of the first year's campaign.

21. Merodach-Baladan, in the mean time, was still in full possession of his own principality, and had intrenched himself in his capital of Dur-Yakin, whither he had transported " the gods living in " several other cities, to save them from capture. He also had

forced a contribution from Ur, Larsam and other Babylonian cities, and, it would appear, had carried away their gods, too, but not in a friendly spirit. He had surrounded the city with a deep and wide moat, which he had filled with water from the Euphrates by means of trenches dug for the purpose, and which, after providing the moat with a dam, he cut off. Nothing had been neglected; yet such was the generalship of Sargon, the consummate skill and bravery of his soldiers, and such also the prestige of invincibility which attended on his name, that Dur-Yakin fell at once, at the first onslaught. Merodach-Baladan fled into the citadel, leaving his own tent, with all its royal belongings, to the conqueror; the city was taken, his palace utterly despoiled of "gold and silver, and all that he possessed, the contents of his palace, whatever it was, with considerable booty from the town." In one inscription we are told that not only his wife, his sons and daughters were made prisoners, but Merodach-Baladan himself. Another merely says: "And this Merodach-Baladan recognizing his own weakness, was terrified; the immense fear of my royalty overwhelmed him; he left his sceptre and his throne; in the presence of my ambassador he kissed the earth; he abandoned his castles, fled, and his trace was no more seen." This account must be the more correct, or else he must have been very poorly guarded for a captive of so much importance, since it is a fact that he escaped and vanished from the scene,—for a time, having by no means thrown up the game, as will appear.

22. As for the city of Dur-Yakin, it was razed to the

ground, or rather, in the literal language of the inscriptions, made a heap of. There were in it a certain number of people from Sippar, Nipur and Babylon, who had probably been brought there and detained against their will. These Sargon sent back to their respective cities, in honor and peace, and "watched over them," restoring to their cities certain lands which had been taken from them years before by some nomadic tribes, now auxiliaries of Merodach-Baladan, and famous for their skill in archery. The nomadic tribes, Sargon tells us, he replaced under his yoke, and restored the forgotten land boundaries. To complete the redress of grievances and wrongs, he restored to the different cities the gods that had been carried out of them, and revived the laws and observances which had been neglected. Having done all these things, he returned to Babylon, where he was rapturously received, and delighted the priesthood's hearts by his lavish bounties to the great temples.

23. A great prestige must have attached to the name of Sargon, if we judge from the ease with which he triumphed over formidable obstacles; from the feebleness of the resistance he encountered where preparation had been made for a desperate stand; and especially from the terror his fame inspired in remote countries, as shown by the voluntary submissions he received. Of these, none seems to have flattered his vanity more than an embassy from seven kings, ruling small principalities in the Island of Cyprus (probably originally Phœnician colonies). This island he calls YATNAN, and with

some exaggeration describes it as situated " at a distance of seven days' navigation, in the midst of the Sea of the Setting Sun." As he adds that the very names of these countries had been unknown to the kings his fathers from the remotest times, this little blunder may be due, not so much to love of boasting as to pardonable ignorance. Anyhow, it is with great complacency that he tells how those seven kings, after the news of his great deeds in Syria, and the humiliation of the king of Chaldea, " which they heard far away," " subdued their pride and humbled themselves," and " presented themselves before him in Babylon, and brought—(more probably sent)—gold, silver, utensils, ebony, sandal-wood and the manufactures of their country, and kissed his feet." He doubtless received these advances with becoming graciousness, and, in return for the gifts they brought, gave the ambassadors a marble stele with a full-length sculptured portrait of himself, and a short inscription commemorating his principal deeds. This stele was dutifully set up in one of the cities of Cyprus, for there it was found in a fine state of preservation, and is now one of the ornaments of the Museum in Berlin.

24. A short time before, Sargon had received in the same manner the gifts and homage of a king of DILMUN, an island in the Persian Gulf, now included in the lowlands of the coast, and also that of certain allies of the Armenian Urza in the mountains of the North-west who had given much trouble to his governors, and who now at last threw up the game as hopeless, and sent their submission all the way to

the royal camp, "by the shore of the Eastern Sea" (the Persian Gulf). Here, in reality, ends the record of Sargon's personal military career. True, the peace was broken twice more during his reign, once by a slight disturbance in Urartu, where Urza's successor already began to stir, and once by a short war with Elam; but the king left the command to his generals, having himself retired to Assyria. This last conflict was caused by a disputed succession. Dalta, the king of Ellip, had been, while he lived, devoted to the rule of Asshur. But "the infirmities of age came, and he walked on the path of death." Then his two sons, by different wives, "each claimed the vacant throne of his royalty, the country and the taxes, and they fought a battle." One of them "applied to Sutruk-Nankhundi, king of Elam, to support his claims, giving to him pledges for his alliance." The other brother, on his side, implored Sargon to uphold his claim, promising allegiance. No less than seven Assyrian generals were sent to his assistance, and of course the Elamite and his friend were routed.

25. Now at length Sargon had leisure to devote himself to a peaceful and artistic task which he had for years been planning with great love, and of late begun to put into execution, giving to it his personal attention, at odd moments, and all the time he could spare from an Assyrian monarch's everlasting round of military duties. This task was the construction of a new royal residence and city entirely separate from the former capitals. Nineveh had long been neglected, Kalah having been the

47.—THE MOUND OF KHORSABAD.

favorite residence of the kings ever since Asshur-na-zirpal had rebuilt and embellished it. (See p. 164.) The new palace and city were called by the builder's name, DUR-SHARRUKIN—"the city of Sargon." It is this palace which was entombed in the mound of Khorsabad, first excavated by Botta in 1842.* The history of its construction is most interesting, and will be best given in the words of Sargon himself, who tells it at great length in two inscriptions, that on the bulls and that on a foundation cylinder, and in as solemn though more concise a form in both his great historical inscriptions. In fact, the monumental literature of the lower empire is so very superior to the documents of the older period that it is a pleasure to reproduce it, and the story of this entire last century of Assyria gains in interest and vividness in proportion as it is told in the quaint, impressive, and often picturesque language of the texts.

26. "Day and night I planned to build that city," Sargon informs us, "to erect dwellings for the great gods, and palaces, the dwelling of my royalty, and I gave the order to begin the work." The site chosen was that of an exceedingly ancient city at the foot of a mountain named MUZRI, some distance above Nineveh,—a city which had been uninhabited and in ruins from the oldest times, its canal having been suffered to get choked up and go dry. The work was begun probably in 712, and

---

* See "Story of Chaldea," pp. 14–17.

48.—SARGON'S PALACE AT KHORSABAD. (RESTORATION BY V. PLACE.)

it is very probably in order to be on the spot and superintend it that Sargon entrusted the expedition against Ashdod to his Turtan (see p. 267). He began by planting around the future city a vast park, in imitation of the woodland scenery of the Amanos Mountains; he planted it densely with "every species of timber that grows in the land of Khatti and every kind of mountain herbs." No

49.—WALL AND GATE OF DUR-SHARRUKIN, AS CLEARED BY THE EXCAVATIONS.

suspicion of violence or evil-dealing was to stain the fair beginnings of the new city and endanger its prosperity by drawing down on it the disfavor of the great gods, who were to be invited to take up their abode in it. Like David and Omri, he bought at a just price the hill he had chosen. Alluding to one of the meanings of his name (see p. 252) Sargon declares: "In accordance with the name I bear, and which the gods gave me that I might be the guardian of right and justice, govern the powerless,

not harm the weak,* I paid the price for the land for the city, after the tablets appraising its value, to the owners thereof; and in order to do no wrong, I gave to those who did not wish to take money for their land, field for field, wherever they chose. . . ."
"The pious utterance of my lips to bless it pleased the exalted prophets, my masters, and to build the city, and dig the canal, they gave the command." Not only the act of laying the foundation, but even the fabrication of the bricks, the heaping up of the platform proceeded under the consecration of prayer, sacrifice, uplifting of hands and pouring out of drink-offerings, on particularly festive and holy days, in months sacred to appropriate divinities. This entire passage is brimful of mythological points, and allusions to religious observances, which it would be highly interesting to elucidate completely, but unfortunately the material bearing on these subjects is as yet insufficient.

27. The first buildings that rose were temples to most of the great gods. Then the palace " of ivory, of the wood of the palm, the cedar, the cypress" and other precious timber; with " a vestibule after the manner of Hittite palaces;" with doors of palm and cypress wood overlaid with brilliant bronze (probably like those of Balawat, see p. 192). The city, of which nothing could be found but traces

---

* This passage rather goes against the theory that Sargon chose his name himself when he became king; for, had he done so, he could hardly have said that the gods gave it him. On the other hand, we find here some confirmation of the view that he drew a lofty moral from that name. (See p. 252.)

of well-paved streets, had eight gates, named for
the principal gods: two to the east, for Shamash
and Ramán; two to the north, for Bel and Belit;
two to the west, for Anu and Ishtar; two to the
south, for Êa, and the "Queen of the gods." The
walls were named for Asshur and the ramparts

50.—GATEWAY AT DUR-SHARRUKIN (RESTORED).

for Ninêb. These gates must have been sumptu-
ous beyond words, guarded by their symmetri-
cal pairs of colossal winged bulls, of placid and majestic mien, and set in the panelled wall, with the
same wonderfully effective monsters striding in pro-
file, on both sides of the gigantic figure of Izdubar
and the Lion. (See Nos. 51 and 52.) A great bless-
ing is specially called down on them in the closing
invocation: "May Asshur bless this city, and this

palace! May he invest these constructions with an eternal brightness! May he grant that they shall be inhabited until the remotest days! May the sculptured bull, the guarding spirit, stand forever before his face! May he keep watch here night and day, and may his feet never move from this threshold!"

28. It would take an entire chapter, and that a long one, to do justice to all the beauties of that marvellous construction, Sargon's palace, the most thoroughly studied and described, because the best preserved of the Assyrian ruins. Not a detail but was of rare workmanship and exquisite finish; but want of room limits us to only a few illustrating specimens. (Nos. 53–57.) Then the sculptures! the quantity of them, the richness, the variety! Not a phase of the royal builder's life but is amply illustrated in them; not a peculiarity in the countries he warred against but is faithfully noted and portrayed. And lastly—the mass of them! That alone would be imposing, even without their artistic worth. Twenty-four pair of colossal bulls in high-relief on the outside walls, and at least two miles of sculptured slabs along the inner walls of the halls! "I am aware," says one of the leading explorers, "how peculiar it must appear to value works of art by the weight and yard, but this computation is not meant to give an idea of the artistic value of the sculptures, only of the labor expended on them." When we further realize that the entire work, from the construction of the platform to the ornamentation of the walls with slabs,—which, as we

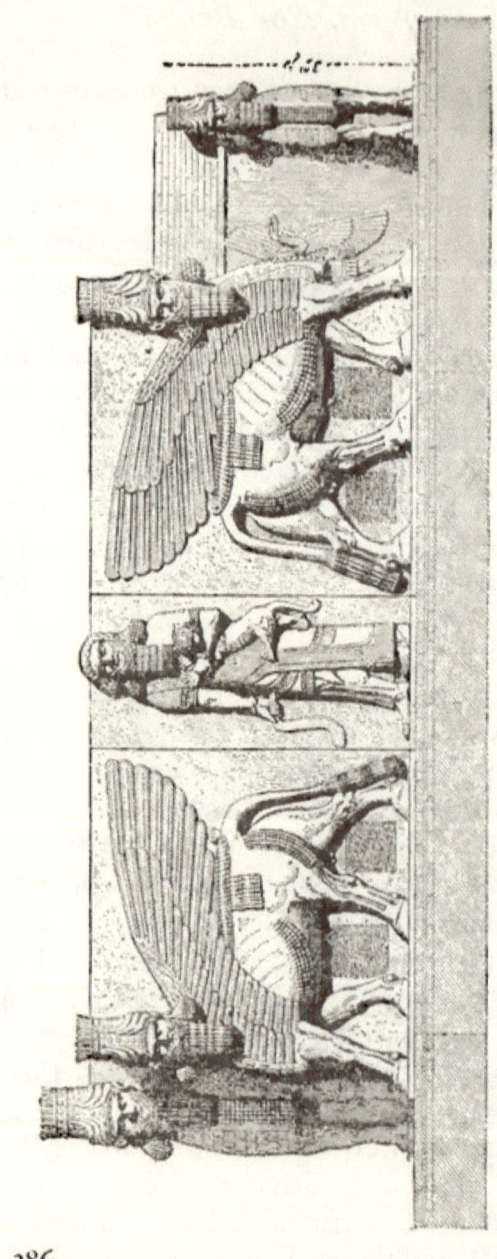

51.—SCULPTURES ON WALLS ON BOTH SIDES OF GATES DUR-SHARRUKIN. (FOR ENLARGED VIEW OF CENTRE PANEL—IZDUBAR AND LION—SEE "STORY OF CHALDEA," ILL. NO. 74.)

know, were sculptured in their places, not done in the artistic workshops and put up and joined afterwards,—that this entire work was performed in barely five years, we feel rather appalled than merely astonished. Yet such is undoubtedly the fact. For the foundation was laid in 712, and Sargon entered the palace to live in it in 707. "To accomplish such a task in so short a time there must have been a great number of sculptors of one art-school working together. A nation capable of bringing together such a number of skilled and thoroughly trained artists must have been very advanced in culture. By the unlimited power which they possessed, Assyrian monarchs could, at any given moment, collect untold numbers of laborers to make bricks, to erect walls and terraces; but no mere material might can create architects, sculptors and painters; *that* requires social conditions in which the arts have long held their place."*

29. In 706 the walls of the city were consecrated. It is probable that the inhabitants destined to people it were only then allowed to take possession. One cannot help wondering a little by what magic wand a city population could be made to order, all in a moment. It is almost like the richly furnished tables, laden with good things, which start out of

---

* Victor Place, quoted in Kaulen's "Assyrien und Babylonien," p. 54. Of all modern popular books on these subjects, that of Dr. Fr. Kaulen gives by far the most detailed, instructive, intelligible and entertaining account of this wonderful palace. See also, of course, the amply illustrated, but more technical description in the second volume of Perrot and Chipiez.

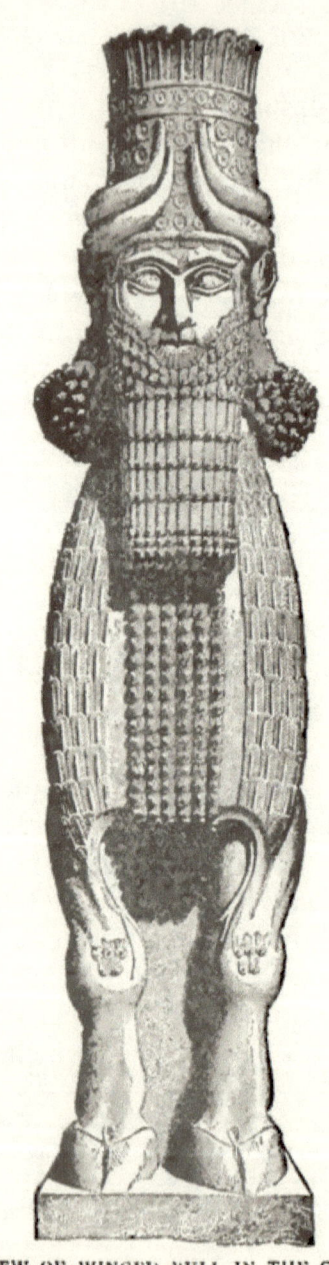

52.—FACE VIEW OF WINGED BULL IN THE GATES OF DUR-SHARRUKIN.

the ground in fairy stories. But an Assyrian king was not puzzled at such trifles; Sargon tells us how he did it, and very simple it is: " People from the four quarters of the world, of foreign speech, of manifold tongues, who had dwelt in mountains and valleys .... whom I, in the name of Asshur my lord, by the might of my arms had carried away

53.—BATTLEMENTS OF THE TERRACE WALL AT DUR-SHARRUKIN, AND DRAIN PIPE. (RESTORED FROM FRAGMENTS FOUND ON THE SPOT.)

into captivity, I commanded to speak one language " (Assyrian, of course), " and settled them therein. Sons of Asshur, of wise insight in all things, I placed over them, to watch over them; learned men and scribes to teach them the fear of God and the King."

30. There might have been worse fates for captives, and these had reason to thank their luck. For

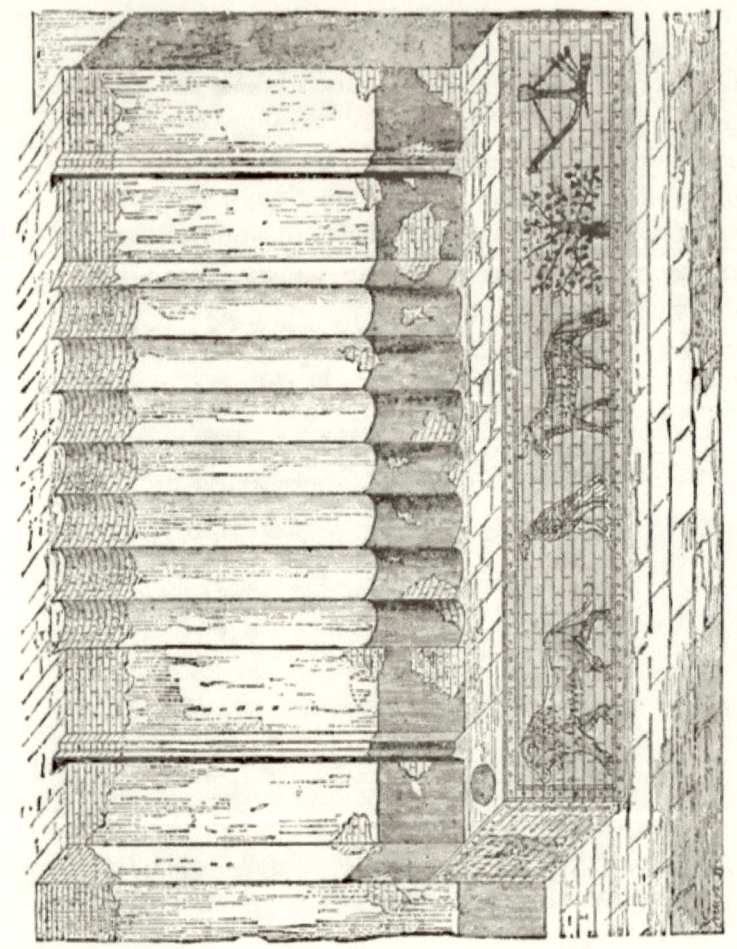

54.—DECORATION (IN ENAMELLED TILES) ON ONE OF THE GATES OF THE HAREM IN SARGON'S PALACE (KHORSABAD).

THE PRIDE OF ASSHUR.

Sargon the home-ruler was a very different person from Sargon the conqueror. Once he had made any people "one with the Assyrians," he adopted them as his natural-born subjects, and extended to them the care to which he considered these entitled. And he had very strict notions of the duties of a sovereign to his people, duties which he himself describes with some detail. He calls himself—

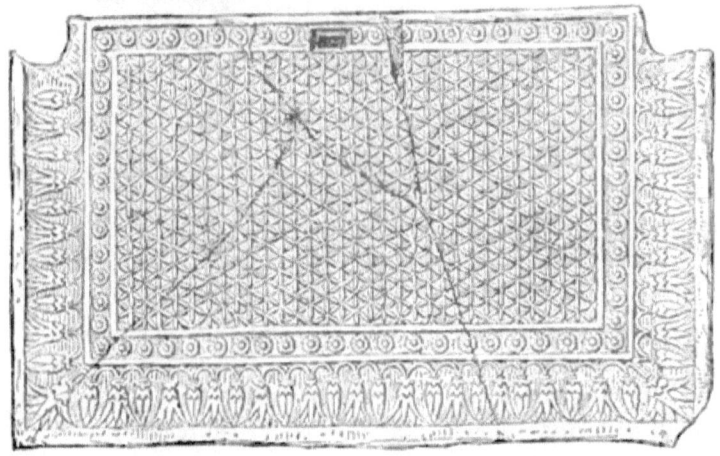

55.—THRESHOLD-SLAB (RUG PATTERN) IN SARGON'S PALACE. (KHORSABAD).

"The inquiring king, the bearer of gracious words, who applied his mind to restore settlements fallen into decay, and cultivate the neighboring lands; who directed his thoughts to make high rocks, on which in all eternity no vegetation had sprouted, to bear crops; who set his heart on making many a waste place that under the kings his fathers had never known an irrigation canal, to bring forth grain and resound with glad shouts; to clear the neglected beds of water courses, open dykes and feed them from above and below with waters abundant as the flood of the sea; a king of open mind, of an understanding eye for all things . . . . grown up in council and wisdom, and discernment, to fill the storehouses of the broad land of Asshur with food and provisions, to overflowing, as beseems the king . . . . not to let oil, that gives life to man and heals sores, become dear in my land, and regulate the price of sesame as well as of wheat."

(Sesame being a grain which is grown in all the East for the sake of its oil.) This last touch especially shows us a monarch anxious for the welfare of his people, even in the smallest details. The whole passage makes us deeply regret that there were not many more of the same kind, allowing

56.—LION-WEIGHT (ONE OF A SET FOUND AT KHORSABAD).

an insight into the peaceful pursuits and home life of the times. For after all, those fierce and cruel kings must have been in some ways human, and the life of that war-breathing and booty-craving people must have been made up of something else besides fighting and plundering. But it is a hopeless wish: the Assyrian kings, in their ideas of history, differed vastly from us, and have not provided us with materials for such a reconstruction.

31. The twofold aspect of Sargon's reign—and probably, to some extent, that of most Assyrian monarchs—is well embodied in a clause of the final invocation in two accounts of the building of the new city and palace, and a statement which immedi-

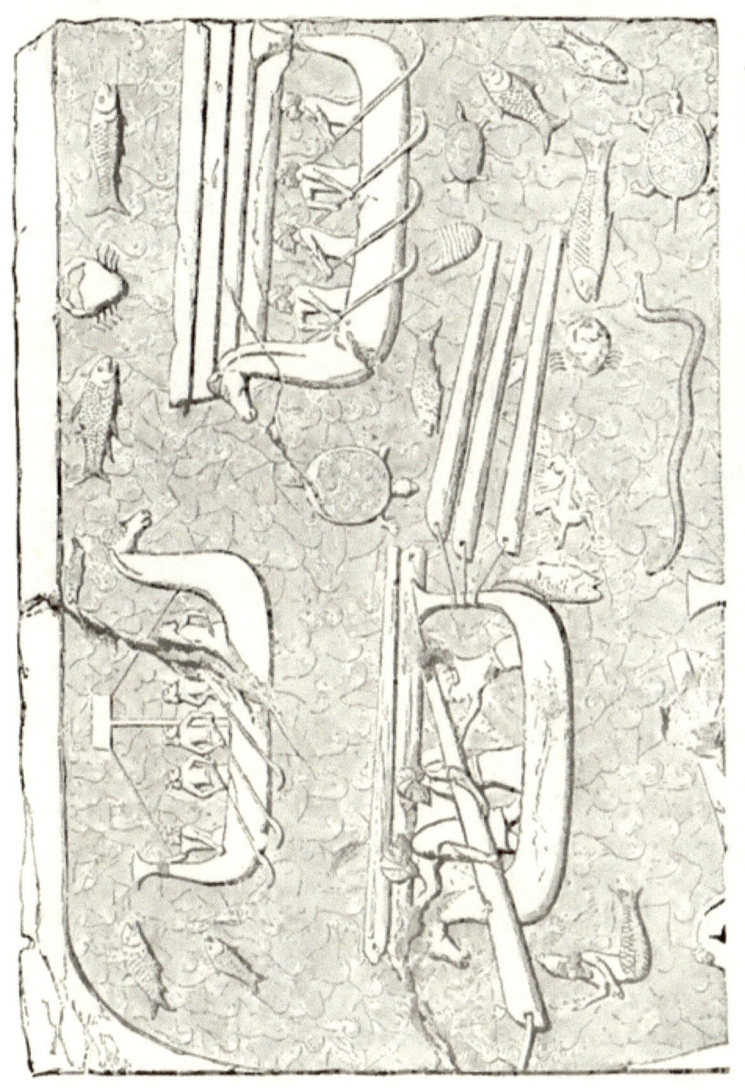

57.—TRANSPORT OF TIMBER FOR SARGON'S PALACE. (THE GOD EA ESCORTS THE FLEET.)

ately precedes it. While the one prays with characteristic straightforwardness: "May I accumulate in this palace immense treasures, the booties of all countries, the products of mountains and valleys!" the other says: "With the chiefs of provinces, the wise men, astronomers, great dignitaries, the lieutenants and governors of Assyria, I sat in my palace and I practised justice." "And may it be," further prays the king, "that I, Sharru-Kênu, who inhabit this palace, may be preserved by destiny during long years, for a long life, for the happiness of my body, for the satisfaction of my heart. . . .

32. But this was not to be. Fifteen months after the consecration of the city walls, Sargon fell, murdered by the hand of an unknown assassin—perhaps no very astonishing consummation, when we consider of what elements the population of his city was composed.

And this is the king who, by some inconceivable freak of chance, had dropped out of history as completely as though he had never existed; whose name was known from a single mention of it in Isaiah's allusion to the war against Ashdod (see p. 267); whose halls, laid open by Botta, were the first Assyrian halls ever entered by a modern's foot; and whose restoration to his proper place in the annals of mankind we owe entirely to the labors of Assyriology.

IX.

THE SARGONIDES.—SENNACHERIB (SIN-AKI-IRIB).

1. OF all Assyrian monarchs, Sennacherib is the only one whose name has always been familiar, whose person has always stood out real and lifelike in the midst of all the fantastical fables, miscalled "History of Assyria," which we of an older generation have been taught, like our forefathers and parents before us. For this one glimpse of truth in the midst of so great a mass of errors and lies we are indebted to the Bible, which has preserved for us, in three different books, an account of this king's campaign in Syria, involving the fate of Jerusalem. The later Bible books (Second Kings, Second Chronicles and the Prophets) abound in passages which portray the Assyrians as a nation, with marvellous accuracy and the most picturesque vividness; but this king is the only individual that is brought out so dramatically. And now that the discovery of a great number of cuneiform texts relating to the same period, some of them very long and well preserved,* has put us in possession of so many facts of his reign, with such details, too, as make these texts anything but

Sennacherib, 705-681 B.C.

---

* See "Story of Chaldea," ill. No. 51, the so-called "Taylor-Cylinder."

58.—SENNACHERIB ON HIS THRONE IN GALA APPAREL (KOYUNJIK).

a dry relation of events, it turns out that the expedition, which has been made as a household story to us by the Bible narrative and Byron's beautiful little poem,* is really one of its most prominent episodes; the interest of it, too, is greatly enhanced by the fact that it is the first disastrous campaign that Assyria had to record. For such it may be pronounced, notwithstanding the silence of the royal annals, as we shall presently see.

2. Sennacherib was a son of Sargon. He was not less warlike than his father, yet seems to have spent at home a far larger portion of his reign of twenty-five years. At all events, in the documents unearthed until now, we do not make out more than eight or nine campaigns, and they cover nineteen years of the twenty-five. He had, to occupy him, a task exactly similar to that which Sargon took such delight in : he built palaces, and turned his attention to restoring the long-neglected capital, Nineveh, to more than its ancient splendor, as it was there he permanently resided, and not in Dur-Sharrukin, of which no mention whatever occurs in his reign. Perhaps his father's fate disgusted him with the new residence.

3. The great features of Sennacherib's military career, besides the Syrian expedition, directed more especially against Egypt, are his wars with the united forces of Elam and Babylon. For the sacred city of Marduk was no longer the loyal

---

* "The Destruction of Sennacherib:" "The Assyrian came down like the wolf on the fold," etc.

friend and vassal it had been to Sargon, but appears to have been thoroughly won over to the cause of revolt and independence, and in the confusion that followed that king's tragic end, Merodach-Baladan re-appeared on the scene, and, after two years of civil brawls, succeeded in once more proclaiming himself "King of Kar-Dunyash." He built great hopes, as usual, on the support of Elam, but does not seem to have had other allies at the time, except the same Aramæan and Chaldean tribes which, on a former occasion, had proved anything but a tower of strength. (See p. 273.) Yet it is in this time that several historians are inclined to place the "embassy" to Hezekiah of Judah, which others contend to have been sent about ten years before. (See p. 269.) Unless some text turn up to settle the question by positive proof, it must be considered an open one; and we may be well content to leave it so, so long as the fact itself is established beyond a doubt.

4. "In my first campaign," Sennacherib reports, "I inflicted a defeat on Merodach-Baladan, king of Kar-dunyash, and on the army of Elam, his confederate, before the city of Kish. In that battle he abandoned his camp, and fled alone, to save his life. The chariots, horses, luggage vans, asses, which they had forsaken in the confusion of battle, my hands captured. Into his palace at Babylon I entered rejoicing, and opened his treasure-house."

Here follows a list of the booty and captives, to which are added 75 fortified cities of Chaldea and 420 smaller towns. As to the unfortunate "tribes," some submitted, and those who did not were "forthwith subdued." From the enumeration of the spoils it is clear that they led a pastoral and probably half-nomadic life: "208,000 people, great and small, men and women; 7200 horses and mules; 11,173 asses; 5230 camels; 80,100 oxen; 800,600 sheep—a vast spoil, I carried off to Assyria."

5. Merodach-Baladan had not reigned more than six months; and now he once more sought safety in the only refuge where he could hope to escape Assyrian pursuit—in his own native marshes of Bit-Yakin. Some search was made for him, but it was soon given up, and Sennacherib, whether as a sign of contempt, or in order to fashion an obedient tool to his hand, placed on the throne of Babylon BELIBUS, the son of a learned scribe of that city, a young man, who, he says, "had been brought up in his palace like a little dog" (? *miranu*).* It is rather remarkable that we never hear again of this royal nominee. In the complicated revolutions which soon after ensue he is entirely ignored, and in later inscriptions his appointment is not mentioned. From this silence historians shrewdly conclude that he proved a failure.

---

* This amusing expression is unfortunately still open to some doubt. This is what the eminent American Assyriologist, Dr. D. G. Lyon, says on the subject (in a private letter): "*Miranu* seems to be some kind of an animal, and the meaning 'little dog' is accepted by several Assyriologists. Still I do not consider it as established that it is the dog." The general meaning of the passage, however, is clear: it somewhat contemptuously intimates that the young Babylonian had been in some way made a pet of, brought up, very likely, among the pages of the royal household. This is about the only instance in Assyrian literature of the quality we call *humor*—slightly tinged with grimness, indeed; but it were not Assyrian else.

6. The next (second) expedition, against the very warlike and turbulent mountain tribes of the KASSHI (COSSÆANS of classical writers),* is of some interest because of the details we are given concerning that most rugged region of the Zagros range. These tribes, we are told, had never yet bowed themselves to the Assyrian kings, and were probably getting troublesome. The dangers and difficulties of a march into those unknown fastnesses must have been exceptionally great, for the king especially mentions that "Asshur, his lord, gave him courage" to undertake it. "Through tall forests, on ground difficult of access, I rode on horseback,—my litter I had borne along with ropes,—over steep places I walked on my feet." † The campaign was successful and carried out on the usual plan: the "great city" of the mountain tribes was destroyed and sacked, then rebuilt, turned into an Assyrian fortress and re-peopled with captives from other lands; a stone tablet was made (probably a stele), with an account of the expedition, and placed within the city. This, however, was not the end of the campaign. The Assyrian army was marched right through the Zagros into Ellip, which was ravaged and made a desert of "in every direction." The king of Ellip,—the same who had been assisted against his brother, and set on the throne by Sargon (see p. 279),—"abandoned his strong cities, his treasures, and fled to a distance." His

---

* See "Story of Chaldea," p. 228.
† After Hoerning's translation.

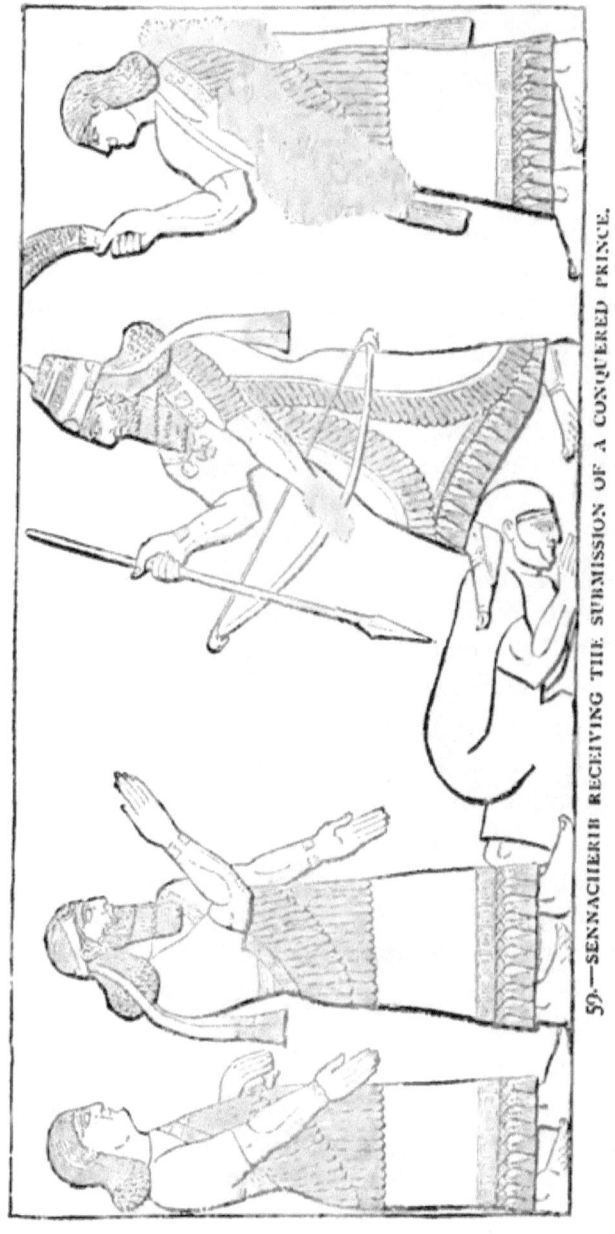

50.—SENNACHERIB RECEIVING THE SUBMISSION OF A CONQUERED PRINCE.

capital was burned down, together with numbers of towns, great and small, and another city raised to the dignity of "royal city" of the new province, under the name of Dur-Sennacherib. What had been his offence we are not told; but it is probable that he joined some attempted revolt of Median tribes, for the vigorous repression dealt to him appears to have terrified even the remoter tribes, untouched as yet by the sword or the yoke, into hasty submission; that best explains the paragraph immediately following, where the king thus closes the account of his second campaign: "On my way back I received a heavy tribute from the land of the distant Medes, the name of which had been heard of by none under the kings my fathers; they submitted themselves to the yoke of my rule." The complacency of this statement is not disturbed by the faintest foreboding that these very "distant Medes" were, only one hundred years later, to occupy the place of those Assyrians, whom they thus timidly conciliated.

7. In the mean time the West had long been in a dangerous state of ferment, not the less dangerous that it was more than usually self-contained. Five years of the new reign had passed, and no outbreak had yet occurred to call down an Assyrian visitation. The kings of the West were biding time and opportunity, and especially the convenience of TIRHAKA (better TAHARKA, Assyrian TARKU), king of Egypt, the third monarch of the Ethiopian line. He was to invade Palestine, and his appearance to be the signal

of concerted risings. The preparations for such an enterprise could not be carried on so secretly as not to reach at last the ears of the Assyrian, and the knowledge brought him quickly down to the seashore; in their rapidity and fury of onslaught lay the main secret of that people's success in war.

"Behold," says the prophet, "they shall come with speed swiftly: none shall be weary nor stumble among them: none shall slumber nor sleep; neither shall the girdle of their loins be loosed, nor the latchet of their shoes be broken: whose arrows are sharp, and all their bows bent; their horses' hoofs shall be counted like flint, and their wheels like a whirlwind: their roaring shall be like a lion, they shall roar like young lions; yea, they shall roar and lay hold of the prey, and carry it away safe, and there shall be none to deliver." (Isaiah, v. 26-29.) *

"The Assyrian came down like the wolf on the fold,
And his cohorts were gleaming with purple and gold;
And the sheen of their spears was like stars on the sea,
When the blue wave rolls nightly down deep Galilee."

They came, "governors and rulers, clothed most gorgeously, horsemen riding upon horses, all of them desirable young men" (Ezekiel). Never had king set out with a lighter heart than did Sennacherib on this his famous "third campaign, into the land of Khatti."

8. King Hezekiah of Judah, although no longer

---

* It has been justly remarked that "we have no contemporary passage that renders more vividly and visibly the impression produced in Palestine by the appearance of Assyrian armies." (B. Stade, "Geschichte des Volkes Israel," p. 605.) And how wonderfully this passage is interpreted and completed by the sculptured representations of these armies!

an impetuous youth, had ended by yielding to the rash counsels of the war party, against the better judgment of the cautious prophet-minister, who was never weary of repeating that "Egypt helpeth in vain and to no purpose;" that "the strength of Pharaoh should be their shame and the trust in the shadow of Egypt their confusion." Prudence was thrown to the winds, and not only was tribute refused, but active hostile demonstrations were indulged in. "The chief priests, nobles and people of EKRON had placed PADÎ, their king, who kept his treaties and sworn allegiance to Asshur, in chains of iron, and unto Hezekiah, king of Judah, had delivered him. And he wickedly shut him up in a prison." After such a breach of allegiance there was nothing left but to hasten the preparations for defence. The first step was to cut off the water supply from the expected invaders. "So there was gathered much people together, and they stopped all the fountains (wells) and the brook that flowed through the middle of the land, saying, Why should the king of Assyria come and find much water?"* The wall of the city also was built up wherever it was broken down, the citadel was strengthened, weapons and shields were made in

Sennacherib's unsuccessful invasion of Judah 701 B.C.

---

* The Bible chapters referred to are Second Kings, xviii., xix.; Second Chronicles, xxxii.; Isaiah, xxxvi., xxxvii.,—a literal repetition, with very slight variations, of the greater part of the narrative in Second Kings. In reconstructing the campaign from these books and the Assyrian monuments, E. Schrader's interpretation has been mainly followed, in "Keilinschriften und Altes Testament."

abundance; captains of war were set over the people, and the king "gathered them together to him in the broad place at the gate of the city, and spake comfortably to them."

9. Fortunately for Jerusalem, Sennacherib loitered on his way down the sea-coast. He tarried at Sidon, the king of which had fled to Cyprus, to settle the affairs of the city, and to receive the personal homage and tribute of several other Phœnician kings, as well as those of Ammon, Moab and Edom. Among the names of these kings we find that of a "Menahem, king of *Samsimuruna*;" if the name stands for *Samirina* (Samaria) it would seem that Israel was even yet suffered to retain a pale phantom of royalty. Then Ascalon had to be reduced to obedience, with the usual routine of ransoming, transportation, and change of king. It was only after this that he sent a detachment of his army to deal retribution on the offending Hebrew state, while he himself proceeded with the bulk of his forces in a south-easterly direction, to besiege the important fortified city of LAKHISH, which it would have been a great blunder to leave for the Egyptians to occupy. What next happened was nothing unusual: "Sennacherib, king of Assyria, came up against all the fenced cities of Judah and took them." The conqueror himself is more explicit: "Forty-six of his strong cities, his castles and the smaller towns of their territory without number, with warlike engines, by assault and storming, by fire and by the axe, I attacked and captured. 200,150 people, great and small, horses, asses, oxen and sheep beyond num-

ber, from the midst of them I carried off and counted them as spoils. Himself, like a bird in a cage, inside Jerusalem, his royal city, I shut up. I cast up a mound against him and barred the issue from his city gate." And the Egyptians still tarried. Then Hezekiah was fain to retract and try conciliation. He "sent to the king of Assyria to Lakhish, saying: I have offended. Return from me; that which thou puttest on me will I bear." And the fine imposed on him was a sum equal to about one million dollars in gold and half that in silver. To meet this demand, after all the outlay caused by his warlike preparations, he was forced not only to empty his own treasury and that of the temple, but to cut from the doors and the pillars of the latter the gold casing with which he himself had had them overlaid in the days of his prosperity. These valuables he sent with a heavy heart to the king before Lakhish, together with the person of Padi, the deposed king of Ekron, whom Sennacherib forthwith proceeded to restore to his former dignity. The lands taken from Judah he divided among this same Padi and the loyal kings of Ashdod and Gaza, not forgetting to increase their tribute proportionately.

10. Lakhish, meanwhile, was taken, and though the siege of this city is not mentioned in the great texts, we have the strongest possible evidence for it in a still more convincing form, for it is represented at full length on one of the finest wall-sculptures, occupying several slabs in a hall of Sennacherib's palace, excavated by Layard at Koyunjik. We give the concluding scene: On a highly orna-

mented throne, the back of which is hung with some costly drapery, his attendants with their huge fly-flappers behind him. Sennacherib is seated before his tent, on a knoll, among grape-laden vines and fruit-trees, while at the foot of the knoll his chariot stands with its driver; two grooms holding the heads of the horses, the royal parasol-bearer at the wheel, and the royal steed held by a soldier behind. The slaughter has not yet ceased, but a high officer, followed by soldiers, stands at the king's foot-stool reporting, probably introducing the file of captives, who wait at a little distance, under escort, some prostrated, others standing, all with hands extended in supplication. An inscription overhead interprets the scene in these express words: "*Sennacherib, king of nations, king of Assyria, seated on an exalted throne, receives the spoils of the city of Lakhish.*"

11. The capture of this important bulwark was no sooner accomplished than news came of the advance of the Egyptian forces, an advance which, tardy at first, had been so unexpectedly rapid at the last, that Sennacherib had but just time to retrace his steps and encounter the enemy in the neighborhood of Ekron. Under the circumstances, it was most undesirable for him to have in his rear a strong royal city held by a doubtful ally, and he sent to demand of Hezekiah the surrender into his hands of Jerusalem. To make the demand doubly impressive he commissioned with it his highest dignitaries, the Turtan (commander-in-chief), the Rabshakeh (a general, *not* cup-bearer) and the Rabsaris (a high officer of the royal household). The description of

this embassy, as given in the Bible books, is an invaluable piece of reality and local coloring, and brings before us the manner in which such half military, half diplomatic transactions were conducted.

12. The messengers came up to Jerusalem and stood before the walls. They "called to the king," and three officers of the household "came out to them." The Rabshakeh was spokesman. He warned the king against trusting to that "bruised reed, Egypt, whereon, if a man lean it will go into his hand, and pierce it;" then insidiously bade him not to put his reliance in the Lord his God, saying, "Am I now come up without the Lord against this place to destroy it? The Lord said unto me, Go up against this land and destroy it." This was a telling argument, and one that could disastrously influence the people, who were intently watching and listening from the top of the wall. Therefore the Jewish negotiators hastily interrupted the orator with the request that he would speak Aramaic to them, not Hebrew, "in the ears of the people on the wall." This admission opened to the Assyrian an advantage which he immediately pursued. He pretended to be sent, not so much to the king as to the Jewish people, to whom he forthwith addressed his speech:

"Hear ye the word of the great king, the king of Assyria. Thus saith the king · Let not Hezekiah deceive you, for he shall not be able to deliver you out of my hand; neither let Hezekiah make you trust in the Lord, saying, The Lord will surely deliver us, and this city shall not be given into the hand of the king of Assyria. Hearken not to Hezekiah; for thus saith the king of Assyria: Make your peace with me, and come out to me; and eat ye every one of his vine and every one of his fig-tree, and drink ye every one the waters of his own cistern; until I come and take you away to a land like your own land, a land of corn and wine, a land of bread and vineyards, a land of oil, olive and honey, that ye may live and not die. And hearken not to Hezekiah when he persuadeth you, saying, The Lord will deliver us. Hath any of the gods of the nations ever delivered his land out of the hand of the king of Assyria? Where are the gods of Hamath, and of Arpad? . . . Who are they among all the gods of the countries that have delivered their country out of my hand, that the Lord should deliver Jerusalem out of my hand? But the people held their peace, and answered him not a word; for the king's commandment was, saying, Answer him not."

13. The Assyrian envoys, according to one account, delivered a letter from their master to the king of Judah, which when Hezekiah received, " he rent his clothes, and covered himself with sackcloth, and went into the house of the Lord;" also he sent to the prophet Isaiah in his sore distress. And the letter, after he had read it, " he spread out before the Lord" and prayed aloud. " Incline thine ear, O Lord, and hear! Open thine eyes, O Lord, and see! and hear the words of Sennacherib. wherewith he hath sent him to reproach the living God! . . . ." But Isaiah sent an encouraging message to the king. This was not a time for reproof but for help, and with all the indignation of the patriot and the priest, he uttered, in the name of Yahveh, a long and withering prophecy against the invader, which is summed up in this passage : " Because of thy raging against me, and for that thine arrogancy is come up into mine ears, therefore will I put my hook in thy nose and my bridle in thy

lips,* and will turn thee back the way thou camest." So the king took comfort, even though a large detachment of the Assyrian army now came and encamped under Jerusalem.

14. The Assyrian and Egyptian forces, meanwhile, for the second time stood face to face (see p. 258, battle of Raphia). There was a great battle near a place called ELTEKEH (Assyrian, ALTAKÛ) and Sennacherib claims to have won the victory; but his account is brief, feeble and somewhat confused. He speaks of capturing Altakû and another city, and carrying off their spoil, but without the usual details and precision. At all events, there is no question of tribute, of submission, of advancing into the defeated enemy's land. On the contrary, he passes on to the affairs of Judah, and then informing us that Hezekiah gathered a great treasure of every kind, his own daughters and many women from his palace and *sent them after him to Nineveh*. Of how he happened to return to Nineveh, not a word.

15. The fact is that his military operations for that year were summarily cut short independently of human agency. A plague broke out, and in a short time carried away such numbers of his soldiers that he was fain to recall the detachment that lay before Jerusalem, and beat a hasty retreat. The Bible historians describe the catastrophe in truly Oriental poetic style: "The Angel of Yahveh

---

* This would seem to have been a treatment commonly awarded to criminals. See illustration No. 46.

went forth" and smote the Assyrians in their camp, "and when men arose in the morning, behold, they were all dead corpses." This account is curiously corroborated by a tradition preserved in Egypt, and heard there by the Greek traveller and historian, Herodotus, 250 years later, of how Sennacherib, king of the Arabs and Assyrians, had advanced towards Egypt to invade it, and how the pious Egyptian king prayed for divine aid, and that same night a swarm of mice was sent into the Assyrian's camp, and destroyed the leathern quivers, shield-straps and the bowstrings, so that they were virtually disarmed, and a great slaughter was made of them. Now the mouse was, in the East, the emblem of the plague-boil,* while there are other examples in Scripture of the destroying angel, or "Angel of Yahveh," as the bearer of pestilence.†

16. During the next year another scene of the great Babylonian drama was enacted. The old champion, Merodach-Baladan, had not thought fit to reappear as candidate for the throne. He left it to a

---

* B. Stade, "Geschichte des Volkes Israel," p. 203 and p. 621, and First Samuel, v. and vi., where the Philistines, smitten with plague-boils for detaining the Ark in their midst, send it back with a guilt-offering, according to the word of their priests and diviners: "Five golden tumors and five golden mice . . . . ye shall make images of your tumors and images of your mice that mar the land."

† See Second Samuel, xxiv. 15–17, where a pestilence is sent upon Israel, and 70,000 people die. "And *when the angel stretched out his hand* towards Jerusalem to destroy it the Lord repented him of the evil, and said to the angel that destroyed the people, It is enough; now stay thy hand. . . . And David spake unto the Lord *when he saw the angel that smote the people*, and said, Lo, I have sinned. . . ."

younger competitor, SUZUB, also a Chaldean prince, "dwelling within the marshes." The great Taylor-Cylinder gives the result of this campaign, beginning with the rout of Suzub:

"He himself lost heart and like a bird fled away alone, and his trace could not be found. I turned round and took the road to Bit-Yakin-Merodach-Baladan, whom in the course of my first campaign I had defeated, and whose power I had destroyed, now shunned the shock of my fiery battle. The gods, the protection of his country, in their arks he collected, and in ships he transported them, and to the city of Nagitu in the midst of the sea, like a bird he flew."

This city seems to have been built on small islets—something like Venice in her lagunes—by the opposite,—the Elamite,—shore of the Gulf, at the mouth of the River ULAÏ (classical EULAEOS), which then flowed into the Gulf, at a great distance from the mouths of the Tigris and the Euphrates, while now it joins the Shatt-el-arab, still many miles inside of the coast line. (See map.)

"His brothers, the seed of his father's house, whom he had left on the sea-shore, and the rest of the people of his land, from Bit-Yakin within the marshes and reeds, I brought away, and counted them as spoil. Once more his cities I destroyed, overthrew them and made them even with the ground. Upon his ally, the king of Elam, I poured the torrent of my arms. On my return, ASSHUR-NADIN-SUM, my eldest son, I seated upon the throne of his kingdom; all the land of Shumir and Accad I made subject to him."

This is the last we hear of Merodach-Baladan. The time and manner of his death are unknown. His vital energies consumed in a struggle of over thirty years, he wandered into obscurity, a broken-hearted exile, giving up the cause of the reconstruction of an independent Chaldean empire which he

OF THE CITY OF LAKHISH."

[To face p. 312

"SENNACHERIB, KING OF ASSYRIA, SEATED ON AN EXALTED THRONE, RECEIVES THE SPOILS OF THE CITY OF LAKHISH."

had made his mission and that of his race. Yet this mission was to be carried on, but by other hands, and the cause was to triumph even yet, but in another century: for with the disparition of the old Chaldean "sea-king" ends the record of the year 700, and the seventh century B.C. begins. Assyria, as an empire, was not to see the end of it.

17. The new century was not ushered in by any very brilliant achievement. The campaign which opened it—into the NIPUR Mountains (a portion of the Naïri range)—might be passed over, were it not that the account given of it on the great cylinder is an admirable piece of description:

"In my fifth campaign, the people of . . . ." (a string of names of tribes), "who, like the nests of eagles, on the highest summits and wild crags of the Nipur Mountains had fixed their dwellings, refused to bow down to my yoke. At the foot of Mount Nipur I pitched my camp. With my followers, the world-renowned, and with my warriors, the inexorable, I, like the fleet gazelle, took the lead. Through defiles, over rushing torrents, by mountain paths, I travelled in my litter; but in places which for my litter were too steep, I climbed on my feet, and like a mountain goat among the lofty cliffs, I clambered. My knees were my place of rest; upon the rocks I sat me down, and water of the precipitous mountain side to assuage my thirst I drank. To the peaks of the wooded highlands I pursued them and completely defeated them. Their cities I captured; I carried off their spoils; I ravaged, I destroyed, I burned them with fire."

18. It was probably during Sennacherib's absence in the North that Suzub "the Babylonian," as he is now called, emerged from his retreat and succeeded in re-assuming the royal title and power. But the Assyrian, before swooping down on him, determined to pluck out the new nest of conspiracy and

rebellion which the emigrants from Bit-Yakin had founded on the shore of Elam, and conceived the bold and original design of attacking it from the sea. He ordered captive shipwrights " of the land Khatti " (Phœnicians of the sea-coast, no doubt), to construct in Nineveh " tall ships, after the manner of their country," manned them with mariners from Tyre and Sidon, and let them sail some distance down the Tigris, when they were transferred by land, with the help of wooden .... (the inscription here is unfortunately mutilated; probably sledges and rollers)—all the way down to the great ARAKHTU Canal, one of Babylonia's principal thoroughfares and fertilizers. Then the soldiers were put on board and the fleet sailed down the Arakhtu into the Euphrates, where it was joined by some more ships, built at a city on the upper Euphrates, and onwards to a station by the Gulf. The king's camp was pitched so near the coast that the waters, at high tide, encompassed it all round and swamped the tents, so that the king, with his attendants, was forced to remain five days and nights on board the ships. At last, the fleet, with all the troops on board, wound its way through the marshes and emerged into the Gulf from the mouth of the Euphrates. A maritime expedition was a great novelty to the Assyrians, an essentially continental people, and the occasion was deemed an unusually momentous one. It was duly honored with much solemnity and ceremony. Sacrifices were offered, and little golden models of ships and fishes made of gold were sunk into the sea as a propitiatory offering to Êa, the lord of the deep. The expedition was only too successful.

> "The men of Bit-Yakin, and their gods, and the men of Elam" (several districts having been ravaged and their cities captured) " I carried away; not one of the evil doers I left behind. In ships I embarked them, to the other side I made them cross, and I made them take the road to Assyria. . . . On my return, Suzub the Babylonian, who to the sovereignty of Phumir and Akkad had restored himself, in a great battle I defeated ; I captured him alive with my own hand, in bonds and chains of iron I laid him, and to Assyria I carried him away. The king of Elam, who had supported him, I defeated; I laid low his might and annihilated his hosts."

19. Victory was followed up by invasion ; the smoke of burning towns, " as driven by a violent storm-wind, obscured the wide face of heaven," and Khudur-Nankhundi had already betaken himself to the highlands for safety, abandoning his royal city, when Sennacherib, for the second time in his experience, was compelled to retreat before a power greater than that of human arms. In his ardor to advance he had been unmindful of the season ; it was the month of December, never a favorable one for mountain warfare. But this particular year the elements were even more boisterous than usual. There was an earthquake, and " the heavens poured down rains upon rains, and snow, which swelled the torrents." So he " turned round and took the road of Nineveh," as he admits with charming simplicity.

20. In those same days it came to pass that Khudur-Nankhundi, king of Elam, died, and was succeeded by his brother, UMMAN-MINAN,—" a man without understanding or insight," he is called, because of his readiness to join in revolts and conspir-

acies, notwithstanding the many severe lessons his predecessors had received. True, the temptation was great. For Sennacherib dwelt in his own land unusually long, probably absorbed in his buildings and restorations; at least, so it would appear from the long interval—no less than six years—between his seventh campaign and his eighth. In this interval the irrepressible Suzub turned up again at Babylon, having apparently escaped from captivity,

61.—DETAIL OF CHALDEAN MARSHES: WILD SOW WITH YOUNG.
(PALACE OF SENNACHERIB, KOYUNJIK.)

though we are not told either when or how he contrived the difficult feat. He seems at first to have led the adventurous life of an outlaw, as he is said to have collected about him a band of desperadoes —"wicked, bloodthirsty, fugitive rabble," with whom he hid among the marshes, then passed into Elam to collect more men, and rapidly returning, entered Babylon, where the people "seated him who deserved it not on the throne, and bestowed on him the crown of Shumir and Accad."

He at once cast about him for allies. But alliances were not to be had for nothing and the royal treasury was exhausted. So, with the consent of the Babylonians, he opened that of the great temples, brought out the gold and silver that was there found and offered it to Umman-Minan, proposing to him a treaty: "Collect thy army! Strike thy camp! Hasten to Babylon! Stand by us!" "Then," writes Sennacherib, who, from the tone of this entire passage, seems thoroughly disgusted and out of patience,

"Then he, the Elamite, whose cities I had captured and made even with the ground, showed that he had no sense: he was unmindful of it. He assembled his army: his chariots and wagons he collected; horses and asses he harnessed to their yokes. . . . A vast host of allies he led along with him . . . . and the road to Babylonia they took. . . . The Babylonians, wicked devils, the gates of their city barred strongly and hardened their hearts for resistance."

The forces of Elam and Babylon joined without hindrance and did not wait for the Assyrian's attack, but boldly advanced to meet him. Then was fought a great battle the description of which, fortunately preserved almost uninjured on the great cylinder, is altogether the finest specimen of Assyrian historical literature we have. Indeed, so full of life is it, of movement and picturesque detail, that it would hold its own even if compared with the best battle-pieces in any literature, those of Homer himself not excepted. It were sacrilege to quote or abridge. We give the whole.*

---

* Translated from Hoerning's version.

21. "Even as swarms of locust pass over the country, they hastened onwards, to do battle with me. The dust of their feet rose before me as when a mighty storm-wind covers the face of the wide heaven with rain-laden clouds. By the city of Khaluli, on the bank of the Tigris, they drew themselves up in battle array and called up their forces.

<small>Battle of Khaluli, 692 or 691 B.C.</small>

But I prayed to Asshur, Sin, Shamash, Bel, Nebo and Nergal, to Ishtar of Nineveh and Ishtar of Arbela, my heavenly helpers, to give me victory over the mighty foe. In good time they hearkened to my prayers, and came to my assistance. Similar to the lion in fury, I donned my cuirass; with the helmet, the honor of battle, I decked my head. My lofty war chariot, that sweeps away the foes, in the wrath of my heart I hastily mounted. The mighty bow I seized which Asshur has given into my hand, my mace, the life-destroying, I grasped. Against all the hosts of the rebels I broke loose, impetuous as a lion, I thundered like Ramân. By command of Asshur, the great lord my lord, from end to end of the field, even as the rush of a mighty shower, I sped against the foe. With the weapons of Asshur my lord and the onslaught of my terrible battle, I made their breasts to quake, and drove them to bay. I lightened their ranks with mace and with arrows, and their corpses I strewed around like sheaves (?). Khumbanundash, the king of Elam's general and principal stay, a man of high estate and prudent, together with his attendant lords,—golden daggers in their girdles, armlets of pure gold on their wrists,—I led away like sturdy bulls that are fettered, and ended their lives: I cut their throats as one does to lambs, and their dear lives I beat out as . . . (?) Like a violent shower I scattered their standards and tents on the ground, limp and in tatters. The asses* that were yoked to my chariot swam in gore . . . . blood and mud stained the pole of my war chariot, that sweeps away obstacles and hindrances. With the bodies of their warriors I filled the valley as with grass. . . . As trophies of victory I cut off their hands and stripped from their wrists the armlets of shining gold and silver; with maces set with sharp spikes I shattered their arms; the golden and silver daggers I took from their hips. The rest of his great lords, together with Nebosumiskun, the son of Merodach-Baladan, who were afraid of my arms and had collected their forces, I took alive in the midst of the battle, with my own hand. The char-

---

* Perhaps "mules"? The German says "Esel."

iots I brought in from the field; the warriors who mounted them had fallen, the drivers had disappeared, and the horses were running about by themselves. For the distance of two kasbus I commanded to cut them down. Him, Ummanminan, the king of Elam, together with the king of Babylon and his allies from the land of Kaldu, the fierceness of my battle overthrew them. They abandoned their tents, and, to save their lives, they trampled on the corpses of their own warriors; they sped away, even as young swallows scared from their nests... I drove my chariots and horses in pursuit of them; their fugitives, who ran for their lives, were speared wherever they were found."

There is in Egyptian wall-literature a parallel battle-piece to this, but much older: it is a poem describing the battle of Kadesh (see p. 30) and the prowess of King Ramses II., written by his court poet, the priestly scribe, Pentaour. The description is as fine and animated but more florid, and contains even more minute particulars; for instance, the names of the king's war-horses. The poem was held in great honor and copies of it were found on several temple-walls.

22. The end of this brilliant campaign is recorded not on the Taylor-Cylinder, but on a monument hewn in the live rock near a place called Bavian, and situated in a wild and very beautiful mountain nook, in a hilly range somewhat to the northeast of Khorsabad. This monument, surrounded by several other more or less injured rock-sculptures, is therefore later than the Cylinder. The campaign which culminated in the battle of Khaluli is briefly sketched, with the closing remark that the Elamites were so thoroughly cowed and broken by their defeat that they retired into their moun-

tains "like eagles," and for a long time undertook no more expeditions, and fought no more battles.

23. But Babylon was not to be let off so cheaply. After ravaging the more accessible parts of Elam, Sennacherib returned with the set purpose of stamping out, once for all, that standing hearth of rebellion, and scattering its cinders and ashes to the winds. "In my second expedition to Babylon, which I went forth to capture, I saw the destruction of its power." He was actuated no doubt by the conviction that Assyria, in her Southern neighbor, had to deal, not with an ordinary rebel, but with a formidable political rival, who, now at last thoroughly aroused by the long machinations of the native princes and their heroic struggles, would not stand on self-defence, nor be content with asserting independence, but would aspire to restore the old Empire, with all its glories, and to resume towards her former colony and vassal the attitude of metropolis and sovereign.

24. It is this political foresight which explains the terrible vengeance he wreaked on the great Southern capital—a vengeance so sweeping and ruthless as to appear monstrous from even an Assyrian's standpoint, especially as it was carried out in cold blood, after the excitement of the battle was passed, and an interval of weeks, perhaps months had elapsed. He proceeded most methodically. He gave the city to his army to sack and carried away the trophies formerly taken from Assyrian kings—the signet-ring of Tukulti-Nineb (see p. 38), the statues of the god Ramân and his consort, Shala, lost by Tig-

lath-Pileser I. (see p. 62) —then gave the word to shatter and destroy. "The city and houses, from their foundation to their upper chambers, I destroyed, dug up, in the fire I burnt. The fortress and outer wall, the temples of the gods," the ziggurat, were overturned and the materials and rubbish thrown into the Arakhtu Canal (see p. 314). He even ordered the temples to be plundered before they were demolished, and the statues of the gods to be broken to pieces, and had canals dug through the city: "In order that, in the course of time, no one may find the place of this city and of its temples, I covered it with water."* Such unexampled severity was nothing short of sacrilege when dealt out to the ancient and holy city, venerable alike to both nations, and which we have seen Sennacherib's predecessors treat with such unvarying respect and piety. Nor did it avail in the end. When events are ripe and their fulness of time is drawing nigh, it lies not in any man's power, by either craft or violence, to stay them.

25. There is not much more to say of Sennacherib's political and military career. During the last ten years of his life, he appears to have, with few exceptions, "dwelt in Nineveh." There were some more wars, but of these we have but fragmentary records, on some indeed no authority but Greek traditions. One thing seems sure, that he never again tempted fortune in the "land of Khatti." A fragment of an inscription tells of a war against

---

* From the French version of Pognon.

some Arabian queen. Several passages from the earlier inscriptions mention his having repeatedly repressed the people of Cilicia, cut timber in their mountains, the Amanos, and made gangs of Cilician captives work at his constructions, together with Chaldeans, Aramæans and others. There is therefore nothing improbable in a tradition, reported by late Greek writers, that a Greek army had once landed in Cilicia and been repulsed by Sennacherib, who is then said to have founded the city of TARSOS, on the small but rapid river KYDNOS.

26. Sennacherib's end was the most horrible that can be imagined: he was murdered, while praying in a temple, by two of his sons, who immediately fled to Urartu,* where they were sure not only of a friendly reception, but of finding followers enough to make a stand and a venture for the crown. Their eldest brother, who had at one time been made viceroy of Babylon (see p. 312), must have died since, for it was a fourth brother who ascended the throne and went forth to punish them: Sennacherib's favorite son, ESARHADDON, the same for whom he left certain personal property in the keeping of the priests of Nebo, by a document which has been called his "Will."†

27. If it really were horror of his father's fate that deterred Sennacherib from occupying the new city and palace of Dur-Sharrukin, the change of residence availed him little. But it was of great

---

* See Second Kings, xix. 37; Second Chronicles, xxxii. 21; Isaiah, xxxvii. 38. These passages are confirmed from other sources.

† See "Story of Chaldea," p. 109.

62.—CAPTIVES BUILDING PLATFORM-MOUND.

benefit to his royal city of Nineveh which, under his supervision and lavish expenditure, blossomed into new beauty and greater splendor than ever before. For he did not content himself with pulling down or restoring old palaces and building new ones, but undertook the renovation of the entire city, its walls and fortifications, and exerted himself wisely for the welfare of the country around it. And this he did after such an approved *modern* manner, that the description almost bewilders us. When, for instance, we read a passage like this: "Of Nineveh, my royal city, I greatly enlarged the dwellings. Its streets, I renovated the old ones and I widened those which were too narrow. I made it as brilliant as the sun,"*—can we not almost substitute "Paris" for Nineveh and Napoleon III. for the Assyrian king? And what more could a modern "improver" do than turn rivers from their course for purposes of public utility? The city suffered from want of water. "Murmurings ascended on high" from the people; "drinking water they knew not, and to the rains from the vault of heaven their eyes were directed." Of the "kings his fathers who went before him," he reproachfully tells us that, "as to caring for the health of the city, by bringing streams of water into it . . . none turned his thought to it, nor brought his heart to it. Then I, Sennacherib, king of Assyria, by command of the gods, resolved in my mind to complete this work, and I brought my

---

* From the "Bellino Cylinder"; translation of Mr. H. F. Talbot, in "Records of the Past."

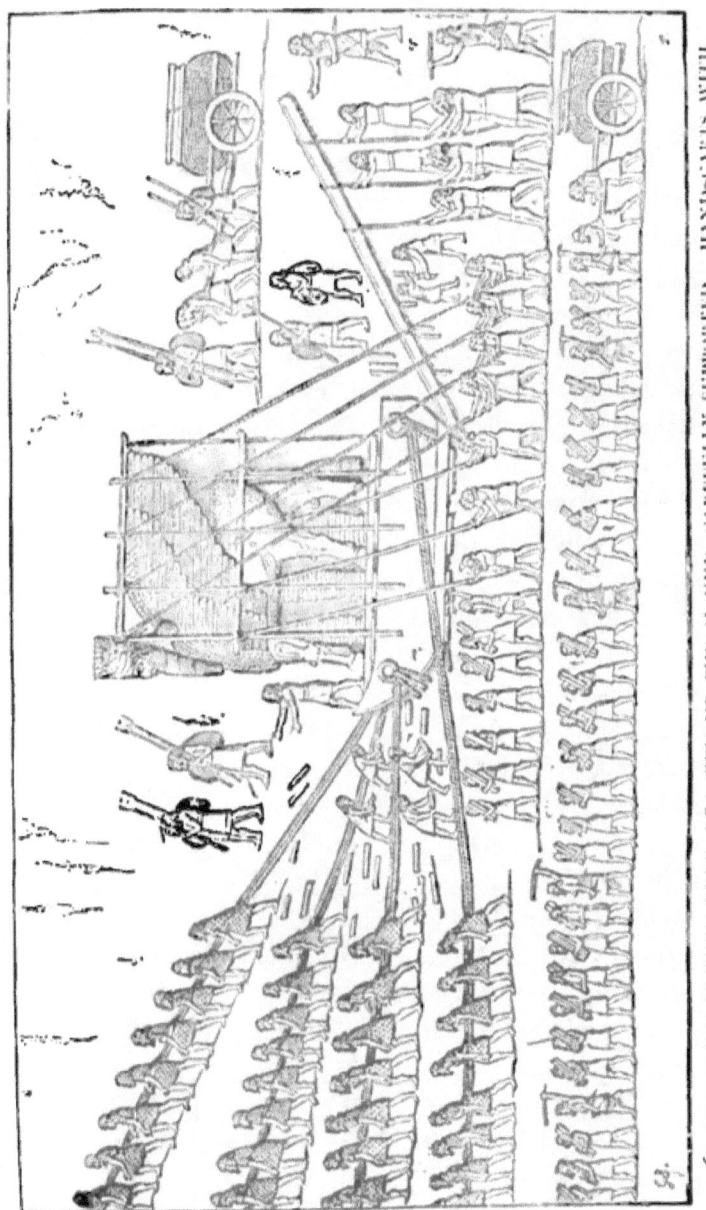

63.—FINISHED WINGED BULL, DRAGGED UP THE MOUND, CAREFULLY SUPPORTED. HAND-CARTS WITH SPARE COILS OF ROPE.

mind to it." So he had no less than sixteen canals dug and embanked, and turned the neighboring stream, KHUZUR, to fill them. This is the little river—little, but turbulent in the rain-season—still called the KHOSR or KHAUSER, which even now flows between the mounds of Koyunjik and Nebbi Yunus, the northern and southern quarters of ancient Nineveh. The Tigris, on the other hand, which had encroached and was undermining the platform on which former kings had built palaces now ruined, had to be forced back into its old bed and regulated by means of a new channel, before the construction of Sennacherib's own residence could be proceeded with.

28. This residence has earned the distinction of being the most imposing of Assyrian palaces. In the words of Mr. George Rawlinson, it "surpassed in size and splendor all earlier edifices, and was never excelled in any respect, except by one of later building. The palace of Asshurbanipal, built on the same platform by the grandson of Sennacherib, was, it must be allowed, more exquisite in its ornamentation; but even this edifice did not equal the great work of Sennacherib in the number of its apartments, or the grandeur of its dimensions." It covered an area of eight acres, and is thought to contain no less than seventy or eighty rooms. Of these the principal ones—the state apartments— were, as usual, lined with sculptured slabs, representing the most varied scenes of the monarch's life in war and peace, abroad and at home. We cannot do better than accompany the few illustrations

64.—HALF-SCULPTURED WINGED BULL DRAGGED ALONG ON A SLEDGE ON GREASED WOODEN ROLLS. OVERSEERS DRIVING CAPTIVES TO WORK.

which limited space enables us to present here, with a couple of descriptive pages from Mr. G. Rawlinson's always spirited and entertaining book:

29. The most striking characteristic of Sennacherib's ornamentation is its strong and marked realism. . . . Mountains, rocks, trees, roads, rivers, lakes, were regularly portrayed, an attempt being made to represent the locality, whatever it might be, as truthfully as the artist's skill and the character of his material rendered possible. . . . The species of trees is distinguished . . . . gardens, fields, ponds, reeds, are carefully represented; wild animals are introduced, as stags, boars and antelopes; birds fly from tree to tree, or stand over their nests, feeding the young who stretch up to them; fish disport themselves in the waters; fishermen ply their craft; boatmen and agricultural laborers pursue their avocations; the scene is, as it were, photographed, with all its features.*

In the same spirit of realism Sennacherib chooses for artistic representation scenes of a commonplace and everyday character. The trains of attendants who daily enter his palace with game and locust for his dinner, and cakes and fruit for his dessert, appear on the walls of the passages, exactly as they walked through his courts bearing the delicacies in which he delighted. Elsewhere he puts before us the entire process of carving and transporting a colossal bull, from the first removal of the huge stone in its rough state from the quarry to its final elevation on a palace mound, as part of the great gateway of a royal residence. We see the trackers dragging the rough block, supported on a low flat-bottomed boat, along the course of a river, disposed in gangs . . . . each gang having a costume of its own which probably marked its nation . . . . under taskmasters armed with staves, who urge on the labor with blows. . . .

---

* Perhaps this was the artists' way of asserting their individuality and extracting a little amusement out of a task which, after all, must have been terribly monotonous and cramping to the imagination, from the conventional sameness in the treatment of the innumerable figures. How else explain such freaks and by-plays as, for instance, in a river carrying corpses of men and horses, or heavily loaded boats,—a large fish swallowing a little one, of which only the tail is visible, protruding from the big one's mouth; or a crab encircling a fish in its deadly embrace?

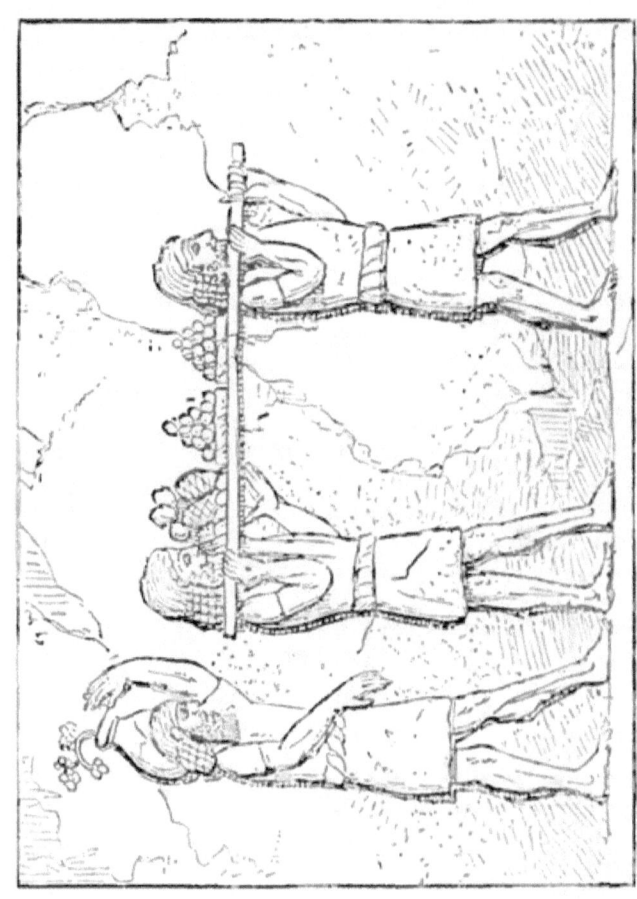

65.—ATTENDANTS CARRYING DESSERT TO THE BANQUET HALL. (ON THE WALLS OF A PASSAGE IN SENNACHERIB'S PALACE.—KOYUNJIK.)

The whole scene must be represented, and so the trackers are all there, to the number of three hundred . . . . each delineated with as much care as if he were not the exact image of ninety-nine others. We then observe the block transferred to land, and carved into the rough semblance of a bull, in which form it is placed on a rude sledge and conveyed along level land by gangs of laborers, arranged nearly as before, to the foot of the mound at whose top it has to be placed. The construction of the mound is elaborately represented. Brickmakers are seen moulding the bricks at its base, while workmen with baskets at their backs, full of earth, brick, stone or rubbish toil up the ascent—for the mound is already half raised—and empty their burdens out upon the summit. (See Fig. 63.) The bull, still lying on its sledge, is then drawn up an inclined plane to the top by four gangs of laborers, in the presence of the monarch and his attendants. After this the carving is completed, and the colossus, having been raised into an upright position, is conveyed along the surface of the platform to the exact site which it is to occupy.*

It is worth noting that when Layard removed the bulls for shipment on the Tigris, they had to be transported to the river bank in very much the same manner we see represented on the sculptures, gangs of Arabs on voluntary service being substituted for the gangs of captive laborers.

---

* "The Five Great Monarchies," 1864, Vol. II., p. 460 and ff.

X.

THE SARGONIDES: ESARHADDON (ASSHUR-AKH-IDDIN).

1. FOR some reason or other the reign of this king has not yielded as abundant a flow of materials as those of his father and grandfather. There is only one long, continuous inscription of him, in two copies, slightly differing from each other, and considerably injured, both stopping short of his most important achievement, the conquest of Egypt. One reason for a scarcity of documents, unusual for so late a period, may be that, of the three palaces which he built, that at Babylon has not been discovered yet, that at Kalah was never quite finished, and was destroyed by a great fire which ruined or destroyed the sculptures, while that at Nineveh is entombed in Jonah's Mound (Nebbi-Yunus), and could never properly be explored on account of the sacredness of the place, and the objections of the Mussulman authorities to having it disturbed.*

2. It is particularly unlucky that half the first column of one of these inscriptions should have proved hopelessly defaced, for it is probable that it con-

_{Asarhaddon, 681–668 B.C.}

---

* See "Story of Chaldea," p. 11.

tained an account of the murder of Sennacherib. It is evident, where the lines become legible, that Esarhaddon is preparing to avenge his father: " I was wrathful as a lion and my soul raged within me " —and he " lifted up his hand to " the great gods,

66.—ROCK-STELE OF ESARHADDON AT NAHR-EL-KELB.

vowing to " assume the sovereignty of his father's house." It appears that he was not at Nineveh at the time, but somewhere in the western part of Naïri. It was the month of January; snow-storms were raging, and endangering his army in those wild passes; but he did not recede, nor even tarry to prepare for a winter campaign. He had " lifted up his hands" to the great gods with more than usual fervor and solemnity, and had received a token. "They accepted my prayer. In their gracious favor a message they sent to me: Go! fear not! We march at thy side! We shall overthrow thine enemies." And from the temple of his favorite goddess, Ishtar of Arbela, had come special messages of like purport. These are the so-called "addresses," which were recorded on tablets, with the names of the priests or priestesses whose lips delivered them. One such tablet has been preserved, and the text is in sufficiently good condition to give a very favorable idea of this specimen of religious poetry, some passages of which are truly impressive. "I am Ishtar of Arbela," the goddess is made to say. "By thy side I go, fear not.... Thine enemy, like the harvest gathering of the month Sivan (May-June), before thy feet descends to do battle. The Great Lady am I. ... Thine enemy I cut off and I give to thee.... Fear not, O Esarhaddon .... I will ease thy heart. ... Respect as for thy mother thou hast caused to be shown to me. Each of the sixty great gods, my strong ones, with his life will guide thee. Sin on thy right hand, Shamash on thy left. ... Upon mankind trust not; bend thine eyes upon me; trust to me: I am Ishtar of Arbela." *

3. There was a meeting far away in the highlands of the Upper Euphrates (a part of CAPPADOCIA), and a shower of arrows began the battle. Whether it

---

* Translation of Mr. Th. G. Pinches, in "Records of the Past," Vol. XI.

was carried on and ended in Esarhaddon's victory or whether the fugitive prince's army refused to fight against superior numbers, is not very clear. "The fear of the great gods my lords overwhelmed them." " Ishtar, lady of war and battle, stood by my side. Their bows she shattered, their line of battle, so closely ordered, she broke through, and in their army the cry resounded, 'This one is our king!'" At all events, Esarhaddon remained undisputed master of the field, and of the throne. There is nothing to show whether his iniquitous brothers perished. Centuries later there was a tradition in Armenia to the effect that their descendants had long been in possession of lands in that country.

4. The reign of Esarhaddon can certainly not be called either inglorious or uneventful. But there is a sameness about the exploits of Assyrian kings and the places where they are performed which makes the recital of them tedious after awhile. Still, there is always a dramatic element in the warfare with Chaldea, and the irrepressible Bit-Yakin family. It was a son of Merodach-Baladan who took the lead this time. Taking advantage of the disturbances which followed Sennacherib's sudden end, he had surprised the Assyrian governor of Ur and seized on the city. And when the new king was firmly seated on his father's throne, the Chaldean maintained an unequivocally hostile attitude: "He did not reverence to me, the gifts of a brother he presented not, to do homage he approached not, his ambassador to my presence he sent not, and concerning the peace of my kingdom he asked not."

All these were grievous breaches of international etiquette, and, from a vassal, meant rank rebellion. "His evil deeds within Nineveh, my capital, I heard," continues the king, "and my heart groaned and my liver was stricken down. My officers, the prefects of the borders of his country, I sent in haste against him; he, the rebel, heard of the march of my army and to Elam, like a fox, he fled away." It is obscurely hinted that he found there a violent end, that the gods whose covenant he had broken laid affliction upon him; that "he trusted to Elam, but did not thereby save his life." His brother, NAHID-MARDUK, in order not to share his fate, hastened to Nineveh to tender his submission, and was invested with the sovereignty of "the province of the sea-coast, the whole of it, the inheritance of his brother," against yearly tribute, which he made it a practice to bring to Nineveh himself, with the addition of valuable presents.

5. Esarhaddon then entered on a line of policy the exact opposite of that pursued by his father. The sacrilegious vengeance taken by the latter on the holy city weighed heavily on his spirit, and he devoted himself to the task of healing and restoration. He began by conciliating the people of Babylon and Borsip, and with that view gave them back certain lands that had been taken from them. Then he went to work to rebuild Babylon itself and all its desecrated temples. In his account of this great undertaking, in which he calls himself a "worshipper of Nebo and Marduk," and refrains from calling on any of the more distinctively Assyrian gods, he shows

great delicacy of feeling in the way in which he avoids casting a reflection on his father's memory. The catastrophe which had overtaken Babylon he attributes to a special judgment of the god Marduk, but even that is vaguely and obscurely worded. "One before him," he says (alluding to Suzub, see p. 317), "under the reign of a former king" (Sennacherib is meant, but not named), "had laid hands on the great temple of Marduk, in Babylon, and given away all his treasures as the price of a bargain. This angered the lord of the gods, Marduk; he forthwith determined to visit the land with chastisement, and destroy its inhabitants." All that followed is then described as the direct act of the god: it is he who flooded the city with the waters of the Arakhtu, who made it even with the ground, who demolished its temples so that the gods and goddesses flew up into heaven—and so Sennacherib, it is implied (for his name is not once mentioned), is cleared of all blame, having been but the instrument of a divine judgment. In the same manner Esarhaddon announces himself as the chosen instrument of the god, who "selects him from the midst of his brothers" to restore the city and its sanctuaries. His affection for the great capital which he had, so to speak, raised from the dead, was very great, and he made it his favorite residence. He never, to the end of his life, had to contend with rebellion in this quarter.

6. We may pass over those among Esarhaddon's nine recorded campaigns which had no further object than securing the frontiers from inroads and rebellions, and which were most probably not com-

manded by himself. An exception must be made in favor of an expedition into "distant Media," where he affirms having penetrated further than any of the kings before him, even to Bikni, "where the mountains of alabaster are," and where he captured several refractory "chiefs of cities," forgave and reinstated some others, while three more, chiefs of "cities of Media whose position is remote," brought him to Nineveh an offering of choicest horses. Another incident of a frontier war which should not pass unnoticed is the repulse and defeat of "TIUSHPA THE GIMIRRAI, a roving warrior whose own country was remote." He and his army were "destroyed by the sword" in a region which has not been identified, but undoubtedly lay north of Cilicia, in the Naïri highlands, in the later province of Cappadocia. "Gimirrai" is the Assyrian name of the nomadic people usually called CIMMERIANS, who, like the Medes, belonged to a different race from any of the nations we have hitherto encountered. As this is the race to which we ourselves belong, and as, at the epoch of history we are now reaching, it is rapidly coming to the front, it will soon be necessary to interrupt the narrative and devote a chapter to its migrations and progress.

7. With Elam, Esarhaddon's relations appear to have been peaceable throughout. Not so with Arabia. He gives a very remarkable account of an expedition into an Arabian region—BAZU, of which the name has not yet been identified, but which must have lain beyond a wide belt of desert. Some

scholars think it was Yemen. He describes the way as lying through an arid waste, "a land of thirst," full of loose stones, where snakes and scorpions covered the ground like grasshoppers; then through high, barren mountains—a description which forcibly recalls "the great and terrible wilderness" of Deuteronomy, viii. 15, "wherein were fiery serpents and scorpions, and thirsty ground where was no water." There is no reason to doubt Esarhaddon's statement, that no king had entered this region before him. Eight Arabian sovereigns were slain in this campaign, two of them women, their wealth and their gods carried away. One of the surviving chieftains, LAÏLIÊ, who had at first fled before the invaders, having heard of the capture of "his gods," performed the extraordinary feat of following the Assyrian king all the way to Nineveh, to try and recover them, as the price of his submission. Esarhaddon, whose disposition inclined to leniency, "showed him compassion and spoke to him of brotherhood." He restored to him "his gods which had been carried off," having previously, however, ordered an inscription to be engraved on them, recording their capture and "the might of Asshur his lord." Not content with this favor, the king invested him with the sovereignty of the entire province of Bazu, which he had just conquered, demanding from him of course allegiance and tribute. This was not the only case of captive "gods" being restored to their owners. On another occasion of the same kind, the king mentions having caused "their injuries to be repaired," before engraving on them his own name and "the might of Asshur his lord."

8. For over twenty years the West had not been visited by Assyrian armies, not since Sennacherib's disastrous retreat. As the royal inscriptions never mention any country unless it is the scene of an Assyrian expedition, we do not know what was going on during this long interval of peace in the lands of Khatti and the sea-coast. They were probably gathering strength for a new rising. It broke out in Phœnician Sidon, which appears to have got rid of the king set over it by Sennacherib, and to have begun operations in advance of all its neighbors, supported only by some mountain tribes of Lebanon. If others were going to join the insurrection, they had no time to do so, for Esarhaddon was beforehand with them. He invested the offending city before any help could reach it, "rooted up its citadel and dwellings and flung them into the sea," then built a new city, which he named "city of Esarhaddon." The rebel king, who had fled to some island,—name not given—he "caught like a fish from out of the sea and cut off his head;" the same treatment was inflicted on the Lebanon chieftain, who was taken "from out of the mountains, like a bird," and both heads were sent to Nineveh with the prisoners and spoil.

9. After returning to Assyria, Esarhaddon convoked the "kings of Khatti and of the nations beyond the sea." They came to Nineveh, twenty-two in number, ten from the island of Cyprus and twelve from the principal Syrian states—the latter proba-

bly glad at heart that they had had no opportunity of committing themselves. The list is headed by Baal, king of Tyre, and Manasseh, king of Judah (the son of Hezekiah). Then come the kings of Edom, of Moab, of Gaza, of Ascalon, of Gebal, of Arvad, of Ammon, of Ashdod, and two more (unidentified): "altogether twenty-two kings of Khatti and the sea-coast, and the islands, and I passed them in review before me." They had not, of course, come empty-handed. Esarhaddon was then building, and their gifts—whether voluntary or demanded from them—were appropriate to the occasion. They consisted of "great beams and rafters of ebony, cedar and cypress," from Lebanon and other mountains, slabs of alabaster and other stones, which "from the mountain quarries, the place of their origin, for the adornment of the palace, with labor and difficulty unto Nineveh they brought along with them."

10. The palace thus endowed is that which the mound of Nebbi Yunus still encloses, unexplored. It is to be hoped that it may some day be laid open, for its furnishings and appointments must have been of the most costly magnificence, judging from the detailed description given on one of Esarhaddon's cylinders. The feast of inauguration, too, was celebrated with great pomp and lavishness.

"Asshur, Ishtar of Nineveh, and the gods of Assyria I feasted within it; victims, precious and beautiful, I sacrificed before them, and I caused them to receive my gifts. The great assembly of my kingdom, the chiefs, and the people of the land, all of them, according to their tribes and cities, on lofty seats I seated within it, and I made the company joyful. With the wine of grapes I furnished their tables and I let martial music resound among them."*

11. We do not know the immediate occasion of Esarhaddon's expedition into Egypt (his tenth campaign), for the cylinders stop just short of it, and we have nothing but fragments for the last years of this king's reign. With the help of these, however, and by the light of former precedents, it is not impossible to give a very probable guess at the course of events. It was, beyond a doubt, the old story: the Syrian princes looking to Egypt for help. Indeed, one fragment expressly states that "Baal, king of Tyre, putting his trust in Tarku (Taharka), king of Kush, threw off the yoke of Assyria." Now this same Baal of Tyre heads the list of vassal kings who paid their court at Nineveh. So he can have lost no time after his return home. He would scarcely risk the venture alone, and there is in the Bible books a statement which makes it probable that the king of Judah for one, at all events, either actually joined him or was ready to do so. One of the Hebrew historians (Second Chronicles, xxxiii.) tells that "the captains of the host of the king of Assyria" took Manasseh out of his capital, "bound him with fetters and carried him to Babylon," but adds that he was soon pardoned and sent back to Jerusalem. This statement tallies very well with what we know of Esarhaddon as a king, who dwelt much in Babylon, and who, unlike his predecessors,

---

* Translation of H. F. Talbot, in "Records of the Past," Vol. III.

was averse to cruelty and much given to acts of grace. The restoration of Manasseh, who, we may be sure, did not spare protestations of repentance and promises for the future, may have taken place after the Egyptian war was victoriously ended, as he would, not unnaturally, be detained as hostage in Babylon while it lasted.*

12. The king of Judah was probably included among "the allies," when we are told (on another fragment) that Esarhaddon sent out his host "against Tarku, king of Kush, against the men of Egypt and against the allies of Tyre." Taharka, it is said, fled. But Tyre, as once before, under Shalmaneser and Sargon, held out a long time, being inaccessible on its island rock. Esarhaddon, who was now marching down the coast, left a body of troops to reduce it by famine and thirst. The city did not surrender until the war had been decided against Taharka. "Its king, Baal, was pardoned and allowed to retain possession of his throne, and we find both him and Manasseh of Judah again at the head of a list of vassal kings under Asshurbanipal.

13. The march from Raphia into Egypt was most wearisome, and could scarcely have been accomplished but for a contingent of camels and supplies of water in skins, which were furnished by a great Bedouin sheikh. Details about the war itself are unfortunately wanting, but the results are known.

---

* Professor E. Schrader thinks that this incident happened fully twenty-five years later, in the reign of Esarhaddon's son, Asshurbanipal. As Manasseh is said to have reigned fifty years, there would be no chronological impossibility in the way.

Taharka retired southwards into his own native kingdom of Kush. Memphis, the capital of Lower Egypt, was taken and sacked, Taharka's family captured, and the Assyrian rule established over the land. It is probable that this, as it would seem, rather easy victory, was in great part brought about by dissensions among the Egyptians. The local dynasties of the numerous principalities, which had been shorn of their independence and subjected to a firm central authority by Shabaka, the founder of the Ethiopian dynasty (see p. 242), would hardly miss such an opportunity of reasserting themselves. This is the state of things depicted by the prophet Isaiah, whose profound knowledge of contemporary politics made him foresee the doom of Egypt, weak and divided against itself:

"And I will stir up the Egyptians against the Egyptians; and they shall fight every one against his brother, and every one against his neighbor; city against city and kingdom against kingdom.... The counsel of the wisest counsellors of Pharaoh has become brutish.... they have caused Egypt to go astray that are the corner-stone of her tribes .... as a drunken man staggereth." (Isaiah, xix.)

Thus it came to pass that Esarhaddon left Egypt divided among twenty petty rulers, native princes, with the exception of a very few Assyrians, who were probably set in the places of such as had been true to Taharka and his now ruined fortunes. One NECHO, hereditary prince of SAÏS (an important but comparatively new city on the left arm of the Nile), he set over the rest, having first ordered him to give his son an Assyrian name, and to change in like manner that of his capital. So when Esarhaddon, on his way home, had a stele of himself cut in a rock of the Phœnician coast, at the mouth of the river now called Nahr-el-kelb (see ill. No. 66), side by side with that of his father, he could with literal truth assume the new and peculiar title which heads the long inscription on that monument: "King of the kings of Muzur (Egypt)." On that same rock, six hundred years before, Ramses II., the victor of Kadesh (see p. 30), had had *his* effigy carved out, together with several more sculptures, to commemorate his triumphs in his wars against the Hittites. When, therefore, the Assyrian conquerors joined their steles to those of the older Egyptian conqueror, it was with the distinct intention of humiliating Egypt by contrasting her former glory with her present low state. And there they are to this day, peaceably together, and the distance between them is as though it were not; the six centuries that divide them have melted into the hazy background of time, the murmuring waves of which beat drowsily around their mighty memories,—as those of the bluest of seas against the rock from which they silently preach of greatness departed, of rivalries hushed, fierce passions quenched in the cool shadow of Death, which mellows all glare, and soothes all turmoil into glorified dreams of the past.

14. Among Assyrian rulers, Esarhaddon undoubtedly is, as has been unanimously admitted, by far "the noblest and most gracious figure." * His end, too, has a certain romantic charm. He voluntarily

---

* Ed. Meyer, "Geschichte des Alterthums," Vol. I., p. 474.

laid down the burden of royalty and abdicated in favor of his son, Asshurbanipal. It were vain to look for motives and explanations in Assyrian annals; they give the bare facts. It is thought, however, that the king's health was impaired, and that he did not feel equal to face the difficult and troublous times which were coming on ; for already Taharka was rallying from the defeat he had suffered only four years before ; the princes who had fallen off from him had found that they had not gained much by exchanging his supremacy against the Assyrian rule, and a formidable coalition was preparing to re-open hostilities, which would call for speedy and vigorous action. It was natural that the weary king, with the presentiment on him of his approaching end, should resign the task into the hands of his young and active son, who, moreover, seems to have been associated for some time with the cares and duties of power. He solemnly and publicly resigned to him the royalty of Assyria. We know, from the annals of Asshurbanipal, the very date of the event. On the 12th day of April, 668 B.C. a lucky day,—"he assembled the people of Asshur, great and small, and from the shores of the Upper and Lower Seas (the Mediterranean and the Persian Gulf)," for the consecration of his son's royalty, to whom the oath of allegiance was sworn before the great gods. From this moment Asshurbanipal "ruled the kingdom of Asshur," and "entered, with joy and shouting," into the royal palace of Sennacherib "in which his father, Esarhaddon, was born, and had grown to man's estate . . . . where he had reigned, and whence he had extended his dominion over all the kings, and increased the number of his subjects at the cost of foreign nations."

15. Esarhaddon reserved to himself the royalty of Babylon, whither he retired, but even that only nominally, for he appointed as viceroy a younger son of his, SHAMASH-SHUMUKIN. There is a letter to him from Asshurbanipal, wherein the young king entitles himself "king of Asshur," and addresses his father as "king of Kar-Dunyash, of Shumir and Accad." Esarhaddon died at Babylon within the year after his abdication.

XI.

THE GATHERING OF THE STORM.—THE LAST COMER AMONG THE GREAT RACES.*

1. IF we pause to think of it, we shall be surprised to find what a very small patch of our earth has hitherto engrossed us. We have, indeed, had side-glimpses of Egypt and even Arabia, and the Phœnicians drew our eyes for a moment towards the far west of Europe. But, on the whole, we have, in reality, for nearly two volumes, been circling round and round within a truncated triangle of land, bounded on three sides by mountain ranges, —those of Lebanon, Nairi and Zagros,—and on the fourth by an imaginary line drawn across the desert from the Persian Gulf to the Mediterranean; and the merest glance at a map of the world will show us what an imperceptible particle of the eastern hemisphere that makes. And of the four great races which count in the history of mankind, as being so-called " culture-races," only three have appeared as prominent actors on this limited but most momentous area: the Turanian, the Hamitic and the Semitic. Of these we have seen the former

---

* This chapter should be followed step by step on the second map, " Navigations of the Phœnicians," etc., or it will be read to very little purpose.

consistently supplanted, if not obliterated, by the two later and more gifted sister races, and among these again the Semitic race steadily gaining pre-eminence. We have now reached the time when the fourth, the last comer among the great races, advances rapidly to the front,—the race which is henceforth to lead in the world ; which even now maintains its rule, nay, spreads it each day more widely and plants it more firmly over all the earth : the race to which the people of this continent belong, as inheritors of the blood and culture of classical antiquity and of all the nations of Europe.

2. This is the race, several members of which are mentioned in Chapter X. of Genesis (2-5) as children of Japhet. With some of these we have become slightly acquainted in the course of the preceding pages: YAVAN, ELISHAH, KITTIM, all branches of the Greek family of peoples ; TARSHISH in the West, and, in the opposite direction, MADAI (the MEDES), and, quite lately, GOMER (the GIMIRRAI of the inscriptions, the CIMMERIANS of the classics). (See p. 338.) But the members of the Japhetic family known to the biblical Hebrews were only a very few offshoots of that most prolific stock, of which, moreover, we must seek the original seat in a more remotely eastern region than any they had any knowledge of,—that vast and imperfectly explored "Table-land of Central Asia," which is more and more generally thought to have been the common cradle of mankind.*

---

* See "Story of Chaldea," p. 186.

3. There is every reason to believe that, when the first great dispersion took place (in the course of how many centuries—who shall say?), a large division lingered behind in the old homesteads for ages, thereby developing a very distinctive type, both physical and moral, and a language more varied, more flexible, more capable of perfectionment than any of the others—the language which became the parent-tongue of all the European languages, ancient and modern, and of some Oriental ones. In that tongue, when these loiterers at length obeyed the common law and began to move and disperse in their turn in quest of novelty and adventure, they called themselves ARYAS, *i. e.*, "the noble," "the venerable," doubtless asserting thereby their own superiority over the native tribes or peoples which they found wherever they pushed their way, and which they invariably subjugated or destroyed, and, in all cases, looked upon with the utmost contempt. For this reason, this entire division of mankind—the fourth great race, with all the nations into which it divided and subdivided in the course of time—has been called the ARYAN RACE. This, at least, is one of the names under which it is most generally known. There is another, which took its origin in the manner of the division of the race.

4. For while one portion restricted their wanderings within the limits of their own continent, Asia, the other, at long intervals but in huge instalments, poured into Europe, mainly through the wide gap of flat steppe-land that stretches between the southern outspurs of the Oural Mountains and the Cas-

pian Sea,—a gap which may be said rather to unite the two continents than to separate them, it is so invitingly accessible. The only obstacle which it opposed to migrating crowds was the Oural River, and rivers are never much of a barrier; where a ridge of mountains will arrest a migration for a hundred years, a river will not do so for a month. All the nations of Europe could trace their origin to these migrations if there were a sufficiency of monuments. As to the Asiatic portion of the race, an important, —in some respects the most important,—branch of it, descended into the great peninsula of India; not, of course, across the wide and utterly impassable belt of the Himâlaya, the highest mountain range in the world, but through that break between the western end of the Himâlaya and the chain of the Hindu-Kush, through which the river Indus forces its way by an abrupt bend. For this reason, the Asiatic and European branches of the Aryan race have been comprised under the double name of THE INDO-EUROPEAN RACE, which felicitously recalls their original unity, while indicating their present divergence. German scholars at one time introduced the fashion of calling the race INDO-GERMANIC, pointedly ignoring all other European nations with a superciliousness somewhat savoring of arrogance. But the scientific world in general very properly ignored this bit of misplaced patriotism, and adopted the other far more correct and comprehensive name. As to the biblical one—Japhetic Race—it has been discarded altogether, as insufficient.

5. The Indo-European race entered the historical

stage of the world under very auspicious conditions. Not only were they the inheritors of all that had already been done by others in the way of culture, but they brought, fully developed, to their task of continuing the great work, the two great characteristics which stamp the race as the noblest and most perfect variety of the human species, and by which they were to make the world their own: the faculty of enduring and adapting themselves to any conditions of life, and—highest gift of all—the faculty of indefinite improvement, unlimited achievement in any line of knowledge, thought, art or action to which they might be led to apply themselves.

6. The great Asiatic half of the Aryan race came in time to split itself into two distinct portions. One, as already mentioned, descended into India and stayed there. The other, wandering to the southwest of the primeval home, and after crossing sundry mountain ridges, spread over the vast region comprising the modern countries of KABOUL and AFGHANISTAN and the eastern half of modern Persia. This region was, in classical antiquity, broken up into many not particularly well known countries with strange, unfamiliar names. Of these, BACTRIA is perhaps the most clearly defined; but by far the greater part of this remote territory went under the vague but significant name of ARIANA, *i. e.*, territory occupied by Aryan peoples. Or perhaps, more properly, "tribes"; for all this region, unlike Bactria, which is a pleasant land of mountains and valleys, not ill-provided with water, is com-

posed of grassy steppes alternating with sandy wastes, where rivers, after a brief course through some oasis, run dry or soak into the sand, so that migrating crowds, as they traversed it in their westward course, remained nomads of necessity, finding no inducement to settle down to farming. But as they moved still further westward and reached the outposts of the Zagros and the mountains of Elam, they did find such inducement, amply, since those rich and fertile slopes and valleys and the adjoining highlands had long been occupied by ancient peoples of an earlier race ; so that they found cities and well cultivated lands to take possession of, and a native population ready to their hand, to be reduced to subjection and subserviency.

7. The name "Ariana" became corrupted into ERAN, or IRAN,* and this has been, and still is, the designation under which comes the entire family of Aryan peoples that have dispersed over this particular portion of Asia. In their wanderings over the face of the Eranian steppes and deserts they continually encountered tribes of Turanian nomads, who, being the older in possession, naturally treated them as intruders. They were, moreover, encompassed on the north and north-east by unmixed herds of the same race—the TURCOMEN of modern TURKESTAN. Thus the most deep-rooted hostility, the most inextinguishable hatred, was established between the two races, and has endured, un-

---

* Practically the same as ERIN, or Ireland, both being equally evolved from the original ÂRYA.

mitigated, from prehistoric times through all the long line of ages. "Eran and Turan" are to this day opposite terms in geography, ethnology and Asiatic politics, and the strife of Eran and Turan, as it has ever been the substance of those peoples' life, has been all along the one theme of their national traditions, poetry and epos.

8. The first among Eranian nations to come forward and win renown and power were the Medes, called "Madai" in chapter ten of Genesis as well as on the Assyrian monuments. It is impossible to guess how long it took them to wander from Eastern Eran to the foot of the Zagros. Towards the middle of the ninth century B.C. they must already have been in possession of many of its valleys and outer slopes, for it was about that time that they first came in collision with Assyrian forces, and we find their name in the inscriptions of Ramân-nirari III. (See p. 194.) After that we can see them gathering power and importance, as shown by the fact that they are mentioned more and more frequently in later reigns, until expeditions against Medes, first in the fastnesses and highlands of the Zagros, then far beyond this barrier, even into the Eranian deserts, become one of the chief preoccupations of Assyrian kings. They speak of three kinds of Medes: the "strong" or "powerful Medes," probably the warlike tribes that had gained a permanent stand in the fastnesses of the Zagros; the "distant Medes," or "Medes of the Rising Sun," with cities and settlements scattered along the southern slopes of the Elburz Mountains, and further east ; and the "No-

madic Medes," apparently rovers of the Eranian steppes. These latter are ingeniously called "*Madai Aribi*" ("Arab Medes"), to indicate that their mode of life was similar to that of the Arabs. It is the boast of later kings, from Tiglath-Pileser II. downward, that they subdued the "distant Medes of the Rising Sun," and that their rule extended eastward to Mount Bikni. Unfortunately it is not very clear as yet where exactly in the East these mountains, said to be rich in marble or alabaster, are to be looked for.

9. If these indications were not sufficient to show that, even as late as Esarhaddon's reign, the Medes did not yet form a united and compact nation, the fact is fully proved by the absence of national government among them. Lavish as all ancient records are with the title of "king," which is awarded to every petty chieftain, we never hear of Median "kingdoms" or "kings," but only of "towns" and "heads" or "chiefs of towns," and that points to a very loose social constitution, and a form of government the most primitive of all after the patriarchal. It is what may be called the "clan-stage" of society. They even fought in clans,—spearmen, archers, and cavalry "all mingled in one mass and confused together," as they were brought into the field by each clan-chief, instead of being divided into distinct bodies and companies as regularly organized armies are. This detail we owe to Herodotus, the Greek traveller and historian, who also informs us, in perfect accordance with what we gather from the Assyrian monuments, that the Medes in ancient

times "dwelt in scattered villages, without any central authority."

10. It is probable that they intrenched themselves first in the very rugged mountain land between the head ridge of the Zagros—now held by robber tribes of Kurds—and the Caspian Sea, then descended and spread gradually to the south-east, occupying the different countries and small kingdoms as the Assyrians vacated them after plundering and devastating them, and choosing the times when they were left prostrate, impoverished and incapable of efficient resistance. Thus, some principalities were formed which became the nucleus of the future kingdom. One of the earliest was that kingdom of Ellip, which, under the old king Dalta, had so long been loyal to Sargon. (See p. 265.) When Media had become a united and powerful state, its capital, ECBATANA, or AGBATANA (modern HAMADÂN), was situated in the midst of that very district, which was called by the classics Media Proper, or Great Media.

11. It is evident that they must everywhere have found ancient populations, with set customs and institutions of their own. These populations were mostly of Turanian stock, very likely mixed with Hamitic, or even (as probably in Elam) with Semitic elements. Aryans never were much inclined to mix with other races; so the newcomers formed a haughty governing aristocracy among the people whom they subjected to their rule. The distinction was further kept up by the two greatest dividers of men, next to race: difference of language and

difference of religion. Still it was hardly to be expected that the conquerors should not be influenced at all by contact with nations who were far from being in a state of barbarism, whose culture, indeed, being old and established, was, so far, superior to that of their conquerors, who were only just coming out of the nomadic stage. So, when the Medes have become one nation and one state, (the name including all the various alien elements either assimilated or reduced to subjection by them), we shall find them a very mixed people, and their religion especially, in its final form, a most remarkable product of the fusion between older forms of worship of entirely different, nay, opposite types. But these subjects can be properly and fully treated only in another volume, which will be principally devoted to the ancient Eranian race. In this place we have to do with the Medes in so far only as they form one of the heaviest clouds in the storm that is fast gathering over the too-exalted head of Asshur. Just one moment longer, however, we may pause, to note how unlike the real facts are to the string of fantastic inventions that have been worked into a national mythical legend in the fabulous story of Semiramis. (See pp. 196-200.) There we see a Median empire flourishing and conquered by the Assyrian Ninus over 2000 years B.C., *i. e.*, about 1500 years ahead of the time when Medes are heard of first as an insignificant barbarous tribe, and some 400 years before Assyria appears at all as a separate country. But then the Greeks got the story from Median sources, and the Medes, who had succeeded the

Assyrians as masters in Asia, may have liked, from national vanity, to exaggerate the duration and consequent importance of the empire they had conquered, and also to represent their conquest in the light of reprisals for one they had suffered in ancient times at the hands of the now annihilated rival.

12. But if the Medes, together with the Chaldeans, alone reaped the fruit of the general revolt which was now soon to encompass Asshur, seemingly at the height of his glory, the catastrophe was by no means due to these two agents alone. The combined efforts of West, South and East would still long have continued unavailing to lay the giant prostrate, even though, in the words of a modern writer, "his own victories were slowly bleeding him to death." In the storm that was steadily gathering, there was, far away in the North, a cloud hitherto unregarded, which kept growing, darkening, nearing, until, joining with the others, it overspread the sky, and thundered forth Asshur's doom. In countries far beyond the ken of the small fraction of the world whose fortunes have hitherto occupied us,—the immense open region north of the Black Sea, now known as Southern Russia,—events had been going on for years,—probably hundreds of years,—which, obscure and confused as the knowledge of them was forever to remain, were, in the fulness of time, to give the decisive push to the scales in which more than that small world's destinies hung anxiously balanced. From the mysterious depths of Central Asia, Aryan hosts kept go-

ing forth at intervals, drawn in the same fateful direction, crossing great rivers, skirting the north of the Caspian, and pouring through the gap between that and the Oural Mountains—a gap which must have been less wide than it is now, in proportion as the Caspian Sea was more extensive. The plains of Russia are seemingly boundless. No barriers there but rivers, very many and wide, the noblest in the world next to the mighty streams of the American continent. There nation after nation could expand, disperse, roam, or settle at will. Truly, if Central Asia were the cradle of the human race, here was that of modern Europe, for there is not one of the nations which now people it whose ancestors did not at some time halt or wander in some part of Russia in their westward progress. The ancestors of the Greeks and Italians had passed long ago, for at the time which we have reached—Esarhaddon's death, 668 B.C.—Greece was a prosperous and already highly cultured land, and Rome herself was nearly a hundred years old. So that the Aryan race was flourishing and bravely working out the promise of its brilliant destiny in the south of Europe, when it was scarcely beginning to push its way to the front in Western Asia.

13. The south of Russia, by its extraordinary fertility, has always been unusually attractive, either to the nomad who wanted pasture, or to the farmer who wanted crops. It was, indeed, just the land to tempt the nomad into settling and farming, and its ancient populations long lived in a stage of culture partaking of both modes of life. The Greeks knew them

vaguely under the general name of CIMMERIANS (more correctly KIMMERIANS). Herodotus knows of certain "Cimmerian cities," and tells that the straits which unite the Azoff Sea to the Black Sea were called "Cimmerian Bosphorus." To the Greeks this region was the extremest north, situated at the uttermost bounds of the world, and the absurdest stories were current about it. Thus it was a vulgar belief that there lay one of the entrances to the lower world (the land of the dead), and that the sun never shone there, whence the proverbial expression: "Cimmerian darkness." Educated, well-travelled men, of course, knew better; witness Herodotus, who, though he never got as far as the lands north of the Black Sea himself, took great pains to collect trustworthy information about it.*

14. It appears that, at some time not specified, another large instalment of Eranian nomads, being pressed upon from behind by certain savage tribes east of the Caspian, took the usual road, crossed the Oural River, the RA (modern VOLGA), the TANAÏS (modern DON), and overran the vast plains long held by the Cimmerians. The Greeks called these hordes SCYTHS, or SCYTHIANS, the Asiatics SAKIII, or SAKI, both exceedingly vague and misleading denominations, since they denoted *all* the roving barbarous peoples of the extreme North and Northeast, many of which, especially in the latter direc-

---

* About the Cimmerians and their kindred peoples, see especially the chapter "Gômer" in Fr. Lenormant's "Origines de l'Histoire" (Vol. II., part 2d, p. 332, ff.).

tion, were undoubtedly Turanian. But the Scythians that passed into Europe were as undoubtedly Aryan, of the Eranian branch. These late comers, coveting the undivided possession of the land, drove the Cimmerians steadily before them, and although a part of these seem to have intrenched themselves in the peninsula now named CRIMEA, by means of a wall across the narrow isthmus (known to Herodotus as "the Cimmerian Wall"), the mass of the people, after making a desperate stand on the banks of the river TYRAS (modern DNIESTER) and suffering a signal and murderous defeat, abandoned the now desert land to the invaders and retreated further west, or rather to the south-west. Having thus been forced to resume their wandering mode of life, they crossed the river ISTER (modern DANUBE), descended into the rugged land known to the ancients as THRACE (now BULGARIA and ROUMELIA), already occupied by a settled population of the same stock as themselves, the wild and warlike nation of the Thracians, which never thoroughly mixed with the Greeks, nor assimilated their refinement of mind and manners. A large surplus of the dislodged Cimmerians overflowed, across the Bosphorus, into Asia Minor, where they caused a commotion not unlike that raised in water by the fall of a stone.

15. History begins, for Asia Minor, far later than for the Semitic river-land and the sea-coast of Canaan. Even the beginnings of the Greek colonies along the Ionian coast-land and the southern shore of the Black Sea are wrapt in the twilight

67.—HITTITE ROCK-SCULPTURE IN THE PASS OF KARABEL (NEAR SMYRNA).
(ERRONEOUSLY THOUGHT BY THE GREEKS TO REPRESENT RAMSES II.)

of myth and epic legend which, on the Euphrates, had made way for authentic monumental records as early as 2000 B.C., and, in some instances, much earlier still. As to the population, political division, and culture of the wonderfully favored land which goes by the general name of "Asia Minor," it is only lately that we have been enabled to form a tolerably trustworthy, though still very vague and general idea on these subjects. The researches, based on recently discovered monuments to which Professor A. H. Sayce has especially devoted himself for the last few years, have shown that it was the seat of an ancient and very high culture, brought thither by Hittite settlers who, probably as early as the fifteenth century B.C., began to spread in that direction from the mountain-lands of Taurus and Naïri (later Armenia), which we found occupied in their eastern portions by an important branch of the race, the people of Urartu (Alarodians). (See pp. 30, 31, 33, 203-205.)

16. In Ionia proper, on the road between the ancient cities EPHESUS and SARDIS, the capital of ancient LYDIA, and 25 miles from modern SMYRNA, there is a pass through a steep and rocky ridge. In that pass the traveller is confronted by sculptures cut in the rock, and representing a warrior in an unfamiliar garb. Herodotus saw them when they were probably in better preservation than they are now, and marvelled much at them. He admits that the Ionians did not know whom they represented, but is under the impression that they were meant for the Egyptian conqueror, Ramses

68.—HITTITE ROCK-SCULPTURE AT IBRIZ IN CILICIA, REPRESENTING A HITTITE GOD.

II., whom the Greeks knew under the name of SESOSTRIS, and erroneously believed to have extended his rule beyond the Taurus. There is a certain humor in the fact that, instead of being the memorial of an Egyptian conquest, these sculptures should have turned out to commemorate the advance and rule of the Egyptians' most constant and powerful enemies. (See ill. 67.)

17. Another most interesting Hittite monument is the rock-sculpture at IBRIZ, in Cilicia, somewhat to the north-west of Tarsus. It is described as

"representing a thanksgiving to the god who gives fertility to the earth. The god is a husbandman, marked as a giver of corn and wine by his attributes. . . . he wears the very dress still used by the peasantry. . . . the high-peaked cap still in use among some Kurdish tribes; the tunic fastened round the waist by a girdle . . . .; and the tip-tilted shoes are the ordinary sandals of the country, with exactly the same bandages and mode of fastening. . . . It is interesting also to notice that some of the patterns on the priest's dress have not yet gone out of fashion amongst the Cappadocian peasantry." * (See ill. 68.)

18. Cappadocia boasts numerous Hittite remains—not only rock-sculptures and sepulchres hewn in the rock, but buildings, cities, palaces, with portals guarded by lions, and apartments disposed much in the Assyrian fashion. The most important of these ruins are those discovered at BOGHAZ-KEUI, where the palace is overlooked by a flat rock, crowned with two citadels, a little beyond which rise walls of live rock, and these, having been slightly smoothed for the purpose, are covered with

---

* Colonel Sir C. W. Wilson, quoted in Wright's "Empire of the Hittites." p. 61.

sculptures representing an entire procession of strange-looking personages and animals almost surely of mythological import. All over Asia Minor, in fact, are scattered traces of an early and powerful Hittite culture, much of which must have survived the greatness of this remarkable race. Thus when a Greek colony was established at Ephesus, in Ionia, they found there a sanctuary of Atargatis (the Hittite nature-goddess, answering to the Semitic Ishtar and Canaanitic Ashtoreth), the centre of whose worship was the national capital, Karkhemish. (See p. 35.) They were especially struck by the characteristic peculiarity of this worship—the hundreds, sometimes even thousands, of ministering women,—and their vivid fancy at once transformed it into a wild and fantastic legend, that of the warrior-women, the Amazons. "In early art," says Professor Sayce, "the Amazons are robed in Hittite costume, and armed with the double-headed axe; and the dances they performed with shield and bow, in honor of the goddess of war and love, gave rise to the myths which saw in them a nation of woman warriors."* According to Greek traditions, not only Ephesus, but Smyrna and several more cities along the Ionian coast-land, were founded by Amazons. This in every instance points to the Hittite origin of the cities, as indicated by the most characteristic feature of the Hittite religion, which it had in common with those of Canaan and the Assyro-Babylonians. The Greeks, who

---

* A. H. Sayce's "Herodotus," p. 430.

always willingly adapted foreign ideas to their own, retained the worship of the Hittite goddess at Ephesus, but gave her a Greek name. Her sanctuary became one of the most popular and renowned holy places in the Greek world : her temple was so lavishly endowed by Greek wealth and adorned by Greek art as to be proclaimed one of the wonders of the world. Yet neither goddess nor worship were ever quite divested of certain Asiatic peculiarities and a certain barbaric splendor, foreign to the usual chaste refinement and moderation of Greek thought and taste.

18. Ephesus, Smyrna, and several other of the more important Greek-Ionian cities, were scattered along the coast-land of a country which became very famous under the name of LYDIA, at the mouths of its finest rivers. When Greek emigrants, driven from home by political feuds, began to settle in the choicest valleys of this beautiful littoral, as early as about 1000 B.C., they encountered but feeble opposition from the population whom they found in possession, for the Lydians, a people principally of Hittite race, though brave, were rather effeminate and of careless habits. They had long been governed by kings, but no trustworthy information about them is attainable until some three centuries later. There are indeed traditions of two dynasties, with long lists of sovereigns, but they are of as mythical a nature as the early dynasties of Berosus, being represented as of divine origin, *i. e.*, directly descended from the Lydians' supreme god MANES and his son ATTYS. The latter was

clearly the "mild sun-god," very much the counterpart of the Adonis-Tammuz of Babylon and Canaan. He, too, was young and fair, and met a tragic end, according to some versions, from a wild boar's tusk. He also was loved by the nature-goddess (here called KYBELE), who, frantic with grief at having lost him, roamed through the world shouting and weeping, in search of him. The festival of Attys, like that of Adonis-Tammuz, came round at the opening of spring, lasted three days, and was of decidedly orgiastic character.* It was introduced, together with the names of the three deities (and popular tradition preserved a distinct recollection of the fact), from PHRYGIA, the country bordering on Lydia from the East, where the Hittite emigrants would naturally have stopped first on their way to the sea. But the name Phrygia must have been of later date, as it is not of Hittite origin.

19. Taken in a broad and general way, it denotes the Aryan population which, at some time, gradually overspread the peninsular region, bounded on the east by the mountains of Armenia and known as Asia Minor, and it supplanted the earlier Hittite rule. The Phrygians, in this comprehensive sense, were themselves a branch of that great and mighty Aryan stock whom we have learned to know as the settlers of Thrace (see p. 361), and a part of whom for a long time continued to call themselves BHRYGES (their local way of pronounc-

---

* See pp. 130-132, 141, 142; and "Story of Chaldea," pp. 323-326.

ing "Phryges"). So universally recognized is the kinship between the nations on both sides of the Bosphorus and Hellespont, that they are often distinguished from each other only by the name of "European Thracians" and "Asiatic Thracians," or as frequently enclosed in the sweeping designation of "the Phrygo-Thracian or Thraco-Phrygian family of nations." Contrary to precedents, their migration appears to have taken place in the direction from west to east, from across the Bosphorus to the Armenian Mountains. This is one of a very few exceptional cases in history of a partial deviation from a great rule. In their progress they of course broke up into several nations; but Phrygia, from its name, appears to have been the headquarters of the original stock. It was this branch of Aryans which eventually filled all the highlands of Nairi, pushed through to the two lakes, entirely ousted and supplanted the Alarodians of Urartu and the neighboring mountain-countries, and became the ancestors of the Armenian nation, which, mixed with later Eranian elements, is firmly established there to this day. At the point of history we have reached, the Armenian division of the Thraco-Phrygian race had as yet arrived no further than the western outskirts of the Armenian range, where they had formed a small but warlike and enterprising pioneering people. It is this to which Chapter x. of Genesis refers in the Japhetic family as TÔGARMAH, son of Gômer, and to which the Hebrew prophets repeatedly refer as *Beth-Tôgarmah*—"the House of Tôgarmah."

20. It is highly improbable that the ancient Hebrews should have had any knowledge of the Cimmerians who dwelt north of the Black Sea. Late researches make it more and more probable that when they speak of Gômer and his sons they mean the Thraco-Phrygian nations south of that sea, to which those Cimmerians also belonged, although, when they crossed the Bosphorus, flying before the Scythians, they came among them not in the guise of kinsmen, but of barbarians overrunning and devastating highly civilized countries. In the absence of monumental evidence, we are fortunate in having a nearly approximative date for this invasion, secured for us by an event connected with it. About 750 B.C. the Cimmerians destroyed the Greek colony of SINOPE, founded a short time before on the Black Sea, in a country which was later well known under the name of PAPHLAGONIA. So they must have crossed the Bosphorus, at all events, several years before. They then began a system of raids which carried them all over Asia Minor, where they maintained a sort of desultory rule, terrifying and plundering the rural populations, every now and then seizing on and sacking cities, for over a hundred years. Lydia and the Ionian coast-land were not spared; they threatened to invade the Assyrian Empire itself, under an adventurous chief, Tiushpa, who was repulsed by Esarhaddon, probably somewhere in the mountains of Cappadocia, as we have seen. (See p. 338.) We shall hear more of them, as well as of their pursuers, the Scythians.

Well might the prophet say: "I see a seething caldron; and the face thereof is from the north. . . . Out of the north evil shall break upon all the inhabitants of the land. For, lo! I will call all the families of the kingdoms of the north, saith the Lord" (Jeremiah i. 13-15).

XII.

THE DECLINE OF ASSHUR.—ASSHURBANIPAL (AS-SHUR-BÂNÎ-HABAL).

1. WHEN Asshurbanipal assumed, undivided, the honors and labors which he had of late years shared with his father, no one, and he least of all, could have imagined that the empire was within half a century—one lifetime— *Asshurbanipal, 668-626 B.C.*
of utter destruction. Nothing could be outwardly more prosperous than the beginning of the new reign, and the young king complacently records that "when the great gods firmly seated him on his father's throne, Ramân poured down his rain, the seed bore five-fold, the surplus grain was two-thirds, the cattle were good in multiplying, in his seasons there was plenty, in his years famine was ended." Upon his monuments he could, not untruthfully, report a long series of triumphs and victories, and his reign was, in one respect, even more brilliant than those of his predecessors: it was a golden time for literature. For the king was of an intellectual turn of mind, indeed was something of what would be called in our day a collecting bookworm, and in the usual self-exalting opening paragraph of one of his cylinders he particularly rejoices that the great gods have given him "attentive ears," and have in-

69.—ASSHURBANIPAL IN HIS CHARIOT.

clined his mind to the study of "all inscribed tablets." Assyrian art, too, attained its highest finish in his day; he was a builder, as a matter of course, a passionate lion-hunter, and kept a harem which must have equalled that of King Solomon in variety and splendor, for we read that all the kings who owned his rule and offered presents in token of either submission or friendship, sent with their gifts the noblest ladies of their families, generally their own daughters and those of their brothers. With such tastes it is not likely that he should have led the life of those veteran campaigners, Shalmaneser II. or Tiglath-Pileser II. Many of his wars were undoubtedly conducted by his generals, but it is difficult to make out which, from the habit of the Assyrian kings of speaking in the first person and taking all the credit to themselves.

2. We have seen that the death of a king was invariably the signal for revolts and coalitions. The rising which claimed Asshurbanipal's attention in his very first year was that of Taharka, the dethroned Ethiopian, who undertook to dispossess the princes set over the different districts of Egypt by Esarhaddon, and actually established himself in Memphis before an Assyrian army could be sent down to oppose him. Asshurbanipal, however, was not slow in his descent, and when he did arrive, having secured his rear by commanding and receiving the personal homage of "the twenty-two kings of the sea-side and the middle of the sea," he defeated in a pitched battle the army sent against him by Taharka, who thereupon hastily fled further south, to

Thebes, then all the way to his own land of Kush, abandoning both capitals to the invaders. The victor stayed in Egypt just long enough to restore to their seats the twenty vassal kings who had, as of one accord, fled into the desert before the advance of Taharka, and to "strengthen the bonds more than in former days," then, "with abundant plunder and much spoil, in peace returned to Nineveh."

3. Very galling those bonds must have been, for scarcely had the Assyrian departed when plotting began again. Asshurbanipal, who loves to represent himself as a benevolent sovereign, a doer of good and a "forgiver of wrongs," whose kind heart is always pained by ingratitude, complains that "the good I did to them they despised, and their hearts devised evil. Seditious words they spoke, and evil counsel they counselled among themselves." They recalled Taharka, promising to acknowledge "no other lord." But their messengers and despatches were intercepted by the Assyrian generals, who captured several of them, and sent them in chains to Nineveh. This swift and summary measure did not prevent the outbreak. Risings and massacres took place in several great cities, though with disastrous results for the Egyptians. Yet, when the captive kings arrived in Nineveh, Asshurbanipal thought it best to try a conciliating policy and forgave their offence. Necho, especially, the prince of Saïs, who by his birth, ambition and cleverness, took the lead among the rest, he treated with marked favor. He not only set him at liberty, but clothed him in a costly robe of honor, decked

him with ornaments of gold, placed golden rings on his feet, girt him with a sword of honor in its sheath of gold, and thus equipped, and well provided with chariots, horses and mules, sent him back to his kingdom of Saïs, which had been appointed him by Esarhaddon. True, he " made the observances stronger than before," and sent " his generals with him as governors." This unusual leniency was soon proved to be sound statesmanship, for the vassal princes did not favor the next move of the Ethiopian monarch. Taharka, indeed, about this time " went to his place of night," *i. e.*, died. But his successor —some say his nephew, some his step-son—at first showed much energy: fortified himself in Thebes, then marching upon Memphis, which was occupied by an Assyrian garrison, " besieged and took the whole of them." The news of this disaster, being carried to Nineveh by a swift messenger, brought down retribution, quick and sure, in the shape of a large Assyrian force. Their approach seems to have created even more than the usual panic, for the Ethiopian not only fled for his life from Memphis to Thebes as soon as he heard that the enemy had crossed the border, but, finding that he was closely followed, gave up the struggle for good and all and retreated into Ethiopia, where he died soon after. This was the inglorious end of the Ethiopian dynasty.

4. Though quelled with so little trouble, the ill-fated attempt was punished this time with the utmost severity. The treatment of Thebes, the sacred city, the repository of untold treasures of art and

70.—ASSHURBANIPAL CROSSING A RIVER.

wealth, was almost similar to that inflicted on Babylon by Sennacherib, and the report of it carried terror through the world. "That city, the whole of it, in the service of Asshur and Ishtar, my hands took," the victor sweepingly reports; "spoils unnumbered I carried off;" the most conspicuous objects were "two lofty obelisks, with beautiful carving, set up before the gate of a temple." About five years had elapsed since the first rising of Taharka, and for the next ten years the Assyrian rule was undisturbed in Egypt.

5. The cities of the sea-coast, too, were not very troublesome during this period, with the exception of a renewal of hostilities on the part of the king of Tyre, who, however, was reduced to obedience by a blockade so severe that the people of Tyre had been forced to drink sea-water. He sent his son to tender his submission; also his daughter and the daughters of his brothers for the royal harem, with great dowries. The king of Arvad, who had been implicated in the same revolt, came to Nineveh himself, bringing his daughter and many gifts. And when he, shortly after, died, his ten sons "arose from the midst of the sea, and with their numerous presents" came to kiss the royal feet and submit their claims to the royal pleasure. Asshurbanipal appointed one of them to the kingdom of Arvad, and dismissed the others with gifts and marks of honor. Several other kings took the same means of securing his favor in this, the early and prosperous portion of his reign; but the most curious inci-

dent of the sort is the episode with the king of Lydia.

6. One day there came to the frontier of the Assyrian Empire, somewhere in the North-west, men of unfamiliar tongue and garb, who demanded admittance, showing themselves to be friendly. "Who art thou, brother?" asked the Assyrian guards of their chief; "of what place?" But he did not understand, and so they took him to Nineveh and brought him before the king. Here he was tried with "the languages of the rising sun and of the setting sun," but a master of his language there was not, his tongue they could not understand. Unfortunately, the fragment which relates this amusing occurrence is very imperfect and breaks off abruptly; so we do not learn in what way a mutual understanding was at last arrived at. Finally, however, the foreigner proved to be an envoy from GYGES, king of Lydia (Assyrian: GUGU, KING OF LUDI), which Asshurbanipal calls "a district where they cross the sea,* a remote place, of which the kings my fathers had not heard speak the name." This Gugu or Gyges, the founder of a new dynasty and the first historically authentic king of Lydia, of which he had possessed himself by a bold usurpation, was sorely distressed by the Cimmerians, who, descending from their first stations along the southern shore of the Black Sea, were overrunning the whole of Asia Minor (see p. 369), and who made

---

* F. Lenormant prefers this rendering to that of Geo. Smith, "a district beyond the sea."

themselves the more obnoxious because they did not make any regular conquests or settle anywhere, but went about robbing and plundering the countries, storming and sacking cities, in true nomadic fashion. In his great need, and, perhaps, encouraged by the report of Esarhaddon's victory over the Cimmerian chief Tiushpa (see p. 337), Gyges determined on the very reckless step of entreating the assistance of his dangerous and somewhat remote neighbor.

7. This request which, according to the Assyrian code, implied submission, not alliance as among equals, was, very politically, presented to Asshurbanipal as inspired by a prophetic dream. This is his version of the affair:

"The greatness of my mighty royalty was related to him in a dream by Asshur, the god, my creator, thus: 'The yoke of Asshurbanipal, king of Asshur, take, and by speaking his name, capture thine enemies.' The same day that he had seen the dream, he sent his messenger to pray for my friendship. That dream, which he had seen, he sent me by the hands of his envoy, and he repeated it to me."

In what manner and to what extent the required assistance was rendered, we are not told; the narrative merely says:

"From the day when he took the yoke of my royalty, the Gimirrai, masters of the people of his land, who did not fear my fathers, and as for me, had not taken the yoke of my royalty, he captured with the help of Asshur and Ishtar, the gods my lords. From amidst the chiefs of the Gimirrai whom he had captured, two chiefs in strong fetters of iron and bonds of iron he bound, and with numerous presents, he caused to be brought to my presence."

8. The "yoke" which the Lydian king was thus driven voluntarily to take, apparently proved no

light one, for after awhile—probably several years—he ceased to send messengers with presents, "to his own power trusted and hardened his heart," and sent his forces to the aid of PSAMMETIK, king of Egypt, who had thrown off the Assyrian dominion. This was the son of Necho, king of Saïs, who had died soon after the sack of Thebes, and about the same time as the last Ethiopian king. Psammetik had set his heart on achieving what his father had certainly planned: the restoration of a national dynasty in Egypt, and deliverance of the country both from the foreign rule and the tyranny of the petty princes subservient to that rule. Naturally, he looked around for allies, and Gyges of Lydia was one of the first whom he secured. The way in which Asshurbanipal received the message is characteristic of this king, who seems to have been even more habitually religious in his utterances and practices than any of his predecessors, and much given to direct appeals to the deity, as well as to the consulting of oracles and seers. "I prayed to Asshur and Ishtar," he says, "thus: Before his enemies his corpse may they cast; may they carry captive his attendants." His prayer, he further informs us, was heard and literally fulfilled: "Before his enemies his corpse (the Lydian king's) was thrown down, and they carried captive his attendants. The Gimirraï, whom by the glory of my name he had trodden under him, conquered and swept the whole of his country." We may conclude from this that Gyges perished in the struggle, but we are left to guess how and by what means the royal curse was so quickly carried out, and whether Asshurbanipal himself aided the consummation by withdrawing his assistance, or even by giving the Cimmerians a hint that they should not find his armies in their way. He must have been in some way concerned in the disasters which befell the land of Lydia after its defection, for we are told that Gyges' son and successor, ARDYS, thought it best to return to his allegiance.

"After him (Gugu) his son sat on the throne. That evil work by which, at the lifting up of my hands, the gods my protectors had brought destruction on his father, by the hands of his envoy he sent me the tidings of it, and took the yoke of my dominion, thus: "The king whom god has blessed art thou; my father from thee departed, and evil was done in his time; I am thy devoted servant, and my people all perform thy pleasure."

9. Asshurbanipal's cylinder annals have the peculiarity that they do not give the events under the respective regnal years, but dispose them into groups, give a connected narrative of each, and, having finished with one, pass on to another.* This makes his inscriptions much more attractive reading from a literary point of view, but leaves the chronological sequence very uncertain. It is seldom possible to find out a date in this reign, unless from coincidence with dates well-established from other sources. This incident with Lydia we can locate pretty accurately, because we happen to know that

---

* As to the annotated Eponym Canon, the fragments of it which have been discovered do not bring us down quite to 722, the year of the taking of Samaria. The portions of the plain list of *limmu* which were recovered also break off in the first years of Asshurbanipal.

Gyges did in 654, or perhaps 653 B.C. The first Lydian embassy probably took place towards the end of the Egyptian campaign, in 665 or 664 B.C.

10. Although Asshurbanipal never refers to the Gimirraï again, it is not at all impossible that they should have been a vexation to his Western borders all through his reign. One thing is sure: although he complacently accepted the submission of Ardys he was not able to help him much. For it was during the rule of this king, who reigned in Lydia 36 years and survived Asshurbanipal several years, that Lydia suffered most from the Cimmerians, who at one time took and sacked the capital, Sardis, itself, all but the citadel, which was too strong for such primitive tactics as theirs, and where the king held out until they were driven out of the city, or left it of their own accord to seek other plunder. The times of aggression and foreign conquest had gone by for Assyria. She was, instead, threatened with invasion on several sides, and wherever the danger was most imminent thither were her armies directed. It was a matter of necessity, not choice. And however troublesome the Cimmerians may have been, there was just then a point which claimed attention far more pressingly.

11. This was the lake region in the extreme northeast of the empire. The Kingdom of Van, it is true, remained friendly, but the neighboring countries east and south-east of it made some decided hostile moves, backed by a nation remoter still, but which represented a very black point in the gathering general storm-cloud. This nation, designated as

SAKI, *i. e.*, Scythians, was occupying that belt of highland beyond the river ARAXES (now ARAS), which, watered by the river KYROS (now KOUR), stretches along the foot of the great Caucasian ridge between the Black Sea and the Caspian. It was an offshoot of that same branch of the Eranian stock which we saw pressing upon the Cimmerians from behind, in the roll of the great tidal wave of migrations, and dislodging them from their wide lands in the south of Russia. (See p. 361.) Indeed, Herodotus, probably retailing a current tradition, asserts that this division of Scythians descended into Asia in pursuit of the Cimmerians, but missed the way and accidentally got into the highlands of the Southern Caucasus. The explanation is scarcely even plausible; but the fact is certain, and it may be supposed that they somehow stumbled on the defile or pass known in antiquity as the "CAUCASIAN GATES," as that is the only point where a descent would be possible through such a broad, rugged and altogether impracticable mountain barrier as the Caucasus. Their name remained to the region in which they settled; it is given on maps of the ancient world as SACASENE. To the Hebrews of that and later periods it was known as MÂGÔG, and it was not one of the least surprises we owe to Assyriology to find that the "Gôg, King of Mâgôg," of Ezekiel (chapters xxxviii. and xxxix.), was originally a real and historical person, no other in fact than the chief of the Scythians in Asshurbanipal's time, probably a warrior sufficiently renowned to have survived as a by-word of terror in the memory of later generations.

12. This name of Gôg occurs on one of Asshurbanipal's cylinders under the form of GÂGI. In describing the campaign in the north-east,—entirely successful and highly satisfactory in the way of tribute and booty,* —the king concludes by recording that he,—or more probably his general,—captured alive and brought to Nineveh two sons of "Gâgi, a chief (or 'the chief') of the Saki," after taking seventy-five of their strong cities, because they had "thrown off the yoke of his dominion." This last expression, even if it implied more of a boast than a reality, would show that the Scythians of Mâgôg had dwelt where history finds them for at least a couple of generations, and had become in great part weaned from their nomadic habits, although we shall find the following generation resuming them with the utmost readiness when tempted to do so by the prospect of unbounded plunder.

13. We now come to the great features of this reign—the wars with Elam and with Babylon; a succession of events of such magnitude and dramatic interest, told, too, with a literary skill so foreign to the monumental composition of earlier ages, that the rest of Asshurbanipal's annals read like a highly flavored romance.

---

* It is amusing to find among the names of cities captured in this expedition, that of URMEYATE—modern Urumieh, or Urmiah (lake and city),—as an instance of the tenacity with which names survive through ages.

Elam had been for some time on unusually friendly terms with Assyria. At Esarhaddon's death the throne was held by URTAKI, the second of three brothers, who all reigned in turn. About that time there was a drought and famine in Elam, and Asshurbanipal showed, for a wonder, real kindness and generosity. He sent down transports of corn from his own royal stores, and received a number of the Elamite's subjects, who " fled from the face of the drought and dwelt in Assyria until rains fell in his country and there were crops," when they were sent back free and unharmed. Such treatment was certainly very neighborly, and the Assyrian monarch had for once good reason to complain of ingratitude when Urtaki, with several tribes of the coast and marshes, suddenly invaded Accad. The whole of the southern country was governed by Asshurbanipal's younger brother, SHAMASH-SHUMUKIN, whom Esarhaddon had installed as viceroy at Babylon. He sent at once to Nineveh, to implore his brother's assistance. So rapid was the invasion that when the messenger sent down to examine into the state of affairs returned to Nineveh, he reported as follows: " The Elamite, like a flight of locusts overspreading Accad, is encamped over against Babylon ; his camp is fixed and fortified." An Assyrian army quickly raised the siege and Urtaki was driven back into his country ; for, says the king, the gods " delivered judgment against him, who, when I did not make war with him, made war with me." That same year Urtaki died.

From some lines, rather obscure, and with the ends broken off, it almost seems as if he committed suicide. At all events, "the time of his kingdom ended, and the dominion of Elam passed to another."

14. Not to any of his sons, but to his younger brother, TEUMMAN; most probably by violence and against the law of inheritance, for this prince appears to have been familiar with crime in its blackest form. "Teumman, like an evil spirit, sat on the throne of Urtaki," is the vigorous expression in the text. His first move was to attempt the murder of his five nephews, sons of the two preceding kings, who however, got timely warning and fled to Assyria with sixty more of their family, and a great retinue, partly of expert bowmen. Asshurbanipal granted them his protection and when Teumman sent two of "his great men" to demand their surrender, indignantly refused; "the demand of his vile mouth I did not accede to. I did not give him those fugitives." This refusal, of course, amounted to a declaration of war, and Teumman was already preparing his forces when he made the request. The emergency was a serious one, and so Asshurbanipal considered it, even though confident of victory in consequence of omens which were interpreted as boding evil to Elam. But his greatest reliance he placed on the goddess Ishtar of Arbela, his and his father's especial patroness. (See p. 333.) Before setting out for this momentous campaign, which he was to command in person, he went to

Arbela to sacrifice and entreat for a message or a sign. What befel there is related in a page of such high poetical beauty that it stands entirely alone in what we possess of Assyrian literature, only matched, in another line, by the description of the battle of Khaluli. (See p. 318.) Like that classical piece, therefore, we shall give this episode unabridged : *

15. "In the month of Ab (July), . . . in the festival of the great Queen (Ishtar) . . . . I was staying at Arbela, the city the delight of her heart, to be present at her high worship. There they brought me news of the invasion of the Elamite, who was coming against the will of the gods. Thus : ' Teumman has said solemnly . . . "I will not pour out another drink-offering until I shall have gone and fought with him." '

" Concerning this threat which Teumman had spoken, I prayed to the great Ishtar. I approached to her presence, I bowed down at her feet, I besought her divinity to come and to save me. Thus : ' O goddess of Arbela, I am Asshurbanipal, king of Asshur, the creature of thy hands, [chosen by thee and ?] thy father (Asshur) to restore the temples of Assyria and to adorn the holy cities of Accad. I have sought to honor thee, and I have gone to worship thee.' . . . . ' O thou queen of queens, goddess of war, lady of battles, Queen of the gods, who in the presence of Asshur thy father speakest always in my favor, causing the hearts of Asshur and Marduk to love me. . . . Lo ! now, Teumman, king of Elam, who has sinned against Asshur thy father, and Marduk thy brother, while I, Asshurbanipal, have been rejoicing their hearts,—he has collected his soldiers, amassed his army, and has drawn his sword to invade Assyria. O thou archer of the gods, come like a . . . . in the midst of the battle, destroy him and crush him with a fiery bolt from heaven !'

" Ishtar heard my prayer. ' Fear not !' she replied, and caused my heart to rejoice. ' At the lifting up of thy hands, thine eyes shall be satisfied with the judgment. I will grant thee favor,'

---

* The translation is that of Mr. Fox Talbot, in " Records of the Past," (Vol. VII., pp. 67, 68), with here and there a trifling alteration after George Smith.

"In the night-time of that night in which I had prayed to her, a certain seer lay down and had a dream. In the middle of the night Ishtar appeared to him and he related the vision to me thus:

"'Ishtar who dwells in Arbela came unto me begirt right and left with flames, holding her bow in her hand, and riding in her open chariot as if going to battle. And thou didst stand before her. She addressed thee as a mother would her child. She smiled upon thee, she, Ishtar, the highest of the gods, and gave thee a command. Thus:—Take [this bow] she said, to go to battle with! Wherever thy camp shall stand, I will come to it.—Then thou didst say to her, thus:—O Queen of the goddesses, wherever thou goest, let me go with thee!—Then she made answer to thee, thus:—I will protect thee! And I will march with thee at the time of the feast of Nebo. Meanwhile eat food, drink wine, make music, and glorify my divinity, until I shall come and this vision shall be fulfilled' (*Henceforward the seer appears to speak in his own person*):

"'Thy heart's desire shall be accomplished. Thy face shall not grow pale with fear. Thy feet shall not be arrested: thou shalt not even scratch thy skin in the battle. In her benevolence she defends thee, and she is wroth with all thy foes. Before her a fire is blown fiercely to destroy thy enemies.'"*

16. Never was omen more brilliantly fulfilled. Asshurbanipal met Teumman on the banks of the ULAÏ (the classical EULAEUS) where he had fortified himself, in order to close the approach to his capital, Shushan, on this the least protected side, and utterly defeated him. The river was "choked with corpses." Teumman himself, being wounded, yielded to the urging of his son, who said to him, "The battle do not continue," and together they fled into the woods. But their chariot having

---

* How strangely close in general outline is the parallel between this incident of the vision and that of Hezekiah spreading Sennacherib's letter of defiance before the Lord, and praying loudly for help, then the prophet comforting him and saying to him in the name of Yahveh, "I have heard thee!" (See p. 309.)

71.—SCENE FROM THE BATTLE ON THE ULAÎ: THE DEATH OF TEUMMAN.

broken down, they were soon reached by the Assyrians who were in pursuit, and after a brief stand they were both thrown down and beheaded. The fugitive princes were among the pursuers, and the report spread that one of them, TAMMARITU, Urtaki's youngest son, cut off his uncle's head with his own hand. The somewhat meagre narrative given by the cylinders is amply compensated by the sculptures in Asshurbanipal's palace, which represent the successive scenes of this war in its smallest details, with short inscriptions above the principal groups, telling exactly what the actors are doing or even saying. Thus over the figure of a wounded man surrendering himself, there is this inscription: "*Urtaku, the relative of Teumman, who was wounded by an arrow, regarded not his life. To cut off his own head he bade the son of Asshur, thus: 'I surrender. My head cut off. Before the king thy lord set it; may he take it for a good omen.*'" Want of space forbids our setting before our readers more than one specimen of these battle-scenes; but it is a very complete one; a careful perusal of the intricate composition will show almost every characteristic detail of an Assyrian battle. It is, besides, of particular interest, because it includes the death of Teumman: the wounded king is kneeling, with extended, imploring hands, while his son still defends him with drawn bow. Above them the inscription runs thus: "*Teumman with a sharp command to his son had said, 'Draw the bow.'*" The interest in another of these scenes is centred on a chariot driving at full speed, with a warrior in it who holds aloft a man's head. The inscription above informs us that this is Teumman's head carried from the field.

17. It was eventually taken to Nineveh, where it figured in the king's triumphal procession, when, " with the conquests of Elam and the spoil which by command of Asshur his hands had taken, with musicians making music, into Nineveh he entered with rejoicings." The head of Teumman had been tied on a string and hung around the neck of one of his chief allies and friends, a prince of the marshes, who had been captured alive, and now walked in the procession. The two envoys whom Teumman had sent to demand the fugitive princes, and who had been detained prisoners, first learned their master's fate by beholding this miserable show. At sight of it they tore their beards, and one of them ran himself through with his sword, while Teumman's head was " raised on high " in front of (or above) the great gate of Nineveh, and exposed before the eyes of the people, who reviled it. Then began the executions. Those captives who had the misfortune to be of high birth and exalted rank were put to death under the most barbarous tortures, some in Nineveh, others in Arbela. What the annals pass over in a few matter-of-fact words, the sculptures but too vividly bring before us, with the usual explanatory inscriptions. For instance: " . . . . *who against Asshur the god, my father uttered great curses, their tongues I pulled out, I tore off their skins,*" above a scene where both these tortures are represented. It was under these ghastly auspices that the fugitive

princes were restored to their country, and one of them, UMMANIGASH, a son of Urtaki, was placed on the throne, while his younger brother, Tammaritu, received the government of an important province of Elam. These things happened about 655 B.C.

18. It is a curious instance of providential retribution that Asshurbanipal, one of the most ruthless, complacently cruel of even Assyrian monarchs, should have met with ingratitude whenever he did really confer benefits. Thus he certainly had been a good brother to Shamash-Shumukin, the young viceroy of Babylon, whose power and income he had confirmed and increased. Yet the latter planned his overthrow and very nearly succeeded in achieving it. Whether he would have been content with establishing an independent royalty for himself in Babylonia, or whether he meditated ultimately seizing on the Assyrian crown also, there is nothing to indicate with any certainty. At all events, he went to work with as much craftiness and far-sightedness as Merodach-Baladan had ever done, and brought about a coalition as extensive and which proved more nearly successful, because the times were more ripe and the measure of oppression and hatred fuller. Many of the actors in the drama were the same as fifty years ago: now, as then, the conspirator's chief reliance was placed on Egypt, where Psammetik was eagerly watching his chance (see p. 380), and whose name was sufficient to give "the kings of Khatti" courage to rise. It was at this time that the defection of Gyges the Lydian took

place, of whom Asshurbanipal complains that he sent troops to the king of Egypt (see p. 380). Lastly, Ummanigash, the new king of Elam, joined the coalition, his loyalty not being proof against the prospect of recovering his country's political independence combined with the heavy bribe offered by Shamash-Shumukin. He even effected a reconciliation with the son of Teumman, and incited him to action, saying: "Go; against Assyria revenge the slaying of thy father." Shamash-Shumukin found no difficulty, it appears, in gaining over to his cause Babylon itself, and the great cities of the South, "seats of the gods," although Asshurbanipal had been most lavish in adorning their temples with gold and silver, and setting up in them images of the gods. All these preparations, which must have taken some years, were carried on with the utmost secrecy and skill, and just before the outbreak the wily viceroy, who, as the inscriptions pointedly say, "was speaking good, but in his heart was choosing evil," the better to lull his brother into dangerous security, sent to Nineveh one of those complimentary embassies so much in use among Orientals. The envoys were received with the most brotherly cordiality, clothed in robes of honor, feasted at the king's own table and dismissed with costly presents. This last blind gave time to mature the plot, and the outbreak found Asshurbanipal unsuspecting and unprepared.

19. "In those days," he then informs us, "a seer slept in the beginning of the night and dreamed a dream, thus: 'On the face of the Moon it is written concerning them who devise evil against Asshur-

banipal, king of Asshur. Battle is prepared. A violent death I appoint for them. With the edge of the sword, the burning of fire, famine, and the judgment of Nineb, I will destroy their lives.' This I heard and trusted to the will of Sin, my lord. I gathered my army; against Shamash-Shumukin I directed the march."

20. Dreams and prophecies notwithstanding, it is very doubtful whether Asshurbanipal would have been able to weather this storm and win a respite of fifty years for Assyria, had not the house of Elam been hopelessly divided against itself, so that its princes thought far more of fighting and murdering each other than of supporting their ally. Ummanigash, the Assyrian nominee, was dethroned by his youngest brother, Tammaritu, who having "destroyed him and part of his family with the sword," and wishing to remove the unfavorable impression which he had produced on the people of Elam by his ferocious vengeance on his uncle Teumman, flatly denied that he had had any part in his death. Asshurbanipal expressly states that he "spoke untruth concerning the head of Teumman which he had cut off in the sight of my army, thus: 'I have not cut off the head of the king of Elam . . . .'" And when reminded of the allegiance he owed to his former protector, he replied that *he* had taken no engagement of the kind; that "Ummanigash only had kissed the ground in the presence of the envoys of the king of Asshur." So he did not renew the alliance with Assyria, and received a further bribe, offered by the rebellious viceroy of Babylon. His rule, however, was but brief, notwithstanding his attempts at winning popularity. The royal

house of Elam had now arrived at that state of feebleness and dissension which invites usurpers, and such are ever ready in the persons of ambitious generals, who can rely on the devotion of their soldiers. It was in this way that the crown of Elam was suddenly snatched from Tammaritu by a certain INDABIGASH. Tammaritu escaped with life, and, for the second time, fled to Nineveh, with many of his kinsmen, eighty-five in all. He kissed the royal feet, threw dust on his hair standing at the royal footstool, vowing to redeem his past offences by loyal service, if the king would but overlook his defection. Asshurbanipal, reflecting that the fugitives would once more prove useful tools when he would have time to attend to the affairs of Elam, received them graciously, and gave them lodgings within his own palace, where they naturally were as much prisoners as guests.

21. For the present, he had neither time, attention, nor forces to spare for anything but the repression of the revolt in Babylonia. Egypt was allowed to have its own way, and Psammetik not only shook off the Assyrian rule, but got rid of all the vassal princes and restored an undivided royalty in Egypt. Gyges was left to the gods and the Cimmerians were suffered to gain ground unchecked. The states of Syria and the sea-coast are stated to have joined the coalition, but no punishment is recorded as inflicted upon them. The Medes are not so much as mentioned, and subsequent events prove but too well what good use they made of the time. Having thus concentrated all his powers

on one task, Asshurbanipal need not, perhaps, have boasted quite so loud of having accomplished his "rebellious brother's" overthrow. At all events it was complete. The siege of Babylon was so long and severe that the inhabitants were reduced by famine to feed on the flesh of their sons and daughters. How the end came is only hinted at somewhat obscurely: it is said that "the gods threw Shamash-Shumukin in the fierce, burning fire and destroyed his life." We often see in sieges portrayed on the sculptures, that the Assyrian soldiers were in the habit of hurling firebrands into the cities of which they stormed the walls. It is very likely that a general conflagration may have been caused in this manner, and that the viceroy may have perished in it, an end which his brother, quite in accordance with his religious ideas, regards as a special divine judgment. The vengeance which he took on the survivors—pulling out the tongues of some for blaspheming the name of Asshur; throwing others into pits among the stone bulls and lions set up by Sennacherib, *i.e.*, probably in the gates of Nineveh, as a spectacle to the people; cutting off limbs and throwing them to dogs, bears, vultures,—all these horrors he represents as acts of pious homage to the offended deity: "After I had done these things," he says, "and appeased the hearts of the gods my lords, the corpses of the people whom the Pestilence-god had overthrown . . . . out of the midst of Babylon, Kutha, Sippar, I brought and threw into heaps." Then he relates how he further propitiated the gods, by gifts and religious observances and by the singing of psalms.* Then, having reduced to obedience the tribes of Kaldu, Arameans, and the rest of Accad, "by command of Asshur and Belit and the great gods, my protectors, on the whole of them I trampled, the yoke of Asshur which they had thrown off I fixed on them. Prefects and rulers appointed by my hand I established over them."

22. Among the Chaldean princes who had followed Shamash-Shumukin's fortunes was NABU-BELZIKRI, a grandson of Merodach-Baladan,† true to the traditions of his race. To inflict the greatest possible injury on the hated foe, he had recourse to stratagem. He feigned loyalty and applied for help. The king indignantly records that "sons of Asshur" were sent to his aid, and "marched with him, guarding his country like a wall;" but he captured them by treachery and shipped them over to Elam. Indabigash, who then was already king, and who wished to propitiate the Assyrian, sent them back to him with an embassy and offers of alliance. But this attention was far from satisfying the enraged monarch, who sent back to him, through his own envoy, a threatening message demanding the surrender of Nabubelzikri himself and his companions: "If these men thou dost not send," spoke the king, "I will march; thy cities I will destroy; the

---

* For a parallel with the Jewish ideas on similar subjects, see above, pp. 8-10.

† Most probably the son of Nahidh-marduk, Merodach Baladan's youngest son, whom Esarhaddon appointed to the principality of Bit-Yakin.

people I will carry off: from thy royal throne I will hurl thee, and another on thy throne I will seat. As formerly Teumman I crushed, I will cause to destroy thee. This is to thee." The envoy had no occasion to repeat the royal message to his master. The people of Elam, hearing of Asshurbanipal's anger, were greatly frightened and revolted against Indabigash, whom they put to death, placing on the throne in his stead the son of another general, who reigned under the name of UMMANALDASH II.

23. This new usurper was not devoid of dignity, and would not purchase protection by breach of faith with his guest. From some small and much injured fragments it would appear that there was also some correspondence concerning the statue of the goddess Nana, carried into captivity from Erech by the first Khudur-nankhundi, and that Ummanaldash would not return the statue. These two refusals were more than sufficient pretences for an invasion. Asshurbanipal descended on Elam and swept it through in a brief and triumphant campaign, accompanied by the refugee Tammaritu, whom he replaced on the throne in Shushan. Incredible as such recklessness may appear, the first thing Tammaritu did was to turn against his protector and rebel for the second time. He had been in too great haste, however, and had not waited for Asshurbanipal's departure, who at once crushed the revolt—a success of which he gives the credit to Asshur and Ishtar, who, he says, "broke Tammaritu's hard and perverse heart, took hold of his

hand, from the throne of his kingdom hurled him and overwhelmed him." He was not put to death, but carried back to Nineveh, where a more humiliating doom awaited him.

24. It took one more laborious campaign to complete the overthrow of Elam, but this time it was final. City after city, town after town was pulled down, burned, sacked,—warriors were slaughtered, captives carried away without number. Shushan, the capital, was reserved for the last. It had never yet been sacked, and was a right royal prey. Asshurbanipal gloatingly relates how he opened the treasure-houses of the kings of Elam, where wealth had accumulated from the most ancient times, where "no other enemy before him had ever put his hand;" how he brought forth not only that wealth, but all that had ever been paid to the kings of Elam for their aid by former kings of Accad, and now lately by Shamash-Shumukin, besides all the furniture of the palace, even to the couch on which the kings had reclined, the war chariots, ornamented with bronze and painting, horses and great mules, with trappings of silver and gold—all of which he carried off to Assyria. But Shushan was not only the chief "royal" city of Elam, it was also the country's sacred city, "the seat of their gods," and was to suffer all the horrors of desecration as well as plundering. Its great tower (probably the ziggurat), of which the lower part was cased in marble, was demolished and broken into from the roof, "which was covered with shining bronze." The sacred groves, into the midst of which no for-

eigner had ever penetrated, nor even trod their outskirts, were cut down and burned by the Assyrian soldiery. The statues of the gods and goddesses (of whom eighteen are given by name, besides SHUSHINAK, the supreme god, " the god of their oracle, who dwelt in groves,") were carried off to Assyria " with their valuables, their goods, their furniture, their priests and worshippers." The winged bulls and lions " watching over the temples" were either broken or removed, the temples themselves " overturned, until they were not." On this occasion, too, the statue of Nana was at length carried out of the place of her long captivity of over 1600 years to be restored to her own old sanctuary at Erech.* Lastly, thirty-two statues of former and later kings, including one of Tammaritu, all fashioned in gold and silver, bronze and alabaster, were carried to Assyria. On some of them mutilation was inflicted; this is particularly mentioned of one king, a contemporary of Sennacherib, against whom he had made war; Asshurbanipal boasts that "he tore off his lips which had spoken defiance, cut off his hands which had held the bow to fight Assyria." He winds up the dreadful narrative by this most frightful statement of all:

"The wells of drinking water I dried up; for a journey of a month and twenty-five days the districts of Elam I laid waste, *destruction, servitude and drought I poured over them* .... the passage of men, the treading of oxen and sheep and *the springing up of good trees I burnt*

---

* See " Story of Chaldea," pp. 195, 343, 344.

off the fields. Wild asses, serpents, beasts of the field safely I caused to lay down in them." *

And after enumerating the captives he led away, from the daughters, wives and families of several kings, down through the list of governors, citizens, officers and commanders of various corps, to "the whole of the army all there was," the people, male and female, small and great, horses, mules, asses, oxen and sheep, besides "much spoil," he sums up with this grim but expressive piece of exaggeration: "The dust of Shushan Madaktu, and the rest of their cities, entirely I brought to Assyria."

25. This was the end of Elam. As a kingdom, as a nation, it was no more. Its name henceforth disappears from the ranks of countries. And when the time, now so near at hand, arrived, of retribution and vengeance on the destroyer of so many nations, Elam was not one of the avengers. The poor remnants of her people were passing under another rule, still too young to direct events, and stood aloof, rejoicing, but inactive. Yet Asshurbanipal, in the last pages of his great cylinder, still

---

* The Hebrew prophet Zephaniah, who lived about this time, thus announces the approaching end of Assyria: " And Yahveh will stretch out his hand against the north and destroy Asshur, and *will* make Nineveh a desolation and dry like the wilderness. And herds shall lie down in the midst of her, all beasts of every kind . . . . desolation shall be in the thresholds, for he hath laid bare the cedar work. This is the joyous city that dwelt carelessly, that said in her heart: ' I am and there is none beside me :' how is she become a desolation, a place for beasts to lie down in !' . . . . " Have we here a revengeful reminiscence of the words of the Assyrian document, or only a similarity of thought and expression derived from unity of race?

speaks of Elam, even of "kings of Elam." For Ummanaldash had once more escaped with life, by timely flight "into the mountains." When the wasters and spoilers had departed, he returned into his now desert cities,—" he entered, and sat in a place dishonored." But Asshurbanipal had not done with him even yet. The companion of his

72.—ASSHURBANIPAL FEASTING.

flight and disasters was Nabubelzikri, that grandson of the old Chaldean king, and as long as *he* lived and was free the Assyrian's heart was not satisfied. So he sent once more to demand his surrender from the heart-broken whilom king. Nabubelzikri, the inscription goes on to tell with that strange pathos which their great simplicity at times lends to these narratives—

THE DECLINE OF ASSHUR. 403

"Nabubelzikri heard of the journey of my envoy who into Elam had entered, and his heart was afflicted. He inclined to despair; his life he did not regard and he longed for death. To his own armor-bearer he said: 'Slay me with the sword.' He and his armor-bearer with the steel swords of their girdles pierced through each other." *

By this magnanimous act the last of a heroic race saved his friend from a shameful deed, which he

73.—ASSHURBANIPAL FEASTING.

could scarcely, under the circumstances, have helped committing, and himself from worse than death.

---

* How strikingly like this tragedy is to that of Saul! "Then said Saul to his armor-bearer: 'Draw thy sword and thrust me through therewith lest these uncircumcised come and thrust me through and abuse me.' But his armor-bearer would not, for he was sore afraid. Therefore Saul took his sword and fell upon it. And when his armor-bearer saw that Saul was dead, he likewise fell upon his sword and died with him." (I. Samuel xxxi. 1, 5.)

His desperate determination has been fully justified by a small fragment found among the rubbish of the Royal Archives in Nineveh. It is the beginning of a letter, and runs as follows: "*From Ummanaldash, king of Elam, to Asshurbanipal, king of Asshur.—Peace to my brother. . . . Forces do thou send; for Nabubelzikri to surrender I took. I will surrender him to thee. . . .*" Let us hope that the unfortunate monarch, reduced to such abjectness, gave his friend and guest a timely hint. However that be, he kept word with the Assyrian to the letter: he surrendered the corpse of Nabubelzikri and the head of his armor-bearer to the envoy, who took them both into the royal presence. Asshurbanipal only records in his great cylinder that he would not give burial to the body, but cut off the head and hung it round the neck of a follower of Shamash-Shumukin, who had gone with Nabubelzikri into Elam. But a sculpture representing a feast scene in the royal gardens completes this statement in the most ghastly manner. Asshurbanipal reclines on an elevated couch under a vine-arbor; his favorite queen is seated on a throne at the foot of the couch; both are raising the wine-cup to their lips; a small table or stand is before them; on another, behind the couch, are deposited the king's bow, quiver and sword. Numerous attendants ply the inevitable fly-flappers, beyond these musicians are ranged. Birds are playing and fluttering in the palm-trees and cypresses. But the king's gaze is fixed on a horrible object suspended in the branches of one of the latter: it is the head of Nabubelzikri, placed

74.—DYING LION. (ASSHURBANIPAL'S PALACE.)

there that he may delight his eyes and enhance his pleasure in the feast by gloating on the dishonored relic of his dead enemy. They must have had some way of preparing human heads in those days, or they could never have got such prolonged enjoyment out of them.

26. At the same time that Asshurbanipal thus hunted down the last scion of the ancient house of Yakin, he was very shrewdly desirous to reassure and conciliate that prince's former subjects. Of this we have a curious proof in a proclamation, by which he, so to speak, introduced to them the governor he sent to watch and rule them, with a force of soldiers. A draft or copy of this document turned up in the Library at Nineveh, and as it may be interesting to see how an Assyrian royal proclamation was worded, we give it here:

"The will of the king to the men of the coast, the sea, and the sons of my servants.—My peace to your hearts; may you be well.—I am watching sharply, from out of my eyes, over you, and from the face of the sin of Nabubelzikri. . . . entirely I have separated you. Now BELIBNI, my servant, my deputy, to go before, to be over you I send to you. I command . . . . of myself my forces I send. I have joined with you, keeping your good and your benefit in my sight."

27. As for Ummanaldash, he dragged on a couple of years longer a miserable phantom of royalty. And yet, brought low as he was, there was found a man foolish enough to covet the poor shreds of power and pomp that still clung to him: PAKHE, an obscure upstart, caused the country to revolt against him, and Asshurbanipal thus relates the end of his career in Elam: "From the face of the tumult of

75.—DYING LIONESS. (ASSHURBANIPAL'S PALACE.)

his servants which they made against him, alone he fled and took to the mountain. From the mountain, the house of his refuge, the place he fled to, like a raven I caught him and alive I brought him to Assyria."

28. According to the most probable calculations, the open revolt of Shamash-Shumukin took place about 650 B.C., and he perished in 648. Then the two campaigns against Elam bring us to 645 as the most likely date for its final destruction and the sack of Shushan. After that we have the account of one more expedition, that against the Arab princes, who had been led to support the rebellious viceroy. As usual, whenever Arabia is in question, it is impossible to identify the places exactly. The king tells us that he "ascended a lofty country, passed through forests of which the shadow was vast, with trees great and strong .... a road of mighty wood," and "went to the midst of Vas, a place arid and very difficult, where only the birds of heaven and the wild asses are. . . ." The latter description seems to indicate a rather remote district in the interior of Arabia. In this, the last distant and victorious Assyrian expedition we hear of, the spoil in camels and captives was so abundant, that on the army's return to Assyria the captives were gathered and bartered in droves, while camels were distributed by the king to the people "like sheep," and those that were offered for sale in front of the gates of Nineveh, sold for only half a shekel of silver (about 31 cents) apiece. One of the most powerful Arab chieftains, VAITEH, whose territory

bordered on Edom, Moab and Ammon, was captured, and Asshurbanipal granted him his life, though not his liberty, after having, with his own hand, struck down his son before his eyes, " by command of Asshur and Belit," of course. He returned by the road of the sea-shore, for he mentions, incidentally, having " destroyed the people of Akko, who were unsubmissive." These are the last warlike deeds of Assyrian arms in Syria of which we have any record.

29. Asshurbanipal, in the conviction that he had brilliantly weathered the direst storm that ever yet had imperilled the Empire, now considered himself entitled to a public triumph of unexampled splendor. On his return to Nineveh he organized a festive show on a scale surpassing all precedents. In accordance with the Assyrian character, it was of a pre-eminently religious nature, and chiefly consisted in sacrifices and drink-offerings to Belit, " mother of the great gods, beloved wife of Asshur." But the great feature of the procession was that Asshurbanipal ordered the last three kings of Elam —Tammaritu, Ummanaldash and Pakhe, captive— and Vaiteh, the Arab chieftain, to be yoked to his war-chariot, and was drawn by them in state to the gates of the temple, where, having alighted, he lifted up his hands and praised the gods before the assembled army. It was a strange irony of fate which thus placed on a foot of equality the two upstart usurpers and the last descendant of a line of kings, reaching back, for aught we know, to the first invaders of Accad—and a stranger still, that this act of insane

pride should be the last glimpse we have of Assyrian greatness, to be almost immediately followed by an utter and irretrievable fall. This is an almost *too* pointed illustration of the trite, familiar saying!

30. For on this unnatural pinnacle we take leave of Asshurbanipal, although he lived and reigned many years longer. His death, indeed, cannot be placed earlier than 626 B.C., and the latest of his two great cylinders brings down his annals to about 640. But by reason of the absolute lack of monuments this long interval is a blank, as far as knowledge of any events that filled it goes. It is very probable that the last of the great Assyrian monarchs spent those years mostly in enjoying the luxurious leisure to which he naturally inclined, and indulging his literary and artistic tastes, as well as his religious propensities. So much has been said in another volume about his library,* and so often have its contents been referred to, both in that volume and the present one, that more details are uncalled for except to mention that the palace in which the library was situated, and the halls of which were so lavishly decorated with historical slab-sculptures, was not really a new structure, but rather Sennacherib's old palace restored and considerably enlarged. It was the captive Arab chieftains, with their tribes, who were employed on the work of carrying burdens and building the brickwork, which, more than 2000 years later, other Arab

---

* See "Story of Chaldea," Chapter IV. of Introduction, "The Book of the Past."

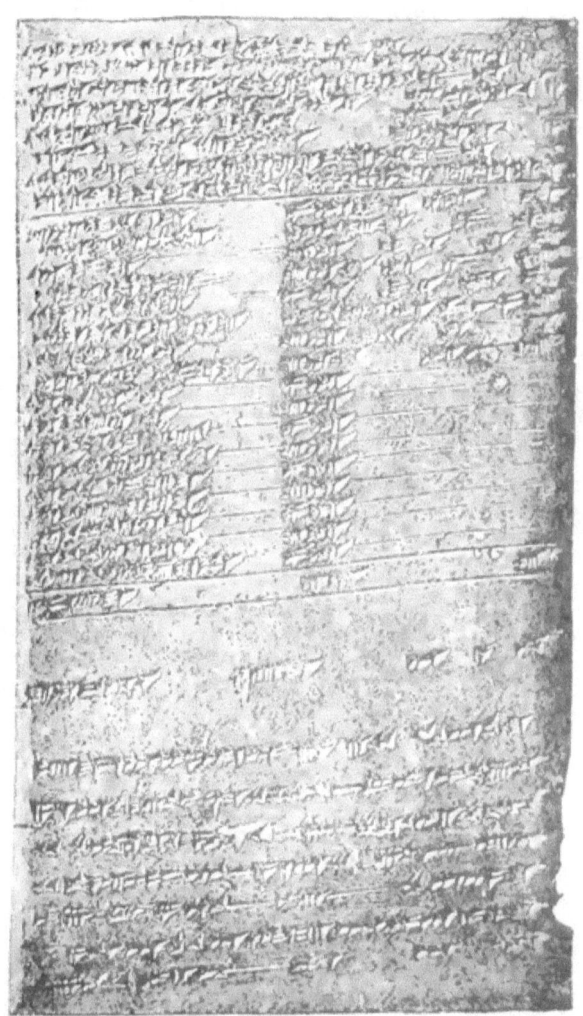

76.—A PERFECTLY PRESERVED TABLET—TWO COLUMNS—ACCADIAN HYMN, WITH ASSYRIAN TRANSLATION FACING IT—FROM ASSHURBANIPAL'S LIBRARY (KOYUNJIK).

tribes under their sheikhs were, in their turn, to clear from the rubbish of ages and uncover to the eager gaze of curious foreigners. Another of those strange coincidences with which history abounds!

31. It was under Asshurbanipal that Assyrian art attained its greatest perfection of execution and detail. As regards mere ornamentation, nothing could surpass the profusion and the exquisite finish

77.—TAME LION AND LIONESS AT LIBERTY IN THE ROYAL PARK. GRAPE VINE AND FLOWERS. (ASSHURBANIPAL'S PALACE.)

of the designs, the richness and delicacy of the tracery. The historical sculptures, representing battles, sieges, treaties, scenes of war and peace both, have been spoken of above (see p. 390). But the hunting scenes and presentations of animals, as usual, bear off the palm in point of interest and artistic beauty. What can be finer, more perfect in form, attitude and expression, than those hounds starting for the chase? (See ill. No. 80.) It seems as though we feel them tugging at the leash, and hear their deep, eager bay. Asshurbanipal's royal kennel has yielded many splendid models to the artists, and he was so fond of his dogs that he had portraits of his especial favorites made in terra-cotta. Several of these statuettes have been found, bearing the animal's name—"TEAR-THE-FOE," and such like— along its back or on its collar (see ill. No. 78). The

78.—TERRA-COTTA DOG. (ONE OF ASSHURBANIPAL'S FAVORITES.)

king was a patron of every kind of sport. Lesser game—wild asses, antelopes—was hunted in many and various ways: stalked, netted, lassoed, driven to a centre. But the game which the king himself almost exclusively affected, was the game of games, the royal lion; not Asshurnazirpal himself had been a more passionate lion-hunter, and never does his handsome figure show to better advantage than in the exercise of his favorite and dangerous pastime, attired in the close-fitting, becoming tunic, richly embroidered, short-sleeved and cut high above the knee, in order to give full liberty to every movement, full play to every muscle.* The lion-hunts represented on Asshurbanipal's sculp-

79.—THRESHOLD-SLAB IN ASSHURBANIPAL'S PALACE (KOYUNJIK).

tures are very numerous, and the Assyrian artists, as usual, appear at their very best when portraying the

---

* See Frontispiece. A particularly spirited and finished composition; unique, too, as in no other do we see the king leading a spare horse. The explanation which suggests itself is that the animal may

30.—LEASHED HOUNDS GOING TO THE CHASE. (ASSHURBANIPAL'S PALACE.)

noble beast in the manifold attitudes called forth by the various stages and moments of the chase. Some of their works in this line have become universally admitted classical models in art ; for instance, the famous dying lion and lioness. (See ill. Nos. 74 and 75.) The latter especially, with her broken back and paralyzed hindquarters, painfully rising on her front paws to hurl a last roar of defiance at the foe, is a masterpiece in the highest sense.

32. Asshurbanipal's name was known to the Greeks in the corrupted form of SARDANAPALUS. They made of him the last king of Assyria, an effeminate tyrant, who spent all his life within his palace, in the enervating luxury and idleness of the harem, until the last crisis came, when he roused himself from his unmanly torpor, and, suddenly developing into a hero, fought for two years for life and crown, and at the last, being overpowered by numbers, erected an immense pyre, on which he burned himself, all his wives and all his treasures. This story, derived from the same source as that of Semiramis (see p. 196, ff.), is as utterly worthless, nor was it believed by *all* the Greeks. Herodotus, for instance, knew better, and speaks of Asshurbanipal's successor.

---

have been a favorite one, and that the rider, being thrown or dragged from the saddle, the king may have secured the bridle, to try and save the frightened horse. The whole scene is too peculiar not to have been the reproduction of a real occurrence, possibly executed at the king's especial command.

XIII.

THE FALL OF ASSHUR.

1. It is much to be regretted, though perhaps scarcely to be wondered at, that Assyrian monuments should utterly fail us for the short period after Asshurbanipal's death, during which the long score standing against Assyria was summarily wound up and paid in full. It is quite in accordance with what we know of Assyrian annalists, that they should be silenced by disasters, and besides, the end, coming so suddenly, must have been preceded by a time of convulsion and tumult, during which the last rulers of an empire, hastening headlong to dissolution, were not in the mood, nor had the leisure to build, to sculpture slabs and engrave inscriptions. We are therefore thrown entirely on Greek traditions and accounts, always incomplete, seldom trustworthy and very fragmentary. To reconstruct in a general way the course of events is about as tedious and uncertain an operation as recomposing a torn-up letter out of fragments rescued from the waste-paper basket, with many of the scraps lost.

2. We do not even know for certain whether Asshurbanipal's immediate successor were the last king of Assyria, or whether there was one more, or even two. In a corner of the great platform at

Nimrud (Kalah), Layard uncovered the ruins of a comparatively small, poorly constructed, meanly ornamented building, the bricks of which bear the name of "ASSHUR-IDIL-ILI, king of Asshur, son of Asshurbanipal, king of Asshur, son of Esarhaddon, king of Asshur." But there are some fragments with still another royal name, and the last king of all is called by Herodotus and other Greek historians SARAKOS, which could very well be an abbreviation and corruption of "*Asshur-ak*hi-idina"; there are, too, a couple of small fragments which evidently refer to a time of disaster and tribulation, and bear that very name. It is therefore not at all impossible that the long line of Assyrian rulers may have closed with an Esarhaddon II.

3. What is certain is, that after Asshurbanipal's death, Assyria's downward course was incredibly rapid and constant, having begun most probably even in the last years of that monarch's lifetime. One Greek chronicler states that "Sardanapalus died at an advanced age, when the power of the Assyrians had been broken down." Now we have seen that Egypt, Syria and Media had slipped from his hold while he was throwing all his weight against Elam and Babylon. Nor does he seem to have made any effort to recover lost ground after his final victory in that direction. He must have known that Psammetik steadily labored to bring the Syrian states under Egypt's dominion, for we read that the Egyptian king made war in those parts during twenty-nine years, in the course of which he took Ashdod and probably other cities,

too. The time was not long gone when such tidings would have sufficed to bring down an Assyrian force, yet no interference appears to have been attempted. True, Urartu had been friendly now for many years; but Scythians and Cimmerians threatened from the north and north-west, yet nothing had been done to check them since that one campaign into the Armenian mountains, which ended with the capture of Gôg, the Scythian chief's, two sons. As for the Medes, they also had been let alone since the first years of the reign, and had wisely kept aloof, having work of vital importance to attend to at home. And when they reappear, it is no longer as a loose federation of separate tribes, under independent chieftains, but as a compact nation, united under the strong rule of a powerful, universally acknowledged king.

4. Exactly how or in how long a time the change was effected, will never be known, as we have no monuments to guide us, but only the Medes' own traditions, as retailed to us by Greek writers. Herodotus tells us that the founder of the new royalty was a certain DEÏOKES, originally a simple city-chief, who gained so much renown for his great wisdom and uprightness, that not only his own clansmen, but people of other tribes and cities as well came to him when they had any quarrels and submitted the issues to his judgment instead of fighting them out; that he cleverly improved his ever increasing and widening influence until he converted it into a real power, so that when, backed by a certain number of devoted followers, he proclaimed himself king over

all the Median cities or tribes, he met no resistance. He built himself a royal residence, the city of Hagmatana (Agbatana), in the country formerly called Ellip, and wasted by Sennacherib (see p. 301), and established there a thoroughly organized central government. When he died, his son, PHRAORTES, quite naturally succeeded him as king of all Media.

5. Now this name of Deïokes is an unusually correct rendering of one which we find on some Assyrian monuments: DAYAUKKU. Sargon, in one of his wars with Urza of Van (715 B.C.), mentions having taken prisoner and carried to Nineveh a certain Dayaukku and his son. And two years later he goes to a country which he calls BÎT-DAYAUKKU, and which appears to border on Ellip, to the north or north-west. "The house of Dayaukku," after the analogy of "the house of Omri," "the house of Yakin," must have been a principality founded by a chief of that name. It was evidently of some importance, since Sargon takes the trouble of naming it individually, together with Ellip, instead of including it in the total of "forty-five city-chiefs," whose submission he received that year. There is therefore nothing improbable in the supposition that a prince of the house of Dayaukku, and bearing the founder's name, was the first to unite the scattered tribes of his nation into a whole. It may very well be that he established the seat of power in Ellip, on account of its beauty and fertility, after that country had been laid waste and its royal line exterminated by Sennacherib; nor is there anything to prove that he built a new capital, while it seems very likely

that he should have restored and enlarged the old royal city of Ellip. What the origin of the name Hagmatana was, we do not know.

6. The Medes had about fifty years of comparative peace, and, of late, total freedom from invasion, in which to accomplish their work of national consolidation and organization—under a leader fitted for the task, a time amply sufficient for a people already ripe for the change. When that leader's son succeeded him on the throne which he had built, the first hereditary king of Media, the young nation was anxious to try its strength, and against whom so naturally as against Assyria, its oldest and most deadly foe, weakened also at this time by her late terrible struggle for life? For the first time the parts were reversed and the invader was invaded. Phraortes (the Greek corruption of the Median name FRAVARTISH), after some successful expeditions against sundry less formidable neighbors, crossed the Zagros and descended into Assyria. The move, however, was imprudent and premature. The old lion, if lamed, was not yet to be bearded with impunity in his own den by one solitary assailant. There was a battle, in which the invaders were routed and driven back, and Fravartish remained on the field. This may possibly have taken place in the last years of Asshurbanipal.

7. The invasion, however, was soon repeated. UVAKSHATARA, called by the Greeks KYAXARES, the son and successor of Fravartish, was a far greater man and better warrior. He attributed his father's defeat to the defective organ-

ization of his army, and at once proceeded to abolish the old division by clans (see p. 354), which gave no chance against such perfectly organized and drilled veteran troops as the Assyrian. Herodotus reports of him that he—

"divided his troops into companies, forming distinct bodies of the spearmen, the archers and the cavalry, who before his time had been mingled in one mass and confused together. . . . This prince, collecting together all the nations which owned his sway, marched against Nineveh, resolved to avenge his father, and cherishing a hope that he might succeed in taking the city. A battle was fought, in which the Assyrians suffered a defeat, and Kyaxares had already begun the siege of the place, when a numerous horde of Scyths, under their king, MADYÈS, son of PRÔTOTHYÊS, burst into Asia in pursuit of the Cimmerians, whom they had driven out of Europe, and entered the Median territory."

8. So far Herodotus. We have already seen (p. 359) that the motive he ascribes to the great Scythian invasion is a fanciful one, and a good hundred years out of the way, since it was as long ago, at the least, that the Cimmerians had appeared on the southern shore of the Black Sea. But the invasion itself is a fact, as authentic as any in history. The barbarians who came thus opportunely to gain a respite for the Assyrian capital, by suddenly drawing Kyaxares away to defend his own kingdom, were the people of Mâgôg (see p. 383), and it has been suggested that their chief, Madyès, may have been a grandson of Gôg (Gâgi), since his father's name, PRÔTOTHYÊS, looks uncommonly like that of PARITIVA, one of those sons of Gôg whom Asshurbanipal captured.* They were a people of horse-

---

* Fr. Lenormant: "Origines de l'Histoire," Vol. II., First Part, p. 465.

men and bowmen, who ate the flesh of horses and drank the milk of mares, whose warfare was one of raids and plunder, like that of the Cimmerians. What started them from their quarters at the foot of the Caucasus, on the river Kyros (see p. 383), is a mystery; most probably they were tempted by the state of general agitation into which the entire Naïri region was thrown through the withdrawal of the heavy pressure exerted on it by the fear of an ever impending Assyrian interference. Left to themselves, the petty nations of the mountain-land were more independent, but also more defenceless, and promised to fall an easy prey to hordes of mounted bandits.

9. Media was by no means the only victim of the Scythian visitation. They swept through the greatest part of Asia Minor, dislodged various peoples, whom they carried along with them on their further road as a wild torrent carries along the trees it uproots and the bridges it breaks to pieces on its way. The Cimmerians, who still roamed about the lands, but were becoming few and scattered, were easily engulfed, and the whole mass rushed and rolled southward. They had overrun Syria and Palestine almost before the unfortunate peoples of those much-suffering countries had heard of their coming, and, according to a tradition recorded by Herodotus, would have gone on straight into Egypt, had not Psammetik "met them with gifts and prevailed on them to advance no further." Whereupon they turned back, but, passing by the city of Ascalon, a body of stragglers stopped to

plunder its famous temple, devoted to the Syrian goddess Atargatis or Derketo.

10. This was the emptying of that "seething caldron" which the prophet Jeremiah, who lived at this very time in Judah, saw "in the North." Several chapters of this prophet (iv., v., vi.) are devoted to the Scythian invasion, and its being "from the North" is repeatedly insisted on:

"Flee for safety, stay not, for I will bring evil from the North, and a great destruction. A lion is gone forth from his thicket, and a destroyer of nations" (iv. 6). "Behold, he shall come up as clouds, and his chariots shall be as the whirlwind: his horses are swifter than eagles. Woe unto us, for we are spoiled" (iv. 13). ".... It is a mighty nation, it is an ancient nation, a nation whose language thou knowest not, neither understandest what they say. Their quiver is an open sepulchre, they are all mighty men" (v. 15, 16). ".... Behold, a people cometh from the north country; and a great nation shall be stirred from the uttermost ends of the earth. They lay hold on bow and spear; they are cruel and have no mercy; their voice roareth like the sea, and they ride upon horses . . . ." (vi. 22, 23).

11. Ezekiel is even more explicit. He wrote years later, when the captivity which Jeremiah announced had actually come to pass. But so vivid was the recollection of the Scythian scourge, the effects of which he had perhaps witnessed in his early youth, that in one of his grandest visions, in which he portrays in the form of a prophecy the fury of all the nations of the world let loose against the people of Yahveh but checked by him in the end, he borrows some of the most telling features from that visitation. The invading hordes are personified under the name of "Gôg, of the land of Mâgôg," and said to bring with them "a great

company" of nations, "Gômer and all his hordes, the house of Tôgarmah in the uttermost parts of the North, and all his hordes, even many peoples with thee."

"Thou shalt come like a storm, thou shalt be like a cloud to cover the land, and all thy hordes, and many people with thee. . . . Thou shalt devise an evil device; and thou shalt say, I will go up to the land of unwalled villages; I will go to them that are at quiet, that dwell securely, all of them dwelling without walls and having neither bars nor gates; to take the spoil and to take the prey; to turn thine hand against the people that are gathered out of the nations which have gotten cattle and goods. . . . Thou shalt come from thy place out of the uttermost parts of the North, thou and many peoples with thee, all of them riding upon horses, a great company and a mighty army. . . . I will bring thee upon the mountains of Israel; and I will smite thy bow out of thy left hand, and will cause thine arrows to fall out of thy right hand. . . . And it shall come to pass in that day that I will give to Gôg a place for burial in Israel . . . . and they shall call it the valley of the multitude of Gôg."

12. We do not know in what way Palestine and Syria were rid of their terrible visitors. They are said to have held Western Asia under their dominion for a number of years (twenty-eight, according to Herodotus, but the figure is now thought to be exaggerated), "during which time," says the same historian, "their insolence and oppression spread ruin on every side. For, besides the regular tribute, they exacted from the several nations additional imposts, which they fixed at pleasure; and further, they scoured the country and plundered every one of whatever they could." It is scarcely possible that Assyria with her accumulation of wealth, the fruit of so many centuries of war and rapine, should

have been spared. Historians, indeed, consider this invasion to have been the shock that shattered the already loosened and never very compact structure of the Assyrian Empire down to its foundation, and disabled it from resistance when the final and more regular assault was made. Mr. Geo. Rawlinson and Fr. Lenormant are of opinion that the frightful condition in which most of the palaces were found by Layard and Botta, due as much to fire as to demolition, is a visible token of the Scythians' passage over the land. The almost total absence of any valuables among the ruins accords well with the predatory character of their raids; but what speaks most loudly in favor of the suggestion is the poverty-stricken meanness of the small and unsightly dwelling—palace no longer!—which Asshurbanipal's successor, Asshur-idil-ili, built for himself in the south-east corner of the great platform at Kalah : " This coarseness and meanness," remarks Lenormant, " bear witness to the haste with which a residence of some sort had to be put up for the king immediately after a great disaster. . . : A comparison of this lowly building of Asshur-idil-ili's with the splendid sculptures filling that which his father had constructed at Nineveh, is more eloquent than any argument to paint the change in the condition of the Assyrian monarchy."*

13. The Hebrew prophet Zephaniah, a contemporary, perhaps expected Assyria to perish at the hands of the Scythians, when he uttered his scath-

---

* " Origines de l'Histoire," Vol. II., Part First, p. 446, note.

prophecy. (See p. 402, note.) But the end was not to come for a few years yet. Kyaxares was unable to expel the barbarians by sheer force, and resorted to craft. It was reported that he and his nobles invited Madyês and the greater part of his people to a banquet, and, having made them drunk, massacred them. Some such stratagem may have been used, but it could have been only a very partial remedy. It is probable that Kyaxares, moreover, by some means—promises and bribes very likely—sowed division among them, and attached a part of them to himself, for later on we are told that he had a body-guard composed of Scythians, who taught archery and hunting to the young sons of the Median nobles. Such a defection, after a massacre, following the slaughter of the chiefs,—for it is not to be supposed that an ambush in the form of a feast would have been laid for any *but* the chiefs,—would weaken the rest sufficiently to make them leave the land. At all events, they disappear, and to use a favorite Assyrian phrase, "the trace of them is not seen."

14. Now at last Kyaxares could turn his mind and forces once more to his long-cherished and long-deferred scheme. The then reigning Assyrian king—the Saracos of Berosus and the Greeks unwittingly suggested his next move, by incautiously appointing to the viceroyalty of Babylon a Chaldean, NABU-PAL-UZZUR, generally known as NABOPOLASSAR, who immediately entered into a close alliance with the Median king. They agreed that they should unite their efforts to overthrow the tottering

empire and share the territory that had obeyed its rule. Nabopolassar, of course, was to be king of Babylon. To seal the treaty they arranged that Kyaxares' daughter AMYTIS (or AMUHIA) should be given in marriage to NEBUCHADREZZAR* (NA-BU-KHUDURUZZUR), the son of Nabopolassar. The agreement thus became a sort of family covenant.

15. In 608 the united Median and Babylonian forces began the siege of Nineveh. We may take for granted that each of the allies brought into the field the contingents of all the tribes and petty peoples whom each held under his subjection, although few are mentioned by name. The desolation was great. Public prayers were offered, penitential psalms were sung, a general fast of a hundred days was proclaimed for the city and army. Nor were more active measures neglected. The great capital had still endurance left for a two-years' siege. Then the end came. We are simply told that Saracos, when the enemy was close at hand, set fire to the royal palace and perished in the flames. There is nothing improbable in this tradition, but nothing to prove it; no details whatever exist concerning this great catastrophe. The Tigris is said to have left its bed that year and broken through the city wall, opening a wide breach to the besiegers. But all we really *know*, is that Nineveh ceased to be, and with it, the Assyrian Empire.

16. We have seen that this end was not as sud-

---

* This form is more correct than Nebuchad*n*ezzar, and also occurs in the Bible books.

den or unprepared as it appears at first sight. Contemporaries seem to have expected it for some time. Thus the Hebrew prophet Nahum, who wrote at the time of Shamash-Shumukin's rebellion, raised a triumphant song of wrath and vengeance, which, though premature by nearly half a century, describes the actual event with thrilling vividness. True, the destruction of one great city was much like that of another, and there was no lack of subjects for such studies in those days. But the special rebukes addressed to Assyria sum up its individual character as a nation with telling master-strokes; and the whole song being one of the classical pieces of Hebrew poetry, we shall give the principal parts of it. The prophet exults at the impending ruin of Assyria as bringing deliverance to his own people.

"Thus saith Yahveh : . . . . And now will I break his yoke from off thee, and will burst thy bonds in sunder. . . . Behold, upon the mountains the feet of him that bringeth good tidings, that publisheth peace ! Keep thy feasts, O Judah, perform thy vows; for the wicked one shall no more pass through thee; he is utterly cut off.

". . . . The chariots rage in the streets, they jostle one against another in the broad ways; the appearance of them is like torches, they run like the lightnings. . . . The gates of the rivers are opened and the palace is dissolved. . . . Take ye the spoils of silver, take the spoils of gold, for there is none end of the store, the wealth of all pleasant furniture. She (Nineveh) is empty, and void and waste. . . . . Where is the den of the lions, and the feeding place of the young lions, where the lion and the lioness walked, and the lion's whelp, and none made them afraid? The lion did tear in pieces enough for his whelps, and strangled for his lionesses, and filled his caves with prey, and his dens with ravin. . . . Woe to the bloody city ! It is all full of lies and rapine. . . . The noise of the whip, and the noise of the rattling of wheels; and prancing horses, and jumping chariots; the horseman charging, and the flashing sword, and the glittering spear; and a multitude of slain, and a great heap of carcasses: and there is no end of the corpses. . . . And it shall come to pass that all they that look upon thee shall flee from thee, and say, Nineveh is laid waste; who will bemoan her? Whence shall I seek comforters for thee? Art thou better than Noamon?*

". . . . Behold thy people in the midst of thee are women; the gates of thy land are set wide open unto thine enemies; the fire hath devoured thy bars. . . . Thy shepherds slumber, O king of Asshur, thy worthies are at rest; thy people are scattered upon the mountains and there is none to gather them. There is no assuaging of thy hurt; thy wound is grievous: all that hear the bruit of thee clap the hands over thee; for upon whom hath not thy wickedness passed continually?"

17. But the finest dirge on the fall of Asshur we owe to Ezekiel, who introduced it into his long and elaborate prophecy on Egypt, against which Nebuchadrezzar was then successfully waging war. As Nahum says to Asshur, "Art thou better than Noamon. . . . ?" Ezekiel says, in substance, to Egypt: "Why shouldst thou not fall? Art thou better than Asshur?" He wrote forty years after the event. So the wrath and the bitterness of rancor were past, and the whole passage is a gorgeous gem of poetry even in the plain prose translation, breathing a spirit of lofty, mild contemplation, almost sorrow that such grand things should be doomed, out of their own wickedness, to perish.

"And it came to pass . . . . that the word of Yahveh came unto me, saying, Son of man, say unto Pharaoh, king of Egypt, and to his multitude: Whom art thou like in thy greatness? Behold, Asshur was a cedar in Lebanon, with fair branches, and with a shadowing

---

* One of the names of Thebes, the sack of which was then a recent memory.

shroud, and of an high stature, and his top was among the clouds. The waters nourished him, the deep made him to grow. ... All the fowls of heaven made their nests in his boughs, and under his branches did all the beasts of the field bring forth their young, and under his shadow dwelt all great nations,—thus was he fair in his greatness. ... The cedars in the garden of God could not hide him; the fir-trees were not like his boughs, and the plane-trees were not as his branches: nor was any tree in the garden of God like unto him in his beauty. ...

"I have driven him out for his wickedness. And strangers, the terrible of the nations, have cut him off, and have left him. Upon the mountains and in all the valleys his branches are fallen, and his boughs are broken by all the watercourses of the land; and all the people of the earth are gone down from his shadow and have left him. Upon his ruin all the fowls of the heaven shall dwell and all the beasts of the field shall be upon his branches. ... In the day when he went down to Sheol,* I caused a mourning: I covered the deep for him, and I restrained the rivers thereof, and the great waters were stayed; and I caused Lebanon to mourn for him, and all the trees of the field fainted for him. ..."

18. It may appear strange, even though the collapse was foreseen and prepared, that it should have taken place with such exceeding rapidity just toward the end. The principal explanation to offer is startlingly simple. There must have been comparatively few real Assyrians left in Assyria, except in the army, in offices, and around the person of the king. It was not only that the country had been "slowly bleeding to death with its own victories," but great numbers of Assyrians had been transported to every quarter of the empire, to every half-subdued and always unreliably submissive province, where, at a crisis, they could be of no use unsupported by forces

---

* The lower world, the world of the dead.

from home, and must have either perished or been absorbed in the native population; while on the other hand, corresponding masses of foreigners were settled in the mother country, a constant undermining element of discontent, hatred, and, no doubt, of treasonable practices. We know from Sargon in what manner Assyrian kings used to people their new cities; and, as late as after the last wars with Elam, Asshurbanipal transported to Assyria thousands of Elamite families. It stands to reason that when the invasions began, there was no defence but within the walled and fortified cities, and even in those treason must have been rife.

What wonder, then, that "the gates of the land were set wide open to the enemies, and the fire devoured its bars"?

And thus, with his own weight, with his own wickedness and folly, Asshur fell. It was a grievous fall, and an utter fall.

PRINCIPAL DATES GIVEN IN THIS VOLUME.

ISHMI-DAGAN AND HIS SON SHAMASH-RAMÂN, FIRST
   KNOWN PATESIS OF ASSHUR . . . . . . about 1800 B.C
BATTLE OF MEGIDDO (DHUTMES III.) . . . . . about 1600 "
BOUNDARY TREATY BETWEEN ASSYRIA AND BABYLO-
   NIA (FIRST KNOWN POLITICAL ACT OF ASSYRIA) about 1450 "
BATTLE OF KADESH (RAMSES II.) . . . . about 1380 "
FOUNDATION OF KALAH BY SHALMANESER I. . . about 1300 "
CONQUEST OF BABYLON BY TUKULTI-NINÊB I. a little after 1300 "
TIGLATH-PILESER I. . . . . about 1120–1100 "
FOUNDATION OF GADES (CADIX) BY THE PHŒNICIANS
                                           about 1100 "
ASSHUR-NAZIR-PAL. . . . . 884-860 "
SHALMANESER II. . . . . 860-824 "
BATTLE OF KARKAR (SYRIAN LEAGUE) . . . . 854 "
JEHU, KING OF ISRAEL, PAYS TRIBUTE TO SHALMANESER II. 842 "
FOUNDATION OF CARTHAGE BY THE PHŒNICIANS . . . 814 "
TIGLATH-PILESER II. . . . . 745-727 "
MENAHEM, KING OF ISRAEL, PAYS TRIBUTE TO TIGLATH-
   PILESER II. . . . . 738 "
HOSEA ESTABLISHED KING OVER ISRAEL AND TRIBUTE
   OF AHAZ, KING OF JUDAH . . . . 734 "
SARGON (SHARRU-KÊNU) . . . . 722-705 "
FALL OF SAMARIA . . . . 722 "
BATTLE OF RAPHIA (SHABAKA OF EGYPT) . . . . . . 720 "
FOUNDATION OF DUR-SHARRUKIN . . . . 712 "
SENNACHERIB (SIN-AKHI-IRIB) . . . . . . 705-681 "
INVASION OF JUDAH AND DELIVERANCE OF JERUSALEM . . 701 "
BATTLE OF KHALULI (BABYLON AND ELAM), AND DESTRUC-
   TION OF BABYLON . . . . 692 or 691 "
ESARHADDON (ASSHUR-AKHI-IDDIN) . . . . 681-668 "
ASSHURBANIPAL (ASSHUR-BÂNI-HABAL) . . . . . 668-626 "
FALL OF NINEVEH . . . . 606 "

INDEX.

A.

Abraham journeys to Egypt, 23; buys land from the Hittites of Hebron, 32.
Accad, see Agadê.
Acre, see Akko.
Adonis-Thammuz, the young sun-god of Gebal, 141; festival of, 142.
Adonis, river in Phœnicia, 141.
Afghanistan, a part of ancient Ariana, inhabited by Eranians, 351.
Agadê, or Accad, most northern of great Accadian cities, 1, 2
Agbatana, see Egbatana.
Aitiological myths, 126.
Ahab, King of Israel, a member of the Syrian league against Shalmaneser II., 179; his victory over and leniency to Benhadad II. of Damascus, 180; his renewed war against Benhadad, and death in battle, 182.
Ahaz, King of Judah, 229; attacked by Israel and Syria, 230; seeks the protection of Tiglath-Pileser II., 231; pays homage to him at Damascus, 235.
Akhabbu Sirlai, see Ahab of Israel.
Akharri, mât,—"Land of," Assyrian name for Phœnicia, 194.
Akkaron, see Ekron.
Akko, modern Acre—one of the Phœnician cities, 78.
Alarodians, the people of Urartu, 204; sometimes called Proto-Armenian, 205; probably a branch of the Hittite family, 205–206.
Alluvium, line marking the beginning of, in Mesopotamia, 1.
Altakû (or Eltekeh), battle of, between Sennacherib and Taharka, 310.
Amazons, originally the women ministering in the temples of the Hittite nature-goddess, 305.
Amber, Phœnician trade in, 92–93;
Ammon, alliance of, with Israel, against Assyria, 180; king of, does homage to Esarhaddon, 340.
Amuhia, see Amytis.
Amytis (also Amuhia), daughter of Kyaxares, married to Nebuchadnezzar, son of Nabopolassar, 428.
Anakim, a pre-Canaanitic people of Palestine, 73–74.
Anu, god; head of the great Assyro-Babylonian triad, 17.
Aphaka, a Phœnician city; cylinder from, 108.
Arados, see Arvad.
Arakhtu Canal in Babylonia, 314.
Aramæans, first advance of, 56.
Ararat, Mo., in Urartu or Armenia, 204.
Aras, ancient Araxes, river, 383.
Araxes, modern Aras, river, 383.
Arba-ilu, see Arbela.
Arbela, one of the great Assyrian cities, 3.
Ardys, King of Lydia, son and successor of Gyges, submits to Asshurbanipal, 381.

435

Ariana, classical name of a part of Asia, 351.
Arpad, Syrian principality and city, 225; joins a coalition against Tiglath-Pileser II., *ib.*; siege of, 226; rises against Sargon, 255.
Art, Hittite, 35, 363-367; Phœnician, 98-99; Assyrian, under Asshurnazirpal, 165-170; under Sargon, 283-287; under Sennacherib, 329-331; under Asshurbanipal, 412-416.
Arvad, Greek Arados, one of the great Phœnician cities, 60, 78; King of, does homage to Esarhaddon, 340; to Asshurbanipal, 377.
Aryan race, also called Indo-European and Indo-Germanic race, 349-350; split into two branches in Asia, the Indian and Eranian, 351-352.
Aryas, the fourth of the great races, 349.
Asia Minor, situation of, 33.
Ascalon, one of the five Philistine cities; temple of Derketo at, 111, 114, 150; King of, does homage to Esarhaddon, 340; temple of, sacked by the Scythians, 423.
Ashdod, one of the five Philistine cities, 150; popular rising in, against Assyria, under Sargon, 267; besieged and taken, *ib.*; King of, pays homage to Esarhaddon, 340; taken by Psammetik, 418.
Asherah, a tree-symbol of Ashtoreth, 112-114.
Ashtoreth, the Canaanitic moon-goddess and nature-goddess, Greek Astarte, equivalent of the Assyro-Babylonian Ishtar and Mylitta or Belit, 107; especially invoked at Sidon, 108; her worship, 110-114.
Assyria proper, greatest extent of, 3-4.
Assyrian Empire, cradle of, 3;

normal extent and natural boundaries of, 65-66; fall of, 428.
Assyrians, their resemblance to the Hebrew in features, 4; in spirit; tendency towards monotheism, 4ff.
Assyriology, scientific worth of, proved by the discovery of the Rock-stele of Tiglath-Pileser I., 43-44; by the decipherment of his cylinder, 44-46.
Asshur, "land of," Assyria, 3; "people of," of Semitic race, *ib.*
Asshur, most ancient capital of Assyria, 2.
Asshur, the Assyrians' supreme god, 5; his name at the head of invocations, 5; his importance as the representative national god, 6; parallel of Asshur and Yahveh, 6-10; his emblem, 11-15.
Asshur-akhi-iddin, see Esarhaddon.
Asshurbanipal (Asshur-ban-na-bal), King of Assyria, son and successor of Esarhaddon; inaugurated in his father's lifetime, 345; brilliant features of his reign, 371-373; his successful expedition into Egypt against Taharka, 374; quells the revolt of the Egyptian vassal kings and sacks Thebes, 376-377; his relations with Gyges, King of Lydia, 378-382; his first war with Elam, 385; gains the battle on the Ulaï, 388-391; orders barbarous executions and tortures of prisoners, 391; quells the rebellion of Shamash-Shumukin, 396; his furthur wars in Elam, 397-399; sacks Shushan, and wastes Elam, 399-401; pacifies Bit-Yakin, 406; his expedition into Arabia, 408; yokes four captive princes to his triumphal chariot, 409; last years of his reign obscure 410; his palace, library, sculptures, 411-416;

INDEX.

his transformation by Greek tradition into the effeminate tyrant Sardanapalus, 416.
Asshur-idil-ili, King of Assyria, son and successor of Asshurbanipal, 418.
Ashur-nadin-sum, eldest son of Sennacherib, made King of Babylon, 312.
Asshurnazirpal, 158, his "Annals," 159; his barbarous cruelty in war, 161-162; his various campaigns, 164; his palace at Kalah, 165; his sculptures, 166; his hunts, 168-170.
Asshur-Uballit, early King of Assyria, his descent on Babylon, 21; his expeditions to the N. and N. W., 37.
Astarte, see Ashtoreth.
Aushar, Accadian name (most ancient) of Asshur, 2.
Atargatis, the Hittite goddess, corresponding to Ishtar, worshipped at Karkhemish, 35; by the Philistines, in her temple at Ascalon, under the name of Derketo, 111, 114, 150; her sanctuary at Ephesus, 365-366.
Attys, the son of Manes, the Lydian sun-god, counterpart of Adonis-Thammuz, 366-367.
Aturia, ancient classical name of Assyria proper, 3; its narrow bounds, *ib.*
Ausi, see Hoshea.
Avva, a city of Syria, unidentified, 249.
Azariah (also Uzziah), King of Judah, pays tribute to Tiglath-Pileser II., 229.

B.

Baal (plural "Baalim," feminine "Baalath"), meaning of the word, 107; Canaanitic equivalent of the Babylonian "Bel and Belit," 116; priests of, at Jerusalem under Ahab, 116; test sacrifice to, ordered by Elijah, *ib.*

Baal, King of Tyre, does homage to Esarhaddon, 341; rebels against him, *ib.*; vanquished and pardoned, 342.
Baalath, see Baal.
Baal-zebub ("the Lord of Flies"), name of the sun-god as worshipped at Ekron, 150.
Baalim, see Baal.
Bab-el-mandeb, strait of, 69.
Babylon, taken by Tukulti-Nineb I., 38; abandoned by Merodach Baladan, invites Sargon, 275; captured and utterly destroyed by Sennacherib, 320-321; rebuilt by Esarhaddon, 336; Shamash-Shumukin, viceroy of, 347; besieged and captured by Asshurbanipal, 396; Nabopolassar, King of, 427.
Babylonia, early relations of, with Assyria, 19-21; later hostile attitude of, towards Assyria, 61-62.
Bactria, a part of ancient Ariana, inhabited by Eranians, 351.
Bagistana (Behistun), 198.
Bahrein Islands, probable starting point of the Hamites of Canaan, 68-69.
Balawat, ruins and gates of, 190.
Bavian, rock-sculptures and inscription of Sennacherib at, 319.
Bazu, a region of Arabia, unidentified; invaded by Esarhaddon, 337.
Behistun, see Bagistana.
Bel, god; one of the great Assyro-Babylonian Triad, 17.
Bêlit, the goddess; her fundamental identity with Ishtar, 19.
Belibni, Assyrian governor sent to Bit-Yakin by Asshurbanipal, 406.
Belibus, made king of Babylon by Sennacherib, 299.
Bel-Marduk, see Marduk.
Benhadad II. (Assyrian Dadidri), king of Damascus, a member of the Syrian league against

Shalmaneser II., 179; his war and reconciliation with Ahab of Israel, 180; defeats Ahab in a second war, 182; murdered, and succeeded by Hazael, 183.

Benhadad III., king of Damascus, son and successor of Hazael, defeats and humiliates Judah, 227-228.

Berytus, modern Beyrout, one of the Phœnician cities, 78.

Beth-Tôgarmah, see Togarmah.

Beyrout, see Berytus.

Bhryges, see Phrygians.

Bikni, Mount, in eastern Media, unidentified, 225, 338, 354.

Bit-Dayaukku, a Median principality, 420.

Bit-Khumri (House of Omri), name given by the Assyrians to the kingdom of Israel generally, 182-183.

Bit-Yakin, princes and leaders in Chaldea, 172; Merodach Baladan, prince of, 237; subdued by Esarhaddon, 334-335; by Asshurbanipal, 406.

Boghaz-Keui in Cappadocia, Hittite rock-sculptures at, 364.

Burna-Buriash, Babylonian king of the Cossæan dynasty, 20.

Byblos, see Gebal.

C.

Canaanites, their dispersion probably caused by the shock of the Elamitic invasion, 71; early populations found by them, 73; their sensuous and materialistic character reproduced in their religion, 103-104; its dualism, 105-108; its connection with the Babylonian religion, 105, 107; their peculiar nature, both sensuous and sanguinary, 129-136; orgiastic character of their festivals, 131-132; their child-sacrifices, 132-137.

Cappadocia, a country on the Upper Euphrates, 333-337; rich in Hittite remains, 364.

Carisbrooke Castle, in the Isle of Wight, built on the site of a Phœnician tin-station, 91.

Carmel, Mount, 78.

Carthage (Kart-Hadascht), Tyrian colony, 133; child-sacrifices at, 134-135.

Cassiterides, see "Tin-Islands."

Caucasian Gates, the great pass of the Caucasus, 383;

Chinziros, see Ukinzir.

Chaldeans proper—see Kaldu.

Cilicia, a country of Asia Minor, raid of Shalmaneser II. into, 178.

Cimmerians (Assyrian Gimirrai, Hebrew Gômer), first appearance of, 337; their principal seat in the south of Russia, 359; pass into Thrace, retreating before the Scythians, 359; into Asia Minor, across the Bosphorus, 360; destroy Sinope, 369; rule and plunder Asia minor for over a hundred years, ib.; distress Gyges, king of Lydia, 377-380; sack Sardis, 382.

Clermont-Ganneau, the discoverer of the Stele of Mesha, the Moabite, 216, note.

Cosmogony, Phœnician, 140.

Cossæans, see Kasshi.

Crete, Greek island colonized by Phœnicians, 86;

Crimea, Russian peninsula, 360.

Cyprus (Assyrian Yatnan, Hebrew, Kittîm), Greek island, colonized by Phœnicians, 86; seven kings of, pay tribute to Sargon, 277; ten to Esarhaddon, 339.

D.

Dadidri, see Benhadad II.

Dagon, the Philistine fish-god; his temple at Ascalon, 114-115, 150.

INDEX. 439

Dalta, king of Ellip; his loyalty to Assyria, 265-266; death and disputed succession of, 278.

Damascus, the Aramæan capital; its importance and duration, 56; besieged by Shalmaneser II., 184; taken by Tiglath-Pileser II., 232; rises against Sargon, 255.

Danube (river), ancient Ister, 360.

David, king of the Jews, the deliverer of his people and real founder of a national monarchy, 151; builds Jerusalem, 152.

Dead Sea, its low level, 42;

Deiokes, the reputed founder of the Median kingdom, 419-421; probable identity of the name with the Assyrian Dayaukku, 420;

Derketo, the Philistine fish-goddess, a form of Ashtoreth, 111; her temple at Ascalon, *ib.*; her companion, the fish-god, Dagon, 111; mother of the mythical Semiramis, 196.

Dhutmes III., the Egyptian conqueror, 21; wins the battle of Megiddo, 27; receives tribute from Assyria, 28;

Dibon, capital of Moab, 213.

Dilmun, king of, sends tribute to Sargon, 277.

Djebel, see Gebal.

Dniester, ancient Tyras, a river of Russia, 363.

Don, ancient Tanaïs, a river of Russia, 359.

Dualism, a conspicuous feature of the Canaanitic religions, 106-108.

Dur-Sharrukin, founded by Sargon, 280-283; buildings, walls and gates of, 283-285; artistic decoration of, 285-287; mixed population of, 288-289.

Dur-Yakin, the capital of Bit-Yakin, 274; taken by Sargon, 275.

E.

Ea, god, one of the great Assyro-Babylonian Triad, 17.

Edom, king of, pays homage to Esarhaddon, 340.

Egbatana (Ecbatana, Agbatana, Hagmatana, modern Hamadan), capital of Media, 355; fabulous legend of its foundation by Semiramis, 198; reported to have been built by Deïokes, 420.

Egypt, her long seclusion, 21-22; is conquered by the Shasus or Hyksos, 24; her conquests and wars in Asia, 26-31; her revival, after a long period of decadence, under the Ethiopian dynasty, 242; invaded by Esarhaddon, 342-344; by Asshurbanipal, 373-377; shakes off the yoke of Assyria under Psammetik, 395.

Ekron, one of the five Philistine cities, 150; seat of the worship of Baal-Zebub, *ib.*: dethrones its king, Padî, and revolts against Assyria, 304.

Elamitic invasion, a momentous turning-point in ancient Oriental history, 72.

Elijah, Hebrew prophet, taunts the priests of Baal, 116.

Elishah, the Biblical name for parts of Greece, 212-348.

Elissa, the foundress of Carthage, 211.

Eltekeh, see Altakû.

Emim, a pre-Canaanitic people of Palestine, 72.

Ephesus, originally Hittite city in Ionia, 364; the great sanctuary of Atargatis at, 365-366.

Eponym Canon, or table of Limmus; its uses in chronology, 117.

Erân, or Irân, collective name of all the countries, inhabited by Eranian nations, and of those nations themselves, 352; opposed to Turân, 353.

Esarhaddon (Asshur-akhi-iddin), king of Assyria, son and successor of Sennacherib, 331-346; makes war against his brothers, 333-335; receives favorable oracles from Ishtar of Arbela, 333; subdues Bit-Yakin, 334-346; rebuilds Babylon 336; leads an expedition into "distant Media," 337; repels the Gimirrai (Cimmerians) in the north, *ib.*: his Arabian campaign, 337-339; chastises Sidon and some districts of Syria, 339; receives homage and tribute from twenty-two kings at Nineveh, 339-340; builds a great palace at Nineveh, 341; quells a revolt in Syria, 341-342; his Egyptian campaign, 342-344; his abdication in favor of his son Asshurbanipal, 345; appoints his other son, Shamash-Shumukin, viceroy of Babylon, 346; dies, *ib.*

Eshmun, the Eighth Kabir, 143.

Ethiopian dynasty in Egypt, founded by Shabaka, 242; end of, under Taharka's successor, 375.

Eulaeos, see Ulaï.

Ezekiel, the prophet, his description of Tyre, 95; his prophesies, 424, 425, 430, 431.

F.

Fravartish, see Phraortes.

G.

Gades (Cadiz), foundation of, by the Phœnicians, 68, 90.

Gâgi (Gôg), a Scythian chief, captured, 384.

Gath, one of the five Philistine cities, 150.

Gaza, one of the five Philistine cities, 150; king of, does homage to Esarhaddon, 340.

Gebal, Greek Byblos, modern Djebel, one of the great Phœnician cities, 78; its priestly character, 139; seat of the worship of Adonis, 141; king of, does homage to Esarhaddon, 340.

Gibil, the fire-god, absent from Assyrian pantheon, 16.

Gimirrai, see Cimmerians.

Gôg, see Gâgi.

Gômer, see Cimmerians.

Goshen, land of, given to Jacob and his sons, 23.

Gozan, a portion of Mesopotamia, 249.

Gugu, king of Ludi, see Gyges, king of Lydia.

Gyges, king of Lydia (Assyrian Gugu), sends an embassy to Asshurbanipal to entreat his aid against the Cimmerians, 378, 379; conspires with Psammetik against him, 380; perishes in the struggle against the Cimmerians, *ib.*

H.

Habor, see Khabour.

Hadidri, see Benhadad II.

Hagmatana, see Egbatana.

Haldi, the "great god" of the Alarodians, 263, 264.

Hamadan, see Egbatana.

Hamath, Hittite kingdom in Syria, 179; a member of the Syrian league against Shalmaneser II., *ib.*; rises against Sargon, 255.

Hazael (Khazaïlu), a Syrian officer murders Benhadad II. and succeeds him, 183; is defeated by Shalmaneser II., 184.

Herodotus, the Greek historian, 108, 354, 359, 362, 417, 419, 422.

Hezekiah (Hizkia), King of Judah, abstains from conspiring against Assyria, 254; his sickness, 270; his wealth, *ib.*; receives Merodach Baladan's embassy, 271;

his imprudence, *ib.*: openly revolts against Sennacherib, 304; submits and sends tribute, 306; is delivered from the Assyrian army, 307-310.
Hincks, Dr., one of the decipherers of Tiglath-Pileser's cylinder, 45.
Hiram, King of Tyre, friend of David and Solomon, 154; furnishes men and materials to build the temple of Yahveh and Solomon's palace, *ib.*
Hittites (Egyptian "Khetas," Assyrian "Khatti"), a great people, 29; their wars against Dhutmes III. and Ramses II., 29-30; of Hamitic stock, 30; their first headquarters, *ib.*; signs of their northern origin, 31; their decline, 33; their culture and religion, 35-36; their early collisions with Assyria, 37; supplanted by the Aramæans, 56-57; 148.
Hoshea (Ausi), King of Israel, succeeds Pekah, 231; conspires against Assyria, 246.
Hyksos, see Shasus.

I.

Iaubid, or Ilubid, upstart king of Hamath, 255; taken and flayed alive by Sargon, 256.
Iahuhazi mât Iaudai, see Ahaz of Judah.
Ibriz, in Cilicia, Hittite rock-sculptures at, 364.
Ilubid, see Iaubid.
Ilulai, King of Babylon, possibly identical with Shalmaneser IV., 240.
Indabigash dethrones Tammaritu and usurps the crown of Elam, 395; perishes in a revolt, 398.
Indo-European race, its great qualities, 351.
Indo-Germanic race, see Aryan race.
-Samirina, see Samaira.

Isaiah, the Hebrew prophet, warns the king of Judah against trusting to Egypt, 243, 254; rebukes Hezekiah for his imprudence with regard to Merodach Baladan's embassy, 271-272; comforts him at Sennacherib's approach, 309.
Ishmi-Dagon, earliest known king of Asshur, 2.
Ishtar, goddess of love and of war, rules the planet Venus, 18; "of Nineveh," "of Arbela," *ib.*: her fundamental identity with Belit, 19; with Ashtoreth, 107; the favorite deity of Esarhaddon, 333; her message to Asshurbanipal, 386-387.
Israel, kingdom of, secedes from the house of David, 157.
Israelites invade Moab, 126.
Ister, modern Danube, 360.

J.

Jacob settles in Egypt with his family, 23.
Japhetic race, see Aryan or Indo-European race.
Jehovah, see Yahveh.
Jehu usurps the crown, 184; pays tribute to Shalmaneser II., 185-187.
Jeremiah, a Hebrew prophet, on the Scythian invasion, 370, 424.
Jerusalem, the political and religious centre of the Jewish nation, the only holy place of Yahveh, 152; the temple at, built by Phœnician artists, 154-155; fortified by Hezekiah, 304-305; siege and deliverance of, under Sennacherib, 307-309.
Jews, tribes of, gathered into a nation under David and Solomon, 151-153; oppressed by Solomon, 154; separate into two kingdoms after Solomon's death, 157.
Joel, a Hebrew prophet, 256.
Jonah and his preaching at Nineveh not mentioned on the mon-

uments, 208; possible explanation of the story, 209-210.
Jonathan, the son of Saul, 151.
Joseph, his brilliant career in Egypt, 25.
Judah, kingdom of, ruled by the house of David, 157.

K.

Kabirim, the seven Phœnician deities, 142-143.
Kaboul, a part of ancient Ariana, inhabited by Eranians, 351.
Kadesh, Battle of, 30; one of the Hittite capitals, *ib*.
Kalah, one of the three Assyrian capitals, 3; founded by Shalmaneser I., 37; rebuilt and embellished by Asshurnazirpal, 164-166.
Kaldu (Chaldea proper), strict definition of the name, 170; princes of, 172; their ambition and rebellious attitude towards Assyria, 172, 173.
Kaphtor, uncertain island, perhaps Crete, 149.
Kar-Dunyash, Babylon, 20.
Karkha, the royal citadel of Mesha, king of Moab, 216.
Karkhemish, principal Hittite capital, 31; important and wealthy commercial station, 148; final conquest of, by Sargon, 261.
Kar Ninêb, fortress built by Sargon in the Zagros lands, 262.
Kar-Sharrukin, fortress built by Sargon in the Zagros lands, 262.
Karkar, battle of, 181.
Kart-Hadascht, see Carthage.
Kasshi (Cossæans), Sennacherib's campaign against the, 300.
Khabour, or Habor, "the river of Gozan," 249.
Khaluli, battle of, 318-319.
Khatti, see Hittites.
Khatti, land of, general name for Syria, irrespective of races, 148.

Khauzer, see Khuzur.
Khazaïlu, see Hazael.
Khetas, see Hittites.
Khemosh, the god of Moab, 126, 205-217.
"Kherem," "devoting" "captured cities to destruction," 138.
Khosr, see Khuzur.
Khumbanigash, king of Elam, makes alliance with Merodach Baladan against Assyria, 259.
Khudur Lagamar, early Elamite king, 25.
Khudur Nankhundi, early Elamite king, 25.
Khuzur, now Khosr or Khauzer, stream that flowed through Nineveh, 326
Kileh-Sherghat, hamlet on the site of Asshur, 2.
Kimmerians, see Cimmerians.
Kings of Assyria, their priestly character, 10-11; sacredness of their persons, 14-16.
Kings of Egypt, their Asiatic expeditions, 26-30.
Kiriath-Sepher ("the City of Books"), a city in Phœnicia, 144.
Kir-Haresheth, a city of Moab, 126.
Kish, a city in Babylonia, 298.
Kittim, see Cyprus.
Kour, ancient Kyros, river, 383.
Kurdistan, see Naïri.
Kyaxares (Uvakshatara), king of Media, son and successor of Phraortes, 421; invades Assyria, 422; returns to Media in consequence of the Scythian invasion, *ib*.; frees Media from the Scythians, 427; enters an alliance with Nabopolassar of Babylon, *ib*.; unites with him to besiege Nineveh, 428.
Kybele, the Lydian nature-goddess, 367; myth of her love to Attys, *ib*.
Kydnos, a river in Cilicia.
Kyros, modern Kour, river, 383.

L.

Laïlîê, an Arab chieftain, kindly treated by Esarhaddon, 338.
Lakhish, a fortress of Judah, besieged and taken by Sennacherib, 305-307.
Lebanon, Mount, meaning of the name, 78.
Limmu, or Eponyms, Assyrian magistrates after whom the years were named; importance of the institution for the establishment of a reliable chronology, 146.
Lydia, a country in Asia Minor, 364; population of, principally Hittite, 366; early traditions of, *ib.*; overrun by Cimmerians, 378-382.

M.

Madai, see Medes.
Madaktu, one of the great cities of Elam, 401.
Madyes, son of Prôtothyes the Scythian king, 422; killed at a banquet by Kyaxares, 427.
Magog, the Hebrew name for the Scythians of Sacasene, 383.
Manasseh, king of Judah, son and successor of Hezekiah, does homage to Esarhaddon, 340; rebels against him, 341; captured and pardoned, 341-342.
Manes, the supreme god of the Lydians, 366.
Marduk, successor of Meridug, chief god of later Babylon, 17; ruler of the planet Jupiter in Assyria, *ib.*
Marduk-habal-iddin, see Merodach Baladan.
Masios, Mount, continuation of Taurus, 30.
Medes (Madai) subdued by Ramán-Nirari III., 104; send tribute to Sennacherib, 302; to Esarhaddon, 337; the three kinds of, 353-354; their loose political constitution, 354; they spread through the Zagros, 355; unite into a kingdom, 419-421.
Megiddo, battle of, 27.
Melkarth, or Baal-Melkarth, the Phœnician sun-god, protector of westward navigation, 90; pillars of, *ib.*; specially worshipped at Tyre, 108; meaning of the name, *ib.*; temple of, at Tyre, *ib.*
Memphis, one of the capitals of Egypt, 373.
Menahem, King of Israel (Assyrian: Minihimmi-ir-Samirina), pays tribute to Tiglath-Pileser II., 227.
Meridug, see Marduk.
Merodach Baladan (Marduk-Habal-Iddin) of Bit-Yakin, 237; does homage to Tiglath-Pileser II., at Sapiya, 238; makes alliance with Khumbanigash, King of Elam, against Sargon, 259; with Sutruk-Nankhundi, successor of Khumbanigash, 269; sends an embassy to Hezekiah, King of Judah, 270-272; opens hostilities against Sargon, 273; is defeated and flies into Elam, 273; returns to Dur-Yakin, 274; flies again, 275; reappears on Sennacherib's accession, as King of Babylon, 298; is defeated and flies to Bit-Yakin, 299; retires to Nagitu, on the shore of Elam, 312.
Mesha, King of Moab, sacrifices his eldest son, 126-127; Stele of, 213-217.
Migrations of races; obscurity of the subject, 70-71.
Minihimmi-ir-Samirina, see Menahem, King of Israel.
Moab, kingdom of, 126, 157; Mesha, king of, 126-127; 212-217; king of, does homage to Esarhaddon, 340.
Moloch, meaning of the name.

107; Canaanitic sun-god, *ib.*; the fierce sun-god, 115; worship of, distinguished by human sacrifices, 133; child-sacrifices to, at Carthage, 134-136.
Moriah, Mount, temple of Yahveh on, 153.
Muzazir, a kingdom of Naïri, 264; conquered by Sargon, 264.
Muzri, ancient city, on the site of which Dur-Sharrukin was built, 280.
Myths, Canaanitic, difficult to unravel, 109-110; of Baal, his sleep and his travels, 116; Aitiological, 126.

N.

Nabopolassar (Nabu-pal-uzzur) becomes king of Babylon, 427; enters an alliance with Kyaxares, *ib.;* unites with him to besiege and destroy Nineveh, 428.
Nabu-bel-Zikri of Bit-Yakin, a grandson of Merodach Baladan, rises against Asshurbanipal, 397; commits suicide, 402-403; his body treated with indignity, 404.
Nabu-khudur-uzzur, see Nebuchadrezzar.
Nabu-pal-uzzur, see Nabopolassar.
Nagitu, a city of Elam by the Gulf, 312.
Nahid-Marduk, a son of Merodach Baladan, submits to Esarhaddon, 335.
Nahr-el-Kelb, rock-sculptures of, 344; stele of Esarhaddon at, *ib.*
Nahum, a Hebrew prophet, his prophecy against Assyria, 429.
Naïri, lands of, geographical position, 43; campaign of Tiglath-Pileser I. in, 47-54; great outbreak in, under Sargon, 260.
Nebi-Yunus, mound of, 331-340.
Nebosumiskun, a son of Merodach Baladan, taken prisoner in the battle of Khaluli, 318.
Nebuchadrezzar (Nabu-khudur-uzzur), son of Nabopolassar, married to Amytis, daughter of Kyaxares, 428.
Necho, prince of Saïs, set by Esarhaddon over the other nineteen tributary kings of Egypt, 343; conspires with Taharka against Asshurbanipal and is carried captive to Nineveh, 374; is set free and returns to Saïs, 375; dies soon after the sack of Thebes, 380.
Nineveh, the last capital of Assyria, rebuilt and embellished by Sennacherib, 325; besieged by Kyaxares, 422; fall of, 428.
Ninyas, son of Ninus and Semiramis, 198, 200.
Ninus, mythical founder of the Assyrian Empire, 196.
Niphates, Mons, northern boundary of Assyria under Tiglath-Pileser I., 65.
Nipur Mountains, a portion of the Naïri range, 313.
No-amon, one of the names of Thebes, 430.

O.

Obelisk, Shalmaneser II.'s black, 185-187.
Omri, father of Ahab; builds Samaria, 182.
Onnes, or Oannes, first husband of the mythical Semiramis, 196.
Oppert, Mr. Julius, one of the decipherers of Tiglath-Pileser's cylinder, 45.
"Orgiastic" religions and rites, 131; meaning of the word, 132.
Orontes, river in Syria, 30, 178.

P.

Padi, King of Ekron, devoted to Assyria, dethroned and delivered to Hezekiah of Judah,

304; restored to his throne, 306.

Pakaha, see Pekah.

Pakhe usurps the crown of Elam from Ummanaldash II., 406; is yoked to Asshurbanipal's triumphal chariot with three more captive princes, 409.

Palaces of Asshurnazirpal at Kalah, 165-170; of Sargon at Dur-Sharrukin, 283-287; of Sennacherib at Nineveh, 327-330; of Asshurbanipal 410-416.

Palestine, derivation of the name, 33; pre-Canaanitic populations of, 73-76.

Pantheon, Assyrian, 16-19

Paphlagonia, a country of Asia Minor, 369.

Parityas, a son of Gâgi, the Scythian chieftain, 422.

Patesis, king-priests, 2.

Pekah (Pakaha), son of Remaliah, murders and succeeds Pekaih, king of Israel, and makes alliance with Syria, 229; assassinated, 232.

Pekaiat, son and successor of Menahem of Israel, murdered and succeeded by Pekah, 229.

Pelishtim, see Philistines.

Philistines (Pelishtim), powerful nation of Syria, 35; their confederation of five cities, 150; their long conflict with the Jews, 151.

Phœnicians, their wealth, 67-68; their origin and migrations, 68-70; their earliest race-name, 69; their country and cities, 76-80; their politics and government, 78; their industries, 81; their navigation, 83; their colonies and trading stations, 83-84; their slave-trade and barter-trade, 85; their colonies on Greek islands, 85-86; their voyages for tin, 86-92; for amber, 92-93; their caravan trade, 93-94; their great wealth and luxury, 94-96; their intellectual and moral character, 96-97; their lack of inventiveness and originality, 97-99; their great genius for business and money-making, 99; their historical mission, 99-102; carry their worship to Greece and Italy, 144.

Phraortes (Travartish), King of Media, reputed son and successor of Deïokes, 421; his unsuccessful invasion of Assyria and death, ib.

Phryges, see Phrygians.

Phrygia, a country of Asia Minor, anciently ruled by Hittites, 367; later overrun by Aryans, ib.

Phrygians, an important branch of the Aryan race, 367.

Phrygo-Thracian nations, 368.

Phut, see Puna.

"Pillars of Melkarth," 90.

Pre-Canaanitic populations of Syria, 73-75; probably Turanian, 75-76.

Proto-Armenians, see Alarodians.

Protothyes, a Scythian chieftain, 422.

Psammetik, King of Saïs, son and successor of Necho, draws Gyges of Lydia into an alliance against Asshurbanipal, 380; becomes King of all Egypt and refuses allegiance to Asshurbanipal, 395; his long wars in Syria, 418, 423; stops the Scythian invasion by bribes, 424.

Pul or Phûl, see Tiglath-Pileser II.

Puna (Punt, Phut, Pût), Hamitic tribe, probable ancestors of the Phœnicians, 69.

Punt, see Puna.

Purple dye, invented and monopolized by the Phœnicians, 81-82; fisheries, 82; navigation in pursuit of purple mussel, 82-83; purple mussel first occa-

sion of colonization, 83-84; of prosperity of Greek islands, 86.
Put, see Puna.
Pygmalion, King of Tyre, 211.

R.

Ra, modern Volga, 359.
Ramân-Nirari III., son and successor of Shamshi-Ramân III.; his long reign and successful wars, 191-192; his queen, Shammuramat, 194-195; their names jointly mentioned in a dedication of some statues of Nebo, 202.
Ramses II., the Egyptian conqueror, 29-30.
Raphia, battle of, between Sargon and Shabaka, 258.
Rawlinson, Sir Henry, one of the decipherers of Tiglath-Pileser's cylinder, 45.
Remaliah, see Pekah.
Rezin, King of Syria, makes alliance with Pekah, King of Israel, against Judah, 229-230; besieged in Damascus and put to death, 233.

S.

Sacasene, a region south of the Caucasus, occupied by Scythians, 383.
Sacrifice, original meaning of the word, 118; different classes of, 118-120; two modes of, burnt offering and consecration, 120-121; to consist of perfect victims or offerings, 122; most lavish when prompted by fear, 123; human, a logical necessity, 123-124; common to all religions in remote antiquity, and considered a divine institution, 124-126, 127; legends connected with abolition of human sacrifices, 128-129; child-sacrifices at Carthage, 132-135; at Jerusalem, 135; forbidden by Romans, 136.
Saida, see Sidon.
Saïs, an Egyptian city, 344; Necho, hereditary prince of, *ib.*
Saki or Sakhi, see Scythians.
Samaria, capital of Israel, built by Omri, 182; attacked by Shalmaneser IV., 247; taken by Sargon, 247; rises against him, 255.
Samaritans, later; their mixed origin, 249-250.
Sanchoniatho, Phœnician priest; "Fragments" of, 125, 139, 143.
Sapiya, capital of Ukinzir's Chaldean principality, taken and sacked by Tiglath-Pileser II., 237; Merodach Baladan does homage at, 237-238.
Sarakos, last King of Assyria, named by the Greeks, 418.
Sardanapalus, see Asshurbanipal.
Sardis, capital of Lydia, 364; sacked by Cimmerians, 382.
Sargon (Sharru-Kênu), King of Assyria, takes Samaria, 247; character of his reign and wars, 251-254; crushes the rising in the West, 255-256; marches against Shabaka, 256; defeats him at Raphia, 258; his campaign against Merodach Baladan, 272-276; receives tribute from seven kings of Cyprus, 278; from the King of Dilmun, *ib.*; settles the dispute between the sons of Dalta, King of Ellip, 278; builds Dur-Sharrukin, 280-289; his wise rule and care of his people, 291-294; his assassination, 294.
Saul, King of the Jews, 151.
Sayce, Professor A. H.—his researches about the Hittites, 36, 205, 365.
Scythians invade Southern Russia and drive the Cimmerians into Thrace and Asia Minor,

359-360; occupy the regions by the river Kyros, 383; descend into Asia Minor, *ib.*; invade Media, 422; descend into Syria, 423; expelled by Kyaxares, 427.

Scyths, see Scythians.

Semiramis (Assyrian: Shammuramat), mythical legend of, 196-202.

Sennacherib (Sin-akhi-irib), King of Assyria, son and successor of Sargon, 295-330; his first campaign against Babylon and Merodach Baladan, 298; invades Ellip and receives tribute from the "distant Medes," 300-302; his unsuccessful campaign into Syria and against Hezekiah of Judah, 303-311; sends to summon and besiege Jerusalem, 307-310; encounters Taharka at Altakû, 310; is forced by a pestilence to leave Jerusalem and Syria, 309-311; his second campaign against Babylonia, 311-313; his campaign into the Nipur Mountains, 313; his last campaign against Babylonia, and Elam, 315-322; gains the victory at Khaluli, 318-319; captures and utterly destroys Babylon, 320-321; is reported to have founded the city of Tarsus in Cilicia, 322; dies, murdered by two of his sons, *ib.*; his constructions and improvements at Nineveh, 322-326; his palace, 326-330.

Sesostris, Greek name of Ramses II., 364.

Shabaka (the So or Soh of the Bible), the founder of the Ethiopian dynasty in Egypt, 242; arouses the hopes of the Syrian nations subject to Assyria, 243; defeated at Raphia, 258.

Shalmaneser I. founds Kalah, 57.

Shalmaneser II., his long warlike reign, 175-176; his campaigns in Western Syria, 178-185; his black obelisk, 185-187.

Shalmaneser III., son and successor of Ramân-Nirari III.; his wars in Nairi and Urartu, 203-206.

Shalmaneser IV. succeeds Tiglath-Pileser II., 239; besieges Tyre, 240, 242-245; besieges Samaria, 246.

Shamash-Ramân, early Assyrian King, son of Ishmi-Dagan, 2.

Shamash-Shumukin, younger son of Esarhaddon, appointed viceroy of Babylon, 346; implores Asshurbanipal's assistance against Urtaki, King of Elam, 385; conspires against Asshurbanipal and organizes a vast coalition against him, 392-393; besieged in Babylon by Asshurbanipal and perishes in the conflagration, 396.

Shammuramat, see Semiramis.

Shamshi-Ramân III., son and successor of Shalmaneser II., 191.

Sharru-Kênu, see Sargon. Meaning of the name, 251.

Shasus, meaning of the word, 24; invade and conquer Egypt, *ib.*

Shepherd kings, see Shasus.

Shushan (Susa), capital of Elam, sacked by Asshurbanipal, 399-400.

Shushinak, supreme god of Elam; his statue carried off to Assyria by Asshurbanipal, 400.

Sidon, modern Saida, first Phœnician capital, 70, 78, 80, 81; revolts against Esarhaddon and is destroyed, 339.

Simmas, foster father of the mythical Semiramis, 196.

Sinjar Hills, limestone ridge in Upper Mesopotamia, 1.

Sinope, Greek colony on the Black Sea, destroyed by the Cimmerians, 369.

Smyrna, Hittite rock-sculptures between Sardis and, 362.

So or Soh, see Shabaka.
Solomon, son of David, builds temple of Yahveh on Mount Moriah, 153; lays heavy burdens on the Jews, 154; his policy of conciliation with his neighbors and its fatal results, 156.
Somali coast, 69.
"Stele," meaning of the word, 16; Rock-stele of Tiglath-Pileser I., 43-44; of Esarhaddon at Nahr-el-Kelb, 344.
Sûr, see Tyre.
Susa, see Shushan.
Sutekh, Hittite supreme god, 35.
Sutruknankhundi, successor of Khumbanigash, and ally of Merodach Baladan, 270; abandons his cause, 274.
Suzub, Chaldean king of Babylon after Merodach-Baladan, 372; buys the help of Umman-Minan, king of Elam, 316-317; is routed in the battle of Khaluli, 318-319.
Sydyk ("the Just"), one of the Kabirim, 143.

T.

Taharka (also Tirhaka, Assyrian Tarku), king of Egypt, conspires with the Syrian kings, 302; defeated by Esarhaddon, 343; rises against Asshurbanipal, 374; is defeated and flies to Kush, 375; conspires with the Egyptian vassal kings, *ib.*; dies, 376.
Talbot, Mr. H. Fox, one of the decipherers of Tiglath-Pileser's cylinder, 45.
Tammaritu of Elam, Urtaki's youngest son, cuts off Teumman's head in the battle on the Ulaï, 391; dethrones Ummanigash and becomes king of Elam, 395; joins Shamash-Shumukin against Asshurbanipal, 395; dethroned by Indabigash and flies to Nineveh, 396; replaced on the throne of Elam by Asshurbanipal, 399; revolts again and is carried captive to Nineveh, 399-400; yoked to Asshurbanipal's triumphal chariot with three more captive princes, 410.
Tanaïs, modern Don, 360.
Tarku, see Taharka.
Tarshish (corrupted name, Tartessus), extravagant accounts of, 87-88, 349.
"Tarshish-ships," 89, 94.
Tarsos, a city in Cilicia, reported to have been founded by Sennacherib, 323.
Tartessus, see Tarshish.
Taurus, Mount, 30.
Teumman, king of Elam, brother and successor of Urtaki, continues hostilities against Asshurbanipal, 387; defeated and killed in the battle on the Ulaï, 389-392.
Thammuz, see Adonis.
Thebes, one of the capitals of Egypt, sacked by Asshurbanipal, 376.
Thrace, modern Bulgaria and Roumelia, 361.
Thraco-Phrygian nations, 368.
Tiberius, a Roman Emperor, 136.
Tiglath-Pileser I. (Tukulti-palesharra), his cylinder and its decipherment, 44-46; his campaign against the Hittites, 47; in the land of Naïri, 47-54; against the "Aramæan Riverland," 56; his pursuits in peace, 57-58; his love of sport, 58-59; his visit to Arvad, 60; his unsuccessful wars against Babylonia, 59-62.
Tiglath-Pileser II. probably a usurper, 207; identical with the Phûl or Pul of the Bible, 207-208; policy of, 219; his campaigns in the north, east and south, 224-225, 226-236; receives the homage of Merodach

Baladan and other princes at Sapiya, 237-238; dies, 239.

Tin, essential ingredient of bronze, 86; Phœnician travels in search of, 87-92; overland route through France for the transport of, 89.

"Tin-Islands" (Greek Cassiterides), first known name of the English channel islands, 88.

Tirhaka, see Taharka.

Tiushpa the Gimirraï, the Cimmerian chieftain, repulsed under Esarhaddon, 337.

Togarmah, the son of Gomer, represents the Armenian division of the Thraco-Phrygian race, 368.

Tophet, valley of, near Jerusalem, devoted to the worship of Baal and to human sacrifices, 135.

Tsôr, see Tyre.

Tukulti-Ninèb, son of Shalmaneser I., conquers Babylon, 38; loses his signet ring which is recovered by Sennacherib, *ib.*

Tukulti-Ninèb II., 158.

Tukulti-palesharra, see Tiglath-Pileser.

Turân, collective name of all the Asiatic nations of Turanian race, as opposed to Erân, 352.

Turcomen, of the Turanian race, inhabitants of Turkestan, 352.

Tyras, modern Dniester, 361.

Tyre (original name: Tsôr, modern Sûr), one of the great Phœnician cities, 78; the old and new city, 80; description of her splendor by the prophet Ezekiel, 95; supplants Sidon as queen of the Phœnician cities, 149; sends out most of the later colonies, *ib.*; that of Carthage, 211; revolts against Tiglath-Pileser II., 236; besieged under Shalmaneser IV., 240, 243-245; pacified under Sargon, 258; Baal, king of, does homage to Esarhaddon, 340; rebels against him, 341; Tyre besieged, reduced by famine, 342; rebels against Asshurbanipal and is reduced by blockade and thirst, 377.

U.

Ukinzir (Greek Chinziros), Chaldean prince of Sapiya, king of Babylon, 237; submits to Tiglath-Pileser II., *ib.*

Ulaï (Eulaeos), river of Elam, 313; battle on the bank of, 388-391.

Ummanaldash II. usurps the crown of Elam after the death of Indabigash, 398; dethroned and succeeded by the reinstated Tammaritu, 406, 407, *ib.*; reigns once more a short time, flies from a revolt and is carried captive to Nineveh, 408; yoked to Asshurbanipal's triumphal chariot with three more captive princes, 409.

Ummanigash, a son of Urtaki, becomes king of Elam, vassal to Asshurbanipal, 392; joins the coalition organized by Shamash-Shumukin against him, 393; dethroned by Tammaritu, 394.

Umman-Minan, brother and successor of Khudur-Nankhundi, king of Elam, assists Suzub against Sennacherib, 315-316; is defeated in the battle of Khaluli, 318-319.

Urartu (Armenia proper), rise of, among the kingdoms of Naïri, 203-206; its writing borrowed from the Assyrian, 205; revolts against Tiglath-Pileser II., and is defeated, 226; friendly to Assyria under Asshurbanipal, 419.

Urmevate, modern Urmiah or Urumich, city, 384.

Urtaki, King of Elam, opens hostilities against Asshurbanipal, 385; his defeat and death, *ib.*

Urumich, Lake, see Lake Van.

450 INDEX.

Urza, King of Urartu, organizes a vast coalition against Sargon, 259; defeated and escapes into the mountains, 263; puts an end to his own life, 264.
Urzana, King of Muzazir, ally of Urza of Urartu, 263; flies from Sargon, 264.
Uzziah, see Azariah.

V.

Vaitch, an Arab chieftain, captured by Asshurbanipal, 409; yoked to his triumphal chariot with the three kings of Elam, 409.
Van, Lake, and Lake Urumieh, their peculiarities, 40–42; Rock-stele of Tiglath-Pileser I. near, 43–44.
Van, city and ruins of, 204.
Vas, a part of Arabia, unidentified, 408.
Volga, ancient Ra, a river of Russia, 359.

Y.

Yahveh, the God of Israel, 10, 137–138; idolatrous worship, local and private shrines of, 152; temple of, on Mount Moriah, proclaimed only lawful high place of worship, 153.
Yahua, son of Khumri,—see Jehu, king of Israel.
Yaman, or Yavan, upstart king of Ashdod, 266; flies to Ethiopia and is delivered up to Sargon, 267.
Yatnan, see Cyprus.
Yavan, Hebrew and Assyrian name of the Greeks, 348.
Yemen, part of Arabia, 69.

Z.

Zagros Mountains, Tiglath-Pileser I.'s campaign in the, 54; the natural eastern boundary of Assyria, 65.
Zephaniah, a Hebrew prophet, his prophesy against Assyria, 401.
Zamzummim, a pre-Canaanitic people of Palestine, 74.
Zuzim, a pre-Canaanitic people of Palestine, 74.

www.ingramcontent.com/pod-product-compliance
Lightning Source LLC
Chambersburg PA
CBHW051848300426
44117CB00006B/315